Business School

Managing and managing people

The Open University, Walton Hall, Milton Keynes, MK7 6AA

First published 2010. This edition 2011

Edited, designed and typeset by The Open University

Printed in the United Kingdom by Cambrian Printers, Aberystwyth

FSC

Mixed Sources

Product group from well-managed
forests and other controlled sources

Cert no. TT-COC-2200
www.fsc.org
© 1996 Forest Stewardship Council

ISBN 978 1 8487 3927 7

3.2

Contents

Introduction

Being a manager today is a demanding job that requires skill and distinctive attitudes and behaviours. This book introduces you to the most important of these. It identifies the main elements and realities of a manager's job and explains how you can develop and organise yourself to be effective and successful in your role.

Managing in modern organisations is not easy: no context is the same; the 'right' decision in one organisation may be the 'wrong' one in another, or at another time. There is no 'one best way'. This is recognised in this book. However, there is also 'received wisdom' – tried and tested practices and behaviours that are usually effective in bringing about the result a manager wants. These are included in this book where appropriate. But even 'good practice' needs adaptation: time or resources may be in short supply and a manager may have to do the best he or she can with what's available. This is the art of management: doing what's possible in the best way possible in the circumstances to achieve, through others, the goals for which an organisation is striving.

A little history

In the twenty-first century, organisations are characterised as fast-moving, dynamic places. Three changes continue to affect organisations. These are changes in the external environment, changes in the demands made on organisations, and changes in the expectations of the people who work in organisations. All these make management a messy and complicated business. But neither management nor its messiness and complexity are new. As far back as ancient Egypt, the building of the pyramids and the great temples needed to be managed; in thirteenth-century China, Sun Tzu, a military strategist, devised managerial approaches to achieving collective goals; and in sixteenth-century Italy, Machiavelli wrote about how to manage effectively.

While management is not new, however, the study of management as a discipline emerged in Adam Smith's 1776 book *An Inquiry into the Nature and Causes of the Wealth of Nations* (often abbreviated to 'The Wealth of Nations'). In this work, Smith outlines the ways in which the division of labour within an organisation can contribute to the economic success of that organisation. Before the division of labour, one worker completed a whole job – Smith wrote about making pins to be used for connecting one piece of cloth to another. Smith found that when the work was divided there was a very large increase in the output of the pin makers. After division, one worker made only the pin's head, another only the point, and others, further parts of the pin. This theme of division of labour was picked up later by Frederick Winslow Taylor, with his work entitled *The Principles of Scientific Management* (1911). The work of Taylor became the starting point for a new area of academic study, the study of management. So what was the cause of this sudden emphasis on studying management? Essentially, it was the

Industrial Revolution, which began in Great Britain in the eighteenth century and spread to Western Europe, North America and eventually to other parts of the world. Industrialisation is a process that continues today.

The Industrial Revolution changed the nature of business. Advances in machines such as steam engines brought about changes in the ways in which goods were produced. Previously, business had been based on people making products in small workshops and then small local traders selling or exchanging goods with other local traders. The advances in technology resulted in new means of production that were far more efficient and far more cost-effective than the small-scale business could ever be. However, these new businesses required a change in the ways in which people worked. Whereas previously people managed themselves and possibly one or two other people, new businesses ran factories which employed 100 or 200 people. Suddenly there was a need to control what these people did, to coordinate their actions and to direct them towards achieving the goals of the organisation. This was the birth of management.

Since that time there have been many perspectives on management which have shaped the ways in which we think about management now. Despite many ideas on management being very old, many of them are still reflected in the management practices we use today.

About this book

While it would be simpler if management (like life itself) operated in a clear, constant way, this is rarely the case in real organisations. Management is messy. Often, several events happen at the same time. A weakness of most management books, including this one, is that we deal with issues one at a time before explaining how they can be used together. A second weakness of most management books, but not this one, is in presenting management as a sequence with a clear start and finish. We have structured this book so that you can make sense of any topic or issue without having to read all the earlier ones. Of course, some of the topics at the start will make more sense when you have read about later topics – but we have to start from somewhere!

We begin by looking at **what it is that managers do**. Being clear about the purpose and role of management will help you make sense of the knowledge and skills you will want to develop. This topic will also help you identify and see the links between the most important issues in your busy and demanding day. We've selected four key components of the management function that are central to what most managers have to do.

- *Communicate*. Talking, emailing, writing and listening to colleagues, clients or regulators, competitors and others inside and beyond your organisation or team ensures clarity and helps you to persuade or motivate people. Whatever the setting, communication is an everyday and vital function and skill of management.
- *Solve problems and make decisions*. As a manager, you often have to take responsibility for things you may previously have left to others.

- *Plan and control, monitor and evaluate.* These are core skills in making sure that tasks are achieved effectively and efficiently so that your objectives – and those of your organisation – are met.

- *Receive and handle information.* Activities such as these are connected with communication, but wider than that. Most managers have to find things out, interpret data and reports, investigate issues and decide who else needs to know what.

No manager can be effective in these or other aspects of management on their own. People are the means through which a manager gets things done. The ability **to understand and work with people** is fundamental to management. We cover three core people-related roles of managers.

1 *Motivating people.* You can achieve more as a manager if people do more of the things you want them to, not because they are told to but because they want to and understand why. Motivating people means that you won't have to rely on ordering people exactly what to do.

2 *Exercising power, influencing and learning.* The key to success is being able to work with people so that the 'right' things happen, or at least the wrong things don't happen. 'Soft' people skills are central to this.

3 *Making groups and teams work.* More and more work is delivered through teams or groups of people working together towards a common objective. But this is not easy. Open or repressed conflict between people working on a shared task can mean that the task is not done well.

Moving on from addressing the foundational skills in managing people, we consider the **processes of people management** (the Human Resources cycle) which are common to most management roles. These include:

1 *Recruiting people.* This is not only about getting the right people to achieve the desired goals, but also about making sure that what you are hiring them to do needs to be done.

2 *Inducting people.* When people are new to the organisation we need to tell them what their job is, the policies and procedures of the organisation, and how people work together. What they need to do needs to be clear to them and they need to be motivated to work effectively with you and your colleagues. Induction is also needed for people who have been transferred to your area from within the organisation to work with you on a temporary or permanent basis.

3 *Managing performance.* Connecting individuals' efforts and objectives to the objectives and key performance indicators of the organisation is one of the hardest but most important things a manager is involved in.

4 *Reviewing performance.* Setting objectives is only the first part of managing performance. Managers have to support and appraise performance against these objectives.

5 *Developing people.* Good managers not only learn and improve themselves all the time, but also develop those they manage and work with.

You and the people you work with are just two of the factors which shape how effective a manager you are – **the context, especially your organisation**, will affect what works and doesn't work. So, finally, we cover how you as a manager can understand and respond to:

1 *The culture of your organisation* – or your part of it. The manager often has little impact on the culture of an organisation, but a manager can have a positive influence on the psychological climate, that is, the perceptions of people in the work group or team.

2 *The external environment.* Changes in the world outside the organisation – such as government decisions, global finance and energy – can all affect every manager in the organisation. It is useful to be able to anticipate how the external environment will have an impact on you and your part of the organisation.

The final topic brings together all these dimensions – you, the people you work with and your organisation – to consider the vital matter of **change**. Few, if any, managers have not been part of organisation-wide change programmes. Rather, managers are vital to such change programmes which enable organisations to anticipate and respond to their changing world. It is useful, therefore, for managers to understand organisational change. However, you may often be involved in smaller, 'local' changes that you yourself may initiate. If these are well-managed, they are more likely to be successful.

The Tools and techniques section at the end of this book contains tools and techniques to help you:

- generate, organise and communicate ideas
- analyse situations, solve problems and make decisions
- organise and communicate information and data.

These visual thinking and communication tools will help you to put into practice the ideas that the book deals with.

What do we mean by 'manager'?

It is important to recognise that while managers manage, many also have other work. Many managers also do the work that their work group does. Here are two examples:

- the nurse for the hearing unit at the hospital manages her team of nurses, but also works with patients with a particular hearing illness
- the sales manager manages her sales staff, but also spends two days each week selling to the organisation's most important customers.

In these two cases this non-managerial work is planned. Sometimes, however, a manager completes some or all of another person's tasks when that person is absent. The opposite situation also occurs. Here, most of a person's job may be to carry out the normal work of the work group – such as nursing or selling. But when the manager is absent, the employee becomes the manager during that absence.

It is also important to recognise that organisations decide to call some employees managers when they are not managers in the ways we describe. The most common example in the UK, for example, is when sales staff are called sales managers. There are two reasons for this. The first is because organisations believe that customers will be more likely to buy from a sales manager than a sales assistant. The second is that organisations believe that sales staff will be more motivated if they have job titles which are seen as having a high status.

Throughout this book we write as if you are a real manager for all the time you are at work. When reading you will need to focus on the real management part of your work.

Chapter 1 What do managers do?
What do managers actually do?

What do we mean by management? Most writers on management in this part of the twenty-first century would agree that it is the planning, organising, leading and controlling of human and other resources to achieve organisational goals efficiently and effectively. If you can relate your activities to this description then you are a manager – even if the word manager is not part of your job title. You may have only one or two people for whom you are responsible, but if you work through them to achieve organisational goals, you are managing them together with the other resources you use. To manage requires certain aptitudes and skills. Often, however, the task of managing – especially if you are new to the role – may leave you with little opportunity to consider or analyse what you are doing. You may feel that you are responding to a range of demands without being in as much control of your work as you would like. Many new managers feel like this. At some stage, most managers feel ill-prepared for their role and wonder whether they are doing the 'right' things. Consider the following example.

The world of management

Carly had to admit that being promoted to Section Manager wasn't quite what she thought it would be. For her first review meeting with her line manager she had been asked to prepare an outline of her views on the job. Over the last three days, Carly had been making quick notes in her diary. As she read her list to her line manager she found it depressing:

- Constant interruptions! I can never spend enough time on a task.
- I always seem to be reacting to events and requests rather than initiating them.
- Most of my time is spent on day-to-day matters.
- I always have to argue about work responsibilities and resources.
- I never have time to think – and decisions always need to be made immediately.
- I seem to spend all my time talking to people and never actually doing anything.

When Carly finished speaking, she apologised. Her line manager laughed and said: 'Welcome to the world of management!'

This confusing world has been the subject of much analysis by management writers who have tried to make sense of the contradictions and time pressures that characterise most management jobs. One of the most well-known definitions of what management is and what managers do was given by Henri Fayol, a French mining engineer who, in 1916, published a book on management. In it he defined management as a process involving

- forecasting and planning
- organising
- commanding
- coordinating
- controlling.

The simple division of a manager's job into these separate elements remains a powerful idea, although now we would refer to 'commanding' as leading.

What is managerial effectiveness?

There are no absolute measures of managerial effectiveness. Organisations have aims and objectives, and managers are effective when they help their organisation to achieve these aims and objectives. Thus, it is important that every manager (and employee) knows the purpose of their organisation, the purpose of their job and the work-specific objectives they must meet.

There are various ways of explaining the purpose of a job, and we consider two approaches here.

The most common term is key performance indicators, or KPIs. Setting KPIs is often an organisation-wide process. One version of this process is Management by Objectives. Variations of this are found in all types of organisations, although the process is often no longer referred to as Management by Objectives.

Management by Objectives aims to identify key areas in a person's work and to set targets against which his or her performance (or effectiveness) may be measured.

Management by Objectives is a simple idea which often proves to be very difficult to apply. Peter Drucker, a well-known writer on management, suggests that effective managers follow the same eight practices. They:

- ask 'what needs to be done'
- ask 'what is right for the enterprise'
- develop action plans
- take responsibility for decisions
- take responsibility for communicating
- focus on opportunities
- run productive meetings
- think and say 'we' rather than 'I'.

(Source: Drucker, 2004)

The first two practices give managers the knowledge they need. The next four help them convert this knowledge into effective action. The last two ensure that the whole team or organisation feels responsible and accountable. Most of the practices are applicable at all levels of management.

What does your effectiveness depend on?

At least four sets of factors influence your effectiveness as a manager, and not all of them are under your direct control.

You. In the first place, there is you. You bring a unique blend of knowledge, skills, attitudes, values and experience to your job, and these will influence your effectiveness. If you have been a manager for some time, you will remember some of the mistakes you made as a new manager, and can see how your greater skills now help you to be more effective.

Your job. Then there is the job that you do. It is likely to have many features in common with other managerial jobs, but just as you are unique, so is your job in its detailed features and some of its demands on you. There may be a good or bad match between your skills and the demands of the job, and this affects your potential effectiveness.

The people you work with. The people you work with exert a major influence on how effective you can be as a manager. Descriptions of a manager include 'a person who gets work done through other people', 'someone with so much work to do that he must get other people to do it', and 'the person who decides what needs doing, and gets someone else to do it'. Perhaps surprisingly they get close to the truth with their emphasis on the importance of people for the achievement of a manager's work. One measure of managerial effectiveness is the extent to which a manager can motivate people and coordinate their efforts to achieve optimum performance. However, in most settings managers do not control people in the way that they can control the other resources that they need to get their work done. Rather, managers are dependent on people. Managers' effectiveness is limited by the qualities, abilities and willingness of these people.

If we had been writing 50 years ago, we would have mentioned that there are organisations where commands are frequently given, for example, the military services, the fire service and the police service. In the twenty-first century there will still be situations where a manager in such organisations gives an order and expects immediate compliance. However, many of the processes in organisations such as these now involve softer methods of managing staff.

Your organisation. Finally, the organisation you work in determines how effective you can be. How the organisation is structured and your position in it affect your authority and your responsibilities, and impose constraints on what you are able to achieve. Similarly, the culture of the organisation, with its unwritten norms and ways of working, also influences your ability to be effective as a manager.

Effectiveness, then, does not come from just learning a few management techniques. Some techniques are important and necessary, but managerial effectiveness is more complex. It is influenced by a range of factors – you, the job you do, the people you work with, and the organisation you work in.

Your job

The pressures of managerial life and the generally fast pace of managerial work mean that few managers have any real opportunity to reflect on the nature of their job. Even if they do, it is not easy to make sense of the work that a lot of managers do. Research in the USA found that the manager's day included a series of short, unconnected activities. At first sight, a lot of the things that managers spend their time doing don't seem clearly connected to the achievement of their goals.

In an article in the *Harvard Business Review*, 'What effective general managers really do', John P. Kotter examined the seemingly inefficient ways in which many managers appear to work. He kept records of what they did and he found that their activities are brief, fragmented and frequently unplanned. They spend 70% or more of their time in the company of other people, sometimes with outsiders who seem to be unimportant. They hold lots of very brief conversations on seemingly inconsequential matters, often unconnected with work, and they do a lot of joking. They ask many questions but rarely seem to make any 'big' decisions during their conversations. They seldom *tell* people what to do. Instead, they ask, request, persuade and sometimes even intimidate. Do these descriptions fit anyone you know (perhaps you, or your boss, or the head of your organisation)?

Kotter says this behaviour is 'less systematic, more informal, less reflective, more reactive, less well-organised, and more frivolous' than a student of management would ever expect. However, he says the behaviour can be explained. He suggests that the two main dilemmas in most senior managers' jobs are:

- working out what to do despite uncertainty, great diversity, and an enormous amount of potentially relevant information
- getting things done through a large and diverse set of people despite having little direct control over most of them.

Thus, the seemingly pointless and inefficient behaviour is, in fact, an efficient and effective way of:

- gathering up-to-the-minute information on which to base decisions
- building networks of human relationships (networks that are often very different from the formal organisation structure) to enable them to get their decisions implemented.

Kotter's explanation is just one way of making sense of the seeming chaos of what managers do. Various other ways have been suggested. We now consider two which we see as very useful.

The 'job description' approach

One way of gaining a clearer picture of what you do as a manager would be to list all your activities in a giant job description. An example is set out below. The list does not describe the job of an actual manager but sets out typical managerial activities.

The manager's job

Makes forecasts

Makes analyses

Thinks creatively/logically

Calculates and weighs risks

Makes sound decisions

Determines goals

Sets priorities

Prepares plans

Schedules activities

Establishes control systems

Sets/agrees budgets

Monitors progress

Exercises control

Determines information needs

Establishes/uses management information systems

Manages his or her time

Copes with stress

Adjusts to change

Develops his or her skills and knowledge

The manager and his or her team

Builds and maintains his or her team

Selects staff

Sets performance standards

Raises productivity

Motivates people

Arranges incentives

Designs jobs

Improves the quality of working life

Monitors and appraises performance

Harmonises conflicting objectives

Handles conflict

Leads

Adopts appropriate management styles

Communicates effectively

Negotiates/persuades/influences

Makes presentations

Conducts meetings

Writes reports and correspondence

Interviews

Counsels and advises

Identifies organisational problems

Creates conditions for change

Implements/manages/copes with change

Designs new organisation/team structures

Establishes reporting lines

Develops internal communication systems

Takes account of environmental factors affecting the organisation (economic, environmental, technological, social, political)

Listing and grouping a manager's activities goes a little way towards making some sense out of the complexities of managerial work, but it does not offer any explanations. Another difficulty is that many other jobs have many of these components. Nurses, sales staff, engineers, chefs and cooks, and office workers, for example, often carry out some of these activities.

The roles of a manager

One of the best-known attempts to make some sense out of the seeming chaos of what managers actually do was made by Henry Mintzberg in 1971. He studied a number of chief executives and kept records of all their activities, all their correspondence and all their contacts during the period of the study. His analysis of the data concluded that managerial work had the following six characteristics.

1   The manager performs a great quantity of work at an unrelenting pace.

2   Managerial activity is characterised by variety, fragmentation and brevity.

3   Managers prefer issues that are current, specific and ad hoc.

4   The manager sits between his organisation and a network of contacts.

5   The manager shows a strong preference for verbal communication.

6   Despite his heavy obligations, the manager appears to be able to control his own affairs.

Note that the study related to *chief* executives. Mintzberg's main question was 'Why did the managers do what they did?' His answer was that they were fulfilling certain *roles*. He identified 10 different roles into which he was able to fit all the activities he observed. He grouped the 10 roles under three broader headings on the grounds that, whatever they were doing, they were invariably doing one of three things: making decisions, processing information, or engaging in interpersonal contact.

Interpersonal roles

These cover the relationships that a manager has to have with others. The three roles within this category are figurehead, leader and liaison. Managers must act as figureheads because of their formal authority and symbolic position representing the organisation. As leaders, managers have to consider the needs of an organisation and those of the individuals they manage and work with. The third interpersonal role, that of liaison, deals with the 'horizontal' relationships which studies of work activity have been shown to be important for a manager. A manager usually maintains a network of relationships, both inside and outside the organisation. Dealing with people, formally and informally, up and down the hierarchy and sideways within it, is thus a major element of the manager's role. A manager is often most visible when performing these interpersonal roles.

Informational roles

Managers must collect, disseminate and transmit information and these activities have three corresponding informational roles: monitor, disseminator and spokesperson.

In monitoring what goes on in the organisation, a manager will seek and receive information about both internal and external events and transmit it to others. This process of transmission is the dissemination role, passing on information. A manager has to give information concerning the organisation to staff and to outsiders, taking on the role of spokesperson to both the general public and those in positions of authority. Managers need not collect or disseminate every item themselves, but must retain authority and integrity by ensuring the information they handle is correct.

Decisional roles

Mintzberg argues that making decisions is the most crucial part of any managerial activity. He identifies four roles which are based on different types of decisions; namely, entrepreneur, disturbance handler, resource allocator and negotiator.

As entrepreneurs, managers make decisions about changing what is happening in an organisation. They may have to initiate change and take an active part in deciding exactly what is done – they are proactive.[8] This is very different from their role as disturbance handlers, which requires them to make decisions arising from events that are beyond their control and which are unpredictable. The ability to react to events as well as to plan activities is an important aspect of management.[9] The resource allocation role of a manager is central to much organisational analysis. A manager has to make decisions about the allocation of money, equipment, people, time and other resources. In so doing a manager is actually scheduling time, programming work and authorising actions.[10] The negotiation role is important as a manager has to negotiate with others and in the process be able to make decisions about the commitment of organisational resources.

Mintzberg found that managers don't perform equally – or with equal frequency – all the roles he described. There may be a dominant role that will vary from job to job, and from time to time.

It is important to note that many non-managers in organisations seem to have these sorts of interpersonal, informational and decisional roles. For example, a hotel receptionist is fulfilling an interpersonal role when she meets the hotel guests' needs by communicating with the room attendants and restaurant staff. A car park attendant who monitors how full the car park is and, when necessary, displays the sign 'car park full' is disseminating information. When the same attendant sends the larger cars to the areas of the car park where there is more space, he is acting as a resource allocator. But in each case routine situations are being handled in routine ways. In contrast, the situations managers deal with differ in the degree of routine, the size and scope and complexity of the activities in which they are involved, and the responsibilities associated with these activities.

The demands, constraints and choices of your job

How much freedom do you have to do your job as a manager? What factors place limits on your effectiveness? More importantly, what can you do about such limitations? Rosemary Stewart (1982) developed a concept which enables jobs to be examined in three very important ways: the demands of the job, which are what the job-holder must do; the constraints, which limit what the job-holder can do; and the choices, which indicate how much freedom the job-holder has to do the work in the way she or he chooses. Her purpose was to show how dealing appropriately with demands and constraints, and exercising choices, can improve managers' effectiveness. Consider the following two examples.

Job A

Simon manages a team of health and safety training officers in a large chemicals company. Although he has a general responsibility for ensuring that staff receive appropriate training, he has little influence on the content of training sessions as a result of health and safety legislation laid down by country laws and when training takes place, but he can influence how the training is provided and other aspects of it.

Job B

Arshia manages a drop-in advice centre for homeless teenagers. She has relative freedom in deciding what, when and how assistance is offered within the range of organisational capability. The management committee has just set out a new strategic direction for the organisation which Arshia believes can be improved on, and which she can influence.

Note the differences between the demands and constraints imposed in each case, and how these demands and constraints will place limitations on the respective choices that Simon and Arshia can make.

Demands of the job. Demands are what anyone in the job must do. They can be 'performance demands' requiring the achievement of a certain minimum standard of performance, or they can be 'behavioural demands' requiring that you undertake some activity such as attending certain meetings or preparing a budget. Stewart lists the sources of such demands as being:

- Manager-imposed demands – work that your own line manager expects and that you cannot disregard without penalty.
- Peer-imposed demands – requests for services, information or help from others at similar levels in the organisation. Failure to respond personally would produce penalties.
- Externally-imposed demands – requests for information or action from people outside the organisation that cannot be delegated and where there would be penalties for non-response.
- System-imposed demands – reports and budgets that cannot be ignored nor wholly delegated, meetings that must be attended, social functions that cannot be avoided.
- Staff-imposed demands – minimum time that must be spent with your direct reports (for example, guiding or appraising) to avoid penalties.
- Self-imposed demands – these are the expectations that you choose to create in others about what you will do; from the work that you feel you must do because of your personal standards or habits.

9 → Planning & Marking

7 → Feedback to HOY on certain pupils.

7 → Notes from parents in planners, Parent Evenings.

8 → Writing reports, attending dep. & yr meetings

|

8 → I expect myself to maximise pupils learning

Lack of funding
8 → Old t'books
Outdated ICT

9 → Sticking to
markschemes,
Teaching for tests

10. Pupils attitude
is all important.

Constraints. Constraints are the factors, within the organisation and outside it, that limit what the job-holder can do. Examples include:

- Resource limitations – the amounts and kinds of resources available.
- Legal regulations.
- Trade union agreements.
- Technological limitations – limitations imposed by the processes and equipment with which the manager has to work.
- Physical location of the manager and his or her unit.
- Organisational policies and procedures.
- People's attitudes and expectations – their willingness to accept, or tolerate, what the manager wants to do.

To this list for today's world we would add factors which will impose constraints such as:

- ethics – your own and those to which your organisation adheres
- the environment – climate change and remediation.

Choices. Many managerial jobs offer opportunities for choices both in what is done and how it is done, though the amount and nature of choice vary. Managers can also exercise choice by emphasising some aspects of the job and neglecting others. Often they will do so partly unconsciously. The main choices are usually in:

- *what* work is done
- *how* the work is done
- *when* the work is done.

Analysis of your job using these concepts of demands, constraints and choices can be revealing, particularly if it leads to the recognition that one or other aspect needs changing.

Note that demands and constraints also apply to many employees who work in the organisation. Choices, however, often do not apply to employees doing routine jobs.

Your management skills

Imagine always having to work at a level above your capabilities. Alternatively, imagine doing a job that frustrates you because it demands few of your skills. Both situations are likely to be stressful. Thus, matching your own capabilities to the requirements of your management job is important for a variety of reasons.

Which managerial skills and competencies are most frequently used in managerial work? Obviously, the answer to this question will vary enormously from job to job. However, there are recognised 'sets' of skills and competencies. One such set of occupational standards for management and leadership has been developed in the UK by the

Management Standards Centre. The latest standards are based on research carried out between 2002 and 2004. The broad categories of skills and competencies which they cover are shown in Figure 1.1.

Figure 1.1 Skills and competencies

The diagram shows six functional areas (A–F) with Managing self and personal skills having a central position, indicating their contribution to the other five areas of competence. Each area contains a number of 'units' of competence, numbering 47 in total. For example, listed under Working with people are 12 'units' set out in Table 1.1.

Table 1.1 Units of competence

D1	Develop productive working relationships with colleagues
D2	Develop productive working relationships with colleagues and stakeholders
D3	Recruit, select and keep colleagues
D4	Plan the workforce
D5	Allocate and check work in your team
D6	Allocate and monitor the progress and quality of work in your area of responsibility
D7	Provide learning opportunities for colleagues
D8	Help team members address problems affecting their performance
D9	Build and manage teams
D10	Reduce and manage conflict in your team
D11	Lead meetings
D12	Participate in meetings

These 12 competencies recognise the importance of the soft skills which managers bring to their role. Overall, the standards are designed to act as a benchmark of best practice.

A simpler scheme of management skills was suggested by Robert L. Katz (1986) in the *Harvard Business Review*. Katz, who was interested in the selection and training of managers, suggested that effective administration rested on three groups of basic skills, each of which could be developed.

Technical skills. These are specialist skills and knowledge related to the individual's profession or specialisation. Examples include project management skills for engineers building bridges, aircraft and ships. Katz pointed out that training programmes tend to focus on skills in this area. These skills are easier to learn than those in the other two groups.

Human skills. Katz defines these as the ability to work effectively as a group member and to build cooperative effort in the team a person leads.

Conceptual skills. Katz saw these as being the ability to see the significant elements in any situation. Seeing the elements involves being able to:

- see the enterprise as a whole
- see the relationships between the various parts
- understand their dependence on one another
- recognise that changes in one part affect all the others.

This ability also extends to recognising the relationship of the individual organisations to the political, social and economic forces of the nation as a whole. This has since been called the 'helicopter mind', that is, being able to rise above a problem and see it in context. These conceptual skills are likely to be demonstrated by a manager or executive higher in the organisation. Indeed, at these higher levels of management, organisations require these skills.

One area of skill that Katz did not list, but which is becoming increasingly recognised (though often grudgingly) as a basic requirement for managerial effectiveness is a political skill in handling organisational politics. These politics cover pursuit of individual interests and self-interest, struggles for resources, personal conflicts, and the ways in which people and groups try to gain benefit or achieve goals.

Characteristics of an effective manager

Which special characteristics, if any, do effective managers possess? What makes a manager effective in one organisation, one situation, at one time, can be ineffective in another organisation, situation or time. There are few universals in management. But some researchers do claim to have identified a range of characteristics that are common to the more successful managers. Eugene Jennings (1952) studied 2,700 supervisors selected as most effective by senior managers in their organisations and by the people who worked under them. These supervisors also met effectiveness criteria in terms of department productivity, absentee rate and employee turnover. The identified traits and behaviours are set out in Box 1.1 in order of priority.

Box 1.1 Traits and behaviours

Gives clear work instructions: communicates well in general, keeps others informed.

Praises others when they deserve it: understands importance of recognition; looks for opportunities to build the esteem of others.

Willing to take time to listen: aware of value of listening both for building cooperative relationships and avoiding tension and grievances.

Cool and calm most of the time: maintains self-control, doesn't lose her/his temper; can be counted on to behave maturely and appropriately.

Confident and self-assured.

Appropriate technical knowledge of the work being supervised: uses it to coach, teach and evaluate rather than getting involved in doing the work itself.

Understands the group's problems: as demonstrated by attentive listening and trying to understand the group's situation.

Gains the group's respect, through personal honesty: doesn't try to appear more knowledgeable than is true; not afraid to say, 'I don't know' or 'I made a mistake'.

Fair to everyone: in work assignments, consistent enforcement of policies and procedures; avoids favouritism.

Demands good work from everyone: maintains consistent standards of performance; doesn't expect group to do the work of a low-performing worker; enforces work discipline.

Gains people's trust: willing to represent the group to higher management, regardless of agreement or disagreement with them.

Takes a leadership role: works for the best and fair interests of the work group; loyalty to both higher management and the work group.

Humble, 'not stuck up': remembers that s/he is simply a person with a different job to do from the workers s/he supervises.

Easy to talk to: demonstrates a desire to understand without shutting off feedback through scolding, judging or moralising.

You are the best person to assess whether your capabilities match the requirements of your management job, as each managerial role will differ according to a variety of factors. It is not easy to make such an assessment, but it may help you if you consider the way in which you are line managed. However, managers tend to use their own line manager as a role model regardless of whether what is being modelled is appropriate and effective. Thus, it is wise to consider how, ideally, you would like to be managed and to take note of the way in which other managers manage their staff. Then you will be in a better position to assess your own capabilities. The advantage will be that you will have examples to follow – and ones to avoid!

Transition into management

Ironically, the same skills that helped individuals to become managers may prevent them from becoming an *effective* manager. One of the most common reasons for promoting someone to managerial status is that he or she has excelled as a 'player'. Most sales managers have been very successful salespeople, most production managers have worked well on the shop-floor, most office managers have been very good secretaries or administrators. Presumably, the rationale is that if you can do it well, you can manage it equally well. While the majority of managers find the transition to a managerial position stimulating (if stressful at times), some find it more difficult. The reason is usually that they find it difficult to stop doing their previous job. They continue to 'play' rather than manage. They try to retain some of the roles they did well as operators, and this can reduce their effectiveness as managers.

This problem is known as the player–manager syndrome. Understanding the syndrome may help you to change your roles, or help other managers to be more effective. In some jobs, there is a complete break when a person moves from operating to managing. For instance, not many airline managers continue to fly aeroplanes. However, in many management jobs a certain amount of operating is still needed. There may be expectations in your organisation that you should continue in some of your former operating roles. When changing to a management job it is important to consider whether time spent operating improves or damages your management role. You may want to use the opportunity to change the emphasis of your work so that it is more about your management role and fits into your available time more easily.

Some of the reasons people give for finding it hard to stop doing their old role and adjust to the new one are set out below. Solutions are also suggested on the kinds of adjustments you can make.

1 **It is important to keep my specialist skills up-to-date**. You can maintain your skills by guiding, teaching or coaching in order to perfect someone else's technique. This helps your team members to develop new competences.

2 **I believe it helps my leadership image if I show that I can perform as well as any of my staff and can do anything I ask them to do**. Your leadership and ability to perform to a high standard will be better demonstrated by sharing management issues with your staff. Share with them how the objectives could be set, how to plan and organise them, how to set up a control mechanism and how to evaluate the achievement. This develops valuable project management skills in your team.

3 **My staff expect me to remain 'one of them'**. If you share with your staff aspects of your managerial thinking – its planning, organisation and coordination – you'll demonstrate the particular contribution you are making to the team effort.

4 **I feel more secure and comfortable doing something I know I can do well**. By doing tasks which are within the capabilities of your staff, you could be denying them the opportunity to gain the experience.

5　**I believe it is often quicker and easier to do the job myself than leave it to somebody who cannot do it so well**. Helping others to learn yields benefits in the long run. Take every opportunity to develop your staff, and do this in a planned fashion.

6　**I need to carry out work myself because I don't have enough people to do the job**. When there are unexpected staff shortages or sudden demand, for example, you may need to respond by doing the job yourself. But who will be managing while you are performing? If a staff shortage is long-standing you will need to try to get extra resources or to reduce the levels of activity. When times are difficult your team needs you to plan work activities, to be an effective figurehead and spokesperson for your department and to influence decisions taken elsewhere.

7　**My manager gets very involved and expects me to do so as well**. This is a difficult situation to deal with because it may involve trying to influence the attitude of the person who manages you. However, it is important to demonstrate your effectiveness as a manager if you are able to. This includes giving evidence of the value of your contributions to planning and budgeting; the effectiveness of your control systems; and your interest in, and influence on, job design, the motivation of your staff and morale in your department. By doing the job yourself you will not demonstrate your qualities as a manager unless you are able to manage the work of your team in addition to your own work.

8　**My job is largely functional and involves a good deal of operating as well as managing**. If you are a manager who maintains a professional role or particular specialism, you must spend some time on it. But the functions of manager and professional or specialist functional leader overlap a good deal, as is suggested in Figure 1.2.

Figure 1.2 The overlap between managerial and professional or specialist functions

Many people like to spend their time and energy operating rather than managing. Operating is often easier and more rewarding than managing, and it is usually less demanding and carries fewer risks. However, you need to maintain the right balance. To do this you need to be able to separate operating and managing very clearly. New managers can find the transition difficult. Older managers may have failed to make the transition.

Making the transition

Seven stages of transition have been identified which apply to management and indeed many other life and work transitions, especially when a transition has been quite sudden (Adams *et al.*, 1976). These are set out below.

1 *Immobilisation*: the initial 'frozen' feeling when you do not know what to make of your new role.

2 *Minimisation*: you carry on as though nothing has changed, perhaps denying inside that you really have new roles as a manager.

3 *Depression*: when the nature and volume of the expectations upon you have sunk in and you feel you cannot cope; depression can be accompanied by feelings of panic, anger and blame.

4 *Acceptance*: when you begin to realise there are things you are achieving and more you could achieve, and that you have moved on from what you used to do.

5 *Testing*: when you begin to form your own views on what management is all about and even experimenting with what you can do.

6 *Seeking meaning*: you find the inclination and energy to reflect upon and learn from your own and others' behaviour.

7 *Internalising*: you define yourself as a manager, not just in title but in what you think you are doing; you and your job have come to terms with each other.

The seven transition phases represent a sequence in the level of self-esteem as you experience a disruption, gradually acknowledge its reality, test yourself, understand yourself, and incorporate changes in your behaviour. Changes in level of self-esteem appear to follow a predictable path. Identifying the seven phases along such a self-esteem curve can help you to understand the transition process better. This is illustrated in Figure 1.3.

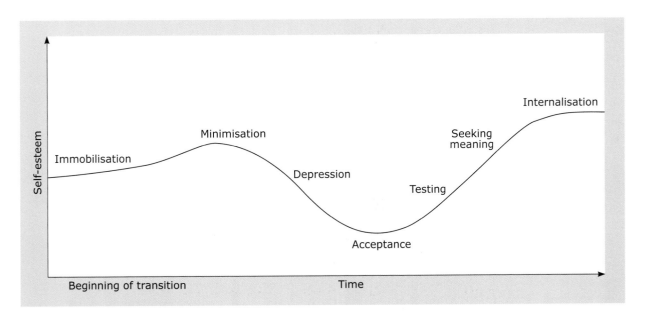

Figure 1.3 The transition process

(Source: Adams *et al.*, 1976)

Although this seven-stage model describes transition as a sequence, not everyone in job transition will experience every phase. Each person's progress is unique: one may never get beyond denial or minimisation; another may drop out during depression; and others will move smoothly and rapidly to the later phases.

Recognising pressure and avoiding stress

Most people would agree that a certain amount of pressure is tolerable, even enjoyable. Different people, of course, react in different ways to pressure. Some people tolerate more than others do. But we are often at our best when the adrenalin is flowing and when we are working under pressure to achieve good results within a limited time. Problems start when the pressure becomes too great or continues for long periods. It then becomes stress. It ceases to be enjoyable. In the UK, employees are absent for an average of eight days a year and stress is the fourth major cause of this absence (CIPD, 2008). The five main causes of work-related stress that CIPD identified were:

- workload

- management style

- relationships at work

- organisational change and restructuring

- lack of employee support from line managers.

These causes should alert you to the idea that, as a manager, you are just as likely to suffer from stress as to be the cause of it! How a manager can reduce stress among direct reports is covered elsewhere in this textbook.

See also: Improving the psychological climate: what a manager can do, Chapter 12

It is important that managers are able to distinguish between pressure and stress so that they can avoid stress while making the best use of appropriate pressure. A simple way of differentiating between pressure and stress is by the effects that they have.

Most high achievers (and a lot of managers would fall into this category) find pressure to be positively motivating. They are able to respond to it energetically. Stress, on the other hand, is debilitating. It deprives people of their strength, their vitality and their judgement. The area of concern is where pressure becomes stress. Here, one needs to be constantly looking for tell-tale signs.

Causes of stress

The most common causes of stress are:

Demand. For the manager, demand will include responsibilities such as:

- responsibility for the work of others and having to reconcile overlapping or conflicting objectives – between group and organisation, between individuals and group, and between one's own objectives and those of other managers

- responsibility for innovative activities, especially in organisations where there is a cultural resistance to change.

When these demands are excessive, they can be regarded as role overload which occurs when a manager is expected to hold too many roles. In the recent past, many organisations in Europe and the USA have responded to demands for cost reduction by 'delayering'. This involves reducing the number of managers, while the amount of work to be managed remains the same. Some organisations have implemented delayering by requiring that the remaining managers do all the work of managers now removed. They are also told to achieve the same quality as before. The managers affected may see this as an impossible task. Equally, role underload can be stressful if a person feels underused. Work overload and underload is different from role overload and underload. In work overload and underload, stress is created as a result of the quality and quantity of work demanded – either too much or too little.

Control. A manager's role as coordinator can be stressful, especially where authority is unclear or resources are inadequate.

Role ambiguity, incompatibility and role conflicts.

- Ambiguity about management roles is often inevitable: they invariably combine a number of overlapping roles. Indeed, it is precisely this overlap that makes management jobs interesting and offers scope for creativity.

- Role incompatibility occurs when a manager's expectations of role are significantly different from those of his or her staff and colleagues. Pressure to do things that do not feel appropriate or 'right' is stressful.

- Role conflict may occur when someone has to carry out several different roles. Although the manager may be comfortable about performing each role individually, there may be conflict when several roles are held at one time. This may include conflict between roles associated with home and family and roles associated with work.

Other major sources of stress that are not confined to managers but affect them include:

Relationship problems. People who have difficulties with their manager, their staff or their colleagues may exhibit symptoms of stress.

Support. All staff need adequate support from colleagues and superiors.

Career uncertainty. Uncertainty often occurs as a result of rapid changes in the economic situation inside and outside the organisation, in technology, in markets and in organisational structures.

Symptoms of stress

It is common for managers to seek work or responsibilities even though they know this will increase the pressure on them. The stimulus of responsibility, of achieving work or personal targets, and of working against deadlines provides much of the interest and satisfaction in their work. However, this pressure can become counter-productive if it is excessive – if you no longer feel in control and if the satisfaction of achievement fails to compensate for the stress of delivering the outcomes. At this stage you need to be able to identify the cause of the excess pressure and take measures to correct it. Your objective must be to maintain a level of pressure that you find stimulating and not threatening.

Symptoms of stress include being too busy or working longer hours, insecurity, an unwillingness to delegate, loss of motivation and indecision. Work performance may decline or become inconsistent. Other symptoms may include irritability and short temper, panic reactions, heavy reliance on tobacco, alcohol or drugs such as tranquillisers. All can be signs of other problems, but their presence should make you suspect stress.

Once you are aware of the causes of unproductive pressure, you are in a position to address the problem.

Reducing stress

Methods of reducing stress that work for the manager are also likely to be effective for the work team: less stress among direct reports will reduce demands on the manager. Possible actions include:

- Promoting collaborative working approaches. If you are careful to involve members of your team in making decisions about matters that affect them, they will be more likely to cooperate with you and with each other.
- Creating 'stability zones'. These are areas of work over which you and members of your work group have some control, or a measure of control.
- Being alert to the actual demands being made on you and those in your work group.
- Ensuring that everyone knows their roles and the functions they are expected to fulfil.
- Setting yourself and others clear priorities and keeping an overview of everyone's workload.

These actions will help you to monitor roles and workloads, to clarify expectations and help to provide staff with a sense of control and certainty, and to promote good relationships.

A final point is that it is common for managers to set themselves high standards in terms of both the quantity and the quality of their work. This is reinforced when the organisational culture creates an expectation of long working hours. If it is usual to hold breakfast meetings, this may create unreasonable pressures on staff who have school-age children. If these examples are familiar you should consider changing your own working practices and persuading other managers to change theirs.

We have considered mainly causes of stress which take place at work. There are many causes of stress in workers' lives outside work. Some organisations make arrangements to help workers with their problems caused by issues outside work. Since this help can involve specialist knowledge, organisations may employ their own specialists for this. Managers need to know what the organisation's policies are on stress with causes outside work, and what they should and should not do.

Managing your time

For many managers the most difficult and stressful problem they have to deal with is shortage of time: the work simply will not fit into the time available. Many courses and books are available on time management to train people in techniques for managing their time. As with so many management techniques, there is no magic solution, merely a good deal of common sense that you could work out for yourself – if you had time.

There are three principles in improving time management:

- work shedding
- time saving
- time planning.

Work shedding

By work shedding we mean:

- stopping doing some tasks
- changing the task method to one taking less time
- reducing the quality of some work
- transferring tasks to other people.

Getting rid of some of your work is an obvious solution. The problem for some managers is that they don't know how to, or are unwilling to. They are perfectionists, worriers, interferers, individuals who cannot let go. The techniques of shedding work are simple. You need to:

- concentrate effort on your key activities
- delegate.

To concentrate on key activities requires you to identify carefully those tasks which *must* be done thoroughly. This does not mean that the others can be done to an unacceptable standard, but that you are better placed to allocate time and effort appropriately. The Pareto Principle, or the 80/20 law, should help you to sort out your priorities. It asserts, on quite strong evidence, that 80% of our results are generally produced by 20% of our effort – and that the remaining 80% of our effort is swallowed up in achieving that last 20% of our results. If this holds true for managers, then a lot of effort is devoted to jobs that don't merit the effort. These jobs are candidates for shedding, or at least for receiving less attention. The trick, of course, is to identify the key 20% that means so much to your success.

Delegation is the other main device for shedding work. Delegation means giving someone the authority (and the necessary resources, including time) to do something on your behalf. We mainly use the term when transferring work to the people who work for us. When you do this you retain the responsibility for it. Responsibility has been compared with influenza – you can pass it on but you cannot get rid of it. In exercising your responsibility you must strike an appropriate balance between trust and interference. When we transfer work to another department, or to a supplier or customer, we would usually call this transferring, rather than delegating work.

See also: Learning and development activities, Chapter 11

Time saving and time planning

One approach to saving time is to identify the main wasters of time in your working life – and eliminate them. Some major time-wasters are:

- giving a higher priority to new email than is necessary
- accepting all telephone interruptions
- encouraging people to discuss their problems with you
- encouraging visitors
- holding meetings which are unnecessary, badly planned or badly conducted, or all of these
- reading slowly (much time spent reading documents)
- writing slowly (much time spent drafting)
- delaying starting important and urgent work, or procrastination (indecision)
- unnecessary or inefficient travelling.

To identify time-wasters such as these, try keeping a log of your time – even if only for a few days. This can help you to identify where time is being wasted. At 15-minute intervals throughout a working week, note the main tasks on which you have been working. You can save time in keeping your log by preparing a pro forma sheet with columns headed with your most likely activities. Then you can insert ticks and an occasional comment. At the end of the recording period you should analyse the entries in the columns. This will reveal the proportions of time that you are spending on each aspect of your work, and it should highlight time-wasters and jobs that could be shed.

To manage effectively you need some time every day when you can give your undivided attention to your key tasks. Interruptions to this time will damage your concentration and your ability to think clearly. You could identify an hour each day when you are simply not 'available'. If you want to keep face-to-face conversations short, don't sit down. When you want to end a face-to-face discussion when you are sitting, sum up and stand up. Make appointments with visitors to talk to them at a more appropriate time. Better still, if the visitor is located nearby, visit them; that way you retain control over the length of your visit. Colleagues will soon start to respect your time and privacy. It becomes a status symbol – and like all status symbols it should be visible but not ostentatious.

See also: What are meetings for?; Making meetings more effective, Chapter 2

Meetings are one of the most notorious wasters of time. If they are your meetings, first decide if they are necessary. If they are, then plan them carefully. Set an agenda, set a time limit, and keep discussion strictly to the point.

If you are a slow reader, you can learn how to skim read. If you draft slowly, try a different method. For example, voice-recognition software can speed up your 'writing' because it enables you to speak your ideas rather than putting them down on paper. Time spent socialising and on visits may be important to build networks and good relationships. If it is one of your key activities, do it. If not, limit it. Procrastination is possibly the worst 'thief' of time for many managers. Difficult or disliked decisions and tasks are delayed in the hope, rather than the expectation, that they will resolve themselves or that new information will come to hand which will make things clearer. First, identify if there really is a difficulty with the decision or task – you could get help or advice. Second, try breaking a task into smaller, more easily achieved steps. Third, try allocating a time to the unwelcome task, preferably followed by something enjoyable, for example: 'I will do this task between 10.30 am and 12.30 pm before lunch with Peter tomorrow'. But generally, procrastination is a habit and requires self-discipline to overcome it.

Travel is a serious waster of time if there are alternative ways of accomplishing a goal. There is little point in working evenings and weekends so that you can spend your days on the train or the motorway. However, when travel is essential, a long journey by train or plane or other form of public transport can provide uninterrupted time for you to discuss an important matter with a colleague, or to read or think. Technology can allow people to carry on with many normal activities while travelling. It can also be used to avoid unnecessary travel.

Like your other scarce and expensive resources, your time needs to be planned and budgeted to make effective use of it. Time planning is itself time-consuming and routine. But, like many routines, it can help to reduce pressure by reducing the uncertainty in your day, and thus lower the stress associated with uncertainty and lack of control.

Chapter 2 Communicating and managing communication

The communication climate

One hour in the office

8.55	Arrive at office; check and send email including a message to David with a request about budget information.
9.05	My part-time secretary, Meena, arrives. I ask her to set up a meeting with Sarah and another one with Peter. Meena sounds tired; she's been having a few family problems and may have to leave early today. She promises to improve the slides for my presentation tomorrow, though.
9.10	I go to see Jamal about the visitors we're expecting tomorrow. I could email him but I like to make personal contact when I can. Jamal has started a heavy cold so we make a contingency plan in case he's off sick tomorrow and can't give his presentation.
9.20	When I get back to my office Jo comes in wanting to know if I've sorted out his contract yet. I haven't. I'm just about to phone the HR department when a supplier calls to say they won't be able to make a deadline. I phone Dina in Purchasing to see if we can extend the deadline and then call the supplier to say they can have three more days. Then I phone the HR department.
9.40	I start to read the papers for the meeting about customer complaints after lunch, but David calls to ask if he can move our 10.00 meeting back to 9.45. I say yes – I've known David a long time and we get along well so our meetings are always pretty relaxed. We discuss how much we should bid for in terms of staff resource. It's clear we won't get what we want. We agree to meet again on Friday to try to come up with some creative solutions.
9.55	Meena calls to say she's set up a meeting with Sarah at 10.30 but hasn't had a response from Peter yet. I start reading the papers for this afternoon's meeting, but Jan comes in. My heart sinks – Jan's 'have you got a minute?' requests always take a long time … it takes all my skills to keep her focussed on her difficulty today and encourage her to see what her options are.

Communicate – that's what we do most of the time in the workplace. But how good are we at communication and how important is it that we are effective? Effective communication in organisations is very important. Examples include the way in which ideas, information and feelings are communicated within organisations and the interpersonal skills required. Communication is seen as an important component in good leadership and management. Employees' satisfaction with communication in organisations influences their commitment to the organisation, their motivation and, ultimately, productivity at the organisational level.

What makes communication better in some organisations than others? 'Communication climate' – the atmosphere or conditions in which communication takes place – directly influences whether working relationships will be cooperative and information flow will be smooth.

A communication climate can be 'open' or 'closed'. An open climate is one in which people feel they can speak freely without fear of being criticised; suggestions are welcomed and acted on and mistakes are used as an opportunity to learn. An open climate is generally regarded as a goal to which most Western organisations aspire. In a 'closed' communication climate the environment is often highly political, with a high but concealed priority given to competition for approval, promotion or resources. In such a climate people can become possessive about the information they have access to, using it as a source of power. Here, information is given or not given in order to reinforce a person's position rather than to contribute to effective working. In such a climate communication between individuals is minimal, defensive and focussed on relationships rather than work objectives. Consider the two examples below.

Petra's offer

Working at the academic bookshop is like being part of a close-knit family. Petra, the manager, has worked hard to achieve that. Sales are not good, however. The cost of academic books is high and a poor economic climate led to a fall in sales. Deborah thinks she has a good idea for increasing sales. She mentions it to Petra who tells her: 'That's a great idea, Deborah. I'm not sure that some aspects of it will work but we can discuss it at Friday's meeting.'

Georgia's apology

It was Georgia's first presentation at the medical supplies company. She didn't know how it happened but she'd shown the wrong figures to a group of senior managers. One of the managers had used the figures in an external report which had now been reported in the media. 'I think I need to tell my manager immediately', she thought as she emailed her line manager to arrange a discussion. At the meeting later that day, she could hardly believe what she was hearing. Her manager did not accept her apology or discuss a solution. Instead, she found herself being criticised for incompetence. Distressed, she became defensive and blamed her manager for not checking her presentation.

The first example is typical of an open communication climate and the second is typical of a closed one. What makes a communication climate open or closed? Table 2.1 sets out the main characteristics of communication in open and closed climates, first identified by Jack Gibb in 1961.

Table 2.1 Characteristics of communication in open and closed communication climates

Open and closed communication climate characteristics	
Closed climate behaviours	**Open climate behaviours**
Evaluative – judgemental assessments of others' behaviour *Example*: You shouldn't have done that. You're always doing things you shouldn't!	**Descriptive** – describes a complaint in behavioural terms rather than being judgemental; avoids blaming *Example*: I wish you hadn't done that before discussing it first
Controlling – an attempt to impose a solution or outcome *Example*: Do it this way	**Solution-oriented** – a focus on working together to resolve problems *Example*: We've got different ideas about the way this can be done so let's find 15 minutes to talk
Neutral – indifference towards the other person *Example*: How could you have forgotten to spellcheck the report?	**Empathetic** – identification with the situation or emotions of another person *Example*: I know how hard you worked to meet the deadline but I think you forgot to spellcheck the report in the rush
Strategic – an attempt to manipulate or deceive the other person *Example*: I've got a great task for you that should really help your career	**Spontaneous** – there is no attempt to manipulate the other person *Example*: I've got a task I'd really like you to do – but it's a little difficult
Superior – the other person is not worthy of respect *Example*: The decision has been made so there's no point in saying anything	**Equal** – the other person is worthy of respect *Example*: I'd like your views on this
Certain – the speaker's view is correct *Example*: I already know the answer	**Provisional** – a willingness to consider the other person's situation or view *Example*: I have an answer in mind, but I'd be interested in your opinion

Few communication climates are fully 'open' or wholly 'closed'. A communication climate may be closed because it has always been that way or because of pressures to get the job done. It can also occur when organisations are in financial trouble or where there are threats of job losses. Unless an organisation is very small, there is likely to be more than one communication climate within it. Indeed, communication climate and communication satisfaction among employees (the extent to which their communication needs are met) can be assessed at work-group level. A study of a Dutch regional police force by Bartels *et al.* (2007) suggests that the communication climate is more strongly linked to employee commitment to the work group than the organisation as a whole. At this level of the work group, then, managers are best placed to influence the communication climate and communication satisfaction.

What you can do to improve the communication climate

As a manager, you may not be able to change your organisation's communication climate. However, it is possible to improve the communication climate in your own work group. Indeed, Ed Robertson (2005), a writer on organisational communication, maintains that an organisation's communication climate will be only 'as strong as the multiple work groups or micro communication climates that comprise it'. In their work groups managers need to communicate:

- job information
- personal information
- operational information
- strategic information
- information to their managers.

At the same time, a manager's direct reports need:

- explanations of policy and answers to questions
- job performance expectations to be set out clearly
- notice of changes from official sources
- freedom to make suggestions and to make complaints
- provision of important information by preferred sources and media
- more senior personnel to be accessible and approachable
- efforts by a manager or supervisor to understand their feelings and problems
- expressions of appreciation by the manager or supervisor of good performance
- openness and willingness of more-senior people to initiate communication.

While all are important to an employee's satisfaction with communication, according to the UK's Chartered Institute of Personnel and Development (2006), the opportunity to feed upwards and feeling well-informed about what is happening in the organisation are the key drivers of employee commitment. Employee expectations may differ across national or ethnic cultures, of course.

There are some key areas that a manager needs to focus on to improve the communication climate in the work group.

Information needs. To perform well, employees need information as set out above. Note that the term is used here to include ideas, issues and opinions as well as more conventional formal information such as reports. Thus, managers need to consider what they are communicating, how, how much, and to whom. This means first assessing two fundamental aspects of communication:

- adequacy
- flow.

Adequacy refers to the amount and quality of what is provided. Where information is inaccurate or incomplete – or if there is too little of it – misunderstandings, mistakes and frustration are likely to occur. Conversely, however accurate and complete the information, too much can cause information overload. For staff, this can mean spending time trying to identify what is important from a mass of detail. Flow refers to the way in which information flows vertically and horizontally in an organisation, allowing for the exchange of ideas, issues and opinions. Obstructions and 'bottlenecks' will disturb the flow, and so need to be identified.

See also: Improving your information management, Chapter 5

There are various ways of assessing the information needs of individuals. A simple mapping device can be found in Chapter 5 of this book.

Feeling valued. If employees want to make suggestions but these are always ignored or their opinions are never sought, they will feel that they 'don't count' in the organisation. A manager can help direct reports and more junior staff to feel valued by treating them with respect, by listening to and acknowledging their opinions, even if suggestions are not used. This not only helps staff to feel engaged and committed: it is considered vital in fostering creativity and innovation. A further step is to invite suggestions and opinions.

Trust. Where there is a lack of trust, employees will rarely admit to making a mistake and are less willing to take risks or to tolerate change. As a result, they are unlikely to be offered the support they need and their productivity may suffer. A manager can create an atmosphere of trust in two ways. The first is to be trustworthy, that is, by being truthful. The second is to ensure that when a direct report admits to a mistake, the focus is placed on putting it right or preventing the same mistake happening again. In the UK health service, when medical mistakes occur, systems rather than individuals are scrutinised for primary causes of error. In an office situation, an employee may circulate an out-of-date document because there is no standard system for naming and dating files and versions, providing greater opportunity for error. Good systems make errors less likely. However, mistakes will still occur as a result of individual error or misjudgement. It is best if the manager's first reaction is understanding and forgiving. The request 'Tell me what happened' is likely to result in a constructive resolution, while the question 'Why ever did you do X?' is likely to result in a defensive response by the member of staff.

Conflict. Conflict is inevitable. The art of dealing with it is to use it constructively. People usually disagree because they have different perspectives or views of the situation. Exploring these perspectives can lead to better solutions. Although in some cases the need for a quick decision or for confidentiality prevents this, a manager needs to invite conversation with staff, to listen carefully and to look for areas of agreement. The manager also needs to encourage people to disagree. This can be done by encouraging staff to question what you or the organisation is doing and to think about ways of improving the way things are done. Rewarding or recognising staff for their questions and ideas is important.

Grievances. When staff members feel they have been treated unfairly, a manager needs to deal with these grievances seriously. Staff need to be sure that grievances involving colleagues will be listened to and treated in confidence, and that a serious attempt will be made to deal with the source of the grievance. Other grievances may be less personal and can be discussed openly, for example, in a staff meeting.

Feedback. Continual feedback – both positive and negative – is vital to maintain and improve the performance of staff. A constructive approach when a job has not been well done is to ask the person to assess the outcome. Did it meet the requirements? A second question is to ask what they would do differently if they were asked to carry out the task again. This allows for self-correction. In addition, it can identify difficulties beyond the person's control which require the manager's intervention. When giving positive feedback it is good practice to be specific about what has been well done and acknowledge difficulties or sacrifices. An example is given in Box 2.1.

See also: Managing conflict, Chapter 8

Open communication climate behaviours will convey to people that they are valued, recognised and acknowledged. Other individual behaviours that convey this include not interrupting and never ignoring another person's attempts to communicate. In such an open climate it is possible to reject an idea a person has put forward without rejecting the person too. Closed communication climate behaviours result in defensiveness in which people protect themselves from attack, often by verbally attacking the critic, distorting the information (for example, by distorting the reason why they did something the way they did), by avoiding information, by pretending not to care about it or by simply ignoring relevant information.

Box 2.1 Being clear

Much of the time we leave out detail when we speak. We say: *'Good presentation, John'* when what we actually mean is *'It was great that you found time to create those graphs; it really helped in communicating the size of the increase in complaints.'* Being clear often means saying things more fully. This is particularly important when managers need to ask a person to change their behaviour or practices. If we leave out the necessary detail we may be misunderstood. Our request can sound too dogmatic or judgemental. A well-known 'formula' for making requests is:

1 *I notice* – say what you noticed or observed.

2 *I feel* – say how you feel about it.

3 *Because* – say why you feel that way.

4 *I want* – say what you want or hope the person to do.

5 *So that* – say why you want or hope for this.

Here are some translations of statements using the formula. The numbers indicate each part of the formula in the translations.

Whatever made you forget to call John while I was on leave?

John just told me he did not know that we might have to change the deadline (1). I feel upset and embarrassed (2) because it was important that we told him as soon as we knew (3). I'd like you to let me know if you think you won't have time to cover particular tasks while I'm on leave next time (4) so we can make sure your workload is manageable (5).

Stop what you're doing; I need you to work on the budget.

The project proposal has to be in by Monday morning, Nikki (1). I'm feeling under a lot of pressure (2) because I'm busy with the training evaluation report (3). I'd like you to gather information for the budget (4). The quicker I finish the report the sooner I can help you (5).

Note that statements of empathy or acknowledgement could be added to each message, for example, *I realise you have been/are very busy ... I realise you haven't done a task like this before ...*

Some tips

- Be descriptive and focus on the situation not the purpose. Avoid saying *You always/never ...*
- Avoid implying that what you felt was the fault of the other person. Avoid saying *I felt manipulated/ignored ...*
- Avoid blaming the person when giving the reason for feeling as you do. Avoid saying *... because you let me down.*
- Be specific about what you want to happen. Say 'I'd like you to give me your new ideas on the project by Friday', not 'Give it some thought'.
- Try to make the reason for what you want positive and motivating.
- Use *I* not *you* for each part of the formula, unless unavoidable.
- Be empathetic.

Theories of communication

The broadband advertisement

A magazine advertisement for a broadband service claims that it will enable 'much faster communication' between your computer and the internet. It states a precise data transfer rate as a measure of this 'improved' communication.

The shareholder's meeting

At a company's annual shareholder meeting the audience watches a DVD, hears speeches and receives brochures. After the meeting the director and the head of corporate communications congratulate one another. 'We're really communicating the message to stakeholders,' the director says.

On the plane

Two people are sitting in adjacent seats on an aeroplane. One person is talkative; the other person pretends to sleep to avoid a conversation.

Hidden feelings

Danja didn't like Tabitha but it was important not to show it in front of her boss, Sam. When the three of them met, Danja smiled at Tabitha as she greeted her. In an instant, Sam saw that Danja's smile wasn't genuine. 'Those two don't get along with each other,' she thought.

In the first example, the communication is not 'human': computers and servers exchanging information have no awareness that they are sending or receiving electronic symbols and no understanding of where the data came from (or went to). They cannot understand what it means. In the second example, the company seems to be 'communicating' a one-way flow of information, from the company to the shareholders. Was anyone listening, watching, reading? In the third example, the 'sleeper' is saying nothing but is communicating the message: 'I don't want to talk to you now.' The person is simply using non-verbal communication. The example also shows that it's hard *not* to communicate – even silence communicates something! In the fourth example, Danja communicated the message she intended *not* to. So, the view of communication we are proposing is wide. It is very inclusive and allows consideration of issues such as interpretation, intention, context and meaning.

We all communicate, but the basis for improving communication skills is knowing something about how communication 'works'. A general definition of communication is 'social interaction through messages'. As the examples show, people use the term communication in many ways, ranging from the speed of transmission of information through a channel, to interactions that involve intention and understanding.

The information theory model of communication

A theoretical framework for understanding communication often taught on management courses is the information theory of communication. Developed by Shannon and Weaver (1949), this approach links clearly to what became the information technology revolution of the twentieth century. The basic idea is shown in Figure 2.1. Communication is seen as a linear process in which a sender develops a message, then transmits that message over a channel to a receiver. Textbooks sometimes refer to this as the SMCR (sender, message, channel, receiver) model. Some authors use the term 'source' instead of 'sender'.

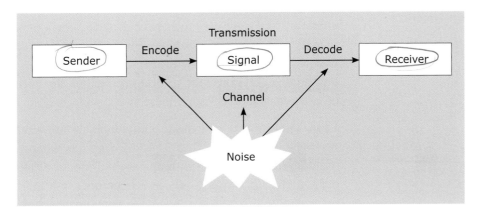

Figure 2.1 A simple model of communication

The model has three basic components:

1 A sender or source of an encoded message – for example, a computer or a television camera.

2 A medium or channel of transmission – for example, signals running along cables or sound waves travelling through the air.

3 A receiver which decodes the message – for example, another computer, a television or a radio receiver.

An additional feature is noise in the channel which restricts the amount of information that can be transmitted. Imperfections or noise in the telephone wires between two handsets can distort sound as it travels to the receiver. Shannon and Weaver provide a *mathematically* robust model by ignoring issues such as interpretation and meaning. Their focus is on the amount of information, that is, the number of 'bits' that moved through the channel. The model has made a large contribution to the development of the various technical systems that we use in communication, such as the telephone, television and computer networks. For the manager, the model may be useful when considering the use of communication media. However, as a model of *human* communication it is best regarded as a very simple view, a metaphor (which can sometimes be useful) rather than a technical description. Key components of human communication are missing, including how the same message can be interpreted very differently by different people depending on prior knowledge and experience, beliefs, values and ethnic culture.

The constructivist model of communication

The constructivist model of communication is so-called because it sees people as constructing meanings. As infants we label and categorise ('dog', 'animal'); we construct mental models (a series of seemingly unconnected events becomes 'a visit to the dentist'). In these ways we understand and make sense of our world. Language is important, if not essential, in creating these concepts and mental models and in developing them into more sophisticated ones through direct experience and through listening and talking to others. One person's constructions will differ from those of another person, of course, with the largest differences occurring between people from very different ethnic cultures with different languages. Consider what the concept 'city' might be for a person who has never seen one and a person who lives and works in London. Consider the mental model of 'the right way to behave at work' for a person from a society that regards deference and obedience as the norm. Now compare it with the mental model of a person from a society that regards initiative-taking, questioning and constructive disagreement as the norm. Imagine a merger of two organisations, when these two people may have to meet.

Even within the same culture, individuals do not always share precisely the same experiences. Thus a person who has worked only in a small organisation will have a different mental model of an organisation from a person who has worked only in a large one. In a major organisational change managers will experience much the same change but their perceptions and understanding of it will differ.

What guidance does constructivism give us on communication? It suggests we need empathy – the use of one's intellect and emotions to understand another person's view.

Empathy is believed to involve:

- Having an emotional response to another person which involves being capable of feeling the same emotions as another and may involve sharing the other person's emotional state.

- The mental capacity to take the position or perspective of another person. This may also involve understanding the context that might have led to a person's actions and beliefs.

- Self-regulation processes that prevent confusion between one's own feelings and views, and those of the other person.

(Source: Decety and Jackson, 2006)

When we show empathy, we are being empathetic. It is easier to be empathetic when what the other person is telling you seems believable. In situations where a statement doesn't seem to believable, the other person may have to provide more information before empathy can occur.

Six steps to perspective-taking and empathy

The following list sets out six steps to understand the perspective of another person:

1 **Assume difference**. This means being active and seeking out differences in how another individual views a situation.

2 **Know self**. To be receptive to another person, we need to realise that our own view of a situation is just that – a view. There may be alternative views that will increase our knowledge or understanding.

3 **Suspend self**. To be receptive to another person's views, we need to put our own ideas aside and try to see the world of the other person. This is known as switching (changing) frames of reference.

4 **Allow guided judgement**. Because we will not be sure that we have understood the other person's viewpoint, we need to be guided by feedback on our understanding. This is likely to involve asking the other person questions like 'So your view is …' and allowing the person to correct us.

5 **Allow empathetic experience**. With the information given, we can then construct the alternative view that the other person holds. This knowledge is valuable when, for example, we need to predict how the person will respond to a future message or situation.

6 **Re-establish self**. We can now return to our own view of a situation, but it is highly likely that our own view will have changed because we have incorporated new knowledge of and from another. In attempting to understand someone else's view we have extended our knowledge, whether this be social, emotional, cultural, practical or scientific.

(Source: based on Bennett, 1987)

Seeking to understand another's view in this way is the basis for arriving at shared understanding and meanings. Put another way, we are better able to communicate.

How similar, how different?

Do we always have to practise the six steps to communicate effectively? They require effort and there isn't time in a working day for a manager to go through them during every communication. Consider the vertical continuum shown in Figure 2.2.

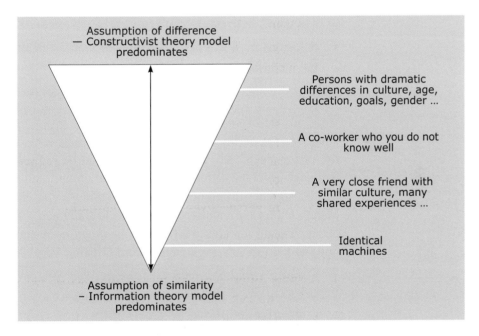

Figure 2.2 When to assume similarity or difference

The bottom end of the vertical continuum in the diagram represents the assumption of similarity. The top end represents the assumption of difference. It is safe to assume similarity when we are considering identical machines sending information, as in the information theory model. As we travel up the continuum, we can think of people rather than machines and increasing degrees of difference between people. A close friend at work will be more similar than a colleague who is not a friend, or a worker in the next department. At the top end of the continuum we can think of people from very different cultures from our own.

The width of the inverted triangle represents the *effort* required to achieve good communication in those situations. Because of the greater effort and time required to communicate effectively and empathetically with people who are very different from ourselves, we do not want to go any 'higher' than necessary in any situation. However, judgements about how much effort to put into communication will need to take account of the greater effort needed to correct misunderstandings and repair poor relationships if the initial effort proves insufficient. There will be many occasions when, as a manager, you will need to make such judgements.

Understanding communication

Interpersonal communication is complex. Generally, we communicate far more meaning than just the words we speak, and what is understood by the person with whom we are speaking may not be what we intended. Understanding how *misunderstanding* can occur equips us better to improve our own communication. We consider three main approaches to understanding verbal (and written) communication which provide insight.

The first of these three approaches is that of John Austin (1962), who introduced the idea of language use as 'speech acts' in which it is possible to distinguish between

- the literal or 'dictionary meaning' of words (locution)
- the intention of the speaker (illocution)
- how the utterance was received by the listener, or the consequence for the listener (perlocution) which may or may not be unintended.

Austin proposed that language is not a fixed system of rules with sentences delivering 'facts' whose truth or falsity can be judged. His idea was that language involves actions, context, situation and audience. The same words can be used for different purposes (intentions) – so the illocution can be hidden within the locution. Consider the statement: 'Tom is very thorough'. Depending on the context, the statement can be meant positively ('Tom's good at his job') or negatively ('Tom is being very slow; anyone else would have finished the job a long time ago'). Speakers' intentions are said to fall into one of five categories:

- to describe something
- to influence someone
- to express feelings or attitudes
- to make a commitment
- to try to achieve something.

(Source: Deaux *et al.*, 1993)

Here is an example of Austin's distinction, adapted from a study of managers' communications and people's reactions at a Californian ski resort by Guild (2002). It is also an example of how misunderstanding can occur (in this case, through poor communication by senior managers). The senior managers had to reduce the number of seasonal workers because of lack of snow. However, the managers gave as their reason not 'lack of snow', but 'to maximise shareholder value'. This 'message' upset the employees who remained after the staff reduction because the company had often communicated to them its core values such as 'people are important' and 'we are responsive to our customers and each other'. The reaction of the remaining staff was that the company was 'greedy'. When snow returned three weeks later, and the company tried to re-employ some of the staff who had been dismissed, they declined, even though they had not found other work. As a result, customer service suffered.

Here, the *locution* – what was said by the senior managers – was: You are being dismissed because we need to maximise shareholder value.

The *illocution* – what was meant by the senior managers – was: The lack of snow is resulting in an unsustainable reduction of income so we need to reduce staff (costs).

The *perlocution* – the unintended consequence or by-product for the staff – was: Remaining staff were upset; their view of the company changed from one that cared about staff to a company that was greedy. A further consequence was that dismissed workers refused to be re-employed by the company, harming customer service.

This approach provides insights into the ways in which we convey our messages, their consistency with prior messages and the need to consider the context and the knowledge, needs, concerns, values and situation of the message recipients. The example reveals one of the typical ways in which recipients of messages construct different meanings from those which managers intended to communicate.

A second approach to understanding communication is known as 'politeness' theory, originated by Erving Goffman (1967). Goffman's view was that a person needs to live up to his or her self-image, and thus needs to 'save face' – that is, maintain self-respect. At the same time, a person needs also to maintain the 'face' of other people. Goffman maintained that face-saving constituted the 'traffic rules of social interaction'. Everyone plays the game, which is based on a working acceptance of what people say rather than a 'real' acceptance. A person may want to save face because of pride or honour, or because of the status power he or she can exert over others. A person might want to save the 'face' of another person because of emotional attachment to the other person, because of the moral rights of the other person, or simply to avoid hostility. Each person's sub-culture and ethnic culture will have their own face-saving practices. Essentially, Goffman sums up for us the meaning of 'tact': we might confess to a personal failing to avoid having to be inconsistent, that is, act in a friendly way while feeling negative to the person; we might suggest things, or use humour, or be ambiguous rather than choosing words which would be untactful. By doing this we are not seen to have 'officially' communicated the message. And recipients also can behave as if they haven't 'officially' received the message. For example, we may invite another person to speak at a meeting – 'You first' – conveying a 'modest' view of ourselves while complimenting the other person. In some group situations, a person will be dependent on others for supporting his or her 'face', and in some circumstances a group may come to share 'a face'.

The implication is that we change our language based on our understanding of listeners to gain their cooperation. Brown and Levinson (1987) suggest there are two types of face: positive and negative.

Positive face is the need to be liked and is conveyed when we compliment others or show concern for them. A key feature of negative face is recognising that another person does not have to do what we want them to do. Using these ideas, it's possible to distinguish between the ways in which we might make a request:

'Write this report by Wednesday.' This is a bald directive that takes no account of the listener's 'face'.

'It would be great if you could write that report by Wednesday.' This is positive politeness which attempts to minimise threat to the listener's 'face'.

'I know you're busy, but we're going to need that report on Wednesday. Will you be able to do it by then?' This is negative politeness: the speaker knows he or she is imposing on the listener so the speaker acknowledges the autonomy of the listener.

'We're going to need that report by Wednesday.' This is also negative politeness, but the statement is not direct; the listener is being asked indirectly to do something. Such statements allow the listener the greatest autonomy.

The words we choose when we speak are said to be based on three factors: social distance between the speaker and listener, the relative power of the speaker, and the degree of imposition he/she is making (a consideration whenever requests are made). There will be cultural and gender differences, of course, in how 'politeness' is judged and performed; context and situation are likely to have an impact too.

An example of such behaviours is provided by Bremner (2006). It centres on a Middle Eastern university (where English is spoken) where a project was mounted to produce information on all courses in a common format. The project involved many staff: administrators, course writers, proposers of new courses and teams developing the courses. A study of email messages exchanged showed the ways in which those who hold power feel able to use language; the difficulties faced by those without power when making requests; and how the choice of words can affect the way a writer is perceived.

Consider the following messages and 'politeness' interpretations.

Message 1

'Thank you for the great job you did during Stage One of the [...] for the new courses. As discussed at the last workshop [...] in order to facilitate the success of Stage Two a workshop has been planned [...]. Helen and Patrick join me in inviting you to this very important workshop. [...] It is imperative that those involved in Stage Two [...] attend this workshop.

We know that this is an extra commitment but need your assistance and support [...]. Could you please make the necessary arrangements to ensure that your classes are covered? [...] We look forward to seeing you on [...].'

Comment

The message, from the university's second in command, thanks and invites the people to whom it is addressed. It makes requests for support and commitment and for arrangements to be made. However, there is little doubt that attendance at the workshop is mandatory, made clear by the word 'imperative'. It is little short of a 'bald directive': Do this! Note also the use of we and you/your: they are designed to make the message seem inclusive, but don't really succeed – not helped by the formal language used elsewhere in the message. The writer of Text 1 has power; he can be confident that his demands will be met regardless of how 'nice' he is.

Message 2

'Hello everyone again.

I'm coming under some pressure a little further up the line to provide an update on the status of the [project]. I'd be very grateful if you could send me […].

Sorry to hassle you on this, but as there is a deadline […] for getting the first section of all courses out, the sooner I have an idea of what's going on the sooner I can provide help where needed.

If you have already responded, thanks. If you haven't, or if I'm writing to the wrong person, please update me/ask me to remove your name from the list. That way you can avoid these increasingly desperate calls for information.

Thanks a lot.'

Comment

This message was written by the manager of the project coordinator, who had no power over academic colleagues. By the time this message was sent, deadlines were being missed, the task was more time-consuming than had been expected and there was growing resistance to it among the academics. The text states that senior managers require this, but note how the writer tries to separate himself from the senior managers' command ('…send me …') with the use of the words *'I'd be grateful if …'*. The writer attempts to be closer to the recipients of the message than to the senior managers. Note the use of informal language and the use of *I* and *you*; there is none of the 'forced inclusiveness' used in Text 1.

Often we use politeness strategies without much thought. However, by consciously considering the use of negative strategies, our requests are more likely to be accepted when we have little status power to insist.

The third approach to looking at discourse focuses on conversation between people as part of actions which are 'situated' in time, place and context. Such conversations are known as 'talk-in-interaction'. The central tool of the approach is conversation analysis, which aims to reveal what a conversation is 'doing' as it develops. It was developed by Harvey Sacks, in the 1960s and 1970s, and elaborated by Emanuel Schegloff and others. Sacks believed conversation, far from being disorganised, is highly structured. He considered, among other things, turn-taking; how participants organise topics; and how, in group settings, the next speaker is 'chosen'.

Gibson (2008) describes conversation as incrementally and progressively produced and subject to the 'rule' of one person speaking at a time. Conversation 'options' change as the conversation progresses: questions need immediate answers; the moment to make a complaint passes quickly; what can be said *right now* is constrained by what was said before. Speakers must also choose what they say from a number of things they *could* say, and quickly: hesitation invites someone else to speak. Moreover, the speaker can both select the next speaker, by posing a question to a particular person, and what the next speaker will talk about. In this way, obligations and expectations are set up.

A problem with the approach, according to Gibson, is that it does not respond to several factors we have argued to be important:

- non-verbal aspects of communication (a criticism which can be made of the other approaches too)
- what participants are like, including their formal status
- the relationships between participants
- how all these affect the content and course of conversation.

Gibson's idea is useful to managers. It asks us to think about features of conversation, the demands and constraints on participants, the choices we have. It also suggests the skills required both to ensure the participation of others and to direct conversation when required.

All three approaches – those of Austin, Goffman, and Sacks – remind us of issues in communication, such as:

- more than *facts* are communicated: values and opinions (including prejudices) may be part of communication content, and are likely to shape communication behaviour in a variety of other ways
- how others interpret what we say, based on their current knowledge and understanding, and what they will do as a result
- how status power is communicated through language
- the nature of the language used
- communication is a kind of 'game' in which everyone is allowed to save face
- participants in a conversation shape the nature of the conversation.

Barriers to communication

Improving communication has two aspects to it: understanding what helps effective communication and recognising barriers to it. Managers will find that some barriers can be removed or lowered, while others must be accepted.

Barriers can be categorised in various ways. Here is a general one, which includes most of the common barriers.

Physical barriers and distractions. There may be little a manager can do about the way the design of a building separates people or locates them in open-plan settings where their communication may disturb others. However, policies on interruptions may be effective in dealing with physical barriers such as closed doors, screens and features that separate people. A noisy environment or a constantly ringing telephone can also hinder communication. A quiet meeting space may overcome this. Good open-plan offices have these. Other barriers, such as speaking too fast or too loudly, can be overcome easily. Such problems shouldn't occur at all if speakers check listeners' understanding of what's been said.

Perceptual barriers. Our assumptions often hinder communication. We may assume that a person knows or understands something, or sees things in the way that we do. Often, we may be unaware of such assumptions. Unless earlier communication has confirmed that staff have the same knowledge and share a similar understanding of it, much of the 'work' of communication will be to clarify these two issues. To do this may mean that one or more of the people involved has to change their thinking.

See also: Theories of communication, in this chapter

Checking one's assumptions by asking what a person knows and understands about something is necessary – and may reveal interesting insights.

Emotional barriers. Fear and lack of trust are probably the two most common emotional barriers to communication. Fear – of criticism, of negative reactions, or simply of an angry response – will make people reluctant to communicate, particularly their thoughts and feelings. Lack of trust may make people reluctant, to communicate not only thoughts and feelings but ideas too. For example, people who promote someone else's idea as their own, not stating that it came from someone else, or whose response to all new ideas is 'I'd already thought of that' will find that in future people will not share their ideas with them. Such behaviours may be due to competitiveness, or lack of confidence, or both. The habit of talking 'behind a person's back', often to gain support for one's own view, is also likely to reduce the amount and content of future communication. If something is important, then it should be discussed with all the people involved.

See also: The communication climate, in this chapter

Cultural barriers. Ethnic cultural barriers are similar to perceptual barriers, but cultural differences may extend to

- values (for example, valuing individual assertiveness over relationships, group work and/or compliance)
- what is acceptable practice in the workplace
- the closeness or otherwise of professional relationships
- how good performance is rewarded and how poor performance is treated.

When we meet someone from a different culture we need to be aware of possible differences in how people communicate. However, we must not assume that a person will communicate differently because of an ethnic difference. To assume this could be seen as discriminatory. Conversations will be easier if diversity is seen to be valued by you and your organisation and if the reason for exploration is clear and has benefits for the other person.

Language barriers. In the global financial crisis that arose in 2008 the public heard and read words, phrases and ways of expressing ideas that required 'translation' into ordinary language by commentators. The banking profession used a language that others could not understand. Professional communities such as engineers, scientists, charity workers and accountants – so-called communities of practice – form around a particular line of work and set of ideas. Members are able to communicate with each other easily as a result of shared knowledge and understanding. In doing so, the community develops its own 'language'. In this language community, a single word or phrase stands for a whole set of ideas and their complex interrelationships. The problem is that others who need to understand the language may not. On a lesser scale, jargon and buzz words used by a group, section or department of an organisation or by members of a profession will also hinder communication with 'outsiders'. Here, checking one's assumptions about the knowledge of another, and perspective-taking, are needed to improve communication.

Gender and status barriers. Gender and status differences often occur at the same time in societies where one gender is considered to possess a higher status than the other. Researchers have found clear differences between what, in general, each gender values. For example, in the West men are said to be more task-oriented while women are more concerned with social and emotional aspects of group work. A man might command the team to meet a deadline. A woman may be concerned that a command might damage team spirit cohesiveness. However, statistical differences between gender *groups* hide *individual* variations. We know that some female managers give commands, and some male managers put team spirit first.

Status (real or imagined) has a major impact on group communication. In general:

- leaders and men speak more than women in a mixed group
- men interrupt women more often than they interrupt men
- men allow other men to interrupt them more than they do female interrupters
- men are more likely to change the topic after a women has spoken.

Status power may result in unequal contribution, but where gender alone results in unequal contribution to discussion, it is likely some employees will have less opportunity to share knowledge and ideas.

Interpersonal barriers. Interpersonal barriers – or personality clashes – arise when relationships between people are not strong and harmonious. As a consequence, mutual trust and confidence in one another are not high. This results in the kind of emotional barriers outlined above. A manager can lower interpersonal barriers by assuming that the other person is sincere, by showing that the relationship is valued, by being open and prepared to change a point of view where appropriate, by listening and by beginning the conversation on common ground. Finding something that both share – an interest in a sport, or having children of a similar age – often helps build good relationships.

Beyond the words: paralanguage and non-verbal communication

Successful and effective communication is more than simply choosing the 'right' words in the circumstances. The way in which something is said, and the body language used, affect the meanings that people construct from what they hear and see. Managers need to understand these other aspects of communication to understand others better, and be better understood.

Paralanguage

Paralanguage refers to *how* something is said. Examples of paralanguage include how we pitch our voices and the range of pitches we use, the speech rhythm and speed of speaking, the strength we use when we say something, the number and length of pauses, and non-verbal sounds such as sighing, 'ums' and 'ers', laughing or clearing our throats. The statement *'You're crazy'* can mean different things when accompanied by a laugh and without a laugh. These signals are affected by our emotions. The signals also communicate attitudes.

Although we can control the paralanguage we use in speech, it may be difficult to change. Indeed, when our paralanguage communicates the same message as our words, it demonstrates 'authenticity' provided the words and the signals are giving the same message. We sound more genuine and sincere. An angry person is likely to speak emphatically; a person showing sympathy is likely to speak more softly. The former actor and professional voice coach, Steve Hudson – the voice behind some very memorable TV advertisements for aftershave and chocolates in the UK – has some advice on generally improving our delivery of speech (in Ley, 2006):

1 Lower the pitch of your voice at the end of a sentence (unless it's a question). In most languages, this signals self-confidence and control of the information conveyed, according to Ohala (1984); raising the pitch at the end of a sentence (unless it's a question) implies deference or a lack of authority.

2 Pause for two seconds at the end of every sentence before beginning the next, and insert 'mental commas' – pauses at appropriate points.

3 Speak softly and slowly but with enthusiasm.

Ley found that after a little practice her voice changed from sounding bored and rushed to more calm and confident. We are likely to want those in authority to sound calm and confident, as well as those we trust, such as doctors and other professional people, including managers. Paralanguage 'supports' the verbal message and can clarify relationships.

While paralanguage is primarily associated with speech, some aspects of it can be transferred to writing. For example, rhythm can be signalled by the use of punctuation. The more informal the communication the more likely such signals will be included. Consider an email message which contains exclamation marks, capital letters and emoticons (symbols such as these)

:-) }:-(

that represent human emotions. They were developed by Scott Fahlman in 1982, who now rather regrets the impact of them on language (2008)!

Non-verbal communication

Consider the case of a manager who tells a direct report: *'You know I always make time to talk to staff'* and then frowns and drums her fingers impatiently on the desktop. The words and the body language lack congruence – they do not match.

There are a number of types of body language:

- facial expression
- gaze
- pupil (the central part of the eye's lens) size
- posture and gesture – how we stand or sit and how we use our arms and hands
- the distance between us.

Different types of body language often 'go together', for example, smiling and larger pupil size, looking at the other person present (gazing) and posture – how we stand or sit. A smile without the usual other behaviours, particularly other facial behaviours such as (in the West) showing one's teeth, might be considered 'false'. The term 'expressivity' describes the appropriate coordination of non-verbal behaviours. Two main kinds of differences are found in expressivity. The first difference is cultural: culture influences what it is acceptable to express, in what circumstances and how much expression is appropriate. In other words, every culture has 'display rules'. Among Europeans, the Finns are well-known for not showing emotions or feelings in public: for example, it is not appropriate to smile asiatta (without reason) or to talk too much (Wilkins, 2005). Both are considered to hinder effective communication. However, the use of hand gestures by Italians in everyday conversation is legendary!

The second difference is gender: women tend to be more expressive regardless of culture. However, the difference is not related to empathy, power, social roles or the other likely explanations. Indeed, some types of expression seem to be inborn: babies begin to smile spontaneously (that is, with no external stimulus) at about six weeks of age and when they do, girls smile more than boys.

Some types of non-verbal language are universal. They are used and recognised in all cultures because they are almost certainly under 'biological' control, appearing as soon as infants are capable of producing them.

These include the basic types of facial expression, mutual gaze and changes in pupil size. These are more likely to be directly linked to emotion and feeling. Others, such as body posture, are shaped by culture and may be hard to understand without other 'clues' – what is being said or the context in which it is being said.

Facial expression. There are seven facial expressions which are considered universal: happiness, sadness, surprise, fear, disgust, anger and contempt. (The first six are used by blind and deaf children, suggesting that these expressions are innate: that is, they do not have to be learned.) Shame, indicated by blushing, may also be universal but is not necessarily visible because of skin colour.

Gaze. People tend to make regular eye contact when communicating (mutual gaze); a listener will both look at the speaker and look away, depending on circumstances. Continuous gazing – and mutual gazing – can have different meanings according to the context, for example, what is being said and the relationship between the communicators. Two people having an argument and two people in love may make continuous eye contact! Thus gaze may indicate intensity of emotion rather than the specific emotion being experienced. In North Western countries at least, women tend to look at the person they are speaking to more than do men.

Pupil size. The pupils of the eyes change size in response to light (they will become small in bright light) and in response to emotion. They tend to become small with negative emotions such as anger and disgust, and increase with positive emotions, for example, warm feelings, but this is not always so. Pupil size may indicate intensity of emotion rather than the type of emotion (negative or positive) felt. When people are shown photographs of the same person which have been changed to show large or small pupils, people normally regard the photograph with large pupils as more attractive, and the version with small pupils as 'hard' or 'cold'. We are usually unaware that we notice pupil size (and we are not in direct control of our own pupil size). Nonetheless, we use such information when communicating – because no-one can help communicating it.

Postures and gestures. Postures involve the body, while gestures are normally confined to head and hand movements. Gestures can serve instead of words, as long as the meaning is known, for example shaking the head or hand to convey 'No' in many cultures. Hand gestures can also follow the rhythm of speech and support its content. Postures can be fixed (as in crossed arms) or moving (as in swinging arms or legs). In many Western cultures people are encouraged to show interest by sitting upright and slightly forward, head up, legs drawn back, and with the hands held together. However, researchers have found no clear relationship between our postures and our emotions. Clearly, we can adopt the postures that social conventions or situations demand. Cultural differences are likely: in cultures in which people sit on the floor, postures will differ.

Interpersonal distance. Interpersonal distance, a concept introduced by Edward T. Hall in 1959, refers to the physical distance which people choose, not necessarily knowingly, when they speak. It can be thought of as a 'bubble' around a person, contracting and expanding according to numerous factors. Some of these are strong and unchanging, such as culture and individual need for privacy. Other factors arise from a particular situation: the nature of the relationship with others (or another), the number of people present, and physical factors such as heat and noise. We normally notice interpersonal distance only when we feel that another person is too close to us. Research suggests that Anglo-Saxons choose the most interpersonal distance, followed by Asians, Northern Europeans, Southern Europeans, and Latin Americans. There is also a gender difference: women sit or stand closer to other women and touch them more than they would touch men.

Much attention has been given to describing non-verbal communication and, among management consultants, to understanding non-verbal communication as a part of daily management. The key question is: What is it *for* and how does it aid and contribute to communication? Boone and Buck (2003) say that a person's non-verbal activity shows his or her emotional state. This helps communication between people of the same culture because they can coordinate their actions on the basis of these states, which they continuously assess. Why should this be important? It is likely that people are looking for signs of trustworthiness in the other, to identify those with whom we can cooperate and, ultimately, trust. Thus, emotionally-expressive people are considered to be more attractive because we believe we can 'read' them better and thus understand their intentions. When someone tries to hide their emotions, their true emotion will often still be visible – there will be 'emotional leakage'. Conversely, intention – and expectation – can be directly communicated: a smile might signal an intention to be friendly and cooperative (Patterson, 2003).

Mimicry

Our own expectations about another person affect the non-verbal behaviour we use when communicating with them. We are usually unaware that we are matching, or mimicking or imitating the verbal and non-verbal behaviour of others. We do this more when we expect a person to be cooperative.

Our often-subtle and unconscious mimicry of others has an effect. For example, we relax our facial muscles in response to another person's smile. This leads to the other person liking us more and believing that we have a greater rapport – or empathy – with them. We tend to mimic people we know. This may be to build relationships and help group interaction. Empathetic individuals mimic more; people mimic leaders more than leaders mimic followers.

Such knowledge has led some management consultants to promote the idea of *consciously* mimicking others to shape their opinions. The danger is that if the other person becomes aware of mimicry, the effect becomes negative. The smart advice to managers is to be aware of non-verbal cues – one's own and those of others – and their effect.

Communication skills

How many times in a working day do you need to understand another's point of view, build relationships and acquire information? Most managers would say: *'That's the nature of the managerial role'*. All these tasks involve communication skills, but two in particular are relevant: active listening and questioning.

Active listening is called this because the listener is active even if he or she does not speak very much. There are three types of active listening most commonly needed in the workplace.

Support listening is needed when a manager needs to encourage others to speak to say what they think or feel. Your role as a manager here is to learn – which means not distracting the speaker and not putting forward your own views unless necessary. Asking what people think of an idea and how its implementation might affect them, for example, helps you to identify potential problems.

Responding listening focuses on establishing a relationship with another person. Here you are showing the other person that you are interested in them and what they have to say. Clearly, this type of listening is most useful when meeting new people.

Retention listening is required when you are seeking information. It is often most appropriate in group situations.

All three types of active listening require skills. In each case you will need to:

Pay attention and concentrate. Make sure you are not rushed or being interrupted. Reduce or remove distractions.

See also: Barriers to communication, in this chapter

Signal that you are listening. Speakers need to know that they are being listened to. If you look interested as you listen, make eye contact, nod or smile and perhaps say 'Yes, I see' or 'Uh ha', the speaker is far more likely to continue. These gestures do not mean that you agree with what is being said; they show that you are listening, and showing interest in the speaker.

Encourage the speaker to say more, to expand on what they are saying. Depending on what the manager is trying to achieve in a discussion, encouragement could be questions or statements which can be as simple as: *'I'd like to know more about that'* or *'What would you do in the case of X?'*.

Check and reflect back what you think you have heard or understood. Repeating or paraphrasing what has been said is a powerful way of checking your understanding. In paraphrasing, the speaker summarises their understanding and makes a statement such as: *'As I understand it then, you believe that the new workload planning system is difficult for you because your job is not sufficiently routine'*. These techniques also show that you have been listening carefully and that what has been said – and the speaker – are important. When a speaker's tone of voice or facial expression does not match what is being said, you may need to check what the speaker 'really' means. Checking normally means asking a question, such as: *'Did that disappoint you?'*

Pitfalls in listening include:

- selective listening – hearing only what one wants to hear, what one thinks is relevant or what does not contradict one's own views
- interrupting the speaker
- wanting to put forward your own opinion
- becoming frustrated with the way something is being communicated rather than focussing on what is being said
- pretending to listen
- giving opinions on what's being said.

In all cases, the listener's own view or lack of interest gets in the way of understanding the message.

Questioning

Asking questions complements the skill of effective listening. It increases the manager's control over the process of gathering information, although it needs to be used with active listening. Questions need to be systematic, logical and appropriately timed. To ask effective questions requires the manager to:

- understand what's being said
- decide what further information is needed
- consider what kind of question is most likely to produce the information needed
- select the type of question that will also strengthen the relationship with the speaker.

There are various kinds of questions. Two broad categories are closed and open questions.

Closed questions allow the person responding little or no freedom in choosing the response. Often closed questions, such as *'Have you spoken to the supplier?'* require a simple 'Yes' or 'No' in response. Closed questions are not appropriate when a more detailed response is needed. They can be frustrating to the respondent, who may have information to provide but who is not being invited or encouraged to participate in a dialogue. However, they allow a person to retain control of the dialogue; they are quick to ask and answer and responses are easily understood.

Open questions allow respondents freedom in making responses. *'Why is the budget forecast not completed yet?'* is likely to elicit more information than the question *'Have you completed the budget forecast yet?'*. Open questions require the respondent to do the talking so the listener can listen. However, open questions can be unnecessary if they produce more detail than you need. Respondents can move away from the subject or avoid giving direct answers to important questions. Further, the questioner may be more influenced by how articulate the respondent is than by the content of the response.

Decisions about the use of open or closed questions are a matter of judgement. Even where open questioning is appropriate, the occasional closed question may help to keep the respondent close to the subject. Other forms of question include:

Direct questions. These are useful when a limited amount of information is needed. The range of possible responses to direct questions is limited. An example is: *'How long have you been working with this team?'*

Probing questions. These are open questions that guide the conversation from the general to the specific, with the aim of encouraging respondents to provide additional detail. A probing question often follows a closed question, for example:

> Question (closed): *'Would you say you're a good communicator?'*
>
> Answer: *'Yes, I think I am.'*
>
> Question (probing): *'Could you describe a recent event that illustrates this?'*

Probing questions are useful, too, when a respondent is moving away from the subject. However, if they are used too early in a conversation or too many are used, they can be seen as threatening.

Leading questions. These normally suggest what the desired or obvious response should be. Consider the question: *'Don't you think it's important that we talk to Anja about this now?'* It is likely that the questioner expects the answer 'Yes'. Leading questions are often used to persuade others to adopt a particular course of action. Used carefully, they can be constructive and lead people systematically through a thought process. However, they can also be used manipulatively, aggressively or thoughtlessly. This can not only damage relationships, but lead people to decisions they would rather not take. Pressure on the respondent is increased when the questioner has more power than the respondent. Leading questions are unlikely to work if the respondent is fairly assertive and a skilled communicator. Such a person might respond to the above question with: *'Perhaps it might be better to wait until we've spoken to Daniel because ...'*

Loaded questions. These are similar to leading questions but employ emotive language, for example: *'What do you think of this ridiculous decision?'* Such questions make it very obvious what the response should be. They are unlikely to produce respondents' genuine thoughts and feelings. This will be the case when the questioner is more powerful, and it is important for the respondent to give the 'right' answer. In general, loaded questions should be avoided.

Hypothetical questions. These are 'what if' questions. They are useful when you want to test your ideas against the views of others. An example of a hypothetical question is: *'How do you think team members would react if we changed their roles while Jo is on extended sick leave?'* Potentially, they can lead to a rich set of views and exploration of implications which may not have been considered. Hypothetical questions can be used in selection interviews when you want to explore how a candidate might handle a particular sort of situation. An example is: *'What would you do if a team member complained to you about another team member's performance?'*

A problem with their use in job interviews is that a good answer may not reflect what a person would actually do. In interviews, it is usually preferable to ask people what they actually did in a comparable but real situation.

Mirror or reflective questions. These questions serve to summarise and clarify what a speaker has said so they mirror or reflect what was said. The listener might ask: *'So you think there is a lack of clarity about what the task involves?'* Such questions are useful in establishing shared understanding and they help to build relationships between people. However, it can be easy to overemphasise what has been said. This will result in appearing to 'put words into other people's mouths'. In the above example, if the person had said he was unclear about what a task involved or his role, this may not amount to a 'lack of clarity'. To be useful, questions must accurately mirror or reflect what has been said. If they do not, they can become leading questions and can be manipulative and aggressive.

Answering a question with a question. This is primarily a response technique but is used by skilled communicators in two main ways:

- to keep control of a conversation or interview
- to encourage people to resolve problems themselves.

When used skilfully to help people solve their own problems, such questions can help to build confidence and morale. In the following example, the problem a person has brought to you is presented back to them:

Member of staff: What can I do about David's attitude towards Sarah and me?

Manager: Have you thought about how you would like to deal with it?

The effect is to change the focus from the problem to the solution. Note that the manager has kept control of the conversation by shifting the focus. The technique can also be used to manage time. Compare the following dialogues:

Dialogue 1

Member of staff: How much time have you got to discuss this?

Manager: I can spare an hour.

Dialogue 2

Member of staff: How much time have you got to discuss this?

Manager: How much time do you think we'll need?

Member of staff: Half an hour should be enough.

Manager: OK, we'll spend half an hour on it.

In the first dialogue, the manager commits an hour which may not be necessary but is likely to be used. In the second dialogue, only half that time has been committed because the person who knows most about the problem has estimated that it can be dealt with in that time. The estimate may not be accurate but further discussion can be planned with greater accuracy.

The main problem with answering questions with questions is that it can be frustrating to the first questioner. There are times when people have thought through the options and need help in making a decision. At other times, questions call for a straight answer. Imagine asking the hypothetical question: *'How do you think team members would react if we adjusted their roles while Jo is on extended sick leave?'* A response such as: *'How do you think they will react?'* could be unhelpful and even rude.

The types of question, how they are used and to what purpose will require a manager's judgement of a situation and the people involved in the dialogue. Practise at using the different types of question will result in improved communication: information should be more easily acquired, achieving shared understanding will be more rapid, staff are likely to feel more valued and involved, and time will be saved.

Communication and new technology

Does something strike you as odd in the following examples of two managers talking?

Example 1

> *Manager A:* It's a problem that's going to be difficult to resolve.
>
> *Manager B:* We'll do it by email.

Example 2

> *Manager A:* We'll need to organise a meeting.
>
> *Manager B:* I'll get everyone together to decide when to meet.

There is something inappropriate about Manager B's responses. We can see why when we consider the choice of communication *medium*. In each case, it is not entirely fit for purpose, that is, it's not the best way to deal with the task in hand. But how do we choose?

Email, online conferencing tools, instant messaging, computer-supported virtual meeting software, audio and audio-visual conferencing are communication media, but their features affect both the way in which communication can take place and the amount of information that can be conveyed. Some are 'richer media' than others; some are better suited to particular tasks than others. To perform effectively, managers need to understand communication task needs and match the task to the appropriate medium, where possible.

Information richness

Media (or information) 'richness' means the capacity of any medium (or communication 'channel') to carry information, which in turn influences the amount of information that can be processed. The richness of each medium varies according to various factors which either help or hinder managers and other employees to arrive at shared meanings. The richness of the medium required will depend on two things:

1 Equivocality: where there is high equivocality, or different possible meanings, managers will need to exchange information to clarify ambiguities, define problems and reach agreement.

2 Uncertainty: where there is high uncertainty, an organisation will need information in order to solve known problems.

Figure 2.3 sets out these two factors in combination.

	Low equivocality	High equivocality
High uncertainty	1. Low equivocality, high uncertainty Occasional ambiguous, unclear events: managers define questions, develop common grammar, gather opinions. *Example:* Goal-setting in an organisation where there are differences of opinion on what the emphasis should be.	2. High equivocality, high uncertainty Many ambiguous, unclear events; managers define questions, also seek answers,gather objective data and exchange opinions. *Example:* There have been rapid change and unpredictable shocks; managers have been learning by trial and error.
Low uncertainty	3. Low equivocality, low uncertainty Clear, well-defined situation, managers need few answers, gather routine objective data. *Example:* Use of routine technology in a stable environment.	4. High equivocality, low uncertainty Many well-defined problems, managers may ask questions, seek explicit answers, gather new quantitative data. *Example:* Staff turnover is high and a manager needs to conduct a survey to find out why.

Figure 2.3 Equivocality and uncertainty

(Source: Daft and Lengel, 1986)

The degree of equivocality and uncertainty a manager faces makes some channels of communication more suitable than others. In situations of high equivocality and uncertainty, the richest media need to be used; in situations of low equivocality and low uncertainty, the use of less rich media will be adequate. What makes a medium 'rich' or otherwise? Daft and Lengel (1986) set out four main factors:

1 Feedback: instant feedback allows questions to be asked and corrections to be made.

2 Multiple cues: a set of cues may be part of the message, including physical presence, voice inflection, body gestures, words, numbers and graphic symbols.

3 Language variety: that is, the range of meaning that can be conveyed using language and numbers. Natural language can convey concepts and ideas whereas numbers can convey precision.

4 Personal focus: a message can be conveyed more fully when personal feelings and emotions are included; messages can be matched to the recipient's current understanding, needs and immediate situation.

Thus, media, or channels of communication, can be placed in a 'richness hierarchy' as shown in Figure 2.4. Since Richard Daft and Robert Lengel introduced the term 'information richness' in 1984, many more computer-mediated communication technologies are routinely used. These have been added. Note how synchronous and asynchronous media have been separated. When communication is synchronous, there is virtually no time delay; participants respond to one another in 'real' time. Asynchronous refers to such a time delay, though in the case of impersonal communication, the communication may be largely 'one way'.

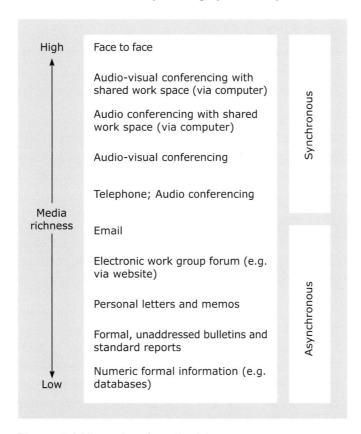

Figure 2.4 Hierarchy of media richness

(Source: adapted from Daft *et al.*, 1987)

Clearly, the face-to-face medium is the richest. It allows for rapid and mutual feedback. A message can be adjusted, clarified, reinforced and interpreted instantly. Less-rich media such as memos don't allow for such timely adjustments and any refocusing of the message. As media become less rich, cues such as visual cues and body language are filtered out. Lowest of all in richness are impersonal bulletins that are not directed to any particular individual.

But when we use these media, do we match the medium to the communication task in hand? Do we assess the equivocality and uncertainty of the situation and then select our medium carefully? The answer is: not as much as you might think, despite the fact that rich media have been found to be superior, for example, where negotiation is called for (Hollingshead *et al.*, 1993). Daft and his colleagues realised that choice of medium has a symbolic value. For example, if a manager believes that a face-to-face meeting symbolises commitment and personal interest, then this medium will be chosen even if it doesn't quite fit the task. Other ideas about lack of fit have emerged. Some can be grouped under subjectivist theories whose proponents, for example Fulk *et al.* (1990), say that:

1 The characteristics of media and task characteristics are not objective but subjective. People's views are influenced by their context.

2 Media characteristics and task features are not necessarily known to users.

3 Choice of media is not necessarily rational – choices are set in a historical and social context – although such choices are 'rationalised' after they have been made.

4 A critical mass of users is needed for a new technology to become useful in the workplace. This also affects people's perceptions of a medium: as more people use a medium, the more useful it seems. They will also perceive the medium to be easier to use.

A third school of thought – situational theories – stresses that in their choice of media, people take account of their own individual communication styles and requirements in addition to the task and organisational context. Thus:

1 The use of any medium will depend on a person's experience and expertise in using it.

2 In turn, their perceptions of its perceived usefulness will change so a 'lean' channel is used to create 'rich' communication.

This means, for example, that email may be used to overcome restraints of time and place imposed by geography, time zones and work schedules even though the medium may not be the best one to use (Dimmick *et al.*, 2000). In the case of email use, van den Hooff *et al.* (2008) found that both subjectivist and situational theories better explained the use of the medium than contingency theory (which says that the medium is matched to richness needs). Conversely, in a study of five hospitals in the USA, Murray and Peyrefitte (2007) found that rich media such as role play were chosen for knowledge – 'know-how' – transfer, while less rich media such as lectures and videotapes were chosen for information transfer. This suggested to them that rational choices may be made when something is important to an organisation and difficult to communicate.

In team work, a variety of media may be in use. For example, face to face meetings might take place with one or more members 'attending' by audio or audio-visual conferencing. Some aspects of a task might be carried out using computer software that provides for document sharing and asynchronous conferencing, while contact between individual team members might be made by email or telephone. What media issues need to be considered when working with groups and teams?

Many studies compare co-located teams working face-to-face with distributed teams using a single asynchronous medium, and sometimes they do not allow for the additional time required to work asynchronously. The tasks teams are set also vary considerably. However, in general, distributed teams:

- take longer to develop effective communication and relationships because of lack of social presence – the feeling that a person is present even if not physically so
- take longer to acquire group norms because observation of each other and interaction are negatively affected by the medium
- find task planning and maintenance activities more difficult; an explicit communication plan and work expectation system are normally needed
- take longer to build a shared understanding of and agree goals
- take longer to reach decisions, primarily because asynchronous media impose constraints on how quickly discussions can take place
- do not necessarily promote more equal participation among members (low-status members who contribute less than others in face-to-face situations continue to do so online)
- have performance outcomes that depend on task type.

Advantages of asynchronous team work include:

- information is more likely to be shared between all members
- more task orientation
- discussion is 'archived' and can be referred to by group members to build on or respond to ideas
- while it takes time to read, comment on and process the 'data', members can decide when to do it and to respond, leaving them time (if time constraints are not too tight) to give considered responses: there is time for pause and reflection.

According to some (Berry, 2006), if asynchronous team working means that time-pressure can be reduced for decision-making tasks then, potentially, the usual problems can be overcome. Shortage of time has an impact on:

- sharing information
- exploring and agreeing what the problem actually is
- generating and examining alternative solutions
- implementation, which is likely to be dependent on wider communication or consensus-building.

What can a manager make of all this? With new technologies, from email to desktop audio-visual conferencing with shared workspace facilities, in more common use many managers may already have a choice of media. Selecting the right 'media mix' to get the task done is more important than deciding on which single medium is 'the best one' to use.

Managers' choices are restricted by the cultural and communication norms – 'the way we do this here' – within organisations. Using suitable media is also difficult for managers because of their own lack of experience in using particular technologies. Thus, good training and support are vital. Many organisations try new media and find that people do not use them enough, or well enough, to make them cost-effective.

Box 2.2 Virtual working and communication

An important issue when considering communication is whether geographically distributed work groups are disadvantaged. For many years organisations have employed staff who do not work at the organisation's site – community workers, sales staff, maintenance workers. Many organisations have developed effective communication arrangements for these staff. But in recent years many organisations have decided it is cost-effective to move other staff out of the office to their homes. This 'virtual office' has been found by many researchers to change the pattern, content and context of communication. It has made effective communication more important in successful working. Virtual office workers are less satisfied with communication than staff who work together in one location. However, some organisations successfully develop suitable communications for virtual workers. For example, Akkirman and Harris (2005) found good communications in their study of workers in a Turkish subsidiary of a Germany-based multinational organisation. During a major reorganisation, one-third of the workers remained office-based while the remainder became virtual office workers. Of the two groups, the virtual workers were more satisfied with communication than were the office-based staff. The company spent two years planning and organising the transition to the new work arrangements, as described below.

The organisation implemented a five-step plan. First, while all the workers were still office-based, it established information technology and network infrastructure and provided ongoing training. Second, the organisation changed its organisational structure to form a process-based organisation that allowed each employee to take an entire process from start to finish in one rapid flow. It wanted empowered workers: hierarchy was eliminated and coaching was emphasised. Third, the organisation moved to results-based performance measurement – managing by results. This replaced the former focus on processes and time-based measurement. Fourth, the organisation created a digital information system allowing all workers to access up-to-date information regardless of location. Fifth, two-thirds of the workforce moved out of their traditional offices into their own virtual workspaces.

During the transition period, which lasted two years, the company established more formalised communication channels, communication protocols and an ongoing communication process to inform and engage workers. The use of information technology applications such as group-ware, email, scheduled video conferencing and audio conferencing was introduced. With more formalised, planned and better-organised communication, the change in workflow and performance management, and accessible information, workers were able to be more 'self-referent and system-referent'. They were able to rely more on themselves and the systems and less on the need for personal feedback or a strong relationship with supervisors.

The organisation also introduced ways of replacing traditional social communication, among them an e-café where employees could enjoy chat-rooms, post to and read e-bulletin boards, play chess over lunch, read newspapers, and so on. The company also regularly brought the virtual office workers to the office for meetings and social events.

One source of difference between the virtual and traditional office workers may have been that the virtual system ended up better designed than the traditional one. However, it is clear that virtual office working does not necessarily result in a less positive communication environment.

What are meetings for?

Face-to-face meetings can be very useful. They are particularly suitable for handling unclear problems or situations – but the cost of bringing a group of people together can be high. Thus you need to ensure that meetings in which you participate, or that you organise, are as productive as possible.

A decision on whether a meeting is necessary will normally be based on what a meeting is *for*. Most meetings are likely to serve one or more of the following purposes:

- to bring together a range of knowledge and experience
- to air grievances
- to gather or give information
- to evaluate current activities
- to explore the effects of current or proposed changes
- to come to decisions or assist in strategic decision-making
- to allocate resources
- to influence policy
- to aid problem-solving
- to develop cooperation and commitment
- to allocate tasks
- to agree actions.

See also: Communication and new technology, in this chapter

Whether a face-to-face meeting is required, or whether the same goals can be achieved by using other media, will depend on how clear and certain a situation is.

Formal meetings are rarely arranged simply to achieve just one of the items on the list above, however. Six main types are outlined in Box 2.3. The point of distinguishing between types is not just their purpose, but the expectations people have of them, the responsibilities of those involved and how they should be run. For these reasons, it is best not to combine different sorts of meetings.

Box 2.3 Types of formal meeting

Briefing meetings. The purpose of these is to inform people of what has already been planned and decided – what is expected of them. Lack of discussion can make these meetings unsatisfactory. People will need to establish shared understanding, clarity and what decisions mean for a group or department.

Business meetings. At these meetings information is shared, issues are discussed and decisions made. Normally there is a formal and often standard agenda. The effectiveness of these meetings can suffer if these meetings are the only opportunity for group communication (people want to discuss issues at length) or if some matters are best discussed or decided elsewhere.

Planning meetings and working groups. Participants use these for the detail that would not be appropriate at business meetings. Policy development may be achieved this way. These meetings focus on communication and participation, often by drawing in people from different parts of the organisation, or from different organisations.

Consultation meetings. Examples include senior management consultations with staff, and organisations consulting with customers, clients or the general public. To avoid the term 'consultation' being misunderstood, it is important that participants understand how much their views will influence a course of action. Too often 'consultation' turns out to be a public relations exercise. Consultation meetings can be an important planning tool. Managed well, they can increase involvement and sense of ownership, provided the brief is clear and they are skilfully chaired. It is important that all those who wish to speak are encouraged to, and feel they have been listened to.

Staff meetings. Regular staff meetings happen in many organisations. They have a range of purposes from reporting on developments to the discussion of interpersonal issues. A high level of trust – and time – is needed to air and explore difficult issues.

Review and evaluation meetings. Such meetings can be regular or occasional but the purpose is identical: to review progress towards organisational or individual goals in an organisation, or part of it, or a project team. Sometimes an external consultant or facilitator can be useful.

Style of meetings

Meetings can vary along two dimensions – from formal to informal and from adversarial to consensual. The formal–informal dimension refers to terms of reference (purposes, functions, responsibilities of the committee or group), procedures and formal roles required (chair, secretary). The adversarial–consensual dimension refers to the type of debate. In adversarial meetings there is challenge, disagreement and opposition, whereas in consensual meetings there is emphasis on what people agree on. This is used as a starting point for coming to agreement on more issues. Which style is planned, or happens, depends on the degree to which individuals share similar values, beliefs and goals. Where a particular committee or group is placed along these two intersecting dimensions can be thought of as its 'meeting style'. This is shown in Figure 2.5.

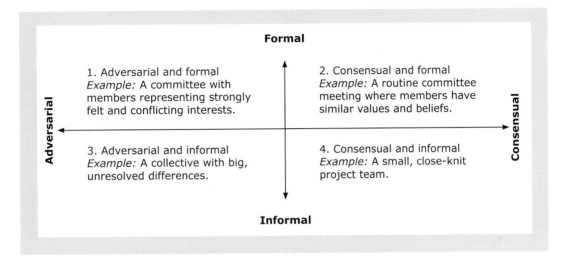

Figure 2.5 Dimensions of meetings

Each style of meeting presents its own opportunities and limitations to members. The formal–adversarial meeting encourages individual achievement and requires political skills. It is important to prepare for such a meeting, not just by reading the papers and planning your argument but also by studying other members, and preparing for the arguments of opponents. You will need to look for compromises between what you and they want.

A key political skill is trying to identify who will support you, and who you can support, then making these contacts before the meeting. If there are people who might support you, or might support those who oppose you, you can consider approaching them before the meeting and explaining why they should support you. The UK term for this is 'lobbying' – the corridors outside the parliament's debating chambers are called lobbies. Another skill is studying the status of other members. The most valued members are usually those who contribute frequently to the debate, make innovative and lively suggestions, and perform whatever tasks are assigned to them willingly and efficiently. The formal–adversarial meeting depends heavily on a skilful and effective chairperson. Quieter, less assertive people are often unsuccessful in formal–adversarial meetings. The mood and atmosphere – the communication climate – can sometimes prevent clear thought and it is rare for the members of such a meeting to work together as a group because there is often little trust.

Both the formal– and the informal–consensual meeting place great emphasis on group achievement through group effort. The chairperson is less important. A chairperson, if there is one, will take on a facilitative rather than a disciplinary or deciding role. The qualities demanded of the ordinary member in a consensual meeting are good listening skills, clear, assertive presentation, openness and honesty, respect for and interest in other points of view, and an understanding of and attention to the decision-making process. The most valued members are usually those who have a high degree of self-discipline and a clear perspective on the needs of the meeting as a whole, and who can clarify arguments, think creatively and share responsibility. If these skills and self-discipline are lacking in many members, the consensual meeting can be very frustrating and time-consuming.

Making meetings more effective

A variety of factors can reduce the effectiveness of meetings. Consider the following example.

The departmental meeting

I was pleased to be invited to the 'getting-to-know-you' meetings the Head ran soon after her appointment. The department had grown and I realised there were a number of new people I didn't know, in addition to the new Head. Five people came. I didn't get an opportunity to talk to everyone before the Head arrived, several minutes late. She welcomed us and asked us to introduce ourselves. Then she said: 'Now, what concerns do people have?' And that's how we got to photocopying.

I can't remember the detail, but whatever was said interested the other five, including the Head. For the next 20 minutes, they discussed photocopying, the machines, the paper, email and printing, printing on both sides of the paper ... The Head spoke about how important it was to control costs. When the meeting ended, I left feeling resentful of the time that I had given. And I still hadn't spoken to some of the new people.

Here, although the meeting was a relatively informal one, the main problem was lack of structure. Other factors that decrease effectiveness are:

- unclear objectives
- lack of preparation
- poor time-keeping
- too many participants
- lack of an agenda
- lack of minutes or notes of the previous meeting, which normally allocate tasks and specify a schedule
- lack of follow-up on actions agreed at the previous meeting
- poor chairing
- poor communication by participants
- ignoring 'the rules', either the formal standing orders or the rules agreed by the group.

When you are chairing a meeting, many of these factors can be eliminated. The possible roles of the chair will depend on the meeting itself. A traditional chairperson has formal responsibility for rules and procedure and the chair's focus is on getting business done. The facilitative chairperson's focus is on maintaining the meeting, helping to maintain the viability of the group that takes responsibility for carrying on the business. The style of chairing adopted needs to match the type and style of the meeting. The style adopted also needs the support of participants. Usually the chair will not explain the style that he or she will use. As a result, chairs sometimes know that the style has not been supported only when participants do not cooperate. Table 2.2 lists various functions that could be performed by a traditional and a facilitative chair, although in practice the functions can overlap.

Table 2.2 Possible functions of a chairperson

Traditional chairperson	Facilitative chairperson
General role and responsibilities	
Ensure fair play	Have an overview of the meeting's tasks and goals
Stay in charge	Help the group to take responsibility for what it wants to achieve
	Help the group to carry out its tasks
Stay neutral	Have little emotional involvement
Agenda and time-keeping	
Open the meeting	Run through the agenda at the beginning and get the meeting's approval for it
State the purpose of the meeting	Arrange in advance for someone to introduce each item
Introduce all agenda items	Update latecomers
Get through the agenda in the agreed time	Keep track of time
Close the meeting	Evaluate how the meeting went at the end
Discussion	
Select speakers	Encourage and help everyone to participate
Ask appropriate questions to clarify points	Encourage the expression of various viewpoints
Summarise the discussion	Encourage people to stay on the subject
Make sure people stay on the subject	Make it safe to share feelings
Arbitrate in disputes	Suggest ways of handling conflict
Control interruptions and people talking privately	
End the discussion	Clarify and summarise the discussion

Table 2.2 continued

Decision-making and voting	
Ensure decisions are taken	Remind the meeting of any agreed procedures for reaching consensus
Decide when to move to a vote	Look for areas of agreement
Conduct a vote	Test to see if there is agreement
Ensure someone is responsible for the agreed actions	Name the people who will carry out agreed actions

Rules	
Check the meeting has been called in accordance with the rules	
Have a good knowledge of the rules	
Take decisions on procedure issues	

Outside the meeting	
Act on behalf of the meeting	Help the group to decide who will act on its behalf
Pursue decisions made in meetings	Help the group to decide who will pursue decisions
Represent the group to outside bodies	Help the group to decide who will represent it

Improving chairing skills

Preparation

Whatever system is used, if you are chairing you must prepare adequately for the meeting. The checklist in Table 2.3 suggests what you might do. You should also consider whether there is a main item you want to present at the meeting. It is difficult to chair a meeting effectively and argue for a particular position – a case of role conflict. You could arrange for someone to take over the chair for the particular item if this is the case.

Table 2.3 Chairing a meeting: preparation checklist

- Prepare (and, if necessary, agree on) an agenda
- Think about the sensible grouping and ordering of agenda items and how they should be handled
- Ask relevant people to introduce agenda items
- Get additional briefing or information for items where necessary
- Read papers
- Allocate rough times to agenda items
- Anticipate likely areas of conflict or difficulty
- Think about who is coming and their likely reactions to various items
- Make sure you are familiar with any rules, procedures and standing orders

During the meeting

If you are chairing, it can be helpful to receive feedback on how effective you were and what you could improve on, so it is often a good idea to ask a colleague to observe and comment on your performance. The meaning of 'effective' will, of course, depend partly on the culture and style of your meetings and partly on the particular circumstances.

The secretary

The secretary's role is usually more straightforward than the chairperson's. Often the main task is to take notes and the primary skills are to identify the essential points and record them accurately. Sometimes the secretary may take responsibility for booking the room, circulating papers and the agenda, chasing up people who agreed to do things, and arranging elections or formal votes. The secretary is also responsible for writing up and circulating the minutes of the meeting. Sometimes a manager's secretary will be suitable for the role of meeting secretary, but often the meeting secretary can be chosen from anyone who is available.

Preparing the agenda

If you act as secretary, you may have a role in shaping the agenda. A clear explanatory agenda is vital in getting through business quickly and efficiently. Some items will be just to communicate information, without discussion or a decision. Others will have already been discussed elsewhere and are on the agenda so that a formal decision can be taken. This can be specified on the agenda. For informal meetings the agenda is often put together collectively, with everyone sharing the responsibility.

Taking minutes

The minutes or notes of a meeting are the official record of what happened so they need to be accurate and impartial: it may be necessary to refer to them if there is a dispute about what was decided. The most important things to note down are decisions, results of votes and the exact wording of any proposals or resolutions. It can also be helpful to summarise the discussion and the arguments.

Writing the minutes

In addition to a record of what was discussed, the minutes should note who was present and who sent apologies for their absence. Most organisations have their own styles for minutes, however. The secretary also must provide for the needs of participants. A useful device is an 'Action' column in the margin of the minutes recording the names or initials of the people who said they would do things – and when. This reminds people and makes it easy for the secretary to make sure that the actions have been completed. A short action list can be circulated immediately after the meeting.

Structure of meetings

Both formal and informal meetings work more effectively if they have a structure or framework. That framework has both visible and hidden components, as shown in Table 2.4.

Table 2.4 The visible and the hidden structure of meetings

The components	Their functions
The agenda and other papers	To set out the business of the meeting in an organised way and keep the meeting on track. The supporting papers relate to agenda items
The minutes	To provide a record of the business and the decisions reached
The room layout	To signal that the event is a meeting and perhaps to indicate who is the chairperson and who is the secretary
The rules and protocols	To formalise the roles of the officers of the meeting (chairperson and secretary) and the written standing orders, and to provide a framework for the conduct of the meeting – who has the authority to control the meeting, who can speak and when, and so on
The language of the meeting	To signal that the activity is a special one: in a formal meeting people may refer to others by their roles ('Chair') and not their names ('Chris'). There is also a language of meeting actions. This may include forms of words such as 'I'd like to support the previous speaker ...' or 'I'd like to speak in favour of the proposition ...'
The understandings	To provide the usual ways of behaving: for example, accepting the decisions of the chairperson; signalling to the chairperson that you wish to speak; following the agenda and not raising issues out of sequence or that are not on the agenda

The ideas set out are a guide to good practice in meetings. Inevitably life is messier than theory suggests, and even the best-planned meeting can have difficulties. There are limits to what you can achieve in meetings and it is important to recognise this. The successful meeting is not the one which never makes a mistake, but the one that survives the mistakes: a 'good enough' meeting.

Chapter 3 Problem-solving and decision-making

Solving problems and making decisions in organisations

Solving problems and making decisions are an essential part of our lives and, for managers, they form a key part of managerial activity. But what do problem-solving and decision-making 'look like' and is there a difference between the two? Consider these examples.

Fire!

The fire alarm sounded, so we had to evacuate the building.

Staff cover

Mia has changed the outside agency she uses when permanent staff are absent – and absenteeism is at a permanently high level. The quantity and quality of the work done by the agency staff is not very high and another agency has promised to provide a better service.

Expansion at Dunrod

Dunrod Builders, a small family firm, has just employed Dina – a non-family member – as company secretary and financial controller. The company wants to expand the range of work it undertakes but it means that John Dunrod, the managing director, and his brother Alan, the general works manager, will need to spend more time planning and supervising. Both claim that they don't have time. Dina investigates and finds that, regardless of the size of each building job, Alan or John visits the customer and prepares an estimate. If they are successful in securing the work then they supervise each job, however small. With as many as 20 separate contracts running simultaneously, resource scheduling is an increasing problem; further, Alan and John have time to make only very short site visits, relying on their building workers instead. But completion dates are often unmet and the number of customer complaints is rising.

Dina concludes that the company has outgrown the style of management control that it adopted when it was smaller and, if it is to grow, will need to make some improvements. Some of these may be structural or organisational (e.g. the roles of the family members), but the issue of planning and control must be dealt with urgently.

Following consultation with the family members, she institutes a system for setting objectives for each project and checking that these fit an overall plan. She also introduces a system of regular reporting and monitoring. Now she is considering the delegation and reallocation of roles to relieve Alan's and John's current workloads and the type of work.

Training solutions

Chief Executive Officer, Kamal Khan, wasn't sure why the staff training and development unit couldn't deliver the service it had been expected to, but he was sure about the potential solutions:

- outsource the service
- continue the service and accept its shortcomings
- replace the unit manager
- redesign the unit and its services.

Replacing the unit manager and asking the new person to redesign the unit and services if necessary seemed like the best solution.

A systems change

Jake's decision to change the system was truly creative: the change involved little work for the benefits gained. There had been no obvious problem with the system but Jake had been asked to look at it carefully as part of an organisation-wide initiative to meet new quality standards.

In each of the above examples, a decision was made. But which also involved problem-solving? Management books sometimes use the terms interchangeably. But notice that decision-making can take place without investigation of a problem, and can be a process of deciding between options, or solutions, only. Does the difference matter?

Many times during a working day, managers are presented with known problems to which there are known or standard solutions. It would be a waste of time to investigate each similar or identical problem, only to choose the standard solution. At other times, in a crisis, right now a decision needs to be made. Then there are situations which might benefit from investigation and to which there are some obvious solutions, but the 'right' solution will require investigation to ensure that it 'fits'. For example, in Example 4, no decision should have been made without first finding out why the training and development was failing to produce the promised service. Without knowing this, there is a risk that the chosen solution would not have worked.

In other situations, solutions can't be developed until the problem is investigated. This is because the problem could be one of several possible problems. Consider the case of poor performance by an employee: the cause could be health problems, difficulties at home, difficulties with equipment or materials – or several of these. Once the problem is investigated, effective action can be taken.

Ways of thinking about problems

The term 'problem' often seems negative. Essentially a problem is simply a gap between a situation that exists now and what is desired, that is, between *what is* and *what should be*. So, the word problem can mean:

- something has gone wrong
- expectations have changed

- something needs improving, for example, with suitable changes a system may be capable of delivering more, perhaps because it never worked properly in the first place

- something is needed that isn't in place, for example, an online booking service

- more than one of the above has happened, for example, performance has worsened just when expectations have increased.

Often we see that improvements can be made. We see this as *an opportunity* rather than a negative situation. However, when we attempt to make the improvement we must go through the same thinking process as when we are problem-solving.

Not all problems – or opportunities – are straightforward and self-contained. There may be many causes of a problem and many of them may be outside a manager's control. Taking an opportunity to make an improvement may have implications for other parts of the organisation and other people beyond a manager's influence. Before we go too far through the process of problem-solving we need to look carefully to see what kind of situation we are dealing with.

There are several ways of thinking about this. One is the degree to which a situation is part of a related set of problems or situations – how 'bounded' a problem is. While it is probably best never to think of a problem or situation as being unconnected, routine day-to-day difficulties tend to be bounded and often have limited implications. The characteristics of a bounded problem or difficulty are:

- you know what the problem is
- you know what needs to be known
- you know a possible solution
- priorities are clear
- there are limited implications
- the problem can be treated in isolation from other issues
- few people are involved
- the timescale is limited.

In organisations where there are robust systems for routine work and established rules and procedures for dealing with situations, problems are more likely to be bounded with few risks and uncertainties surrounding them.

At the other end of the spectrum are unbounded problems. Here, there seem to be question marks everywhere. Typical features of unbounded problems are the opposite of those of a bounded problem:

- you are not sure what the problem is
- you don't know what needs to be known
- you don't know what a solution might be
- priorities are called into question
- the problem cannot be isolated from other issues
- the implications are uncertain, may be great, and are worrying
- a number of people are involved
- there is a longer and uncertain timescale.

77

Further, resources are ill-defined and may alter over time; it is not clear who the significant players are; urgency is unclear. The situation may well be highly political too, with reputation, career progression and the status of business units and staff groups at stake. Unbounded problems are more typical where work is less routine, for example in non-routine project work such as that set out in Box 3.1.

Box 3.1 Anything but routine

Emma has worked for a local government authority for five years. She is an 'ideas' person, and has been particularly successful in recovering an important economic regeneration project that ran into trouble. The project still had problems, but Emma achieved as much as possible, given time and budget constraints, a lack of clarity in the original project brief and the personalities and politics involved. The trouble with the project arose when a major supplier failed to deliver raw materials on time. This required rescheduling of various sub-contracts; it also threatened to take the project beyond the planned completion date and over budget. The consequence would have been that new homes for a non-profit-making housing association to let to low-income families living in expensive emergency accommodation would not be completed on time. Repairing relations with the housing association and other departments and getting approval for delays from funding bodies required great political sensitivity and strong negotiation skills.

The project is an example of an unbounded situation typical in such work. There is a great deal of risk, uncertainty and, almost certainly, ambiguity. It is a sensible idea always to assess where the boundaries of a problem can or cannot be stated. The five 'boundary' questions to ask are:

- Why has this problem arisen: is there an underlying problem that should be dealt with first?
- Has it arisen before and in what circumstances?
- How has the problem appeared: is it part of a network of related problems that need to be considered together?
- What further information is needed to clarify the problem?
- Are other people affected by the problem and should/how should I involve them?

Answering these questions will help you to explore and determine the boundaries.

A second way of viewing problems is to consider problems and solutions as a matrix of known and unknown problems and solutions.

Figure 3.1 is a guide to what is required in particular circumstances, although circumstances are often not clear-cut, of course!

	Known problem	**Unknown problem**
Unknown solution	*Example 3:* Expansion at Dunrod Requires: problem-solving *Dosbarth bl II yn tangyflawni Quantitive a non-verbal.*	*Example 5:* A systems change Requires: creative problem-solving *Marking Policy?*
Known solution	*Examples 1 and 2:* Fire! and Staff cover Requires: decision-making (choosing between possible solutions); may also require problem-solving *Disgybl heb neud GC*	*Example 4:* Training solutions Requires: insight *Disgybl yn camfihafio o hyd?* → *Ella rhesymau gwahanol.*

Figure 3.1 A problem–solving matrix

(Source: adapted from Peckham, 1996)

In the case of the known problem/unknown solution, the problem is likely to require some further investigation – or reinvestigation – so that a solution can be found which resolves it satisfactorily. Known problems are not necessarily *fully understood* problems, which in turn makes finding a solution harder.

To understand the unknown problem/unknown solution case, consider a situation in which a manager wants to make an improvement to a system. The ultimate goal is known – improvement – but any current problems within the system are not known, so the solution that will improve the system is not known.

Unbounded problems have features of both known problem/unknown solution and of unknown problem/unknown solution.

The known problem/known solution cell of the matrix is usually a bounded problem. However, the known problem/known solution situation presents a challenge in the sense that while deciding between options may be sufficient, there is a danger that the problem is not quite as 'known' as it is assumed. However, if the situation is a recurring one for which several standard but flexible options are available, then decision-making in the sense of choosing between options may be all that is required.

If the case of the *unknown problem/known solution* is puzzling to you, think of the moment a child learns to use a hammer: the same 'solution' is tested on every 'problem' regardless of whether the solution is appropriate. A manager may have a favoured solution and actively seek a problem where it can be used. For example, a manager may favour pay incentives as a way of improving performance. This may be effective in some cases but not if the person requires training or better resources to do the job. In these cases, if there is a need for a decision, then it must address the problem.

As we have explained, problems are often complex and messy. First one needs to investigate the problem. Problem X may look like Problem Y which you identified and resolved with Solution Z last week, but closer investigation reveals that the similarity was superficial. For example, two employees frequently take sick leave. Both are suffering from stress-related illness, but investigation reveals that one had been given work targets that are impossible to meet, while the second often disagrees with their manager. Different solutions are required. Another possibility is that two situations might appear very different at first, but be similar at a deeper level. For example, one person is working long hours at the office, apparently overworked, while another has lost interest in work. Investigation reveals that both people have been poorly supported during a change to their work unit.

So, most situations require investigation to find if there *really* is a problem. Where a situation is well-understood, familiar and routine, where information is easy to obtain and the situation is clear-cut, there are often procedures, routines or rules to deal with it. This means that in general there will be no need to spend more time on investigation. Rather, a decision, or deciding between options, is all that is necessary. Many situations arise in organisations, however, that are not well-understood, familiar and routine. These will require investigation – how and how much depends on many other factors, as does the solution you arrive at!

✳ Problem-solving – a framework

Problem-solving is what we do when it would be inappropriate to make a decision without investigating a situation. To decide on a solution before the investigation risks making a decision that doesn't actually solve the problem.

So, how do people normally go about problem-solving in a way that is most likely to be effective? Management specialists have long discussions about different 'methods' of problem-solving and about the difficulty of applying 'rational' models in complex situations. We accept that in real life, most situations are complex. However, if you were to take many examples of how managers carry out problem-solving, a core 'model' emerges. This model, of course, needs to be described step by step, although in practice, people frequently work through the steps in an iterative way. This may involve working backwards, then forwards, or on several steps at once.

Imagine, for example, a situation where you have been asked to produce reports every three months. This will require the collection of information from various sources. It's not obvious to you how you can meet this demand. You will have to make changes to roles, systems and workload planning. But you can see that the report must be produced. The 'problem' in this case is that 'something is needed that we don't currently do; what do we need to do to achieve it?' There is a well-defined goal which requires implementation, but the implementation will involve some problem-solving.

In a different situation, a number of possible solutions may occur to you as soon as you encounter a problem. While investigating the problem, you might also be working out the implications of each solution. Then you might assess how well the 'best' solution addresses the problem. You may find that the solution will not work, or needs changing significantly.

Thus, we are not assuming – in many situations – that anyone works through the model in the order set out. Rather, the stages are those that are important to have covered in effective problem-solving.

This is the basic framework:

- analyse the problem
- draw conclusions from your analysis
- set the criteria for a solution
- identify an appropriate solution
- draw up an action plan.

Exploring the framework

1 Analysis

To decide if there is a problem and what kind of problem it is, you will need to *analyse* it. In doing this you will also *define* the problem. One way of doing this is to ask yourself three seemingly simple questions:

1 What is happening to make you think there is a problem that needs dealing with?

2 How and when is it happening and to whom?

3 Why is it happening?

By asking these questions you are likely to find that those involved in the situation have different perspectives and describe the problem differently. This can be useful in identifying misunderstandings and current or potential conflicts. It may also help to give a broader picture. This can show how the problem is related to others.

Normally a complex problem is the result of several related problems (or just one, deeper problem), so you may need to break it down into its component parts. Diagrams are useful tools to help you do this: they can help to reveal the relationship between different aspects of a problem and the different components of a complex one. You will find the following diagrams and how to use them in the Tools and techniques section of this book:

- systems maps   388
- fishbone diagrams   391
- multiple cause diagrams 393
- network analysis.   397

In a particular problem, some diagrams will help you more than others. When analysing the problem it is useful to have in mind the desired situation. The desired situation, of course, may be far from clear, but you can ask yourself the following questions in order to clarify what kind of solution would be appropriate:

- What are we trying to achieve?
- What are we trying to keep or preserve?
- What are we trying to avoid?
- What are we trying to eliminate?

When you have done all this, you will have defined and analysed the problem: you will know what the key features of the problem are, its symptoms, what is affected, and how. Take particular care to think things through carefully during this part of the problem-solving process. In many circumstances, different approaches to the problem are useful. You will also need to identify and deal with any assumptions you (or others) have made.

Dealing with assumptions

An assumption is something that we think is true, when it may or may not be true. When we are solving problems it is essential to know when we are making important assumptions. Many assumptions are possible to check, but if we don't know we are making them then we don't investigate them (see Box 3.2). When we identify assumptions (and check them) we can develop better solutions and argue for them in a more convincing way. Other people are able to follow the logic of the case or argument.

However, there are times when assumptions can be identified but cannot be tested. Here, the appropriate action is to state the assumptions we are making. It shows that we are aware that our case is built on at least some assumptions that, if wrong, would alter the case, conclusions and recommendations. It alerts others to the possibility that our conclusions may be wrong.

Box 3.2 An example of assumptions

You are the manager of an assembly plant that uses air wrenches in the assembly process. The air wrenches are extremely noisy – a health and safety issue for workers – and the problem you want to resolve is how to reduce the noise level.

You can easily see solutions such as soundproofing the room in which the wrenches are used, or putting silencers on the wrenches. In your thinking, however, you have made the following assumptions:

- Air wrenches are noisy. (But are *all* air wrenches noisy?)
- We *must* use air wrenches. (Is there something else that can be used?)
- *People* must use air wrenches. (Could the wrenches be operated by robots?)
- The wrenches must be used in the *assembly plant*. (Could they be used in a separate building, or could the work be outsourced to a specialist company?)

(Source: adapted from Harris, 2008)

Drawing conclusions

Conclusions are what you *infer* from your analysis: that is, they are judgements about the situation derived from your analysis.

For example, your analysis of a system may show that a part of it is failing because when clients telephone the organisation, only one person has sufficient information to identify the correct department for each client. So you *conclude* that there is insufficient resource in this part of the system.

Similarly your analysis of why no entrepreneurial activities are being carried out in your part of the organisation in the past month may reveal that 75% of your time is being spent handling disturbances and 25% on administrative matters. You conclude that this is leaving you with no time for entrepreneurial activities.

Thus, conclusions follow logically from analysis. They are not the solution to your problem. Rather, conclusions help you to clarify and state your goals for a solution in the next stage in the problem-solving process.

3. Set the criteria for a solution

A solution is an action or set of actions to produce the *desired* situation. It should solve the problem in appropriate ways. Before identifying an appropriate solution, however, you will need to have goals or criteria which your solution needs to achieve. When you identify these goals you will be setting *objectives* for a solution. In the case of too much time being spent on disturbance handling, the first aim may well be to find a way to reduce this, but the final aim is to provide more time for entrepreneurial activities. It is important to have the final aim clear. Note that goals can often be achieved in a number of ways and themselves have the potential for creative approaches and thinking.

4. Identify an appropriate solution

Now you need to try to develop solutions and choose the one that best matches the criteria you set. The solution must relate to the problem and match what you are trying to achieve, keep or preserve, avoid or eliminate. When clients experience a long wait to be connected to the correct department the solution might be to train one or more extra people to operate the telephone switchboard or for clients to select for themselves the department they need. In the example of needing to carry out entrepreneurial activity, the solution might be to delegate more of the disturbance-handling work to others. A proposal to abandon a project because there is a problem with just one aspect of it may be a recommendation that is ill-matched to the problem. If several courses of action are available, you may need to weigh them against each other and your criteria for an ideal solution. At this point a decision tree may help.

See also: Making decisions: comparing options and making choices, in this chapter

A solution to a problem is likely to be presented as a set of recommendations. This will be usual when a decision needs to be made by a person other than yourself, or by your team, or when the participation and involvement of others is necessary as part of the decision-making process.

Recommendations are proposals for action; they set out what needs to be done to produce the desired situation. Your recommendations, of course, will depend on, or be constrained by, a number of factors in your organisation. Such constraints might include other objectives, current systems, personnel, costs, culture, the cooperation of others, the availability of information and, importantly, the time available to resolve the problem. Your proposals will also be shaped by the nature of the desired outcome: do you want to resolve the problem 'once and for all' or do you need a simple solution that will serve for a short period until your department is reorganised in three months' time?

When making recommendations, always make sure that they are as SMART as possible. The letters in SMART are an acronym. They represent:

Specific – proposals or objectives must state clearly what is to be achieved.

Measurable – they must state how success will be measured.

Agreed – they must be agreed with the person who will carry out the proposals and, ideally, with anyone affected by the process or result.

Realistic – they must be achievable within the constraints of the situation and in alignment with other objectives.

Timed – there must be a target time set for achieving the objectives.

5. Develop an action plan

When you have drawn up a set of SMART recommendations, you will need to turn them into an action plan. You will need to consider the steps in the implementation process, who will be involved, time and cost, and communication. You will also need to consider how progress will be monitored to ensure that the objectives are met. Some of these steps will merit *discussion* under the heading of 'Implications, advantages and disadvantages', along with implications, advantages and disadvantages that may not be so obvious. Remember, an action can result in unintended negative consequences. You may be able to avoid these if you consider them early and make suitable plans.

Implications, advantages and disadvantages

It is wise to consider the consequences of your proposals, for example, the time and cost implications of doing nothing and of implementing the plan or how the use of resources might change.

There are likely to be some positive outcomes – advantages – to your proposal which will help to 'sell' it to others. Examples of advantages are outcomes such as skills development or new opportunities that might arise as a result of implementing your proposals.

Disadvantages are the negative consequences of your proposal, such as the disturbance associated with changing a person's role or a process. Setting out the disadvantages of a solution should not weaken your argument. By recognising that a solution has some disadvantages you will be showing that you have developed solutions carefully. Your argument will be further strengthened if you can also set out ways to minimise these disadvantages.

We can never be certain that every part of a solution will work, or that circumstances will remain the same. We cannot remove uncertainty. You should therefore identify the main uncertainties involved, and be aware of the level of risk that you are taking.

As you assess the amount of risk, it can be helpful to try to estimate the probability of events happening as predicted (such as the planned number of operations actually being performed, costs turning out as estimated, a project being completed on time). Various techniques exist for assessing this. For example, you can examine past experience. If a similar event has happened repeatedly in the past, you may be able to use information about it to predict the probable outcomes of future events. Alternatively, you can make subjective estimates based on your past experience, or simply make a guess.

Where a lot of data are available, more sophisticated analyses can be made. However, many managerial problems, including those involving human relations, are hard to quantify. It is helpful to apply some form of risk analysis in all situations. This is because it is rare for there to be certainty about a desired outcome.

Of course, if the disadvantages of a solution outweigh the advantages, you may need to rethink your solution to the problem!

6. Further steps in the problem-solving process

It will be necessary to identify markers that need to be achieved at each stage of implementation to enable progress to be monitored, and to have a clear idea of how you will assess whether the solution has been effective. These aspects of the problem-solving process are covered in Chapter 4 *Planning and control: making things happen* as they have wider applications than in the area of problem-solving. They will take you through all the remaining steps you will need to take, including the evaluation of the outcome.

7. Communicating with and involving others

This framework for problem-solving has been presented as if you are primarily acting alone. However, usually other people will be involved. These might be those who carry out the work, those who receive the services provided, or those whose work links with your work area. The input of other people will usually help you at every stage in the problem-solving process. In some problems, where others may be strongly opposed to your solution, involving them at an early stage may increase their opposition. In this case, you may decide to investigate the problem without their knowledge. Talking to and consulting with others can help you to define and analyse a problem, decide between possible solutions and arrive at the one that best fits the situation. Once a decision has been made about a solution to the problem, or the recommendations for resolving it, it is important to communicate the outcome to everyone who needs to know about it. This should include anyone who may be affected in any way by the proposed action. Involving others should mean that when a decision is communicated to them they are not surprised. If you have involved others in *each stage*, the decision will involve their ideas as well as yours and is more likely to be acceptable. To be effective, a decision needs to be of good quality *and* acceptable: if it is not acceptable, it cannot be effective. Again, if the decision is damaging to others, we can expect them to resist.

The framework for problem-solving is set out in Figure 3.2. It shows the basic steps. The curved arrows show the logical direction of the process while the straight lines show some of the iterative process that problem-solvers go through. Problem-solving in action is considerably messier than the framework suggests. First, the process is iterative. Second, it is likely that a problem itself may be found to be less well-defined than it seemed at first. Third, there may be an underlying problem. Other possibilities are that our information about a situation may be incomplete, we may make wrong assumptions. In all cases there are demands and constraints – risks, cost, time – that limit our choices. Usually there are other people to be considered at every stage. Even an ideal solution may not work if people are unwilling to cooperate.

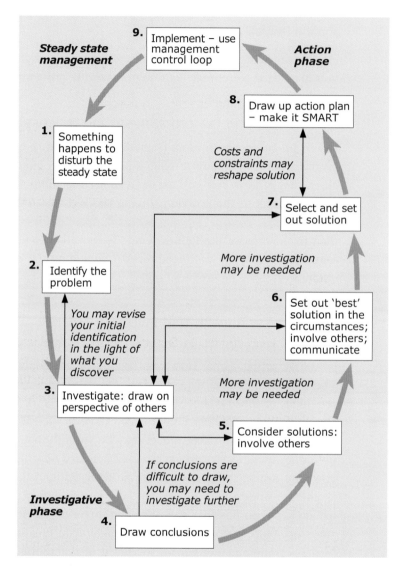

Figure 3.2 A framework for problem-solving

✳ Making decisions: comparing options and making choices

Managers make many decisions in the course of every working day. Decisions can be small, and routine decisions taken several times each day can be mundane, for example, whether to contact a supplier or talk to a particular member of staff. Sometimes the decisions will affect the entire organisation. The types of decision you make as a manager will depend on your organisation and your level of responsibility. Routine decisions are often carried out quickly but when careful thinking is required, it helps to have a framework to follow for comparing and deciding between options.

A decision is a commitment to do something. It may form part of a problem-solving process but may not. Here, we assume it does not and that the options to be compared are either obvious – for example, selecting the most effective recruitment methods from the organisation's normal approaches – or have been given to you by more senior managers.

Framework for comparing options and making choices

Table 3.1 shows the main steps in decision-making to help you choose the one best option from among those you have.

Table 3.1 Comparing options and making choices

Step 1 – Set objectives	Specify what you need to achieve
Step 2 – Set the decision criteria	Establish realistic criteria for a successful outcome. Make sure the criteria are SMART (Specific, Measurable, Agreed – with those who will be affected by the decision – Realistic and Timed)
Step 3 – Compare the options	Assess each option against the criteria established in Step 2
Step 4 – Select the preferred option	Make the decision, based on Step 3
Step 5 – Plan the implementation	Prepare an action plan that is SMART

The steps seem simple. In fact, they can be complex and demanding in practice. This is so when the decision to be made is not relatively well-structured, if information is not easy to find, and if there are too many non-routine elements and no policy guidelines. If the steps turn out to be too complex in practice, then it's best to treat the situation as a problem situation.

See also: Problem-solving – a framework, in this chapter

Set objectives

The most essential element in setting objectives is to be sure that, when you specify the desired outcomes, they actually address the situation. The question '*What are we trying to achieve here?*' is a useful one to ask! The opportunity, situation or problem that the decision is designed to address may need investigation. If so, the decision tree method is not an appropriate one to use: questions need to come before answers. Even after over half a century, Drucker's comment (1955, p. 345) remains relevant:

> (t)he most common source of mistakes in management decisions is the emphasis on finding the right answer rather than the right question.

It is wise, too, to identify which outcomes are *essential* and which are *desirable*. It is also important to state what would be unacceptable. Other people may help when setting objectives – and indeed throughout the process. How much you involve others will depend on the importance of the decision to be made and the sensitivities of those involved.

2. Set the decision criteria

Here, you need to specify the criteria, or requirements, for the desired situation or outcome as clearly as possible. Make sure the criteria are SMART. For example, if the decision is between different photocopiers:

Specific: 2,000 copies a day; two-sided copying facility

Measurable: evidence from suppliers and their customers

Agreed: acceptable to those who must use it

Realistic: can be bought within the budget

Timed: can be delivered within a week of ordering.

The criteria themselves can be set out in Table 3.2. The criteria are listed in the left-hand column.

Table 3.2 Evaluating options

Decision criteria	Option 1	Option 2	Option 3
1 Essential Purchase cost Ease of installation Running costs Quality of after-sales support Ease of use Specification Sort facility Stapler Remote operation Print facility			
2 Desirable Binder facility			
3 Not acceptable Paper trays with a capacity of less than 1,000 sheets			
4 Other features A new model, three months or less since introduction			
5 Uncertainties Availability of option 3			

3. Compare the options

You are now ready to consider the options. Each option should be assessed against the objectives you set in Step 1 and the decision criteria you set in Step 2. It should be a relatively simple matter to eliminate options which fail to match the objectives and the criteria.

When selecting options, you will need to take account of financial implications and the degree of risk, of course. It will therefore usually be necessary to evaluate the cost and resource implications of different options, for example, additional staff costs or savings, additional equipment.

You should also identify the main uncertainties involved, and be aware of the level of risk that you are taking. This should help you to estimate the probability of the decision-making outcome happening as predicted. Past experience can help; otherwise a best guess may suffice. Analytical tools are available for sophisticated analysis but these often require data which are rarely available – and only some decisions can be aided in this way.

4. Select the preferred option

This completes Step 3, but is listed separately to emphasise the comparison of options! The decision should be communicated to those who need to know about it, including anyone affected by it. If there is any likelihood that the decision will be rejected, then it's best to know at this stage. Again, matters are complicated if disagreement has been expected.

5. Plan and control the implementation of the decision

Depending on the nature of the options and the situation they were to address, the implementation may be as simple as ordering something or as complex as planning the implementation of a project. The more complex the decision, the more detailed the implementation plan will need to be. Make sure the plan is SMART. As the plan is being implemented, you will need to monitor progress, using the SMART objectives, and you will need to assess that the overall objective is achieved – whether the decision was effective. These steps are covered in Chapter 4 *Planning and control: making things happen* as they have wider applications than in the area of decision-making.

An example of deciding between options is set out in Box 3.3.

Box 3.3 Tom's options

At just 25 Tom had become the manager of a busy health centre offering the services of doctors, nurses, midwives and other health professionals. Staff and visitors regularly complained that they could never get anything to eat or drink there. Tom realised that the number of people using the centre meant there was a potentially profitable opportunity to provide catering on the premises. There was spare capacity to accommodate a facility. But Tom became confused at the number of options that he had to consider.

Should he investigate an automatic drinks dispenser? Should there be food as well? Or should he outsource the catering? As well as commercial organisations, there were one or two local non-profit organisations who might want to operate a small cafeteria. But then he needed to work out how to operate a tendering exercise, who to invite to tender – and how to decide between them. A non-profit organisation would be more consistent with the community ethos of the health centre, but a commercial organisation might be able to offer additional benefits. But any organisation tendering would have to adopt the health centre's healthy eating policy.

Tom struggled to sort out how best to proceed. Each time he started to think about any one option he would quickly switch to others and he was going round in circles. Then he produced a decision tree. This was no more than a diagram of his options, but it helped him to clarify them in his mind and he was able to think them through.

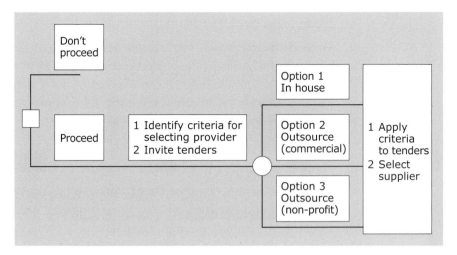

Figure 3.3 Tom's decision tree

Decision trees allow you to show the relationships between your options, and help you to identify different levels of decision. From Figure 3.2 you can see that in this example there were two separate decision points, and at each one there were two or more options to choose from. Obviously, before a decision can be made each of the options has to be evaluated and the likely outcomes have to be predicted. The diagram enables this to be done with a fair degree of clarity. Also, if something goes wrong you can re-examine the decision made, and ask whether the right solution was in fact chosen. This is a simple technique that can be applied to many low-level problems where several linked options are available.

Limitations of deciding between options

See also: Problem-solving – a framework, in this chapter

The limitations of any structured approach to decision-making are essentially the same as for problem-solving.

The approach to decision-making is shown as being rational and clear. Complications, iteration and uncertainties are not indicated. As Fradd (1988, pp. 20–1) said of both problem-solving and decision-making, in practice, one thought suggests another and ideas tend to come in groups. Managers tend to repeat their consideration of a problem, its causes and its solutions. This alternation backwards and forwards will often increase a manager's understanding. Whether you approach decision-making in a linear and rational way, or iteratively, some particular difficulties that might be encountered are:

- It can be hard or expensive to collect all the necessary information.
- It is not always easy to identify the objectives clearly in response to the needs you perceive. You may have to seek a compromise between competing or conflicting interests and objectives.
- Generating options can be time-consuming and expensive.
- You may not be able to find the time for creative thinking.
- Evaluation of alternatives can also be a time-consuming process.
- Predicting future outcomes will often carry a high degree of uncertainty.
- Even if you reach what you believe to be an ideal decision, it may be rejected!

7. Other approaches

Some alternative approaches, based on the ideas of de Bono (1982), may help you when it is not easy to decide between options.

These are:

- *A less than ideal approach.* Try to visualise the ideal solution and then choose an option that will be accepted and is as close as possible to the ideal.

- *An intuitive approach.* Make your choice intuitively, as you often will, but be honest with yourself. State the real reasons why you opted for that choice. Could you justify them openly, or were they bad reasons based on, for example, laziness or fear? Should you perhaps think again?

- *A negative approach.* Instead of looking for the best options, look for reasons to reject options. Eliminate the weaker options one by one until you are left with the least bad option.

- *A changing circumstances approach.* You can eliminate options by considering how valid they would be if your forecast of the future turned out to be inaccurate. Change those circumstances to which the situation appears most sensitive. Choose the option which remains best in the changed circumstances.

Whatever approach you adopt, you should always be clear about what you are trying to do. In particular, you should be clear about your objectives and you should monitor your progress – even if you have to rely on subjective judgements.

The problem with problem-solving and decision-making

Problem-solving and decision-making are rarely easy. Herbert Simon, an eminent psychologist, was the first to identify what is known as *bounded rationality* (Simon, 1960). He noted that organisational contexts, politics and limitations on time and resources mean that managers are often not able to approach a problem or decision rationally. A simple example is the case where information is simply not available for some reason, and a 'best guess' is needed instead. Problems and decisions, then, may not be addressed in an optimal way: solutions and decisions may be simply 'the best in the circumstances'. This is known as *satisficing*.

It is important to separate bounded rationality from irrationality, however. The latter can be defined as thinking which does not conform to logic. Whereas bounded rationality does conform – the logic can be seen – irrational thinking is simply 'bad' thinking. A simple example of irrational thinking is continuing to pursue a solution which will not solve the problem encountered. A manager who is told that there is no budget for training decides to continue to pursue a training solution for an employee. However, the training will not be funded and the person to be trained has rejected the suggestion because she is retiring in three months' time. While the manager *might* see some logic in his thinking, it is not clear. This is not the case with bounded rationality: rational, 'good enough' thinking can still be achieved even under difficult circumstances.

Another factor to consider is that managers seldom deal with one issue at a time. A manager who moves one of her team to relieve a local work pressure point (Problem A) may also use this as an opportunity to begin reshaping a difficult team (Problem B) and provide work experience for a trainee (Problem C). Solutions – and managers – may have multiple purposes. Multiple benefits may ensue, but equally, one failed solution can have a negative impact on the other solutions.

Often, the importance attached to a problem or decision-making will change as time progresses. What was important to a manager yesterday may be overtaken by a more important issue today.

Unexpected events are an important factor in problem-solving and decision-making. The opportunities people have for problems to be raised and for solutions to be discussed – and who is present – will shape the way the problem is investigated and the possible solutions to it.

As a result of such factors, there is some unpredictability about problem-solving and decision-making – and something a little disorderly about it. James March (1978, 1981) suggests that managers need to be opportunistic and flexible, open to possibilities and pursuing broad agendas. Not all solutions will work and not all decisions will be effective, but persistence will often payoff: some will succeed and some that don't succeed on that occasion might succeed on another.

An important reason for managers to take opportunities and be flexible in problem-solving and decision-making is to try to overcome what is known as decisional bias – their own or that of others – which can result from the following:

- preferring some approaches to a solution (and problems) rather than considering equally possible alternatives
- previous experiences in similar situations
- a simple view of uncertainty
- misconceptions
- overconfidence.

See also: Dimensions and types of organisational culture, Chapter 12

One way for managers and organisations to overcome such bias is to ensure that different views can be freely discussed. This will depend on the openness of the organisational culture: how problems are solved and decisions are made in an organisation, who is consulted, and the extent to which the problem-solving and decision-making processes reflect the values of the organisation. In some organisations it may be important that senior people have been involved or consulted even if they are not experts in the problem area.

All this can be summarised as the difference between how problems are solved and decisions are made in practice and how the organisations believe they *should* be solved or made – the difference between the *normative*, that is, how things should or ought to be done, and the *descriptive*, that is, how things are really done.

Problem-solving in action: an example

What does problem-solving look like in action? When we are managers we need to bring *management* thinking to our analysis and resolution of problems. We draw on management frameworks and ideas. Here, we present an example of problem-solving which focuses on a management control problem and uses what is known as the management control loop to analyse and solve it. This framework is covered in Chapter 4. You do not need to be familiar with the management control loop to understand the example.

City Kids

Twelve months ago Jo became the manager of a newly launched project whose mission is to improve children's quality of life in several deprived areas of a city. The project is run by a not-for-profit organisation – City Kids, based in Bexford – and has been funded by direct donations, a national non-profit organisation and the local political authority. The funding by both bodies is for two years only, with a possibility of an extension if the project is successful. A team of six community officers – who, like Jo, are paid – work with children, helping them define and meet their needs through self-help and effective action.

City Kids based the project on a successful one running in another city, Canningforth. There, for example, a group of 8–16-year-olds had decided they wanted to set up and run a neighbourhood radio station. The Canningforth community workers had helped the youngsters publicise their idea, identify and involve individuals and organisations who could help, and raise money.

Each initiative in Canningforth also encouraged adults to get involved with community life, volunteering their time to help set up and run facilities with the children under the guidance and supervision of the community workers – and to organise their own social activities. City Kids had been particularly impressed that one group of women organised their own cookery club after being involved in a children's play scheme in Canningforth. Not all the initiatives that the Canningforth project facilitated had been successful, of course, but there appeared to have been a reduction in vandalism and antisocial behaviour in areas where the project operated. City Kids and its funders want the same for Bexford.

The broad objectives of the Bexford project were sketched out by City Kids before Jo was employed. Jo's first task was to refine the objectives before the community officers were employed. She thought she had arrived at a set of very clear objectives, based on those of the Canningforth project, but the trouble was that when City Kids employed the community officers, most of them had their own ideas about the tasks that were supposed to achieve these objectives. There seemed to be ongoing discussion among Jo and the community officers at meetings a long time after the community officers had set to work, and even now they didn't always follow the plan they themselves had devised when they encountered a problem. The organisers of City Kids are frustrated by the seemingly changing nature of project work, although they understood that tasks might change depending on the success or failure of each.

As for Jo, she seems to be chasing round to see what the community officers are doing and trying to assess whether their work is consistent with the aims of the project. To add to her problem, two community officers don't seem to be performing well but they claim that what they were asked to do was bound to fail given the needs of the children they are working with. Jo is unsure about what to do. Now she is under pressure from City Kids to report on the success of the project in order to secure funding to extend the project to other deprived areas of Bexford.

Jo is panicking. She has got to the point where she feels out of control of both the project and the community officers. However, she is reluctant to talk to the organisers of City Kids and resolves to sort out the problem herself.

Solving the problem

Problem identification

The problem is evidently one of managerial control.

Problem analysis

While Jo had a clear set of project objectives, it appears she did not plan the tasks that were to achieve the objectives. While it was a good idea to involve community officers in the planning process, Jo allowed them too much freedom. This was in part because no *agreed* performance measures were set for the tasks that would indicate whether they were being carried out effectively, to the expected standards. Without these, Jo had no means of assessing whether and why a task was not working, so that corrective action could be taken. The community officers were able to simply change a task, regardless of why it didn't seem to be working.

It is assumed that the project is on budget, although it cannot be assumed that the project is on target or will meet the expected outcomes.

Conclusion to the analysis

Jo was not systematic in planning the project tasks, identifying performance measures and standards or measuring performance against them. Without a clear and well-communicated process of management she has been unable to manage the project (or personnel) effectively.

See also: Planning and control, Chapter 4

Recommendations

1 Jo should reassess the project objectives to clarify again what needs to be done and how the objectives need to be met. Some adjustments may be needed if the schedule and budget are not being kept to. Standards of performance need to be created if none are in place. As a key objective is helping children to define and meet their needs through self-help and effective action, standards of performance will cover the professionalism of community officers in doing this. This, in turn, will also cover

building and maintaining good relationships with key stakeholders (the people, agencies and organisations with an interest in the project, e.g. children, parents, the communities in which the officers work, and funders who do not necessarily have similar interests). If Jo finds that changes to the objectives are necessary, she will need to discuss them with the organisers of City Kids.

2   Jo needs to assess the tasks being carried out by the community workers to see whether they are consistent with the project objectives, that is, that they are likely to result in the desired aims and that the standards of performance are being met. Some tasks could be stopped or changed and others added. However, performance measures will need to be identified for each task and applied during monitoring of tasks as they are being carried out. Discussion will still ensue about whether an initiative is working, how well and whether some adjustment is needed, but performance will be measured. We are not told whether each task is systematically assessed for space needs, costs, helpers, equipment and material needs, specialist advice (and, indeed, if the community officers require additional training and development) but this also needs to be done, of course. Under-resourced tasks are unlikely to achieve expected levels of success.

3   As Jo monitors progress on tasks and outcomes, she may find that the original objectives were unrealistic and need adjustment. If this is the case, she will need to discuss her concerns with the City Kids organisers. Discussions about the projects should be taking place regularly in any case.

4   Although a final evaluation is likely to be carried out, it is necessary to evaluate whether the project is meeting its objective of improving the quality of children's lives (and in what ways) as it proceeds because qualitative information may be unavailable later without a lot of effort. This also needs to be built in at the (re)planning stage, sometimes task by task.

5   At every stage, Jo needs to communicate with the City Kids organisers, the community officers (and, if the objectives were to be changed, the funders and other stakeholders). Given the current situation, Jo would be unlikely to be able to achieve what is necessary without the agreement and cooperation of the community officers. It is likely that to achieve change she will need to establish firm grounds for this, for example, that there is a pressing need for the project to deliver on its promises if it is to receive further funding.

6   Every part of a problem solution – which should result in an action plan and expected outcomes – needs to be SMART: Specific, Measurable, Agreed, Realistic and Timed. Most of these have been borne in mind in the recommendations, but Jo needs to write an action plan and a schedule for implementation. There is some urgency, so Jo should aim to assess the project objectives and tasks, make adjustments and set task performance measurements within two to three weeks.

See also: Evaluation: how well are we doing?, Chapter 4

Strengths, weaknesses and implications

The recommended solution should improve management of the project and should put it back 'on track'. However, if it has gone too far off track and the original objectives need to be revisited, considerable work may be involved. There will need to be re-negotiation with funders and, if this is not handled well, the reputation of City Kids might be tarnished.

If Jo's efforts to communicate with and involve the community officers are not successful – Jo's efforts to exercise control – then she may have to deal with some conflict.

Chapter 4 Planning and control: making things happen

Making things happen

Huf Haus building

Two different organisations

Huf Haus, a German company, is known for its distinctive timber frame houses, which it sells throughout Europe and the UK and in Russia. The energy-saving houses are individually designed for clients – right down to the light switches. The shells of the buildings are manufactured from raw materials in the Huf Haus factory in southern Germany. A prefabricated shell is delivered to the client in 'kit form', together with fixtures and fittings and construction materials. The shell is assembled by Huf Haus employees on site, normally within days. Finishing a house takes a little longer.

In the UK, the government-funded National Bee Unit (NBU) has a team of research staff and bee inspectors whose task is to protect the honeybee. Honeybees are very important to the pollination of farm and wild plants. There are concerns about bee diseases which could seriously affect crops, making the work of the NBU of national importance. The inspectors are home-based and visit beekeepers to inspect hives and provide help and advice. The NBU also provides specialist advice to government departments and industry.

Bee inspector

What do a kit-form house manufacturer and a honeybee research and inspection agency have in common? Indeed, what do *all* organisations have in common whether they are commercial, public sector or non-profit enterprises?

What an organisation does and how it does it may be unique. But there is something they all do. They all use *resources* of various kinds to *do* something, either to produce goods or services or to produce a combination of both. This overall process of using resources to create outputs is often referred to as the transformation model, shown in Figure 4.1. This 'big picture' view of organisational activity is an important one for managers to understand. It can help you to make sense of your place in the organisation and your day-to-day role. Before you can make sense of planning and controlling activities, you need to be clear on *what* is being planned and controlled.

See also: Input-output diagrams, Tools and techniques

Figure 4.1 The transformation model

A transformation process is any activity or group of activities that takes one or more inputs, transforms and adds value to them, and provides outputs for customers, consumers or clients. Typically, we think of outputs from transformation processes as goods and services. Goods are physical (tangible) products of the process; they are typically produced prior to the customer, client or consumer receiving them. On the other hand, we cannot touch or store a service. Services are consumed at the time of production. Many operations produce both goods and services.

Huf Haus mainly produces goods that you can hold and touch – the timber frame of your new house. But it also provides services:

- finance for buying a Huf Haus can be arranged
- architectural and interior design, sourcing and supply of fixtures and fittings, 'single package' delivery, and house construction.

NBU mainly produces services. You cannot hold and touch the advice that the inspector gives the beekeeper when they both inspect the hives and talk about the state of the bees. However, NBU also produces some products:

- publications on bee keeping
- research reports.

Another useful example is a café. Here we have products – meals (goods) – as outputs, but the service provided by the café is an important part of what the customer is buying. We expect the people who take our orders to be helpful, and we would like the space we occupy to be clean and comfortable.

In addition to the outputs which go to clients and customers, there are outputs to several other stakeholders, for example, taxes to government, pay and other benefits to staff.

The input resources that are transformed in the production of goods and services are called *transformed resources* (Slack and Chambers, 2007). They are usually a mixture of:

Materials – some tasks and processes transform the physical properties of materials, such as wood transformed into timber frames, or fish and vegetables transformed into a meal in a café; other operations transform the location of materials, as in the case of parcels in the postal and courier services; others transform the possession – the ownership – of the materials, such as retail operations; and others, such as warehouses, just store materials.

Information – some tasks and processes store and make information available (libraries); others transform the form of the information (consultants, accountants, IT specialists); some sell information (market research companies); others transport information (telecommunications company).

Customer/consumer/client – some tasks and processes transform clients physically (hairdressers, surgeons and dentists); others transform their psychological state or their knowledge (entertainment companies, schools and colleges); others transport customers (ambulance, bus, train and taxi services and airline companies); and yet others accommodate consumers and customers (prisons and hotels).

Where the inputs are raw materials, it is relatively easy to identify the transformation involved, as in the cases of the house builder and the café. Where the inputs are information or people, the nature of the transformation may be less obvious, as when a hospital transforms ill patients (the input) into healthy patients (the output).

Often all three types of core input – materials, information and customers (or consumers or clients) – are transformed by the same organisation.

For example, withdrawing money from a bank account involves information about the customer's account, materials such as cash cards and currency, and the customer. Treating a patient in hospital involves not only the 'customer's' state of health, but also any materials used in treatment and information about the patient.

Several different transformations are usually required to produce goods or provide a service. The overall transformation can be described as the macro operation, and the more detailed transformations within this macro operation as micro operations. For example, when you eat breakfast in a café, the staff have put out the plates and cups, sliced the bread, taken the butter and jam from the refrigerator, made the coffee and heated the milk – a macro transformation with five parts.

Materials, information and customers are not the only inputs required in transformations, however. Inputs known as *transforming resources* are required. These are the resources necessary to carry out the transformation but do not themselves form part of the output. They can be:

Facilities or fixed assets – the buildings, computers and servers, machinery, plant and process technologies of the operation, and chairs, desks and telephones.

Staff – the people involved in the operation. They are the 'human resources' who plan, control, operate or maintain activities. The nature of the staff differs between tasks and processes. For example, the assembly of car seats for children may not need staff with a very high level of technical skills, in contrast to the research and design staff.

Finally, undesirable or unwanted outputs result from the transformation process. These are usually the waste elements generated in the production process. Some waste products can become the input for another transformation. For example, wood waste can be turned into farm fertiliser, new materials for building and furniture making, and ethanol for fuel. However, the most common products of transformational processes are carbon dioxide from transport and processes, and waste which is placed in land-fill sites. Thus organisations will need to be concerned about:

- minimising the environmental impact caused by waste outputs
- preserving the health and safety of employees and the local community
- taking ethical responsibility for the social impact of transformation processes.

Transformation at a more 'local' level

Whatever organisation you work in, you will be part of a macro operation and will plan, control, monitor and perhaps evaluate micro operations. The challenge for managers is to be clear about the inputs and outputs for their micro operations.

Most organisations as macro operations must avoid financial problems. This means that the value of outputs must be greater than the value of inputs. However, it is often difficult to make sure that the value of the outputs from your micro operation is greater than the value of the inputs. For example, if you worked at the National Bee Unit you could find out the costs of the inputs and transformations of your free publications service – available to the general public as well as beekeepers. But what is the value of your output? How can you calculate the value of raising awareness of bee health among non-beekeepers?

It may also be hard to calculate the cost of not putting something right or the value of an output which serves as an input in part of a larger task. Consider the following example in which you are responsible for the coffee machines which provide staff with free coffee. The policy of the organisation you work for is that free coffee will improve staff satisfaction and make staff less likely to leave. Thus, free coffee reduces recruitment costs. It is easy to calculate the cost of the inputs – the coffee machines, the electricity and water they use, and the staff time maintaining them. But it is difficult to judge how much larger the organisation's annual recruitment budget would be if coffee were not provided free of charge.

Performance indicators

If the value of outputs needs to be greater than the value of inputs, then we need to compare them to see if this is so. This will tell us whether the transformation has added value to the inputs: that is, whether our activities have been effective. First, however, we must decide what to measure performance against or what standards to set. The choice is often not simple. To make it simple, often the choice is to measure what can be measured easily. This results in an overemphasis on financial measures, leading to the complaint that *The organisation is being run by accountants* (or external regulators or inspectors, who often share a preference for the easily-measurable aspects).

Performance indicators are usually grouped under four headings:

Economy. This is the simplest measure. It refers to how cheaply inputs can be purchased. The most economical organisation is that which can obtain its inputs at the least cost. We know that this may mean that transformations are more expensive, and outputs may not please our customers or clients. For example, you can easily buy lower-cost, lower-quality coffee for the staff coffee machines. This may mean that the cost of maintenance is higher and that staff satisfaction with the coffee decreases. Economy is unlikely to be the only measure considered.

Efficiency. This refers to the relationship between inputs and outputs, usually expressed as a ratio. An organisation becomes more efficient if it produces more with the same resources, or if it can reduce resource use without a proportionate reduction in output. In a competitive or market-driven environment, there is constant pressure to improve efficiency. In non-competitive environments – monopolies and many public services – there are different and sometimes less-urgent pressures to increase efficiency. The approach taken in non-competitive sectors is often to focus on costs: inputs are reduced while outputs remain unchanged. This would create an increase in efficiency.

Effectiveness. This is a measure of outputs, and can be defined as how well the outputs of the macro operation and the micro operations achieve their defined objectives. It is a measure of the ability of the organisation to satisfy its clients' or customers' needs. It is more difficult to measure than efficiency, but many management experts say that effectiveness is more important.

Equity. This is a particularly important concept in public services. The ethos of a public service organisation, and often its statutory obligations, require it to treat all its clients or customers and users fairly. This is an important difference between public and for-profit services and it complicates the application of commercial measures of performance to public services. An example is the obligation on public postal services in mainland Britain to provide a similar mail service to all inhabitants, however remote they may be. In contrast, a commercial operator can decide to have higher prices for carrying mail to remote locations.

These four Es provide a useful framework for categorising the different components of performance. However, it is often not easy to apply them to your micro operation and the macro operation of your organisation. Here is an example where different stakeholders have different, possibly conflicting views of what effectiveness means. It also looks at the need for measures to be easily understood and agreed. The example set out in Box 4.1 illustrates the problem of what to measure.

Box 4.1 What is neighbourhood policing for?

It is usual for taxpayers to want their taxes to be spent well. In neighbourhood policing, officers work in one neighbourhood where they establish a relationship with residents. Residents are involved in agreeing local policing policies with officers.

Some of the obvious performance measurement questions turn out not to be as simple as they first appear:

- The number of crimes solved in the neighbourhood? In this case, the higher the crime rate, the more crimes will be solved.

- The proportion of crimes solved in the neighbourhood? If this is the measure being used, it is better for the police to concentrate on the easier crimes, and not to allocate resources to tough problems.

- A falling crime rate in the neighbourhood? Then there may be a tendency not to encourage the reporting of crime, or to redefine exactly what is recorded.

Assessing the effectiveness of your activities is an essential part of the responsible management of your organisation and its resources. No activity is likely to take place without the usual planning, controlling and monitoring, of course. But it is good practice to plan with performance measurement in mind.

Planning and control

A vital task for managers is making things happen. To do this effectively, we need to make plans, implement them and exercise control to ensure that events stay on course. When things go wrong or when circumstances change, we need to make adjustments. Understanding this process is important because it is the daily activity of managers.

Plans have a significant role in organisations. In commercial organisations, the need to produce profits for financial stakeholders makes effective planning and control important. In non-profit organisations, where there are limited funds, planning and controlling activities may have even greater importance. It is usual in the for-profit sector for there to be plans and controls, and managers see them as a normal part of their work. In contrast, some people in parts of the public and non-profit sector do not accept that their work should be controlled. They argue that processes and people measuring how well your micro operations are performing damages the good relationships that people should have with each other. However, when we are discussing planning and control we are concerned with the idea of giving direction to and structuring activities rather than how people feel about these processes.

Planning and control are often referred to as a rational process. The term 'rational' is used to mean 'logical and structured' rather than based on judgement or intuition. All managers have at times 'muddled through'. Lindblom (1959), a famous management theorist, refers to management as 'the science of muddling through'! However, in order to be effective as a manager, you need first to understand the rational principles on which planning and control are based. Later you will want to incorporate inspiration, creativity or intuition, but our purpose here is to give you a sound basis for your day-to-day management activity.

See also: Lateral thinking, Tools and techniques

The principles of the rational theory of planning and control are illustrated in Figure 4.2, in what is known as the 'control loop'. We can also define 'planning' and 'control' at this point. Planning is the process of working out what to do and how to do it (Stages 1 and 2 in Figure 4.2) in order to achieve some goal; control is the process of ensuring that the planned tasks lead to success (Stages 3 and 4 in Figure 4.2).

See also: Brainstorming, Tools and techniques

Each stage of the control loop is set out briefly here before being considered in more detail.

Stage 1: Set objectives

If you are going to undertake any initiative, be it big or small, you first need to be clear about what you are trying to achieve. It is also useful to set out some criteria for success so that you will know whether or not you have achieved the objective.

Stage 2: Plan, identify markers and carry out tasks

Having clarified what you wish to do, it is important to plan what to do and actually do it. Here there is a need for 'markers' so that you have some criteria for judging whether you are achieving your objectives. Typically these are derived from your plan, indicating how far you planned to reach by a specified date.

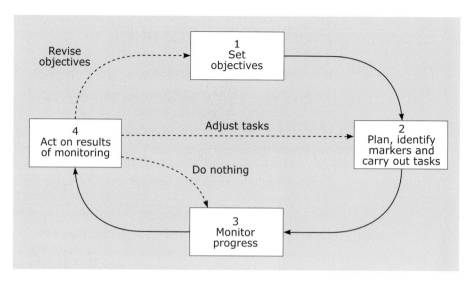

Figure 4.2 The control loop

Stage 3: Monitor progress

Simply noting these markers is not enough: you need to ensure that suitable progress is being made. Throughout a task or project there needs to be a process of checking what is happening and comparing actual progress against the markers.

Stage 4: Act on results of monitoring

Monitoring progress may reveal that the markers have all been reached, but it is more likely to show that progress is not as planned, or even that the original objectives have changed. Your three alternatives are to continue as you are, to revise the tasks, or even, if you have the scope, to revise the original goals. Then you continue the process of monitoring, reviewing, making decisions and re-planning if necessary, going round and round the control loop until the task is done.

The control loop in practice

We now look at each stage of the control loop in more detail in the context of a case study (set out below). It relates to the opening of a new warehouse for a chain of city newsagents' shops. Although the example is specific, it illustrates many of the general issues relating to operational planning.

The new warehouse

A growing chain of newsagents' shops in a city has decided to introduce a centralised system for stocking its shops with newspapers, sweets and snack foods, soft drinks and tobacco. Until now, each shop has had a separate stock and inventory system and suppliers have delivered direct to each store. It is now more cost-effective for the business to have a small warehouse – a single delivery point – from which all the shops can be supplied with stock. A building next to one of the shops has been identified as suitable, after some minor building work, for the new warehouse.

Two main benefits of having the new warehouse are expected:

- Costs will be lower when larger quantities of stock can be bought (an economy of scale).
- Storage space at individual shops can be converted to retail space when the warehouse project is completed.

All the shops need daily deliveries and also urgent deliveries for unplanned needs. Suppliers welcome the plans, as they will deliver to just one location and can organise their transport more efficiently. The newsagent business will need a van for delivering items from the warehouse to individual shops.

All the shops use the same stock and inventory system but this system will now be centralised so that orders to suppliers will be combined. Incoming stock will be separated at the warehouse according to the needs of the individual shops, stored and then allocated for delivery to each shop daily by van.

Luke has been asked to manage this project. It is now 1 March and the warehouse has to be operational by 7 May. All the necessary surveys of the new warehouse have been made. All necessary approvals have been given and finance has been made available. The task for Luke is simply (!) to make it happen.

We will now consider the control loop stages in more detail with the case study in mind, and introduce some techniques as we do this.

Stage 1: Set objectives

First, let us consider the need to set objectives. We would probably have an overall aim of getting the warehouse open and operational on time and within budget. Although this is quite specific, it will be helpful to state what 'being open and operational' means in more detail, such as to:

- recruit and train staff by (date)
- have minor building works completed by (date)
- have the warehouse ready to receive and dispatch stock by (date)
- complete the project within budget
- develop and maintain good relationships with senior management, store managers, contractors doing the work, and suppliers of the racking and the stock for the warehouse.

The final objective is slightly different in nature from the first four. Planning has to be both an analytical process – thinking things through, often involving individual calculation and reflection – and a social process – encouraging the contribution and commitment of others. If goodwill is maintained, they are likely to be co-operative if something unexpected goes wrong. Also, the final objective is more about *how* we do things than about *what* is finally achieved. This points to one possible way of classifying objectives. In the example, the first four objectives are clearly about what we are going to achieve; the fifth one is more about how we are going to do it.

See also: Problem-solving – a framework, Chapter 3

This 'what' and 'how' classification may be termed more formally as output objectives (what we will achieve) and process objectives (how we do it). The objectives could and should be further refined and be SMART, that is, Specific, Measurable, Agreed, Realistic and Timed.

Yet even if we have SMART objectives, we still need something more to help us ensure we achieve them. We cannot afford to wait to the end of the project to know whether or not we have succeeded. We need to know as we go along how we are doing, and for that we need a plan and some sort of 'markers' along the way to help us check on progress.

Stage 2: Plan, identify markers and carry out tasks

The planning process is, in essence:

Planning

- setting clear objectives
- identifying the tasks that need to be done
- linking tasks to people and resources
- drawing up a plan, including markers, that meets your needs as a manager.

Control

- monitoring progress
- revising plans, as indicated by the control loop.

The next step in planning is to identify what tasks are needed in order to achieve them. The mnemonic SCHEME gives us a list of the issues in any plan:

- **S**pace: accommodation in a location and with the facilities needed for the work or event.
- **C**ash: costings and any cash which may need to be available.
- **H**elpers: how many people, when, with what skills and experience.
- **E**quipment: from vans and computers to the coffee maker to be borrowed, shared, leased or bought.
- **M**aterials: sufficient stationery, documents (but too much material is wasteful).
- **E**xpertise: any specialist advice – about this sort of project, or the building, or insurance, or IT system – that you will need.

Once the tasks that need to be done have been identified, they can be displayed and sequenced. The most commonly used planning tool for this is the Gantt chart, which is a form of bar chart. Computer software is available for creating Gantt charts without having to use diagramming tools. A Gantt chart for the warehouse project is shown in Figure 4.3. Note that it is a simplified one: a Gantt chart for a real project would be more complex because many tasks would be divided into separate components.

The second tool used is network analysis, also known as critical path analysis. A network analysis reveals which tasks depend on the completion of others to enable them to start. These tasks make a 'critical path' through the plan. This will have a significant effect on when the project will be

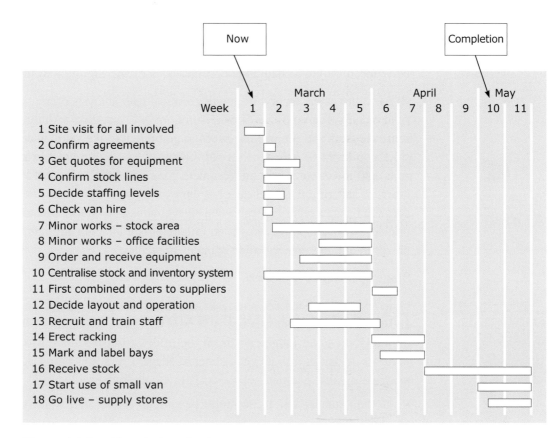

Figure 4.3 Bar (Gantt) chart for the warehouse case study

completed. Such a path will tend to define the shortest timescale, irrespective of other tasks elsewhere. A preparatory diagram for a critical path analysis is shown in Figure 4.4, in which part of the Gantt chart for the warehouse project has been set out. The junctions (called nodes) where arrows meet would usually be numbered. Each task is shown as an arrow and its length does not relate to the duration of the task. You may come across other formats which use slightly different terms.

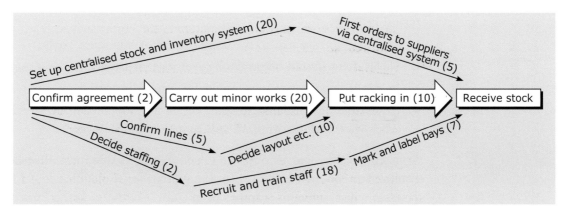

Figure 4.4 Warehouse project – a preparatory diagram for a network or critical path analysis

The numbers on the arrows represent the number of days it takes to complete each task (based on a five-day working week). As you can see, there is one 'path' highlighted. This is because each of those tasks depends on the previous task being completed before it can start, so if the numbers of days for these tasks are added up, it will be seen that (unless some change is made to them) stock cannot be received until 32 working days have elapsed.

Gaining time on other tasks will not affect this. Thus, the highlighted path is the critical path through this part of the plan, and the overall timescale can be reduced only by changing the timescales of the highlighted tasks.

At least, that is the theory. In practice, critical path analysis presents a somewhat rigid picture. The timescale shown is not, in fact, 'absolute'. Although common sense suggests that the racking needs to go up before the stock is delivered, the stock could still be delivered sooner. Likewise, putting up the racking need not wait until the minor works are complete. Many of these tasks could overlap each other, so reducing the timescale, but there are costs – in terms of extra work, possible risks to security, health and safety, damage to stock, and so on. This principle of overlapping tasks is an important one in achieving tight deadlines, however, and this is what often happens in practice.

Stage 3: Monitor progress

Objectives have been set, the tasks that need to be done have been identified and a plan has been drawn up. It is now necessary to monitor what is going on and form some judgement from the information received. Monitoring involves revisiting the objectives set at Stage 1 and measuring actual progress against planned activities. It involves four basic steps:

- Setting standards – these might be called performance indicators or benchmarks.
- Devising instruments to measure performance – these might include regular statistical reports or other feedback mechanisms such as staff or customer satisfaction surveys.
- Comparing performance against standards.
- Taking appropriate remedial action when things are not going to plan.

If SMART objectives have been set then the 'standards' set will be less open to interpretation. It should be possible to specify measurable targets such as timescale and deadlines, quantities, costs, resource use and quality of outcomes. Ideally, those who must meet the performance targets should regard them as:

- Meaningful: essential to the achievement of important goals.
- Clear: there should be no doubt over what is expected.
- Fair: everyone is working to equally demanding targets.
- Adjustable: the targets are fixed, but an adjustment will be possible when staff perform well but still cannot meet a target.

In practice it may not be possible to set objectives that meet all these criteria, and this will lead to different approaches to monitoring. In some cases, it will be obvious whether people are meeting targets so there will be little active or formal monitoring. In other cases more formal and active monitoring will be needed. The most common ways of seeking information to assess whether targets are being met are set out below.

Involvement and observation. Simply watching what is happening and being accessible to staff and colleagues is important. In the UK this is often described as 'management by walking about'. It can be time-consuming but it is an essential part of the monitoring process if you are managing the control yourself.

Regular reporting. This can include written or verbal reports to your management team. This reminds those who prepare the reports what the performance standards and measures are.

Exception reporting. This is summed up by the statement: 'Let me know if you have any problems'. Reports are provided only when there is a deviation from the plan. This can be very cost-effective, but the manager needs to trust the people providing the reports. This is because you are given no information on most performance measures.

Questioning and discussion. This allows you to build up a fuller picture of what has been going on and why, and will often take place during project meetings or visits. The approach is essential when problems arise. Note that standard questions can be answered in regular reporting.

Keeping records and routine statistics. Examples include budget printouts, or last month's sales or occupancy figures. Routine statistics are excellent for identifying trends that are not obvious. However, they may not be immediately available or self-explanatory.

Obtaining information is one thing, interpreting it is another. The facts rarely speak for themselves. For example, when you look at the costs of your branch office you may see that you will spend more than the budget figure. This could be a bad outcome because senior managers hoped that you would spend less than, or not more than, the budget. Or it could be a good outcome because only nine months ago the branch was even more over-budget and faced the threat of closure. The information becomes meaningful first by comparing it with the standard and second by making an assessment – understanding why things have developed as they have. This often means collecting more information and discussing it with those involved. Even with clear standards (such as those relating to quantities or times) it is often difficult to decide whether performance that is more successful than the plan, or less successful than the plan, is significant. Will a less successful performance grow steadily worse, stay about the same, or disappear? It helps if managers know the people involved and the type of work they are doing. Then they can assess the accuracy of such statements as: *'I'll catch up with the work next week'*, or *'We'll never get all this done on time'*. Some people are always over-optimistic, others always expect the worst. Sometimes you know from experience that although markers have been missed, the plan will still be completed successfully. At other times you realise that a crucial deadline will not be met. What does this mean for you?

Stage 4: Act on results of monitoring

The results of your monitoring will reveal which parts of your plan are being achieved, which ones are less successful and by how much. You have three choices following monitoring:

1 **Revise the objectives.** This sounds a major step, but sometimes difficulties cannot be foreseen at the planning stage. In this case some change to objectives is sensible. This can happen when external factors have made the objective unrealistic, or when the work so far has been inadequate and the objective cannot be met within the time remaining, or when the resources required have been seriously underestimated. In the warehouse example, financial difficulties, delays or the need for major works in the building could all result in revised objectives or targets.

One problem with revising objectives or targets is that people may ignore objectives set at the start of future plans. Another problem is that people who have worked hard to meet the plans can become demotivated.

2 **Modify the tasks or activities.** This might involve adding resources or staff, changing the procedures or working methods, arranging additional training for some of the staff, or some other corrective action. Making changes in the tasks still to be completed is the most common course of action, however. The implications of modifying tasks or activities need to be thought through carefully. You might choose a corrective action that solves the immediate problem but does not deal with the underlying cause. Or you may choose one that provides a long-term solution and will prevent the problem recurring. Typically, if the monitoring shows that some delay has arisen, then tasks in the coming weeks will need to be reduced in some way to make up the time.

3 **Do nothing.** This may be sensible if any deviation from the plan is quite small. Taking corrective action could risk making things worse and it could be too late in any case. Moreover, people on the project may already have worked out what to do to bring things back on course.

Successfully deciding what to do when plans are not being achieved is a key management skill. There are many possible actions. Each has its advantages and disadvantages. Changing plans may lead to more, or less, success than leaving them as they are. Accepting a late completion, or costs over budget, may make the people who work with you happy but may make your customers or clients unhappy. The manager has to think about the demands of all stakeholders.

The control loop process – planning (or re-planning), monitoring, making decisions – continues after you have revised objectives or tasks or you are continuing with the existing ones. The project may come to a conclusion, but often as one plan is completed, something new develops out of it, and the process starts again.

Planning and control are excellent learning opportunities. When we monitor progress we gain experience about how long things take. We learn that certain issues cause problems, and this learning should translate into better planning next time. Indeed, experienced project managers are valuable and sought-after; they have learned from their experience of planning and control and bring this wisdom to the project they currently manage.

Dealing with complexity

Even the best plans can fail or falter. The context in which we make and carry out our plans is complex and can change. How can problems be avoided? If you were to observe an experienced manager planning, implementing, monitoring and revising plans you would not see him or her moving through a series of sequential stages, but moving iteratively, backwards and forwards between them.

Initial identification of tasks may mean that we need to change an objective: when tasks need significant resources you may find that resources are insufficient. Then you have to go back and revise the tasks. When you begin assessing the work involved you will see if the objectives are possible. In these early stages you may need to arrange for some key features of the objectives of the plan to be changed. This is much harder to do later when the stakeholders have been told what the plan is. So it is wise to begin to plan early. It is also necessary to attend to people who have an interest in your plan: they can challenge it or make implementation more difficult than expected.

The initial stages of planning: techniques

Two techniques can assist in the initial stages of planning:

- Potential problem analysis, developed by Charles Kepner and Benjamin Tregoe (1981), to identify some of the likely problems ahead and either avoid them or minimise them.
- Contingency planning.

Potential problem analysis

A simple question at the outset can save you a lot of difficulty later. The simple question posed by potential problem analysis is *'What could go wrong with what I am planning to do?'*. The steps in potential problem analysis are:

1 Identify all the key outputs, actions and events in the plan.
2 For each of the key outputs, actions and events, identify all the possible problems that could occur.
3 List the possible causes for each potential problem.
4 Assess the risk of each of these problems occurring.
5 Assess the impact of each problem. Those problems that pose the highest risk and whose impact will be highest should be given the most attention. Where possible, identify ways to prevent potential problems from occurring or to minimise their effects. Preventive or minimising actions may not remove risk altogether, so consider how much residual risk might remain. Develop contingency plans where necessary. Contingency plans are needed where:
    - you have identified a problem which would have a serious effect but which you can't do anything about
    - there is a high residual risk even if you can identify a preventive or minimising action.
6 Record your analysis as you carry it out. A simple method is shown in Table 4.1. There are many variations. This one has a column for combining risk and impact so that you can easily identify the problems that demand most attention. You can add columns as necessary. A useful one might be how you are going to detect whether a problem is occurring. Risk can be assessed simply (high, medium, low) or in more sophisticated ways.

See also: Brainstorming, Tools and techniques

Table 4.1 Potential problem analysis

Plan step	Potential problems	Possible causes	Risk of occurrence	Potential impact	Risk plus impact	Possible actions	Residual risk	Contingency plans

Carrying out potential problem analysis can seem quite negative. However, as well as asking *'What could go wrong?'*, try asking *'What could go right?'*. Are there any unrecognised benefits or advantages in what we are planning? Does it benefit some other work? If you can identify anything of this nature you may find you can secure some unanticipated support for your plan.

Contingency planning

Contingency plans indicate what to do if unplanned events occur, and are valuable resources for the manager in a context where change is continuous. Managers need to decide how much time to spend on contingency planning, and this will vary according to circumstances. At their simplest, contingency plans may just be notes made on your journey home – when you think *'What if …?'* and decide which options you would follow if the *'What if …?'* situation arose. The following suggestions for dealing with contingencies were all made by practising managers:

- Break down key tasks to a greater level of detail to allow better control.
- Be prepared to overlap stages and tasks in your plan in order to meet timescales, but give the necessary extra commitment to communication and coordination that this will require.
- Spend time planning for *'What if …?'* at the start of a project in order to prepare for many of the problems.
- Learn from experience: for instance, develop a list of reliable contractors or consultants.
- Try to leave some slack – some spare time – before and after tasks you cannot control directly, to minimise the effect of any problems before, or during, such tasks.
- Bring forward scheduled tasks if possible – there will be one thing less left to worry about!

Achieving tight timescales

Many managers have the date when a project is to be completed given to them by their bosses. Sometimes your first reaction is that the date set by bosses is impossible. But such timescales are often achievable, a point that is demonstrated time and again by the managers who achieve them! Many of the tasks can be overlapped, for example, so reducing the timescale, but there are costs – in terms of extra work, possible security risks, damage to stock, and so on. Overlaps require good communications between all those involved.

Attention to people

Few things are likely to cause you more stress and difficulty when a plan is well under way than people challenging your plan because they claim they were not consulted. You face a difficult task in gaining their support. People may have all sorts of personal reasons for opposing your plan. Where feelings are involved or a person's sense of self-worth is challenged, such opposition can be very intense. This is illustrated below.

Improved office procedures

A local law centre, which handled enquiries from members of the public who could not afford a lawyer, seemed to be constantly under pressure and understaffed. The manager made changes to simplify the office systems, which made life much easier for those involved. The office staff liked it, but the administrator maintained an intense opposition. Even though she was involved and consulted throughout she did everything possible to hinder the new methods.

The reason became apparent later. The original complex methods gave the administrator a degree of mystique and power. Apart from the manager, she was the only person who understood the unnecessary intricacies of the previous system. Perhaps if the plan for the changes had included finding new responsibilities for the administrator which required her specialist knowledge, she might have been more helpful.

The example shows the importance of understanding the impact of change on individuals. At the outset of any plan, you ask the following questions:

- Who will be pleased about this project or initiative?
- Who might feel threatened by it?
- Who do I depend on to help me?

Recognising that someone may feel threatened by your plans should prompt you to address that problem early on, rather than reacting to a crisis later.

Communication and consultation

For each project plan you devise it is good practice to draw up a communications matrix. Figure 4.5 shows what a communications matrix might look like for the first few stages of a warehouse project. It can also be developed as you go along.

	Operations director	Area manager	Store managers	Marketing director	Stock suppliers	Racking supplier	(And so on)
Initial plan	✔	✔	✔	✔	✔	✔	
Revise plan after site meeting			✔			✔	✔
Agree lines			✔		✔		✔
Install racking			✔				✔
Start supply	✔	✔	✔	✔			

Figure 4.5 Part of a communications matrix for the initial stages of a warehouse development

Communication and public and non-profit sectors

In the public and non-profit sectors, issues of consultation and involvement can be exaggerated. For example, many parts of national government, the European Commission and some voluntary organisations have traditionally planned by consensus. Sometimes, people expect to be consulted about and involved in planning things which, in other organisations, would seem to lie outside their remit. In organisations operating internationally, planning issues may become further complicated by language and cultural misunderstandings. It is important to be as clear as possible what is and what is not negotiable when consulting and negotiating with other stakeholders and to arrive at a shared understanding. This is important in any organisation and perhaps particularly when commercial and non-profit organisations work together – an increasingly common phenomenon.

Evaluation: how well are we doing?

Sales manager Mike checked the weekly sales figures. They met the budget. A month later, with happy customers but sales figures showing little improvement, he wondered what had gone wrong.

Mike was doing what managers in all well-run organisations do: monitoring their activities, for example, by recording sales or numbers of people using sports facilities in a club, or by noting if repairs were being done within one week of being reported. These are mechanisms for collecting information. Monitoring describes the situation at a given point. It answers the question: *'Are we proceeding according to plan?'*. But it is not the whole picture. Evaluation seeks to assess the effectiveness of an organisation, a particular operation, a plan or project. It answers questions such as: *'Did it work?'*, *'How are we performing?'*, *'Are we using the right processes to achieve this?'*, *'Are we being cost-effective?'*.

See also: Planning and control, this chapter

The difference between monitoring and evaluation is an important one. This is because people often make their conclusions too quickly. When you are presented with monitoring information, a natural reaction is to look for an explanation for the situation described. For example, routine monitoring of the number of registrations for a training course might show that this is 10% more than the equivalent period last year. If you have just undertaken a substantial advertising project, it would be easy to assume that this is what has led to the increase. But without further investigation you do not know that this is the case. It is easy to move too quickly from knowing what the situation is (monitoring) to assuming you know why it is so (evaluation).

Evaluation involves asking and answering questions about the effectiveness of your department or project. It involves analysing performance and asking fundamental questions. Evaluation is about assessing the extent to which outcome objectives have been achieved. It is also about success on process objectives: *'Are we using resources efficiently?', 'How could we do our work better?'*. Hence evaluation, like monitoring, is central to good management practice. It closes or completes the control loop, demonstrating that the activities are, or are not, producing the desired effects.

See also: Planning and control, in this chapter

There are two main reasons for undertaking evaluation:

- To ensure that we are doing the best we can to meet the purposes of our organisation (outcomes) and using efficient methods (process).
- To demonstrate to those who manage or finance our activities that the resources they provide are achieving the purposes for which they were intended.

An important part of most evaluation is done informally through the judgements – based on many impressions, comments or observations – that we make in the course of our work. A restaurant manager might ask: How successful was that new menu? What would make it better? What did the people who cooked, ate or paid for the meals think? What will we do differently next time? Sometimes, however, it is important to make a more formal and more systematic evaluation in order to get a more accurate picture of our achievements.

Barriers to effective communication

Managers give many different reasons for why things have to be the way they are and cannot be improved. Or evaluation methods were not included in the plans, so relevant records have not been kept. Evaluations often avoid fundamental questions. Or they may emphasise the evidence that supports what key people believe. Some managers see retaining present methods as more important than asking if they are effective.

A complication in some public and non-profit organisations can be that managers see evaluation as something which they need not do. This is because it is 'done to them' – by, for example, internal quality managers, funders and other external agencies (such as the Audit Commission in the UK). Evaluations can then seem very threatening, particularly if those undertaking them seem not to understand the ethos of the organisation or the project. It can be useful for these managers to do their own internal evaluation or commission external evaluations. This helps them to influence, and respond persuasively to, those imposing evaluations on factors they need to take into account.

The example in Box 4.2 illustrates the importance of making more formal and more systematic evaluations.

Box 4.2 What are we achieving?

Alison, Brian and John were business advisers in a regional government unit that helped people who were planning to start their own small businesses. The constant flow of enquiries kept them busy. Brian argued the case for more resources:

> 'New small businesses create jobs. They offer an opportunity for achievement to those starting them and bring dynamism to the local economy. You can see from the growth in the number of enquiries, and from the growth of those we advise, that this unit is a success story. We need more advisers and more resources'.

The three knew that the regional government's internal quality managers were about to start their three-yearly evaluation of projects. Alison was worried about the questions that might be asked:

> 'They'll add up three years' worth of increasing spending on our salaries, premises, running costs and our marketing of the service. Then they'll ask how many of the new businesses advised by us are profitable. They may even ask which of these would have started without our help anyway! They'll calculate how many new jobs the businesses have created, taking away any jobs lost by existing firms facing these new competitors. By the end, they may judge that our business advice unit is expensive and is having little impact. Then they will recommend that the business advice service is closed'.

John took a more positive view:

> 'It seems that our future depends on how rigorous an evaluation they do, and how much we can impress them with the statistics that make us look effective'.

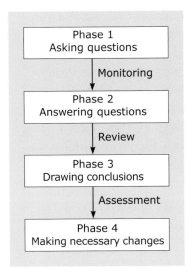

Figure 4.6 The process of evaluation

Evaluation as an iterative process

Evaluation can be seen as a staged process that occurs in four phases, as shown in Figure 4.6.

Phase 1 identifies concerns about the value of what is being done or how it is being done.

Phase 2 addresses these concerns. This means identifying the relevant experience and knowledge about value within the organisation, appraising it critically (*'How do you know?'*, *'Can we be sure about that?'*), seeking out further information either within or outside the organisation, and bringing it all together in a coherent way.

Phase 3 is deciding what needs to be done to improve things.

Phase 4 involves implementing these changes. When made, these changes begin a new control loop and the whole process of monitoring, review and assessment begins again.

In practice, evaluation is rarely as neat and straightforward as this and the four phases are seldom clearly distinguished; Figure 4.7 is a more realistic representation of the process. The different phases often run into each other, and you sometimes end up answering a rather different question from the one you expected. The whole process is often iterative – you go through it repeatedly, learning more and more about the issue, or tackling a succession of issues, each brought to light by the preceding question.

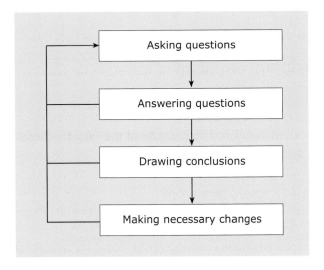

Figure 4.7 Evaluation as an iterative process

What is being evaluated and how?

A problem of process and outcome

Erica read the newspaper report with increasing disappointment. It set out the results of an evaluation of the effectiveness of her local government's 'housing services'. She was amazed to read that responses to queries from members of the public were made within one minute. This indicated that the organisation was 'among the best in the country' against this benchmark. Erica lived in a house owned by the local government. Every time she telephoned about repairs, her call was answered quickly by a receptionist, who then tried to transfer the phone call to the appropriate office. This was very difficult. First, the person Erica needed to speak to was away from his or her desk. Then, when she did contact the right person, it took a long time to process her enquiry. 'They measured the wrong thing,' thought Erica. 'I'm sure they just measured how long it takes for front-line staff to answer the telephone, not how long it takes for a problem to be resolved.'

Erica analysed the situation correctly. Evaluation – the *'How well are we doing?'* question – can focus on two types of objectives: process and outcomes. The evaluation in the example was about a process objective, not relevant to the outcome objectives. An evaluation must assess what it sets out to assess. Assessing the wrong things wastes resources and often creates conflict with stakeholders (those who have an interest in the organisation in some way). Every evaluation must have a clear focus on the objectives. The evaluation must be clear about process and outcome objectives. One difficulty is that these can be in conflict. Process objectives might include cost reduction, while outcome objectives might include adding useful features to the service. It is usually very difficult to achieve both at the same time! Stakeholders who provide funds for a service may be concerned about costs, while stakeholders who use a service will be concerned about service delivery. Where objectives conflict, an evaluation is likely to highlight any differences in goals, values or objectives that exist in an organisation or part of it.

Types of evaluation

We have separated evaluation into two types, which are evaluation of outcome and of process objectives. In other management writing these two types are divided further, and these may help you develop evaluation of your macro or micro operation.

Table 4.2 Types of evaluation

Type of objective	Type of evaluation	Focus – asking questions about ...	Getting answers about ...
Outcome	Strategic	Are we doing the right thing as an organisation?	Aims or overall goals of organisation
Outcome	Impact	Outcomes	Effectiveness
Process	Performance	Relationships between inputs and outputs	Economy and efficiency
Process	Process	Activities	Links between how things happen and what happens
Outcome and process	Composite	Mixture of the above	Some or all of the above

Table 4.3 gives examples of four of the five types of evaluation in a restaurant.

Table 4.3 Evaluation example

Type of objective	Type of evaluation	Focus – asking questions about ...	Getting answers about ...
Outcome	Strategic	– Would we make more profits if we sold the restaurant and opened another type of business? If the restaurant continues: – Is the location suitable? – Is the type of restaurant suitable – vegetarian, ethnic, fast food ...? – Are our customers suitable – age, wealth ...?	Aims or overall goals of organisation
Outcome	Impact	– How satisfied are our customers? – Did the customers eat their meal? – Did they enjoy it? – Was the food what they wanted? – Were they satisfied with the service? – Was the price acceptable? – Is the quality the customers experience always the same?	Effectiveness
Process	Performance	– Do we have all the resources needed to carry out the task? – How much time did it take? – Were the right ingredients available? – Were they of good quality? – What did they cost?	Economy and efficiency

Table 4.3 continued

Process	Process	– Was the catering equipment adequate? – Was the kitchen well-designed? – Were the staff sufficiently well-trained? – How did you go about the process of cooking the food? – Were all health and safety regulations complied with?	Links between how things happen and what happens

Now we look at each of these evaluation types more generally.

Strategic evaluation

Strategic evaluation asks questions about the overall purposes of a project or organisation. Is it doing the right thing? Sometimes this is a response to changes in the organisation's environment, such as a major change in the market-place or in government policy.

Impact evaluation

Impact evaluation concerns whether outcomes – the intended effects – are achieved. Was there any significant impact? Did we make any difference? Were there any unintended effects? It is likely to include looking at the extent of customer or user satisfaction.

This evaluation is difficult when there are other factors beyond the control of your organisation influencing the achievement of the organisation's objective. An example would be an organisation whose outcome objective is to reduce by 1% the number of adults who smoke. It does this mainly by advertising. An individual's decision to stop smoking may be influenced by our organisation's advertisements. But as – or more – important might be an increase in the price of cigarettes, a reduction in the money the individual has to spend, the smoking-related illnesses and deaths of people the smoker knows, the advice of doctors and/or restrictions on where smoking is allowed.

Another problem can be establishing an initial benchmark against which to measure impact. This can be the case in non-profit organisations. What is the impact of an organisation that provides meals and overnight accommodation for homeless people?

Performance evaluation

Performance evaluation takes the specific objectives and targets set for some or all micro operations and aims to measure achievement, considering both quantity and quality. It may often focus on 'value for money'.

Process evaluation

Process evaluation involves asking questions about how particular aspects of the organisation, or part of it, work: the ways in which decisions are taken, how policies and practices are decided and then administered. It will often be useful to compare our micro processes with similar ones in other parts of the organisation, or outside the organisation.

Composite evaluation

Evaluations are rarely clear-cut in practice and often it is necessary for an evaluation to focus on more than one area. This is because issues of performance, process, impact and strategy are frequently interrelated. For example, a performance evaluation may reveal aspects of an organisation's practices and processes which need to be improved. Asking questions in one area can raise questions about activities in another area.

Designing a formal evaluation

Formal evaluation of activities – answering the *'How well are we doing?'* or *'Did it work?'* questions in organisations – can be time-consuming and costly. Figure 4.8 sets out the stages of a formal evaluation and provides an indication of the work involved.

Preparation

Before embarking on an evaluation, you will need to consider the following questions:

- Are the aims and objectives of the macro or micro operation clearly defined?
- What is the purpose and type of the evaluation?
- What is the scope of the evaluation – how wide-ranging is it?
- Who needs to be involved in the evaluation? Who has an interest in the activity and might have something to gain or lose from an evaluation? This might include members or service users, politicians or committee members, funders, employees and volunteers. They do not all have to be deeply involved, but they need to be considered. Each may raise different questions and offer different answers about the issues which are the focus of your evaluation.
- Who is the audience for the evaluation?
- What information already exists about the project?
- How much time and what resources can you allocate to the evaluation?

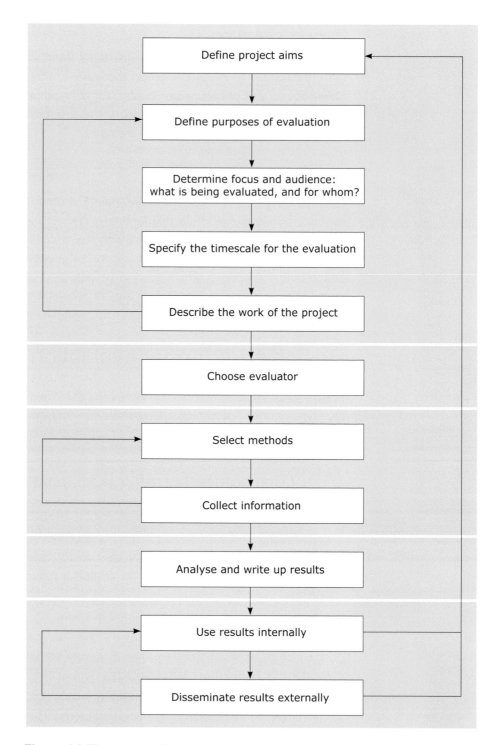

Figure 4.8 The stages of evaluation

(Source: based on McCollam and White, 1993)

Choice of evaluator

In many cases organisations do not have a choice about who undertakes their evaluation: they will be told who is to carry it out. But even where this is not the case, the choice of evaluator poses dilemmas for organisations – whether to bring in an external person or to allocate the task to a member of staff. There are advantages and disadvantages to both choices, as shown in Table 4.4.

Table 4.4 Comparison of evaluators

	Advantages	Disadvantages
Internal evaluator	Can be cheaper Has detailed knowledge about the project High level of commitment – may be easier to implement results More credible with colleagues Can promote maximum involvement and participation of staff Helps to build internal capacity to conduct future evaluations	May have insufficient evaluation skill and experience May not be objective; potential funders may not view the evaluation as objective Staff collusion to misrepresent a situation is harder to avoid Draws on personnel resources that may be limited: lack of time to undertake the work Staff may not speak freely to someone they will see again May have access to confidential information about clients or staff (a potential source of bias) The evaluation findings may be less credible with senior management and other stakeholders
External evaluator	May be more objective Brings technical evaluation expertise May be more efficient because of evaluation skill and experience Likely to have greater credibility with the outside world May offer a new perspective and fresh insights	Can be expensive Can be seen as an intruder, possibly disruptive May not have adequate understanding of project May lack sensitivity to particular population of stakeholders Staff may feel threatened Staff may be less involved in the evaluation because they see it as someone else's responsibility There may be concerns about accountability

(Source: adapted from Bronte-Tinkey *et al.*, 2007)

Whether you use an internal or external evaluator, the cost of evaluation activities should be built into your project or budget proposal from the outset.

Choice of approach and methods

Both the approach to the evaluation and the method used should be decided systematically. The evaluation methods set out below should be seen as a menu from which to select the appropriate combination of methods to suit the focus of the evaluation. Particularly important is the balance between quantitative and qualitative methods.

Quantitative and qualitative methods

Most evaluations feature both quantitative (measurable) and qualitative information and the two are often linked. One person's well-argued views on what was wrong with a promotional campaign are qualitative information. However, such information needs to be put into a quantitative context. How many people's views were obtained? What proportions could be categorised as negative, positive or neutral? Does survey evidence, or the number of new clients or customers, suggest that the campaign was effective despite this one opinion?

Quantitative information can be powerful and persuasive. However, it can be easily manipulated and should be interpreted with care. For example, stating only the numbers of jobs created as a result of a project might be more positive than stating both the number of new jobs and how much was spent on creating each job. Collecting – and skilfully presenting – quantitative information conveys thoroughness and professionalism. It is usual for some qualitative information to be included, as Table 4.5 indicates.

Qualitative information can be very useful for interpreting the quantitative information.

Table 4.5 Quantitative and qualitative information

Evaluation	A quantitative component	A qualitative component
New staff induction policy	Staff turnover rate in first two years of employment	Analysis of entry and exit interviews with staff and with a sample of current staff
Popularity of staff canteen	Number of staff using it	Small, representative group of staff discussing their experience of eating here
Women's health promotion project	Number of women diagnosed as having a specific preventable illness, compared with previous time periods	Informal discussion with women involved, other women who have not had contact with the project, and health project staff
Effectiveness of a marketing campaign	Increase in enquiries or sales in three months during and after campaign, compared with previous three months and same three months in previous years	Analysis of what else was going on while campaign was being conducted, e.g. what were competitors doing?

A framework for choosing the best methods

In most evaluations there are three areas where you need information:

- Performance criteria: what did we set out to do and how will we know if we succeeded? These criteria form the markers against which success is to be measured.

- Results: what information on our achievements have we got or can we get from monitoring or other means? Were the quality criteria met?

- Context: what other information do we need to interpret these results?

Figure 4.9 shows how a framework for an evaluation might look. Your choice of method will be determined by resource availability, and you should take into account:

- the cost of obtaining the information in relation to its contribution to the evaluation
- the time it will take to obtain and analyse the information
- the reliability of the information obtained
- the political aspects of the process – for example, some ways of gathering information may help build up support for the evaluation.

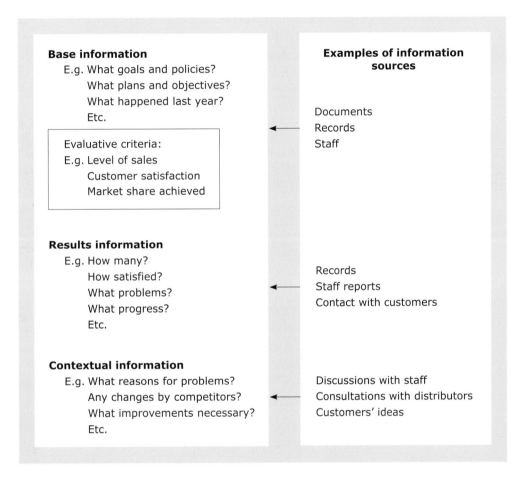

Figure 4.9 The evaluative framework: defining the information required and how it will be obtained.

You may readily identify the kind of data you want, but knowing how best to collect the information and the precise questions to ask, whether in interviews or questionnaires, requires careful thought. Much good-quality, often free, information is available via the internet. A good source of general evaluation information is the UK Evaluation Society. Its website lists many online evaluation resources for the UK and the USA, including Bill Trochim's Centre for Social Research Methods (which hosts an eBook). Another useful UK website is that of the Charities Evaluation Service.

If you are doing your own evaluation, then you may be amazed at the amount of information that has been generated and now requires analysis. In conducting your analysis, look out for the following:

- Evidence relating to the achievement of objectives (or lack of achievement), for example, if you set out to offer training to staff, the numbers in each category of staff attending courses would be important.

- Patterns in the evidence. In the above example, you might find that most participants on the training programme were female workers in their 30s.

- Any unexpected results. In the same example, you might find that people working with finance were those who learned most from courses on personal development.

Analysis is often hard, painstaking work. It is easy to underestimate the time this task can take, even on quite small pieces of work. Do not try methods of analysis that are too elaborate. Highlighter pens can be as effective as databases or card indexes, and may well save time.

You will then need to produce a report: make it something people will want to read. Think about the people who will be reading it and use language they will understand. Avoid jargon and use straightforward terms. It should be accessible and interesting reading. Managers need to think carefully about how to communicate poor performance. Will your audience respond well to 'all the bad news at once?'. If not, can the bad news be divided up so that it is easier to accept? If the culture of the organisation is not to be objective about bad news, what then? In a constructive culture your audience will prefer you to communicate the problems you have found.

Disseminating the findings of the evaluation is important. Some organisations produce several documents: a full report might include sensitive data and be for key internal stakeholders only; another document might be for your internal audience, and a third might be for a non-specialist audience outside the organisation. A suitable version needs to go to all those who have taken part in the evaluation.

Making use of the results

Many evaluations are initiated to create a 'lever for change' and will suggest changes to the strategy, objectives, systems or procedures in organisations. You will need to plan for implementation. If you are using a consultant or external evaluator, often this person can help to manage the implementation of recommendations. Alternatively, consider creating a small subgroup to work on proposals for change.

Some evaluation issues

Most organisations serve a number of different parties, or stakeholders. These can include employees, managers, customers, service users and suppliers outside it, partner organisations, funders and volunteers. Evaluations can highlight differences of expectations between these groups, especially in the public and non-profit sectors.

How much participation?

In these sectors there is often a strong emphasis on the involvement of stakeholders in evaluation, particularly those who benefit from the organisation's service or who are members. If an organisation chooses to involve stakeholders, different expectations can emerge which can become difficult to manage.

In theory, greater participation in evaluation by as many stakeholders as possible is a valid aim: implementation of any changes flowing from the evaluation may affect all stakeholders. In practice, over-ambitious participation can lead to complex, time-consuming evaluations with competing or conflicting parties. This means you need to be imaginative in designing methods of involving people.

If a decision to involve a number of stakeholders has been taken, it is important to involve those who are both easy and difficult to collect information from. If you do not involve stakeholders equally, your results are weakened. The different levels of power of stakeholders can also be important. Stakeholders who provide funds often have more power than the service user, and this often affects the design of evaluations.

Clarifying mission statements

Mission statements, aims, objectives and goals can be written in very general terms which allow them to satisfy the wishes of different stakeholders. Often evaluations which aim to clarify the meanings of general mission statements can lead to disagreements between stakeholders on what the mission should be. For example, in the case of a counselling service, what service users want from the service (insight into their problem) may not be what funders want the project to achieve (reductions in alcohol consumed).

What do stakeholders want from evaluation?

Different stakeholders may want different things from evaluations. For instance:

- Funders may want to demonstrate effective use of public funds, to highlight good practice, to identify new or changing needs, to have criteria for judging between applicants.
- Politicians and committee members may want to make best use of resources, to clarify future directions, to have evidence of effectiveness, to control quality, to validate new approaches, to have evidence to conduct a campaign, and so on.
- Staff may simply want feedback on their performance, or to test out ideas about why things are as they are, to get new ideas about how services might be offered, to address/resolve issues which they perceive as preventing them from doing their job or simply to see the broader picture.
- Service users may value an opportunity to have their views heard or to influence the services offered, or simply to show the usefulness or not of those services.
- Volunteers may want to see the effectiveness their own efforts and how service users value them.

If stakeholders are already aware that a project or organisation is having difficulties, they may each have particular concerns about the consequences. Some may fear exposure as 'failures'. Some worry that something will emerge that they don't want others to know. In a sense, this concerns power. Whose voices are to be heard in organisations? To which stakeholders does the organisation 'belong'?

Involving service users

Users of services may have unrealistically high expectations of their involvement in evaluations and of the service provided. How service users participate in evaluation will depend partly on the history of their involvement in the organisation. Table 4.6 shows a 'ladder' of participation adapted to focus on service users as stakeholders in an evaluation.

Table 4.6 The ladder of participation

Degree of user involvement in organisation	History of organisational planning process
Have control	Service users identify needs and make all the key decisions on goals and means.
Have delegated authority	Organisation identifies and presents needs/problems to service users, defines constraints and asks them to make decisions which can be included in a plan which it will accept.
Plan jointly	Organisation presents draft plans to service users. Expects to change plan substantially in consultation with them.
Advise	Organisation presents a plan and invites questions. Prepared to modify plan if necessary.
Are consulted	Organisation tries to generate support for the plan so that users can be expected to agree to the plan.
Receive information	Organisation makes a plan and announces it. Service users are simply informed of plan and its contents.
None	Service users are told nothing.

(Source: adapted from Brager and Sprecht, 1973)

An organisation with a history of limited or no user participation is unlikely to find it easy to involve users in an evaluation process. You will need to involve people in ways that are more accessible and enjoyable than questionnaires or formal interviews. In contrast, an organisation with, say, a history of joint planning with users may find it appropriate to plan the evaluation in the joint, iterative way with which the organisation and its users are familiar.

In summary, greater participation in evaluation by as many stakeholders as possible is a valid aim in theory: implementation of any changes flowing from the evaluation may affect all stakeholders. If they have been excluded from the process, they may resist implementation. In practice, over-ambitious goals of participation in evaluation can lead to over-complex, time-consuming evaluations with conflict between stakeholders.

Why do evaluations find poor performance?

Hidden inefficiencies

A potential finding of an evaluation is that the organisation is operating less efficiently than it might, and its assets are being under-used. Budgets may be higher than is needed, supplies could be purchased more cheaply, parts of the office accommodation may not be properly used and some procedures may be unnecessarily complex. All these features are results of poor management. Such tendencies exist in all organisations, but they are often more marked in larger ones where the overall task is broken down into separate areas of work and where waste can more easily go unnoticed.

There are two reasons why inefficiencies and potential savings tend to accumulate.

1   Where changes are happening gradually, slack is never obvious to poor managers – it is taken for granted that everyone will be fully occupied and, since work expands to fill the time available, this will appear to be the case. Slack is found only by searching and asking *'What is this really contributing?'*.

2   Poor managers may believe that no manager ever became popular by trying to make savings. Members of staff usually like their way of doing things and believe that what they do is important. No-one likes to be accused of waste and inefficiency. However, a manager is paid to ask awkward questions. A poor manager will probably prefer not to – it disrupts normal work and puts a strain on relationships.

Over-commitment

Organisations can develop a culture of over-commitment in which activities are taken on without the necessary resources. This leads to poor performance and often happens because resources are not connected to service delivery. Managers need to refuse new work that has not been resourced, and to cut services or close projects when resources are no longer provided.

Good managers will often be able to see problems before they happen. In the case of funding coming to an end, plans will have been prepared for the service users and the staff affected will have been helped in finding other work or adjusting to new responsibilities.

One reason why controlling commitments is difficult is that once a service has been provided to users, it is difficult to reduce or stop the service. As a result, organisations find it easier to make general cost savings (in travel, telephoning, equipment, training, support services) rather than shut down a particular service. This is understandable, but it may not be effective. Staff in the underfunded service can become demotivated and then service quality falls.

Collusion

People in service areas may collude to present a misleading picture of a project or department to the evaluators. This usually arises where people feel threatened. Those involved in these unspoken alliances will try to persuade the evaluator and support the views of those they collude with. Classic collusion is motivated by personal and organisational benefits. In many not-for-profit organisations there are opportunities for collusion between the staff of a government agency, the government officers who set it up and the politicians who supported it: they will all benefit from a positive story. While it is never possible to avoid collusion completely, the following guidance to evaluators should help avoid some of the obvious difficulties:

- Be clear why people's involvement is sought.
- Understand your role and how you will be viewed – is it as a neutral person, or as someone who also has a stake in the process?
- Decide what level of participation is sought – will you want merely to consult, or will you want people to be involved in deciding the next steps in the process?
- Develop ownership of the proposals through making time for in-house discussions and keeping people well-informed about the progress of the evaluation.
- In choosing methods, take account of how these are likely to be viewed by the participants.
- Be able to recognise and manage conflict.

Resistance to findings

Evaluation is often contested. Where evaluation recommends changes to activities, structures, systems and procedures, the report is just the beginning of what can be a long and arduous process. Being told that you need to do something differently, or that your efforts were largely wasted, or that you are not doing what you thought you were doing, will rarely be welcome news. If, however, the evaluation process has been managed so that stakeholders have felt involved and consulted through each stage, there should be fewer surprises. An initial reaction can be to deny that some findings are correct, or to blame the evaluator. However, while people may not like to hear that things are not done as well as they could be, there are very few who do not later reflect on any negative findings.

The learning process in evaluation can be considered in two phases. First, there needs to be time for those intimately involved to consider the findings. If you are using an external evaluator, getting them to help facilitate this process can be useful. Second, proper consideration should be given to the need for longer-term changes. At its best, evaluation can lead to changes that strengthen and improve an organisation's performance. At its worst, it can be an expensive waste of time and money. This latter situation can arise when the people aspects of evaluation are overlooked in a search for short-term fixes at the expense of longer-term solutions.

Chapter 5 Managing information
What do we mean by information?

Information is the lifeblood of management – every manager is an information manager, collecting, analysing, acting on and communicating it. We are accustomed to living in an 'information age' and for many of us it may be difficult to think about 'information' without associating it with computers and IT. However, consider what might be going on in a typical office building:

- Kristen is telling Kurt about her work on the project he's leading so he can monitor progress.
- Michel is asking someone what is in the large boxes being carried into the office.
- Tracy is trying to track down a problem with the automated stock control system: orders are not keeping up with sales.
- Patra is preparing her proposal for outsourcing a service. She's wondering if the information she's providing really does support her case.
- Beryl thinks the photocopier doesn't sound as it usually does – she needs to check that there isn't a paperclip inside again.
- There are people having an animated exchange of views in the corridor: Sue and John still haven't agreed next week's targets.
- Christina is concentrating hard: there are two options for the training programme and not only is there insufficient detail about costs, but the figures aren't making much sense to her.
- Seema doesn't look happy – is she overloaded with work again?
- Josef has just read the latest customer feedback and is trying to draw some conclusions from it.
- Wanda thinks she can smell her favourite lunch in the cafeteria upstairs.

Every example involves information, formal or informal, being created, received or delivered in a variety of ways – some of them not specified. Note that in some cases, information leads to the need for more information. In all cases, the information needs to be made sense of so that it can be used and acted on to best advantage.

In the examples, we used the term 'information', but in some cases it would have been more appropriate to use the term 'data'. There is an important difference between the terms.

Data are the raw material of organisational life; they consist of disconnected numbers, words, symbols and syllables relating to the events and processes of the business. Data on their own can serve little purpose; in fact, a serious problem for managers is the need to make sense of the often huge – and sometimes overwhelming – amount of data that they receive in the normal course of their job (Martin and Powell, 1992).

Data require some kind of interpretation before they can be understood and used. Information is data that has been analysed or interpreted in some way in order to communicate knowledge or meaning to the recipient. In short, information is data that has been made useful, as illustrated in Box 5.1.

Box 5.1 From data to information

If you have no knowledge of staff training costs and are told by your HR department that in-house health and safety training will cost €15,000 this year, this will be meaningless data to you. Is €15,000 good or bad? To know this, you need information to enable you to interpret the item of data and give it meaning. The minimum you need to know is whether the figure is high or low. When the HR department tells you that the price charged by outside suppliers of such training ranges from €14,000 to €18,000, you now have the information that the in-house cost is relatively low. As soon as you are able to interpret the data, it becomes useful information. It would be more meaningful to know the cost of training each person, of course.

Sometimes what may be considered to be information by people who pass it to you (because it means something to them) might be data so far as you are concerned (because it has little or no meaning for you). The way you manage data and provide items of data to your staff is part of the process of creating information. The same process may be carried out well – or not so well – by all who communicate with you.

Information is important to you as a manager because it can help you to make better decisions. Note that this does not mean that in the world of work you can obtain perfect information and thus make perfect decisions: life is not like that. Information management processes are only partly rational: people's opinions, attitudes and even emotions will influence what information they collect, how they collect it and how they interpret that information, as well as what they decide to pass on and how they do so.

Information flows

When data and information are transmitted within an organisation, we refer to the movement as information flow. To visualise this flow, in this case mainly of operational data flowing in a system, consider an automated system for stock ordering or billing. Supermarket tills are linked automatically to stock rooms, stock rooms to logistics and logistics to suppliers. The meter readers employed by utility companies are likely to have hand-held electronic readers linked to the organisation's invoicing system. Drivers of delivery companies use wireless hand-held devices that transmit proof of delivery data and customer details back to the organisation. The same device may be used to log and transmit the work hours of drivers and to communicate with drivers. As a manager you will have your own information requirements, and you will need to ensure that others receive the information they need. You are part of the flow of information from one group to another. You may simply pass information on, but usually you will be playing a more active role by filtering, collating and analysing the information that comes to you. You are likely to be involved in the flow of information from senior management to you. You may also be involved in receiving and sending information from and to clients, customers, suppliers and the general public.

Figure 5.1 illustrates how these information flows might operate in a large, conventionally-structured organisation. Note the double-headed arrows representing the information exchange between the front-line staff of the organisation and its customers and clients. The upward-pointing arrows on the left-hand side of the pyramid represent the filtering of this front-line information up an organisation's management hierarchy. The arrows on the right represent the filtering of information about the organisation's strategic objectives – its action plans to achieve its particular goal – into the minds and practices of front-line staff. Note that information about legislation, research results and competitors can reach an organisation at different levels, sometimes quite near the top. The lateral information flows are important: people and units with different but related responsibilities need to know about each other's work. Inevitably, such a diagram will be an oversimplification of all the possible flows of information.

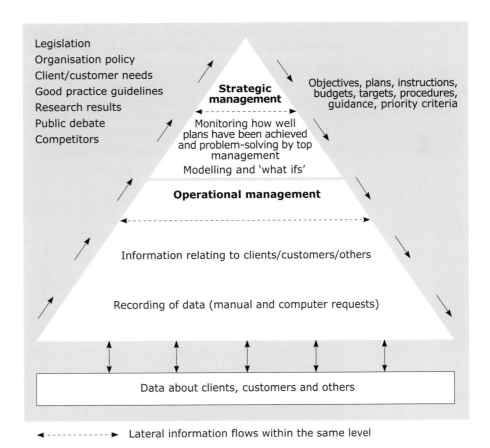

Figure 5.1 Information flows and management levels

Figure 5.1 represents a simple version of what should happen. An example is set out below in Box 5.2.

Box 5.2 Information flowing smoothly

In a telecommunications company, the equipment sales section tells the manager of the maintenance team about a major new order. The manager communicates this information to his staff, who report that they will be overloaded if the maintenance work on the new order is added to their current workload. The manager communicates a request for additional resources to senior management. He also sets up an information reporting arrangement to monitor how his staff use their time and other resources over the six months. The company's senior management considers this manager's need for more resources among many similar requests across the company.

In practice, information may not get collected or passed on, or may be lost, damaged or altered in processing, or delayed beyond the time when it is useful. There can be bottlenecks or delays where a single member of staff is processing large amounts of information returned from many other members of staff. In the example in Box 5.2, if the equipment sales section had failed to inform the maintenance team manager, then the planned smooth process could have gone wrong and damaged customer satisfaction.

As well as being a direct provider of one-off information, as a manager you need to establish systems that enable appropriate people and groups to access the information they need about your work area. To provide suitable access you need to know which groups you serve and what information they need.

Figure 5.2 shows many of the different groups that the manager needs to supply information to. It also gives some examples of the types of information the manager may have to provide.

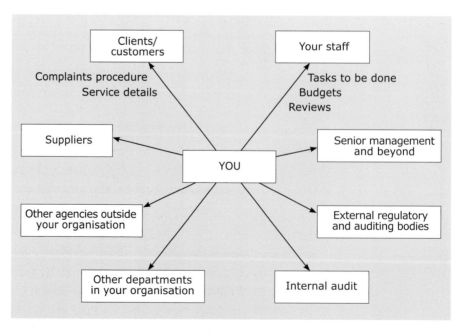

Figure 5.2 The different groups whose information needs a manager may have to consider

The types of information that you may need to obtain from others and communicate to others include:

- information from higher up the organisation about objectives, plans, resources and organisational changes
- information from other teams and departments you work with
- allocation of tasks, resources and responsibilities
- information for priority-setting
- information on staff performance
- information and guidance on standards and quality.

Your effectiveness in collecting and conveying information like this can be a critical factor in the performance of your team. Exactly what and how a manager chooses to communicate to their team depends on a number of factors. For example:

- management style, especially willingness to share information and to consult
- the urgency with which information needs to be communicated
- the complexity of the information
- the sensitivity of the information and its relevance to all, or particular, members of staff (for example, information on pay rises)
- the need to keep a record of the communication
- whether the team works in one place (or at least has a common base that team members visit on a frequent basis) or rarely is together

See also: The communication climate, Chapter 2

- the communication channel options available.

Some organisations place great value on openness, and this leads to a culture in which information tends to be shared wherever possible. Others (especially those under some form of threat) often restrict access to information. Individual managers may take either of these approaches, and their management style may conflict with the organisation's management style. Where control of information becomes a weapon of organisational politics – the pursuit of self- or group interests to gain benefit or resources or achieve goals – service delivery suffers. This is because the flow of information, which should be governed by service needs, becomes distorted. It is important to put personal interests to one side and let the necessary information through.

Different perspectives

An important aspect of information, and of information flows, is that different people will have different perspectives. We capture such a difference in views in Figures 5.3 and 5.4 which highlight humorously how a computer technician and a general manager see the same information flows in an office.

The technician's diagram is simple and clear but it has ignored many important features of the manager's view. The manager has opened up the technician's diamond-shaped 'decision' boxes and unpacked his view of the decision-making process, identifying committees, reports, auditors' inputs, bottlenecks and the main actors. Complexity and uncertainty is represented. To improve the management of the information flows depicted, the two individuals, and others involved, would need to communicate to ensure that each understood what the other wanted and had to offer.

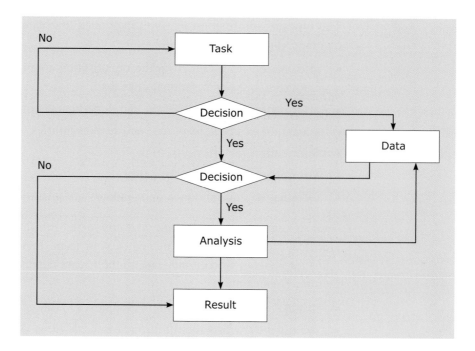

Figure 5.3 A technician's view of office information flows

(Source: Strassman, 1985)

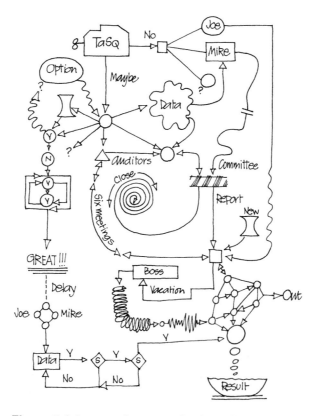

Figure 5.4 A general manager's view of office information flows

(Source: Strassman, 1985)

The qualities and cost of good information

You are about to make a vital decision. How do you know that the information you have to hand is *good* information? Was getting those extra pieces of data really worth the time and effort involved?

For information to be useful to organisations and managers, it needs to be fit for purpose. Poor-quality decisions result from information of insufficient quality. This is different from saying that poor decisions result from insufficient information. In practice most decisions are made with only partial information. What is critical is whether the information you have is any good. As a manager, you need to evaluate the information you receive. To do this you need to be aware of the qualities of the information you receive and pass on to others.

Data and information can be classified in a number of ways. We will use a list of 10 criteria for good-quality information. But first you should be aware of one of the most useful distinctions: hard or soft.

Hard versus soft

The Oxford English Dictionary's definition of 'hard', as applied to data, uses such adjectives as 'factual, objective, reliable'; 'soft' is defined as 'insubstantial, impressionistic, imprecise'. Examples might be:

Hard data	Soft data
Results	Estimates
Statistics	Feelings
Procedures	Opinions
Trends	Judgements
Productivity levels	Values

Hard information can be stated with an apparent degree of precision. Measurements of such things as temperature, length, number of customers served and quantity of output provide hard information. Calculations can be performed on such hard information in order to summarise it and turn it into tables of figures, charts and graphs. Hard information is always necessary for organisations, and neat sets of figures can look reassuring. However, 'soft' information can also be extremely valuable, even though it is expressed in far less rigorous terms – customer satisfaction, quality of service or product, job satisfaction. 'Hard' and 'soft' are only the extremes of a continuous scale – very little information is either totally 'hard' or completely 'soft'. Neither type is better than the other, but each is useful for different purposes and both types can complement each other to provide a fuller picture.

All information collection and interpretation involves selection, judgement, errors, bias and value judgements. For example, a statistic that a particular ethnic minority makes up 2% of the population of a local authority's area might be taken to imply that managers do not have to worry too much about adapting their services to the cultural needs of this group. This would be an inappropriate interpretation of the data – and the figure may, in any case, be disputed by representatives of the ethnic community involved.

The 10 criteria we propose for good-quality information for decision-making, whether hard or soft, are that it should be:

1 relevant

2 clear

3 sufficiently accurate

4 complete

5 trustworthy

6 concise

7 timely

8 communicated to the right person

9 communicated via the right channel

10 less costly than the value of the benefits it provides.

1 Relevance

Relevant information is useful for management decisions to be taken by us or the people we supply information to. Everyday activity quickly adds less-relevant information. Examples include:

- information about things that interest you, but is not needed for decisions
- information about previous suppliers, clients or customers
- information that your predecessors thought was relevant, but you don't.

Removing irrelevant information seems to be given a low priority in many organisations. If you have to supply information to others, you should try to ensure that it is relevant to them. This may involve sending different information to different people. For example, you could send a summary of your proposals to senior management, while giving staff who have to implement them a more detailed breakdown. You could use different email circulation lists for different kinds of information. In this way you act as a filter to ensure that the correct information reaches the right person.

2 Clarity

Information needs to be clear to those who have to use it. If it is not understood, the chances are that it will not be used properly. Lack of clarity is one of the commonest causes of breakdowns in communicating information. Data can often be made clearer by changing the way in which they are presented. For example, spending of £10,000 on advertising is more clearly communicated as £50 for each new client or customer gained.

Bar charts, pie charts and tables are all good ways to make information clearer, too. Good examples are provided in the Tools and techniques section of this textbook.

3 Sufficient accuracy

Both hard and soft information can vary in accuracy. Information needs to be sufficiently accurate *for its purpose*. It is not cost-effective to create information which is more accurate than is needed for management decisions. Providing a greater level of accuracy increases the cost of obtaining and presenting information.

4 Completeness

How much information you need is also a matter of judgement. Sometimes it is obvious that you need more information in order to make a decision. You would not go ahead with staff recruitment without knowing the cost of advertising, for example. But when making decisions, it is often not possible to have available all the information that you would like to have. Some of the information may consist of estimates or may be too expensive to collect. What is important is that you have enough information to form a rounded picture of the situation.

5 Trustworthiness

It is important that you have sufficient trust in the information provided. Some decisions may have to be based on less reliable information, such as estimates or predictions. It is helpful if you have some idea of the level of accuracy of the information before you act on it. One way of doing this is to identify a key measurement – such as the cost of something – and ask what the most likely value, the highest value and the lowest value are for this key measurement.

Your trust in information is likely to be higher if its source has proven reliable in the past, and if there is good communication between you and the person who produced it. It is often helpful to find out key information from more than one source to increase your trust in it.

6 Conciseness

There is a limit to how much anyone can be expected to read, absorb and understand before taking a decision. Verbal briefings and written reports should be concise, so that they can be quickly and readily understood, with the important information being immediately obvious. For written reports, graphs and charts may help. Headings, bullet points and summaries can enable those receiving a report to identify what is important to them.

Conciseness applies to the collection and storage of data and information too. Is it really necessary for all the data available to be collected and held? Would just a sample of the data suffice for the purpose? Can the data be coded, compressed or concentrated so that the same relevant information can be held in a smaller space, processed more quickly or accessed more easily?

Exception reporting can be a powerful way of providing concise information. A report is supplied only if something is wrong and action is needed.

7 Timeliness

An important feature of useful information is that it should be available when it is needed. Information for planning and control needs to be available as regularly as decisions are taken. For example, if monthly meetings are held to monitor performance, weekly reports are unnecessary.

8 Communicated to the right person

Unless information reaches those who need it, the cost and effort of producing it have been wasted. A common problem is that information is often provided to someone at the wrong level of management: it might be sent to senior managers, who fail to pass it on, or to junior staff, who are not sure what to do with it.

9 Communicated via the right channel

The channel of communication needs to take account of the nature and purpose of the information, the speed of transmission required and, above all, the user's requirements. Information sometimes has greater value if transmitted by one method rather than another, because it is received more quickly, or more easily understood. Research evidence suggests that many managers obtain most of their information through conversations. For these people, reports simply confirm or reinforce the information they already have.

10 Less costly than the value it provides

Information has no value in itself; its value comes from how it is used. Each of the activities of collecting, recording, storing, processing, transmitting and presenting data and information makes use of other resources of the organisation – employees' time and skills, measuring equipment, computer processing time and storage, office space, telephones and photocopiers, all of which incur costs. It is only when information is communicated to, understood and used by the recipient that it becomes valuable.

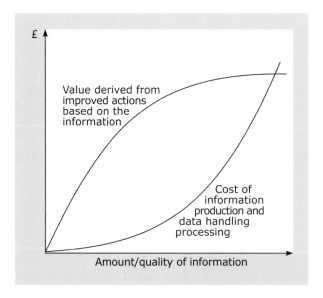

Figure 5.5 Cost and value of information

(Source: Lucey, 1991)

Figure 5.5 illustrates that there comes a point where the extra value you obtain from gathering more information is worth less than the cost of gathering it. Information gathering has an 'opportunity cost': to assess it means looking at what else could be done with the time and resources used in gathering the information.

Since the value of information depends on what is done as a result of receiving it, you can assess its value against its opportunity cost by asking questions such as:

- What information is provided?
- What is it used for?
- Who uses it?
- How often is it used?
- Does the frequency with which it is used coincide with the frequency with which it is provided?
- Is it good-quality information?
- What is achieved by using it?
- What other relevant information is available that could be used instead?
- What is the cost of collecting it?

Keeping information secure

Legislation in many countries requires organisations to store and process personal data securely. Personal data identify a person and relate to the individual, such as education, employment and health records. It is important that you consult the staff member legally responsible for the security of personal data before you change the way you store or process it.

For the organisation's needs, information must be stored securely and be updated regularly. Well-designed systems will include procedures to store data in more than one way, so that if one set of records is lost or damaged, another is available. Interestingly, many organisations do not recognise the need to secure the information that managers and staff keep in their memories.

Some types of information must be kept confidential, for commercial or legal reasons. Confidentiality is also important because unauthorised disclosure of some important items of information could have major consequences. In the for-profit sector, plans for future products, for obtaining new funding, promotional campaigns and pricing policies could be of great value to competitors. Much information is also sensitive – sensitivity refers to the impact that losses or inaccuracies would have on your organisation's operations.

Information requirements

The information you receive, create and share is used partly to help you make management decisions, to enable everyone to do their work.
By management decisions we refer in the main to deciding how work is organised and carried out effectively and efficiently to the benefit of the

organisation. An example of how information benefits management decisions is set out in Box 5.3. The management decisions of a civil engineer might involve how to balance the demands of urgent projects against those that have been planned for some time, taking into account the support staff available. Which type of bridge-building technique to use would be a professional decision.

Box 5.3 Information–decision–benefit

A manager of an orthopaedic unit in a hospital describes how she was able to make significant financial savings because of the way information was used to monitor and reduce waste.

'As a budget-holding department, we thought long and hard about how to minimise wasteful use of resources. For instance, now we book the items of equipment that we use to particular account numbers so that we know how money is being spent.'

'Now that the staff are getting used to the system, we're able to see real benefits from it. For example, for some of the operations we perform, patients are provided with shoulder immobilisers. These are reusable, but previously patients often took them home when they left hospital and we'd never see them again. Now that we book the immobilisers to a specific account number, I've been able to see just how much this "wastage" is costing us. We now have procedures to recover the immobilisers from patients who have been discharged.'

See also: Evaluation: how well are we doing?, Chapter 4

Two of the most important types of management decision are those concerned with monitoring processes – how well an activity is progressing – and evaluating effectiveness – whether the activity met its objectives.

Monitoring the processes involved in delivering your service

Monitoring of processes tells you if you are doing things right. When you have decided on a particular course of action or way of doing things, you need to know if it is actually happening. Is the new product selling well? Are the staff you train doing a better job? Are new customers being attracted by your increasing emphasis on customer service?

Evaluating the impact or effectiveness of your service

Evaluating the impact or effectiveness of a service tells you if you are doing the right things. Some organisations – or departments within organisations – are very good at what they do, but what they are doing may not be meeting the changing demands that are placed on them. Is that new product really profitable, given the unexpectedly high costs of delivery? Are the newly-trained staff making the best use of their time, or should they be redeployed to respond to recent changes? Are those new customers making repeat purchases of valuable items?

Table 5.1 shows (on the left-hand side) some of the main aspects of management that would be involved in producing a new training course on time and within budget. The other two columns suggest sources of information a manager might require for monitoring progress against objectives and evaluating the overall outcomes.

Table 5.1 Sources of information for monitoring and evaluating a training course

Management aspect	Information for monitoring	Information for evaluating
Staff	Work plans and diaries; progress reports	Observation and assessment of results, stress levels and job satisfaction
Finance	Budget reports: planned, actual and variance in expenditure	Resulting income-to-costs ratio
Physical resources (equipment, accommodation, etc.)	Appropriate cost headings within budget reports; observation of resource utilisation	Retrospective report quantitatively assessing use, actual cost and contribution of different resources
Customer relationships (internal and/or external)	Periodic verbal and written progress/ satisfaction checks with key customer contacts	Formal survey of customer satisfaction with process and results
Quality	Testing of elements at various interim stages	Formal survey of customers' satisfaction with results – reasons for dissatisfaction, if any
Relationship with senior management	Regular written progress reports, including budget summaries; informal showing of completed interim stages to senior managers	Appraisal record
Process	Work plans and progress reports	Formal survey of user satisfaction with process; informal reflective written report, incorporating others' inputs, describing processes followed

The entries in Table 5.1 are not meant to be comprehensive, but should give you an idea of how the manager's responsibility for the project also involved responsibility for developing and/or completing various information requirements.

Managers probably need the greatest volume and variety of information for regular monitoring. Much of this information is likely to be informal, qualitative and verbal. Day-to-day monitoring normally requires up-to-date information. To cope with this need to respond to monitoring, you probably have a variety of systems and arrangements for obtaining information. By contrast, evaluation probably needs fewer, more specific, more formal, more quantitative types of information.

Information exchange with customers and the public

Most organisations routinely collect information from customers, clients and enquirers for their records, for sales purposes and for market research. In a public sector organisation, staff may be required to collect information from the general public; for example, local governments in the UK are obliged to collect up-to-date information for electoral rolls.

Table 5.2 details some of the standards and criteria which might be applied to the provision of appropriate information.

Table 5.2 Requirements for information provision to customers and the public

1 Quality of information	The information provided by you and your team is accurate, useful and up to date
2 Assessing information requirements	You assess the information requirements of those who have contact with you and your team, including first-time enquirers
3 Consultation	You have a systematic and sustained process for finding out about customer needs and/or for involving service users in consultations
4 Collaboration with others in information provision	You work with others in developing and providing information to customers and the public
5 Equal opportunities	You provide information to the clients/customers in ways that ensure equality of access
6 Management policy	You have an information policy and strategy, derived from your organisation's policy and strategy, which is managed and resourced so that you can meet your responsibilities within it

You are likely to find it easier to meet these criteria if your organisation's information initiatives are developed in the context of an organisation-wide information policy. Where you judge that you have not met a criterion, you should consider whether this is something you can rectify on your own or whether you need organisational support, for example, in developing or modifying policy.

Management information systems

Information systems in organisations are designed to facilitate information flow – although this is not always the case! Table 5.3 summarises how information can be collected, stored, processed and distributed.

Table 5.3 Information flows: methods

	Paper archive (stored documents)	Person, without computer	Computer system
Collection and input	Manual	Written, read or heard	Manual or electronic
Storage	Medium capacity	Memory is variable; can be hard to extract stored information	Huge capacity
Processing and interpretation	Organised by simple rules, e.g. by subject and date, or as library classification	Very sophisticated at interpretation	Huge capacity for processing if well designed
Retrieval	Varies	Varies	Easy to retrieve the information the system was set up to extract, but may vary in ease of extracting information in new ways
Distribution	Manual – must be physically carried	Formally and informally, verbally and in writing	Huge capacity, fast

While it is easy to get the impression that all information systems must involve computers, this is often not so. Many information systems combine paper, people and computers. Well-designed computer systems can process very large quantities of data with high levels of accuracy and low operating costs. They also allow people to share the same information easily. But the costs of designing the systems can be very large, and the information needs of organisations can change quickly. Very few office-based organisations have become 'paperless' as a result of digital technology; moreover, most managers still rely a great deal on informal information exchange with other people.

Formal management information systems provide information to support management decision-making. The best decisions are often made by those managers who are directly involved in the information systems that provide them with the information they need to make decisions. They pay more attention to the information and trust it more. This requires two things to happen:

1   Some degree of information collecting and processing should be incorporated into their staff's ordinary work.

2   Systems must be in place that capture and process this information quickly.

This means that management information should be generated within the system as part of the work in which staff are primarily engaged, be it the direct care of service users, paying salaries, purchasing supplies or manufacturing goods. Management information should emerge as a by-product of the information that is collected, recorded and processed as part of the day-to-day work of an organisation. This is an ideal that is difficult to achieve in practice, because people like to continue working in ways that are familiar to them and do not take the time to rethink how things could be done. It is also expensive to replace old, outdated computer systems (known as 'legacy systems' or 'electronic concrete').

The ideal is often difficult to achieve in large organisations, too, because some if not most management information will be collected in parts of the organisation remote from the decision-making manager. For example:

information for marketing decisions is captured by the sales department

information for supplies decisions is generated by the operations department

information for HR decisions is captured by every employing department.

However, the concept of a 'system' is a useful way of interpreting what happens in organisations and can be applied to information systems. A system is a set of interdependent parts that operate together to accomplish an objective. Any system has a set of inputs that are then processed ('transformed') in some way before emerging as outputs:

INPUT → TRANSFORMATION → OUTPUT

In large and complex organisations, it is easier to think about large and complex systems in terms of a number of smaller, interdependent subsystems. Each subsystem is a system too. It has its own inputs, transformation processes and outputs. An example would be a subsystem for registering the users of an email account service. The inputs of this subsystem are the service user, his or her purchase history and other details, which are processed to produce a new service user record. This output can then form the input to a number of other subsystems within the larger system.

An important feature of many systems is the inclusion of a feedback loop (Figure 5.6). This is where some of the system's outputs are fed back as an input in order to modify the system: the feedback acts as a control mechanism to allow the system to change, according to its outputs.

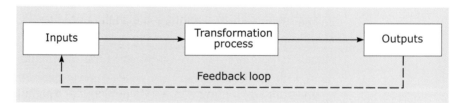

Figure 5.6 System with feedback loop

An information system transforms data into information: it is a set of people, data and procedures that work together to provide useful information. Its most important stages are:

- *Input*: the people and procedures involved in collecting the data.
- *Transformation*: the processing or analysis that is carried out on the data.
- *Output*: the information to be transmitted to the people who need it.

Storage is a feature that is usually taken for granted. An example of an information system is set out below:

An information system in an executive recruitment business

In an executive recruitment service, the data collected and input by staff may include:

- advisers' caseloads, including service users' details
- vacancies available
- reports of visits made
- mileages and travel times.

The processing of this data may include analysis of:

- service users by age
- the skills offered by clients
- the vacancies filled, by type
- lengths of visits and travel times.

The data, and the processing that has been applied to it, provides outputs of information for such management tasks as:

- distributing workloads among staff
- rationalising travel arrangements
- recruiting and training advisers
- attracting new clients.

We are interested in *management information systems*, which provide information in such a way that it contributes to management decision-making. Box 5.4 shows some important definitions relating to management information systems.

Box 5.4 Key definitions

Managing information involves seeing information as a valuable resource that must reach the right people at the right time in the right format.

Information management comprises the planning, organisation and control of information resources.

Management information is information that supports management decision-making, not just routine data. Management information supports operational and strategic planning.

Any system that provides information can be described as an information system, but it may not be a management information system. It may be a tactical information system used in day-to-day operations where substantial decisions are not being made. An example of a valuable tactical information system is a payroll system. The data inputs include details such as salary, number of overtime hours worked, payroll number, tax code, and so on. The information outputs are the amount each person is to be paid, totals of pay to date, etc. Although the information produced may be vitally important to the staff receiving it, the system provides little that is useful to management decision-making in the organisation. So it is not, as it stands, a management information system.

However, a payroll system which, as a by-product of its operation, also includes summary reports of, for example, the salary bill for each department and the total staff costs for the financial year could be described as a management information system. Provided that these reports are sent to the right people, arrive at a suitable time and contain information in a form that the recipients can understand – in other words, they meet all the criteria for good quality information – the information can be used for planning, control and decision-making. Such a payroll system represents an ideal management information system, since the management information comes entirely as a by-product of a routine process, with no data having to be collected solely to satisfy management's information needs.

See also: The qualities and cost of good information, in this chapter

Lucey defines a management information system as:

> A system to convert data from internal and external sources into information and to communicate that information, in an appropriate form, to managers at all levels in all functions to enable them to make timely and effective decisions for planning, directing and controlling the activities for which they are responsible.

(Source: Lucey, 1991)

His picture of a management information system is shown in Figure 5.7.

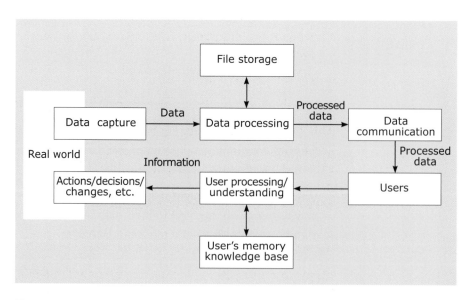

Figure 5.7 Outline of a management information system

(Source: Lucey, 1991)

To develop a successful management information system, managers must be knowledgeable enough to make an effective contribution to its design, and information specialists must understand managers' needs. The aim should be to provide:

- the right information
- at the right time
- in a meaningful form

so that its recipients can:

- assess situations
- evaluate alternative courses of action
- plan to take the most appropriate action.

People factors

Any information system is only as good as the data that are put into it. The reliability and timeliness of data will improve if their relevance to the management process is understood by the people who collect them. So what can you do to increase the likelihood of getting high-quality data into your information systems?

Consider the consequences if a data collector is expected to gather data that he or she does not perceive as useful or meaningful. The effect on the data collector is often one of alienation from the whole process. At best, the need to provide data for unspecified purposes is tolerated but not understood. The consequences for other stakeholders in the information network are that the data are likely to be inaccurate, incomplete and late.

To some extent, the problem of alienation can be overcome by:

- involving staff in the design and evaluation of information systems
- raising their awareness of the purposes for which the data are being collected
- appropriate training
- providing feedback on the uses to which the information has been put.

This may help when data are being collected for operations the data collector can observe regularly, but may be less helpful when the data are being collected for operations that are far away. That is one reason why the ideal management information system is one in which the data required are collected as a by-product of normal working procedures.

Knowledge management

Employees possess knowledge as well as information. Knowledge goes beyond information by adding intangible, hard-to-quantify 'value'. Knowledge includes knowing where to look and who may be able to help, who should see a piece of news, hunches about trends, and being able to read the subtexts to documents and meetings. This type of knowledge cannot easily be expressed in numbers or language, so cannot be 'captured' by information systems. Nonetheless, it requires management so that knowledge can be 'captured' when needed and transferred from one person to another.

You and your colleagues, because of your understanding of how your organisation operates, possess valuable knowledge. It is, therefore, just as important to take account of knowledge and manage it through 'soft' systems as it is to manage more tangible information.

Improving your information management

There will be times when you need to solve information management problems and improve the flow of information in your work area in order to support the effective delivery of the products and services for which you are responsible. We offer some practical approaches to common information management problems. We describe step by step how you can identify priorities among possible problems in information management and we provide you with simple frameworks and techniques to address them. We assume that you have not identified management flow or information defects before. However, when you have done so once, you will not need to begin with Step 1.

Step 1

See also: The qualities and cost of good information, in this chapter

Remind yourself of the 10 criteria for what constitutes good-quality information:

1 relevant to its purpose

2 clear

3 sufficiently accurate

4 complete

5 something the user can trust

6 concise; not excessive

7 timely

8 communicated to the right person

9 communicated via an appropriate channel

10 available at a cost that is less than the value of the benefits it provides.

Step 2

Consider the specific activity where there is an information problem or a need for improvement. Think about the information system in terms of the flows within it. You may find it helpful to use the ideas of input, process, output and feedback. It may also be helpful to draw a diagram of the information flow or system. An example of an information flow is shown in Figure 5.8 for a non-governmental agency that collects and disseminates information on human rights abuses.

Note that the organisation has a head office and a number of local offices. Each activity shown could be represented by a separate flow diagram representing a smaller part of the organisation, for example, a single local office. Choose the scale of your diagram according to the scale of the information flow you want to look at. An information flow diagram does not show processes, but these can be described on your diagram if necessary.

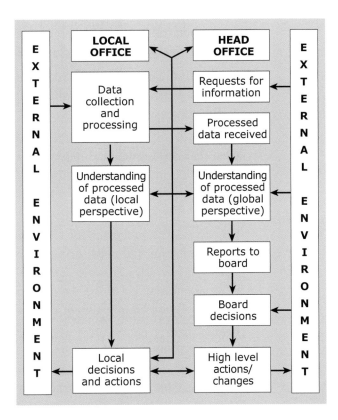

Figure 5.8 A formal information flow

Step 3

There is more than one way of approaching Step 3 depending on your purpose. If you are reviewing an information flow to ensure that it is working as effectively as possible, start by rating the qualities of the information received or transmitted in the flow. If it is clear that there is a problem with the system, this method alone will not be sufficient. You will need to identify and analyse the causes of the problem. In some cases you may need both approaches.

To rate the quality of the information needed or generated by the activity you have chosen, rate the data or information in each part of the flow against the 10 criteria in Step 1. Use a scale of 1–3, where 1 is weak and 3 is strong. Note your reasons and how the quality might be improved.

This should help you to identify where you improve service or product delivery by:

See also: Fishbone diagram, Tools and techniques

- improving data collection and analysis
- making data and information available to those who need it
- making sure that data and information are used effectively.

To identify and analyse the causes of a problem, use a fishbone diagram. This will help you to sort out and make sense of relationships between the various possible causes that may lie behind a problem. Most problems do not have a single cause, and a fishbone diagram helps you to group causes into common themes or categories, so that you can decide what needs to be done to deal effectively with each. Brainstorming the possible causes with other people may be useful.

See also: Brainstorming, Tools and techniques

It may be helpful to label the branches or 'bones' of your fishbone diagram so that they relate to the major components of an information flow:

Input data. This may not exist, or may not be collected systematically; the form in which data are collected may not be easy for you to turn into useful information.

Input sources. The people who collect or transmit data may not know what data are needed and may not be providing them in a useful form. Information may be lost because circulation lists are not kept up to date, or because the people providing data are not made aware of changes in responsibility or function.

Processes. The processes for collecting information may not collect all the information you need, or may focus only on part of what you need. There may be unreasonable delays in the flow of information, or information may go to the wrong people. Perhaps the system on which you are relying simply cannot deliver what you want.

People. It may not be clear who needs to know what. People may not know what information they need in order to perform effectively. They may not be aware of what is already available to them. What might be made available that is not already? What would it take to achieve this? They may not have the necessary skills to make effective use of the information that is available. These might include the skills to access the information (for instance, a necessary level of computer skills and confidence in their use) or the skills to handle and interpret data. Attitudes towards handling and using information may not be sufficiently positive. Are staff aware of the importance of information in their jobs? Does their behaviour demonstrate this understanding? Do they actively seek out information? What might be inhibiting the transmission and use of information? People may be coping in spite of – rather than because of – the way their tasks and roles are structured.

Work through all the possible causes you have identified, clustering related problems and deciding what categories of cause they represent. An example is provided in Box 5.5 to help you. The example also contains the notes the manager made.

Box 5.5 Change of address

Initial complaint

The manager of an agency providing residential care for older people received a letter from the son of one of the residents. The son complained that important information about his mother's circumstances and treatment was being sent to an old address, even though he insisted that he had notified the agency of his new address. On investigation, the manager found that the son's new address had been mentioned in a letter dealing with a number of other matters, but had never been entered on to the agency's computer database, which still contained the old address.

Consequences

When the manager raised this complaint at the next weekly meeting of senior staff, the discussion confirmed what the manager already suspected – that similar errors occurred frequently. Some staff argued that this sort of problem was inevitable in the circumstances in which they were working: relatives often saw their particular problems as being the only ones that mattered. It was not uncommon for them to fail to provide information such as changes of address, no matter how often they were asked. Staff were quick to assure the manager that they always put things right as soon as a problem came to light. Indeed, they seemed to take considerable pride in their ability to fix things that had gone wrong.

After the meeting, the manager sat down to write a letter of apology and began to think about the time and effort that was being wasted on 'putting things right' and wondered what might be done to get to the root causes of the problem.

To help, the manager drew the fishbone diagram shown in Figure 5.9.

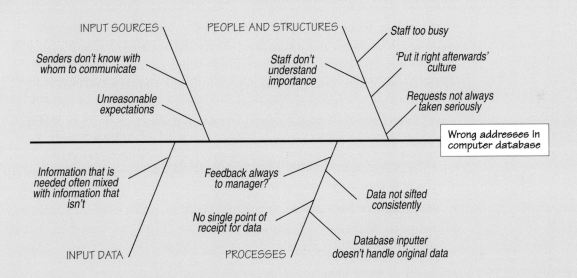

Figure 5.9 The manager's fishbone diagram

In order to keep the diagram relatively simple, we have not included in the diagram all the possible causes that the manager thought of.

Step 4

Now you can draw conclusions from your analysis. A meaningful 'picture' of the problems or areas for improvement is a sound basis on which to consider the most appropriate solutions or improvements. Note that a balance needs to be struck between drawing conclusions too soon in your analysis and doing too much analysis. Effective managers assess when they have sufficient information to draw conclusions. This will often involve talking to others while they are analysing a situation and when drawing conclusions.

During Steps 2 to 4, possible solutions will undoubtedly come to mind. Make a note of them for later use.

Step 5

At this point you can progress towards generating solutions or options for improvements (although the process is often iterative and you may return to some more analysis). First, however, you will need to assess whether the area for improvement, or problem, is small and well-bounded. If so you will be able to tackle all the improvements together. In other cases where the information system is more complex, you may have to choose which part of it to deal with first in order to gain the maximum benefits.

You could base your choices on the Pareto Principle, which states that 80% of the problems experienced in a situation are likely to be due to 20% of the possible causes. A thorough analysis of the impact of poor information on your activities should enable you to establish with some confidence which 20% of information flow weaknesses cause which 80% of problems.

Step 6

Now you can focus your effort on solutions to improve the quality of information or adjust the information flows and systems that will give you the best pay-off in terms of improvement. What is important is the scale of the improvement that you can expect from the changes you make. In deciding on a solution or improvement (or deciding between several possibilities) you will need to consider the outcomes you want to achieve. Positive outcomes are likely to include:

- fewer problems for customers, internal or external
- fewer delays in providing services
- fewer unnecessary costs
- better coordination of resources
- facilitating other parts of your activities
- better or more appropriate decisions
- reduced stress levels of staff.

You will also need to assess improvements on the basis of:

- the resources available to you
- the likely scale and extent of changes
- the extent to which making changes is under your control
- damage limitation (in cases where there is an information problem that is causing errors and which needs to be solved quickly)
- the transferability of solutions: that is, the potential for a solution to be widely used
- the likelihood of success.

Note that a change in how your area works with information that is received from other areas or passed to other areas will have an impact on other people's work. It may cause problems for them if you require information in a different form or pass it on in a different form from that which is expected. On the other hand, if you have identified issues that are shared by other parts of the organisation, this may provide an opportunity to collaborate with others to make improvements.

It is advisable to discuss your list with your team to see what areas they think are important. This will increase their awareness of the value of information to their work, especially if they can see some benefits to themselves and their performance in their jobs as a result of improving the quality of the information available to them. You may have to involve IT specialists, including database managers and data controllers. Discussion with others will also help you to clarify the strengths, weaknesses and implications of various options for improvement. Be prepared to carry out further analysis.

Pareto's Principle is useful, too, for deciding between options. If you use it to prioritise your options, then it is likely that your shortlist will include about 80% of your original list of information problems. It is possible that you might identify just one or two problem areas which, if put right, would instantly transform the effectiveness of your activities. However, this is unlikely – if the problems are so obvious, they would have been spotted and put right long ago!

Step 7

If you have done a good job in identifying improvements that could lead to valuable results and a significant impact, you now need to decide whether you can make these improvements yourself and in what order to carry them out. You may have to seek support for the changes you want to make. This is made easier because you now have the information – and solutions – to be able to communicate your case clearly and convincingly. If you are able to make the changes yourself, draw up an implementation plan using SMART objectives – Specific, Measurable, Agreed, Realistic and Timed. Use the second list in Step 6 to decide what improvements to make first if more than one is to be made.

See also: Problem-solving – a framework, Chapter 3

You may like to know that the manager of the agency in the earlier example (Box 5.2) decided that information would always come in a variety of forms and nothing could be done about this. Instead, he and his team would work with relatives to build good relationships so that the information they provided was as useful as possible. He also decided to explore with staff the ways in which it would be easier for them to recognise the information that needed to be entered in the database. Fewer errors would mean fewer complaints. He set SMART objectives for each action in his implementation plan. This included staff discussions on the ways in which they could work with relatives and the development of a set of criteria for recognising relevant information. They would also set themselves a target for a reduction in the number of complaints about errors in the records.

What you need when you need it: dealing with information overload

If you had lived in seventeenth-century England, during your entire lifetime you would have had access to less information than what is between the pages of a weekday copy of the *New York Times*. According to Richard Saul Wurman, author of more than 80 books on information, it is no wonder we suffer from information overload – that is, having too much information for an individual to be able to process and sometimes too much for an informed decision to be made.

There is information we must collect, analyse, use and/or disseminate as part of professional activities. But there is much more information that we receive in the course of a day, much of which we do not need. Dealing with information overload is a matter of being clear about what information you need, based on your priorities, and managing your time to avoid receiving information that is not useful.

See also: Managing your time, Chapter 1

Kevin Miller, author of *Surviving Information Overload* (2004), has a simple strategy for reducing information load:

1   Don't try to hold in your mind information that you can easily look up.

2   Research and learn what you need for the decisions you're making *now*.

3   Understand and manage well the information that your line manager expects you to have.

4   Play to your strengths: seek information that helps you to be better at what you're supposed to be doing.

He has some general recommendations:

- Skim read material to identify what is important – this is likely to be the information that helps you to make a decision or take action.

- If information is valuable and needed but costly in terms of your time, see if there is a quicker way of getting it.

Miller also has some specific recommendations.

Email

Ask yourself how often you *really* need to check your email during the day.

Don't let your day and your priorities be changed by new email messages (or any other information, requests, and so on). Prioritise on the basis of urgency and importance. Set up your email programme to highlight email automatically from key people. (In Microsoft® Outlook, go to Tools → Organise → Using Colours.) Alternatively, assign high importance to some senders and low to others (Tools → Rules and Alerts → New Rules).

Scan email subject lines and delete without opening any that are not work subjects. Don't 'unsubscribe' to spam (unsolicited email). Most spam senders do not make changes to their mailing lists when they receive your 'unsubscribe' message. It can encourage the sender to send more spam because it confirms your email address is 'live'.

Send fewer emails (and receive fewer) by ensuring that every email you send is necessary.

Save and reuse responses you use often.

Have someone else check your email if possible.

Mail

Open your mail standing up, near the recycling bin; discard unopened, obvious junk mail; sort and prioritise the rest according to urgency and importance.

Telephone

Don't give your phone number to anyone whose calls you don't want.

Ask your assistant, secretary or receptionist to take all your calls and to respond to those they can, transferring only those which need your personal attention.

Create a voice mail message that states clearly when you'll be able to return calls and, if necessary, who to contact in the meantime. Return calls when you say you will. This avoids people leaving more than one message.

Organising information

Being organised is not the same as being orderly: being organised means being able to find what you want; being orderly may just mean time wasted putting things away and then getting them out again two hours later.

Have desk clean-up days – organise, clean up and throw out. Some organisations hold regular clean-up days and provide coffee, or lunch, as well as colour-coded refuse, recycling and 'for shredding' bags. It's easier when everyone is doing the same thing.

File, or stack, documents by category, keeping the number of categories between six and 12. These might be current projects, reports from your team, committees and immediate tasks. Then make sure that all the files or stacks are easily identifiable. Put the ones you use closest to you. Process items only once. If you pick up a document, deal with it (bin it, delegate it, file it or add it to your 'to do' list).

Don't keep information that someone else is *required* to keep: just ask them for it when you need it.

On your computer

File documents or files on your computer in the same way that you would organise other information (see above). Electronic folders can be nested, so a folder named Clexmaso Project Meetings can have a separate, dated, sub-folder for each meeting, or for each year.

Label Microsoft® Word and other electronic files with clear, descriptive names, a date and, if necessary, a version number. Clexmaso Project Meeting Agenda May 09 v2.doc will be distinguishable from Clexmaso Project Meeting Agenda May 09.doc and far more identifiable than Agenda.doc. Then add the 'filename and path' and date to the header or footer (the spaces at the top and bottom of the page) so that if and when the document is printed out you know which document it is and where to find it. (In Word, go to Insert → AutoText → Header/Footer.)

Online searches

Use the appropriate search engine for your needs.

Learn how to focus searches using quotation marks, operators and wildcards by asking a librarian (whose full-time job is to find information).

Don't be an information 'addict'

Possessing information makes us feel good because:

- it gives us a sense of control
- we can use it to influence people
- we can learn from it (and learning is inherently rewarding)
- we can sell it to make money
- it can give us power – the person with the best information at a meeting shapes the decisions most
- getting and acting on information at speed gives us a sense of importance and excitement.

Not having information can:

- make us feel inadequate
- give rise to the fear of admitting 'I don't know'.

Reassure your way out of information addiction by accepting that:

1 Ignorance (not knowing) is the starting point of learning. It's acceptable not to know; you can ask questions instead.

2 Less information means less certainty. However, you need only be about 85% certain to make a good-enough decision, not 100%.

3 Too much information can lead to paralysis by analysis when decisive action is needed.

4 Acting on the 'right' information can lead to change. A small change can produce big results.

Dealing with information overload is sensible. The primary difficulty with avoiding information you do not need is that you may miss being exposed to interesting ideas or opinions in your quest. However, by dealing with information overload effectively, you will be able to make better judgements about what you might be missing and which you might now attend to, if only occasionally.

Chapter 6 Understanding people at work
Individuals and organisations

The Healthy Heart Foundation

A not-for-profit organisation – the Healthy Heart Foundation (HHF) – has entered into partnership with a large, successful, commercial company. The link between the two organisations – a health information service and a company that makes organic soup – is expected to result in increased sales for the commercial company. The company will pay an agreed share of its profits on organic soup sales to HHF. Liz Dawes, HHF's Commercial Enterprises Director has worked hard to convince her staff and volunteers that the partnership is a good idea.

Six months later, Liz found that most, but not all, of her staff and volunteers were positive about the partnership. George Irons who is in charge of website development at HHF appears to have a particular problem. Things reached a crisis point at a meeting yesterday when George shouted angrily that the association with a commercial company was 'just not ethical'. It reduced HHF's credibility and restricted its freedom to be objective about diet and products. George had made similar criticisms before, but no one had taken them very seriously. Now, however, he is threatening to leave unless there is less information on the HHF website about the commercial soup company.

People's behaviour can sometimes be puzzling, as the above example illustrates. However, if we are told something about George the situation can be more easily understood. He is committed to the idea of not-for-profit and social enterprise and believes in his work and that of HHF. He came to HHF from a successful and more highly-paid job in the commercial sector. So, George has goals, values and interests which shape the way he sees and responds to situations and which motivate what he does and how he does it.

Similarly, we can imagine at a business meeting at the soup company someone saying angrily: 'It's just not ethical that we give up our shareholders' profits to HHF.'

Thus, people's goals, values and interests, along with their needs and prior experiences, can help to explain variations in their behaviour at work. At the same time, their behaviour provides clues about what is important to them and what they expect from the organisation. As a result, we may also be able to anticipate an individual's reaction to certain organisational factors, including changes in working.

Workplace behaviour cannot be explained by individual factors alone, however. Workplace behaviour is an interaction between the individual and the organisation, between individual needs and social conventions, between doing what is in our own interest and doing what is allowed. Organisations shape workplace behaviour directly, through making staff accept formal rules and procedures (for example, keeping data secure and complying with decisions) and indirectly, through social conventions (such as acceptable forms of dress and the 'right' way to behave to colleagues). An awareness of this balance of individual and organisational factors is at the heart of managing people.

No two people are likely to have exactly the same beliefs and values and expectations and each may behave differently in a similar situation. Moreover, organisations influence the way people behave, so a person may not behave in exactly the same way in a different organisation or work group. Managers will find three points useful in understanding the behaviours of others:

- considering only 'facts' in the behaviour of an individual is not enough
- people work to achieve different goals and have different values
- although some behaviour may not appear to make sense, we still need to try to understand it.

However, managers do not have the long training that specialists in behaviour (such as psychologists) have, and people have human rights, such as the right to privacy. The aim for managers is to find out 'more' about people's behaviours rather than to seek a full understanding.

To understand individual behaviour it is important to consider how a situation is understood by the person or people involved. We also need to consider how social pressures, constraints and conventions may have influenced the behaviour. Social conventions create pressures on individuals to behave appropriately, yet people are not always aware of these pressures. Some writers suggest that most human behaviour is aimed at achieving goals: it is goal-directed and purposeful. People may have different goals, for example status, power, money and material success, to contribute to society or, primarily, to provide for their families. If we assume that people are goal-driven, then these goals can be used to explain behaviour.

Of course, individual goals and values will not be universally understood and shared within the workplace. (In other aspects of people's life, such as politics and religion, differences between people are accepted.) However, managers often assume that everyone is working towards the same goals – those of the organisation. Many managers assume that the people who will implement management decisions will cooperate. However, the reasons why people cooperate may not be to achieve collective goals. Often, they are trying to achieve their own goals. Fortunately, in many cases both organisational and individual goals can be satisfied at the same time. In some cases, however, the different values or goals of work group members do not match. This can make it very difficult for a task to be completed, as illustrated in the case below.

The language teaching project

The project team seemed to be very suitable. All were experienced in language teaching, were highly trained and each had some specialist knowledge which would be useful. The aim of the project was to advise on a new language-teaching programme for the ministry of education in a developing country. They all were motivated by the aims of the project and seemed to get on well. It seemed that they would work well together to achieve a shared goal. But they did not.

Often the team leader would guide everyone to a decision that all would accept, but then someone would disagree with a previous decision which at the time they had supported. When people's behaviour was studied more carefully it became clear that individuals had different interests, beliefs and values.

For example, one team member really wanted to work in the ministry itself. It was nearer her home and she valued the security of employment it would provide. She was using the project to show the ministry that she would be a good employee. She did not agree with some of the more innovative and radical suggestions of her colleagues because she wanted to be seen as 'a safe pair of hands': that is, a person who could be trusted to comply with ministry rules and regulations.

Another member had just completed a university qualification and wanted to use the project to apply some of the modern ideas she had learned. She felt the team should take the opportunity provided by the project to do something new and different. Another member had close links with a multinational publisher which wanted the ministry to promote its existing textbooks. A big change in the current language programme would make this difficult so this team member resisted suggestions to innovate. One team member was passionately committed to the development of her country and its education system. She thought that only citizens of the country should do this. She was deeply suspicious of all foreign team members – about half the team's members.

Another team member had worked all her life on the development of education systems in different countries. She saw herself as an expert, was proud of her expertise and had a wealth of experience. She was aware of many potential problems with the project and believed these should be discussed fully with team members. Finally, another member saw the project as having high status. She wanted the project to be completed quickly and efficiently because this would support her case when she applied for promotion.

One way of exploring the way in which values, beliefs and loyalties shape behaviour is to consider the different reasons why people might be drawn to a specific job or career. Schein (1978) used the term 'career anchor' to describe the different key values that people hold and how they try to find a way to live according to these values. He identified eight career-anchors which can provide useful insights for managers.

Technical/functional competence People in this category are skilled and enjoy being seen as experts. They have adopted the values of their profession and they identify with their profession (often more so than the organisation they work for). They seek to develop and increase their skills.

General managerial competence These people see a danger in being limited to one work area and recognise the importance of knowing several functional areas. They develop skills relevant to the type of organisation they work for. Opportunities for leadership, high income, higher levels of responsibility and contributing to the success of their organisation are key values and motives.

Autonomy/independence These individuals find it difficult to accept rules, procedures, working hours, and so on. They like to decide how to do their job, what speed to do it at, and what quality standards to achieve. They may choose a lower-paid job rather than give up autonomy and independence.

Security/stability Some people need safety, security and predictability and will seek jobs with permanence and little risk of redundancy. These individuals tend to identify with their jobs and their careers. Their need for security and stability may restrict their career choices.

Entrepreneurial creativity Some people like to create new organisations, products or services which will be seen as the result of their work.

Sense of service/dedication This describes those who choose occupations whose core 'values' match their own. They are often more orientated to these values than to the areas of competence involved in the work.

Pure challenge These individuals define success in terms of overcoming impossible difficulties or just winning. For some the challenge lies in taking on difficult jobs or tasks, while for others it lies in competition.

Lifestyle For these people a career must be integrated with their lifestyle, balancing the needs of the individual, work and the family. They look for an organisation with values that respect personal and family needs.

Schein's is one of several frameworks that describe how values, preferences and assumptions influence the way a person views and approaches their work. Such frameworks can help to explain puzzling behaviours that, when we look more carefully, are consistent with the values an individual holds. They are also helpful in understanding our personal values in relation to professional/occupational and group/team values. However, people are not always able to choose a job that fits with their values. Further, people's priorities often change during their working lives as their personal and domestic situation and their interests and aspirations change.

 ## The Psychological Contract

Motivation is what leads people to persist and overcome obstacles in their work. Part of the manager's role is to ensure that staff are motivated at work. Thus, a challenge for managers is to develop an understanding of what people want and expect from their jobs and to help them to achieve these things. Cultural differences in attitudes to work will make this task harder.

No single approach or theory of motivation provides a full explanation and many have faults. By looking at several theories it is possible to take what is useful from each. It is, of course, difficult for managers to apply motivation theories in the workplace. Discovering what motivates individuals, when they may not be aware of their deeper motivations, is part of clinical psychology, not management. Watson (2002) argues that managers should not focus wholly on people's 'motives'. Rather, they should consider what people do and think in the broader context of the organisation as a type of exchange between parties.

This exchange requires negotiation in which concessions and re-alignments are made on both sides. It requires dialogue and good knowledge of individual circumstances, preferences and motivations. For example, would you continually provide new challenges for an individual so they can have significant development experiences to prepare them for greater responsibilities and possible promotion? Or do you give the individual the same job several times over because you know they perform perfectly competently? Such decisions are likely to be informed by the manager's knowledge of the individual and by the individual's expectations.

A position between Watson's and more traditional theories of motivation is that of the Psychological Contract – a modern concept with significant research support. It adopts the view that motivation is complex, varying from person to person and from situation to situation. The key feature is that the employee has expectations of what the employer will provide, and the employer has expectations of what the employee will provide. Expectations that are not met will result in a break or 'breach' of the Psychological Contract which will often result in upset or conflict. The manager can explore these expectations and try to understand, if not resolve, the conflict.

The Psychological Contract has been defined as:

> the perceptions of mutual obligations to each other held by the two parties in the employment relationship, the organisation and the employee. Such perceptions may be the result of formal contracts, or they may be implied by the expectations which each hold of the other and which are communicated in a multitude of subtle or not so subtle ways.

> (Source: Herriot *et al.,* 1997)

The Psychological Contract covers expectations between the organisation and an individual employee on a variety of obligations, privileges and rights. It considers what the individual expects to give to and receive from the organisation and what the organisation expects to give and receive in return. These expectations can be transactional, such as pay or hours, or they can be relational, such as trust and commitment. If employees and employers do not share a common view of these mutual expectations, problems are likely to emerge.

Some formal employer/employee obligations and expectations are covered, of course, under the formal contract of employment, for example, how many hours should be worked and how much pay will be received. Other expectations, however, are often more implicit and unspecified by either

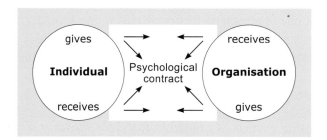

Figure 6.1 A representation of the Psychological Contract

party, for example, trust and fairness, aspects of work satisfaction, work–life balance, motivation and stress. They are the kind of things that are subject to psychological obligations and expectations – the content of the Psychological Contract. Specific examples of such expectations and obligations might include the expectation that support and training will be provided when an employee is asked to carry out a new task, or that the employee will not be asked to work beyond normal working times.

What happens when the expectations are not met? Usually, expectations on both 'sides' are not recognised until there is some 'violation'. For example, there may be disappointment or conflict when the employee is offered no help and support to carry out a new task or is asked to work late. Therefore, managers need to exercise care when making changes that might violate the contract. Many managers will discuss changes with those affected. This should reveal any 'contract' difficulties.

The Psychological Contract has some problems, however, both conceptually and in practice. For example, it does not provide a systematic approach to managing employee/organisation relationships. Nonetheless it offers a framework for identifying and avoiding problems. It highlights the need for managers to talk regularly with their employees and when there is change, to consult widely and systematically. Such discussion may be part of everyday supervision conversations and could be explored during appraisal meetings.

Expectancy Theory

A well regarded theory of motivation for day-to-day management is Expectancy Theory. It argues that we act in the expectations of certain (specific) outcomes, based on prior experience. Expectancy theory was proposed by Vroom (1964) and stresses that it is not just having a reward or incentive that is important in motivating behaviour, but rather it is the link between effort and reward. Some rewards come anyway, regardless of the effort put in, and are unlikely to be effective as motivators. For example, in the UK voluntary and public sectors, pay has traditionally been linked to the job people do rather than to their performance in the job. Some rewards are linked directly to effort, and this can motivate people. Other rewards are linked to effort in a 'probabilistic' way. This means that, for a reward to affect a person's decision to work hard, that person must believe that the effort will increase the likelihood of obtaining the reward. The probabilistic link between effort and reward can be shown as a dotted line in a chain.

Figure 6.2 The link between effort and reward

A further element is needed in the chain shown in Figure 6.2. This is referred to as 'performance'. This is needed because when a reward is given, it is usually for the results of the performance (for example, increased sales or increased subscriptions) rather than for the effort itself. Performance-related pay is usually linked to measurable targets like these. Therefore, an employer rarely rewards effort unless it has resulted in a good performance. In Figure 6.3 the idea of 'costs'– the opposite or reward – has also been added. For example, if we have not worked sufficiently hard and our performance is poor we may be punished.

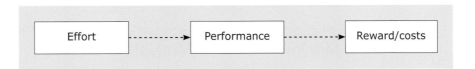

Figure 6.3 The link between effort, performance and reward/costs

Working hard may result in more than one reward or cost. Expectancy Theory suggests that people think about those costs and benefits when making choices about how to act, and base their decisions on this calculation. Sometimes the costs of working harder, such as fatigue, stress or less time for the family or leisure, may be greater than the benefits, such as more pay or status. People refer to 'work–life balance' when deciding, for example, whether to accept a proposed promotion.

Expectancy Theory is concerned less with the nature of particular rewards or costs as a way of explaining motivation and more with the links with performance and effort. If the links are clear and strong, a reward or cost will have a powerful motivating or demotivating effect. If the links are weak or absent, a reward or potential cost will not have the power to motivate. It is important to note here that if a reward or cost is to have any effect on a person's motivation, the person must either want the reward or want to avoid the cost.

The theory assumes that people make decisions on their own, logically and consistently. We can easily disagree with the idea that people really calculate the probable outcomes of particular courses of action in such a detached way. People might go through these processes quite formally when making important decisions, for example, when deciding whether to take a new job or not. This is less likely when making day-to-day decisions, such as whether to make time today to order a new photocopier.

Expectancy Theory emerged at a time when economic and political conditions were quite different from the way they are now in Western countries and is built on assumptions that we might now question. It assumes relatively stable employment in which employees have job security in exchange for loyalty. It also assumes that people work solely to maximise the outcome of the exchange with their organisation, and assumes that all members of the workforce are similar. However, in many Western countries the workforce is now more complex and differentiated, the traditional employment relationship is disappearing and people have a range of different reasons for working. Examples of this are those who volunteer for work without the usual incentives of salaries and organisational benefits. Nonetheless, Expectancy Theory provides a useful analytical framework through which to influence job satisfaction and poor performance.

Other theories of motivation

Two popular concepts of motivation are Maslow's Growth Motivation Theory and Herzberg's Motivation-Hygiene Theory. Both have proved popular with managers for many decades but they have received major criticisms about their validity. We present the theories here because both have become part of the 'language' of management, which every manager needs to learn, if only to understand other managers!

Maslow's Growth Motivation Theory

Maslow's Growth Motivation Theory is based on the principle that everyone has the same needs or desires that must be satisfied. Organisations and managers took this to mean that once we understand these needs, the workplace could be arranged so that workers could satisfy their needs.

Maslow (1943) proposed that human needs exist as a hierarchy. When the first category of needs is satisfied, people move on to satisfy the second category, and so on, until they reach the fifth and highest level – self-actualisation, when a person's full personal potential is realised.

His hierarchy from the basic level upwards is set out below.

Physiological needs – food, drink and shelter

Safety needs – protection against physical and emotional threat or harm, desire for predictability

Social needs – love, affection and acceptance as part of a social group

Esteem needs – to have high self-esteem and the respect of others (prestige, status)

'Self-actualisation' needs – to fulfil our potential to become what we believe we are capable of becoming.

However, self-actualisation is a controversial concept and it is probable that, in organisational settings, this suggested need is unlikely to be satisfied. There is no evidence of systematic progression up the hierarchy. That is not to say that the needs Maslow identified are not important human needs that may motivate behaviour.

Herzberg's Motivation-Hygiene Theory

Herzberg's Motivation-Hygiene Theory is also based on needs, but is more complex. Herzberg and his research team were interested in job satisfaction and researched what factors of a job offered satisfaction and which caused dissatisfaction.

They asked people to recall times when they had felt especially satisfied or dissatisfied by their work and to describe what factors had caused these feelings. The researchers found that two entirely different sets of factors emerged. Herzberg and his team called the factors connected with satisfaction 'motivators' and those connected with dissatisfaction 'hygiene factors'. For example, a person who had listed low pay as a source of dissatisfaction did not necessarily identify high pay as a cause of satisfaction. Thus, whereas previously it had been assumed that there was a single motivation continuum running from satisfaction to dissatisfaction, Herzberg argued that this traditional model was incorrect. It might be that improvement in some areas (which they called 'hygiene factors') would help to remove dissatisfaction, but would not increase satisfaction: that is, they would not motivate people. For example, the absence of information about what is happening in an organisation may be a cause of dissatisfaction to an individual, but when that information is provided they are not necessarily more satisfied; it is just that the dissatisfaction has been removed.

It is important to note that the researchers asked 'when were you satisfied?' and not 'when were you motivated?'. This undermines Herzberg's claim to have researched motivation. The theory is also difficult to apply practically, for example, in job design. However, it may be useful in highlighting the importance of intrinsic rewards – those that are associated with the job itself (Herzberg's motivators) as well as extrinsic ones – work-related rewards that have measurable value (Herzberg's hygiene factors).

Both Maslow's and Herzberg's theories have similar problems in that there is no clear relationship between needs and behaviour, and needs are not sufficiently specified. Both also ignore the capacity of people to construct their own *perception* of needs (Currie, 2006).

Chapter 7 Understanding leadership

Leadership in practice

Three examples of leadership

- Samir always had a sense of purpose and direction and was invariably positive and inspiring: his staff were happy to work with him in a new project that required major effort.

- Rosie made it clear that, at the next performance review, 60% of staff would get a major bonus, 20% would get a small salary increase, and the lowest performing 20% would lose their jobs. The rewards were high for those who performed well, so staff worked hard.

- William was a very supportive leader. He asked team members what new work would most interest each of them and tried hard to allocate it accordingly. He set targets after careful discussion with team members. When anyone had a difficult deadline to meet and needed to work late, he bought food and refreshments to keep the team members going. He arranged celebrations whenever the team completed its work. But he never did much technical work himself.

These three examples of leadership represent very different approaches to it. But while leadership is recognised as an essential part of everyday management, the nature and requirements of a twenty-first century leader are the subject of much debate (Grint, 2005).

Who can lead, what can they lead and where, when and how can they lead? Fulop *et al.* (2004) sum up the problem: 'Leadership is widely regarded as a central determinant of organisational performance but it is a difficult concept to pin down.' While we may refer to leadership in everyday conversation and people appear to understand what we mean, it is difficult to arrive at a precise definition of it.

Nonetheless, it is important for you as a manager to understand the basis of leadership and to learn to lead and influence wisely. It is also equally important for you to encourage leadership skills and capabilities of the people you manage.

In an attempt to define leadership Grint (2004) asks four questions:

Is it who leaders are that makes them leaders?

Is it what leaders achieve that makes them leaders?

Is it where leaders operate that makes them leaders?

Is it how leaders get things done that makes them leaders?

Grint's questions focus on whether leadership is about the person, the results achieved, about a person's position or about leadership as a process. He has argued that effective leaders create a compelling sense of identity for their organisation, department or work group, work out its direction and goals, and how these goals can be achieved, and then communicate persuasively so that people will follow (Grint, 2000). This view contrasts with early views of leadership that focused on the 'who' of leadership: the idea of the heroic leader who had the right and confidence to order others to do what they wanted. For modern organisations, however, no useful results came from this approach. Now, views on leadership concentrate more on the 'what', 'where' and 'how' of leadership and the context in which leadership takes place. They place importance on influence, centred on activities such as building and maintaining networks, creating and maintaining a sense of purpose, enabling and empowering followers (Fulop *et al.*, 2004). This idea of influence is common to many views on leadership: leadership involves influencing others to follow a particular direction or to aim for a particular goal. Ways in which this influence is exercised differ, however, according to the theoretical view of leadership that is held.

Traditional theories of leadership

To understand what modern leadership is and who leaders are we consider briefly some older approaches which still have some influence today. For example, many managers feel they cannot really be leaders and that they are 'playing at leadership' or are 'leaders in waiting'. When asked to explain their view, they may say that this is because they do not fit the image they have of what a leader is. They may have in mind a heroic military or political leader, often male, and the idea that a person is 'born to be a leader' or is 'educated' in leadership by their upbringing or education (Gabriel, 2005). Although historical figures such as Napoleon, Mao Tse-Tung or Churchill are not part of the organisational life we know, some traditional ideas help us to make sense of newer approaches to leadership that are relevant today. Here we set out the three traditional approaches.

Trait theories

Trait theories assume that leaders are 'born, not made': that what makes someone an effective leader is their personality and personal qualities. The implication for management is that the 'right people' with certain fixed characteristics need to be selected for leadership roles. This implies that only a select few can be leaders and that other people cannot be trained and developed to be leaders. The problem is that numerous studies of leaders found there were almost as many different traits identified as there were studies. There is some consensus that intelligence, initiative, self-confidence, and orientation towards achievement and interpersonal skills are important characteristics of leaders. However, there is no universal agreement on the relative importance of these factors. Trait theories have been criticised for focusing too much on who leaders are (their psychological make-up) rather than what they do (their behaviour). The following two types of theories were an attempt to redress this imbalance.

Style theories

Style theories try to identify the most effective way for leaders to behave towards the people they lead. A common finding of research studies is that leadership has two elements: a concern for task and a concern for people. These elements are not necessarily possessed in equal measure by leaders. Task-oriented leaders focus on completing the task. They set goals, plan activities and set and maintain standards. People-oriented leaders focus on establishing good working relationships. They take an interest in their staff's welfare, are easy to approach and are responsive to suggestions. One of the best-known and most widely-used style theories is the managerial grid (Blake *et al.*, 1962). This proposes that the most effective leaders are those who show a high concern for both task and people. Blake and his colleagues argued that this leadership style is effective irrespective of the context. However, the idea that context is unimportant has led to criticisms of style theories and the development of contingency theories, which are more context-specific.

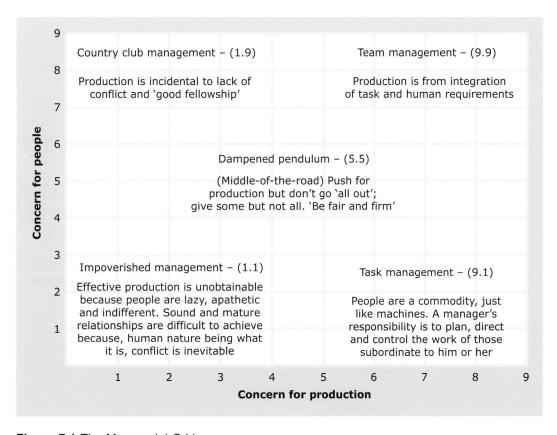

Figure 7.1 The Managerial Grid

(Source: based on Blake *et al.*, 1962)

Contingency theories

Contingency theories or 'fit theories' propose that what constitutes effective leadership depends on the situation. One of the earliest and best-known contingency theories is that of Fiedler (1967). Fiedler confirmed the findings of the style theorists by identifying two main leadership styles: task-oriented and people-oriented. However, he argued that a task-oriented style is more appropriate in some circumstances while a people-oriented style is appropriate in others. The appropriate style depends on the situation a manager faces and whether or not it is 'favourable'. 'Favourableness' depends on a combination of three elements:

- leader–member relationships – whether the leader is liked and trusted by group members
- task structure – the degree to which the tasks to be performed are clearly defined and well-structured
- the leader's 'position power' – the extent to which the leader can reward and punish subordinates (through pay, dismissals, and so on).

The greater the degree to which each of these elements is present, the more favourable the situation. Through extensive research, Fiedler found that:

- task-oriented leaders perform better in situations which are either very favourable or very unfavourable
- relationship-oriented leaders perform better in situations of moderate favourableness
- the performance of the leader depends as much on the situation as on the style of the leader.

The practical implications of the contingency approach are that effective leaders ensure that their leadership style fits the situation they face. There is disagreement over how this can best be achieved. Fiedler argued that a person's leadership style is quite a stable characteristic and therefore difficult to change. Thus, he said, leaders should concentrate on changing the favourableness of the situation, to improve the fit between themselves and the situation. However, other contingency theorists, such as Hersey and Blanchard (1988), disagreed. They argued that effective leaders adapt their style to the situation. Some individuals may be flexible and able to adjust their leadership style, whereas other, less flexible, individuals would be better trying to manage the situation to suit their particular style.

As general theories of leadership, style and contingency theories have been criticised in recent years because, like trait theories, they do not offer complete explanations of leadership, despite some evidence to support each of them. Some of the limitations are set out in Box 7.1.

Box 7.1 Limitations of leadership style and contingency theories

They concentrate primarily on how managers should exercise their authority over others. They say little about how leadership might be exercised when there is no formal hierarchy, for example, between departments or between groups of colleagues.

They are primarily concerned with getting a group to work effectively. They do not deal with the strategic dimension of leadership – giving a sense of direction and purpose to the group or organisation.

They identify leadership with the person in authority, and do not inlcude the possibility that other people in a group may contribute to its leadership.

Grint (1997) suggests that leadership is more complex than these theories claim. Leaders do more than assess a current situation: they anticipate, communicate, direct, persuade and act authoritatively:

> it is not that leaders are those who identify the wave and ride it; rather, leaders are those who persuade us a wave is coming, who go out of their way to appear the most visible surfers to onlookers, and whose actions are taken by the onlookers as actions appropriate for leaders to take.

(Source: Grint, 1997)

Leadership in context

One modern approach to leadership is to see it as a process in which different people take part and play different roles at different times. There is no fixed set of special qualities that enable a person to become, or remain, a leader, and no person will be a leader in all situations or at all times. The approach rests on two ideas: that leadership means influencing other people in ways that are more or less acceptable to them, and that leaders are expected to be and are seen to be influential on important matters.

Influencing others in ways that are acceptable means using your power (for example, the authority provided by your position or role) in such a way that you 'carry' people with you, rather than force them to do what you want. What is regarded as acceptable influence, of course, will depend on the context. For example, in a disaster or emergency, people are likely to accept a directive style of leadership that they would find unacceptable in normal circumstances. People's values and beliefs will also shape what they see as acceptable influence and what they regard as effective leadership. These values and beliefs may also be shaped by culture. Further, who is regarded as a leader will depend not just on what a leader does but also on the expectations and perceptions of the followers. A leader will emerge over time out of the social interaction of the group.

These ideas of leadership and leaders stress that leadership is about tackling the important or core issues that face the group or organisation. These are:

Strategic issues. These are the 'ends' or results the group or organisation seeks. Strategic questions include: in what direction should we go in a changing environment, correctly identifying opportunities and avoiding threats? These strategic questions will usually be more significant for groups at the higher levels of the organisation.

Task issues. These are the 'means' of achieving the group's or organisation's desired results. Task-oriented questions that leaders need to consider include: how can these tasks best be performed? Is there a tension between ends and means?

People or maintenance issues. These are largely about the relationship between leaders and followers. A central task for leaders is to build and maintain a solid relationship with others. People/maintenance questions include: how can a leader maintain the morale, cohesion and commitment of individuals while pursuing the group's or organisation's aims?

The idea that different people play different roles at different times (Hosking, 1997) has three important implications for managers:

1 A leader is someone who influences how the group or organisation understands and tackles the core issues it faces, but who does not necessarily have formal authority. Formal position is a source of power and gives a person the potential to exert more influence, of course. But that potential may not be used effectively, and the group may consider the influence unacceptable. A question to consider here is: what can leaders do to persuade others to follow them?

2 A group can have more than one leader. It is possible for all the members of a group to make leadership contributions. It is useful to talk about leadership being 'focused' or 'dispersed', depending on how many members of the group consistently contribute to its leadership. Equally, different people may demonstrate leadership in different areas. For example, one person may lead the group's tasks while another maintains group morale and commitment. In fact, the three group or organisational issues described above often require different personal qualities and abilities. Developing a strategy involves taking an overview of a situation, whereas getting a task done requires attention to detail. This is one reason why leadership is often dispersed in groups: it can be difficult to find all the qualities and abilities required in one person.

3 When dealing with strategy and task issues, knowledge and understanding of the wider environment, what factors are likely to have an impact on the organisation or group, and how they will impact, are needed to exercise leadership. A leader must be prepared to keep in touch with and understand these wider events and influences. Being a successful leader depends not just on what a person does within a group but also on what that person does outside the group. Therefore, effective networking abilities and being a good ambassador are important leadership skills; they help the leader to understand the threats and opportunities that may face a group and to mobilise resources and support.

See also: Developing leadership skills, in this chapter

If it has occurred to you that many of the skills and behaviours described are those used by managers, then you are right. There is considerable overlap between effective leadership and effective management: distinguishing between them can be difficult! The idea of distributed leadership suggests the potential for leadership to be exercised at any level in an organisation and by anyone. This approach argues that leadership responsibility is dissociated from formal roles. Rather, the action and influence of people at all levels is recognised as integral to the overall direction and functioning of the organisation (Bolden, 2008). Thus, every staff member has – or can have – a leadership responsibility.

Developing leadership skills

If leadership involves skills and capabilities which can be learned and developed, how can these skills be developed? And if the leadership skills and capabilities you need change over time and in the face of new challenges, how will you identify those you need to learn and develop?

One way of approaching leadership development is to identify the different leadership functions you need to undertake. The core leadership functions are:

Developing a sense of direction in the group or organisation

Defining the tasks necessary to achieve the group's or organisation's goals, and making sure that these tasks are carried out effectively

Maintaining the morale, cohesion and commitment of the group or organisation.

A similar approach is taken by Yukl (2004), although he emphasises behaviours required in situations of change, and in turbulent times: the ability to analyse a situation, determine the leadership behaviour needed and then act in a skilful way. He lists three specific categories of behaviours.

Task behaviour

Plan short-term activities

Clarify task objectives and role expectations

Monitor operations and performance.

Relations behaviour

Provide support and encouragement

Provide recognition for achievements and contributions

Develop skill and confidence of group members

Consult with group members when making decisions

Empower group members to take initiatives in problem-solving.

Change behaviour

Monitor the external environment

Explain why change is necessary

Propose an innovative strategy or new vision

Encourage innovative thinking

Take risks to propose necessary change

Facilitate collective learning.

The list is not exhaustive, and other behaviours may be relevant in particular contexts.

Influencing activities

Contemporary leadership has been described as exercising influence. This centres on activities such as building and maintaining networks, creating and perpetuating a sense of purpose, enabling and empowering followers (Fulop *et al.*, 2004). In general, being influential depends on knowledge and expertise, and on developing interpersonal relationships based on mutual trust and understanding. Influencing others can take a number of forms, often linked to a task or process. They are not confined to those in formal positions of leadership, of course.

Consider the following examples.

Difficult customers

Joe is the assistant manager in a medium-sized branch of a chain of supermarkets. He tries to spend at least an hour on each shift at the customer service desk. This gives Joe the opportunity to demonstrate to staff how to deal with difficult customers diplomatically and respect their consumer rights. Many staff members see or hear Joe perform as he expects them to. In the staffroom and store, it is not uncommon for staff to discuss customers in ways that are not complimentary. Joe, having dealt with irate customers, is often tempted to join in but resists doing so in order to set a good example.

Sceptical staff

Sue is Head of Department in a large school. She agreed on behalf of the department to trial a new vocational qualification for 16-year-olds involving a team-based information technology project. Under pressure from the Principal of the school, she had to make the decision at short notice without full consultation with teachers in the department on the detail of the plan. Several staff were very sceptical: students would probably just want to spend their time 'surfing' the internet and it would be difficult to teach them how to work in teams and achieve high-quality project work. Sue was convinced that the curriculum was well-designed and she thought that the teachers were simply reluctant to embrace change. She encouraged them to support each other and gave them additional classroom support during the trial. She encouraged teachers to discuss progress and to provide feedback; she also expressed some of her own doubts. At the end of the trial, Sue agreed with the teachers that the trial had been of limited success and that much more preparation had been needed.

Deteriorating morale

Pradesh was as dismayed as his research and development team when senior managers warned that the difficult economic environment was likely to mean a reduction in finance for the work of the team. For the next few days, team members talked of little but the prospect of job redundancies and team morale deteriorated rapidly. Pradesh called a team meeting and asked members to consider what would happen to the company's competitive advantage if it abandoned research and development. Gradually the mood of the meeting changed. Pradesh then addressed how the work of the team could be made more cost-effective. Ideas quickly began to emerge.

Each example illustrates one or more of the leadership skills and behaviours set out below.

Be a role model

One way in which you can influence other people in an organisation is through your behaviour. If you are seen as a leader, or if you occupy a position of authority, then you may be a role model for other people. So you need to take account of the effects of your behaviour on others. Whether you are aware of it or not, you will lead by example. Joe demonstrated this in the first example.

Do as you say

One function of leadership is to focus people's attention on the issues the leader considers important and help to set the expected standards of performance and behaviour. You are more likely to do this effectively if your deeds match your words – that is, if you do as you say. Joe also demonstrated this in the first example.

Communicate openly and honestly

Your behaviour will be an important factor in determining whether a climate of trust develops in the group or organisation. If you are willing to communicate openly and honestly, group members are more likely to follow your lead. Sue in the second example demonstrated this (although only after the decision was made to go ahead with the trial).

Keep a sense of proportion

Maintaining cohesion and morale is the important 'maintenance' function of leadership. If you can keep a sense of proportion about challenges or problems facing the group, and maintain your own sense of optimism and enthusiasm, then you will help the group to cope with its problems in a positive manner. Pradesh in the third example illustrated this.

Set and manage expectations

A group that knows where it is going and what it is trying to achieve, and believes its objectives to be important, is more likely to be happy and motivated. Help the group set realistic expectations and ensure that these expectations remain realistic. It may be a matter of reminding people of the organisation's mission or goals – trying to keep everyone heading in the right direction. Pradesh in the third example illustrated this, though indirectly.

Admit to mistakes

It is common for a group to blame its leader when things go wrong. The criticism may be unjustified but the leader will need to absorb some of the anxieties and tensions of the group without overreacting. When criticism is justified, it is better to admit to mistakes. Sue in the second example illustrated this.

Networking

Networking is the process of establishing a mutually-beneficial relationship with other people inside and outside the organisation. The purpose is primarily to exchange information, ideas, and to give and receive (or ask for) support. Networking can help you to contribute more effectively to the leadership of your group or organisation. For example, as a leader of a team or group, you can use your network of relationships to further your group's interests, to acquire the resources necessary to carry out its work, and to find out what is going on in the wider environment to help the group members make sense of new challenges. More detail on networking is set out in Box 7.2.

Box 7.2 Effective networking

A manager with a good network of contacts is likely to get better-quality information and therefore be in a better position to make good decisions.

Networking can be used to develop your knowledge; to provide mutual support; to build trust; to increase your visibility; to influence other people; and to build coalitions that support your plans.

Networking is an art rather than a science. It is an activity that many people do naturally, and it is difficult to prescribe rules for how to do it.

A network is not just about communication, it is also a means of making exchanges. An exchange is an interaction in which each party gains something of value. To become a valued and active member of a network, you will need something to exchange: for example, friendship, support, information, a service or contacts.

In many networks some members are more influential and better connected than others. These individuals often act as gatekeepers, guarding or monitoring access to people and giving those they consider to be worthy introductions to other people in the network. Part of the skill of networking is the ability to identify and gain the confidence of gatekeepers.

You can develop your networking skills in the following ways:

1 Look at your organisational chart and choose somebody in an area you know very little about or a person from an office or work area near yours, or someone you have seen at work but know little about.

2 Have a conversation with them. Find out the main aspect of their job. Afterwards think about how you might be of use to the person and they to you.

3 Repeat the activity, say about once a week, until you have built your network up to a good size.

(Source: adapted from Pedler *et al.*, 2007)

Being an ambassador

An ambassador represents the work group to those higher up in the organisation and to other groups in and outside the organisation. Many groups in organisations are interdependent and how well one group works will depend, in part, on how relationships between groups are managed by

See also: What do managers do?, Chapter 1

See also: Coaching and work-based learning and development, Chapter 11; and Mentoring and personal and professional development, Chapter 11

their ambassadors. If an ambassador is viewed favourably, then the group is more likely to be viewed favourably. A leader who is seen to have influence in the organisation is also likely to have influence in the group.

Whatever you decide to do to develop your leadership skills, an important aspect will be to develop self-awareness. You will need to be honest about your strengths and weaknesses in core leadership skills. It can be helpful to seek feedback on your skills from people you trust and from whom you can expect a balanced view. This can be developed as part of a coaching or mentoring relationship with a more experienced person.

Chapter 8 Working in groups and teams

Making teams work: an introduction

In today's organisations, more and more work is carried out by teams and groups of people working together towards a common objective. Making teams and groups work effectively is a challenging task for the manager. Bringing individuals together can slow down and complicate everyday processes and conflict can make even the simplest task difficult to achieve.

Team working has benefits, however. It provides a structure and means of bringing together people with a suitable mix of skills and knowledge. This encourages the exchange of ideas, creativity, motivation and job satisfaction and can extend individual roles and learning. In turn, this can improve productivity, quality and customer focus. It can also encourage employees to be more flexible and can improve the ability of the organisation to respond to fast-changing environments. The benefits and difficulties of team working are summarised well by Mabey *et al.*:

> A team can … achieve what none of the individuals within it can do alone; with the right dynamic, a collection of ordinary individuals can achieve extraordinary feats. But the converse can also occur: a team can fail to achieve what any of its members could easily accomplish.

(Source: Mabey *et al.*, 1998)

The challenge of learning how to make teams work begins with understanding what teams and groups are.

Defining groups and teams

The terms 'group' and 'team' are often used interchangeably. Is there really a difference between the two terms and if so what is it? A starting point in exploring this difference is to say that *all teams are groups* but *not all groups are teams*. From this it follows that what is said about groups will apply to teams but that teams will have special characteristics of their own.

Kakabadse *et al.* (1988) suggest that groups may be *formal* or *informal, primary* or *secondary.*

Primary groups have regular and frequent interactions with each other in working towards some common interests or tasks. A small work group and a project team are primary groups. They usually have an important influence on their members' values, attitudes and beliefs.

Such groups can be *formal*, in that they were deliberately created to serve an organisation need, or *informal*, in that the group forms outside formal structures to meet the specific needs of individuals. Boddy (2005) argues that informal teams are a powerful feature of organisational life because they bring together people who have common interests and concerns and who exchange knowledge and information.

Secondary groups are those whose members interact less frequently. These are often larger than primary groups (an example is a large committee). Their members do not have the opportunity to get to know each other well and as a result they are usually less cohesive than primary groups.

When does a group become a team? The example in Box 8.1 illustrates the difference very simply.

Box 8.1 Group or team?

A number of people kicking a football about in the car park at lunch time is probably a group. There is little structure to what is happening; it is just a few people acting in whatever role they choose (or possibly several) because they want to get some exercise and/or they like spending time with their friends before going back to work.

However, taking this group and turning it into a football team would be a major task. Unlike the group, the team would have a clearly-stated task: for example, winning as many matches as possible. Ensuring that the team performed this task would involve choosing the right people according to their abilities and particular skills to perform clearly-defined roles. Team training would need to be available to help the individuals work better together. The performance expectations of individuals would be defined by the roles they held. For example, no-one expects, except in very unusual circumstances, that the goalkeeper will score goals or that the strikers will defend the goal. When a game is won the team is seen to have achieved the task, although individuals may still be singled out for praise, or for criticism, as appropriate.

A team, then, is a special type of group which 'unites the members towards mutually-held objectives' (Bennett, 1994).

Some differences between groups and teams are given in Table 8.1.

Table 8.1 Differences between groups and teams

	Groups	Teams
Leadership	Strong, focused leader	There may be some sharing of leadership
Accountability	Individual accountability	Both individual and mutual accountability
Purpose	Identical to the organisation's mission	Work towards a specific purpose
Work products	Individuals within the group deliver individual products	Collective work products
Communication	Efficient (time bound) meetings	Open-ended discussion and active problem-solving
Effectiveness	Indirectly through their influence on others	Direct assessment of the collective work products
Work style	Groups discuss, delegate and then do the work individually	Teams discuss, decide and delegate but do the work together

(Source: Weiss, 1996)

The distinctions in Table 8.1 may be overstated: for example, a group may have a specific purpose and a team's effectiveness may not necessarily be directly assessed in terms of the collective work product. However, a difficulty in distinguishing groups from teams is that many so-called teams are really working groups because the emphasis is on individual effort. A real team is a small number of people with complementary skills, equally committed to a common purpose to which they hold themselves mutually accountable (Katzenbach and Smith, 1993). People doing exactly the same job in a call centre answering customer enquiries, with the same individual targets and being overseen by the same supervisor or manager, may be called a team, but it is best described as a working group. There is overlap between teams and groups, of course. But distinctions are useful when considering whether to invest time and effort in building a team when a group will do. For a team to be effective there needs to be a clear, shared understanding of team objectives, mutual respect and trust and an appreciation of individual strengths and weaknesses. There also needs to be an atmosphere in which knowledge and expertise can be shared openly, with opportunities for each team member to make a distinctive contribution.

Is a team or group really needed?

There may be times when group working – or simply working alone – is more appropriate and more effective. For example, decision-making in groups and teams is usually slower than individual decision-making because of the need for communication and consensus. In addition, groups and teams may produce conventional rather than innovative responses to problems, because decisions may regress towards the average, with the more innovative decision options being rejected (Makin *et al.*, 1989).

In general, the greater the 'task uncertainty', that is to say the less obvious and more complex the task to be addressed, the more important it will be to work in a group or team rather than individually. This is because there will be a greater need for different skills and perspectives, especially if it is necessary to represent the different perspectives of the different stakeholders involved.

Table 8.2 lists some occasions when it will be appropriate to work in teams, in groups or alone.

Table 8.2 When to work alone, in groups or in teams

When to work alone or in groups	When to build teams
For simple tasks or problems	For highly-complex tasks or problems
When cooperation is sufficient	When decisions by consensus are essential
When minimum discretion is required	When there is a high level of choice and uncertainty
When fast decisions are needed	When high commitment is needed
When few competences are required	When a broad range of competences and different skills are required
When members' interests are different or in conflict	When members' objectives can be bought together towards a common purpose
When an organisation credits individuals for operational outputs	When an organisation rewards team results for strategy and vision building
When innovative responses are sought	When balanced views are sought

Types of team

If you have chosen to build a team to perform a task, the second question is: 'What type of team do I need?'. One way of approaching this is to consider the type of task to be performed and its level, from routine to strategic. These factors in turn influence several other key dimensions of teams identified by West (2004):

Degree of permanence. A team's lifetime can range from weeks to years depending on the task

Skill/competence required. This depends on what levels of skill are needed to perform the task

Autonomy and influence. This may depend on whether the task is routine or strategic and at what level in the organisation the team is formed.

Peckham (1996) suggests four possible types of problem relating to how well it is already known and understood and to what extent there is already a solution to this problem. These are set out in Figure 8.1. Four types of teams are identified to tackle these different problems: namely, problem-solving teams, creative teams, tactical teams and problem-finding teams.

	Known problem	**Unknown problem**
Unknown solution	Need: problem-solving team with autonomy	Need: creative team with freedom
Known solution	Need: tactical team with role clarity	Need: problem-finding team (analytical and creative)

Figure 8.1 Possible problem types

(Source: adapted from Peckham, 1996)

Thus, each type of team needs a different mix of individuals with specific skills and knowledge. The mix and balance of skills must be appropriate to the nature of the task.

How many people?

Does the task need a lot of people doing the same task (for example, a call centre) or a small, expert team addressing different parts of the task (for example, writing a textbook)? The size of the team needed will be an important consideration. The larger the team, the greater the potential variety of skills and knowledge, but as the size of the team increases each individual will have fewer opportunities to participate and influence proceedings. The size of a team is therefore a trade-off or balance between variety and individual input. A team of between five and seven people is considered best for the effective participation of all members, but to achieve the range of expertise and skills required, the group may need to be larger. This brings with it the challenges of how to manage and supervise a large team.

Homogeneous groups, whose members share similar values and beliefs, may be more satisfying to work in and may experience less conflict, but they tend to be less creative and produce greater pressures for conformity. In contrast, heterogeneous groups, whose members have a wider range of values and beliefs, are likely to experience greater conflict, but they have the potential for greater creativity and innovation.

This introduction has outlined differences between groups and teams but it has also highlighted the fact that *all teams are groups* but *not all groups are teams*. The remaining sections of this chapter sometimes relate specifically to teams and sometimes to groups and teams. Thus, we refer to all groups as *teams* rather than *groups and teams*.

Creating successful teams – a holistic view

Teams need to be seen in the wider context of the organisation. It is then easier for the manager to see what he or she needs to do to ensure that the team functions successfully, and what needs to be controlled, monitored and/ or influenced within and outside the team. At the same time, the manager needs to consider the team in terms of its task phases and processes, from start to finish. This allows the manager to put a particular team-related issue in context in order to understand it better. Looking forwards, the manager needs to consider the development of team members and the skills and competences that will be useful to take to the next team and task.

A manager's task is to understand, plan and monitor all these different processes. This seemingly complex and unwieldy task is easier to understand and manage when broken down into its component parts. The open systems model of team work (Schermerhorn *et al.,* 1995; Ingram *et al.*, 1997) can help to explain and characterise effective team-work processes.

The open systems approach to team working

Schermerhorn and colleagues suggest that teamwork can be considered as a three-stage sequence. Teams are viewed as systems which take in resources such as time, people, skills, problems (inputs) and through transformational processes (throughputs) such as decision-making and different behaviours and activities, transform them into outputs, such as work, solutions and satisfactions (Ingram *et al.*, 1997). This is illustrated in Figure 8.2.

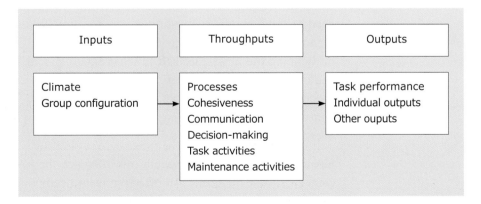

Figure 8.2 An open systems model of teamwork

(Source: adapted from Schermerhorn *et al.* (1995) in Ingram *et al.*, 1997)

Inputs are factors which are controlled and influenced by management. They include 'climate', the atmosphere under which the team works, and 'group configuration', how the team is put together, who is selected to work in it and why. Management will also influence how a team should work by making sure at the outset that the team strategy is in line with the vision and strategic direction of the organisation and that it uses the organisation's preferred work practices; for example, face-to-face or virtual working.

Throughputs refer to the activities and tasks that help to transform inputs into outputs. They may have the greatest influence on effective team work as they include team processes such as developing and maintaining cohesiveness, and communication. They also involve task activities which get the work done and maintenance activities which support the development and smooth functioning of the team.

Outputs are those (successful) outcomes which satisfy organisational or personal goals or other predetermined criteria. The success of outputs may be assessed by a number of stakeholders, including the organisation itself and team members, and by a range of other stakeholders. Team outputs include the performance of team tasks and individual outputs (such as professional development).

How can this framework be applied in a way which highlights how to manage or lead a team and its task? Imagine you have been asked to put together a team to produce the company's internal newsletter. What inputs, throughputs and outputs would you need? What questions would you need to ask yourself about different aspects of the process? We now consider what you might need to think about for the newsletter example. Some of the questions could be adapted and applied to other situations as well.

Inputs

Inputs are often controlled or influenced by management. This may be the direct manager of the group or team or the result of senior management decisions and strategies. This means in practice that the way a team is put together and will function is influenced by the organisation's values, vision and strategy, and its practices and procedures.

Two main factors to consider at this stage are communication climate and group configuration.

Communication climate. In the case of the company newsletter you may need to think about the existing communication culture within the organisation and how the newsletter can enhance it. Consider the reasons for introducing the newsletter and to what extent it is in line with organisational strategy and vision. You may also want to see what existing processes and procedures can be used, what barriers and resistance there may be and what you may need to do to influence and smooth the way so that these are overcome or worked around.

Group configuration. Managers can influence the team process by their choice of team members. An effective team needs to be appropriate to the task: this includes size and the blend of talent. In the case of the newsletter, you would need to think about the skills needed and the people available to work on it. It is also useful to consider whether the task could be used as a development opportunity for someone. If so, is there also a person available to monitor and support them?

Some input-related questions for you to consider at this stage are given in Box 8.2.

Box 8.2 Input-related questions

How much support is there for this newsletter among senior management?

Who might need to be influenced?

What objectives will it fulfil?

What resources will be provided for it? What others might be needed? Where could they come from?

How will individuals working on this be rewarded or recognised?

What might they learn? What skills could they hope to develop?

How many people will be needed to perform this task?

What technical skills are needed (e.g. desktop publishing)?

What training and development opportunities are available?

What roles are needed (e.g. a co-coordinator)?

Who might work well together?

Throughputs

Some common throughputs include:

See also: Managing team processes, in this chapter

Team processes. A sense of unity is created through sharing clear goals which are understood and accepted by the members.

Cohesiveness. This involves encouraging feelings of belonging, cooperation, openness and commitment to the team.

See also: The communication climate, Chapter 2

Communication. This involves being clear, accurate, open and honest.

Decision-making. This involves making sure that established procedures are in place, that everybody is clear about leadership and an environment of trust is being created.

Task and maintenance activities. These include activities that ensure that the task is produced effectively, such as planning, agreeing on procedures and controls. They also include activities that minimise threats to the process, such as monitoring and reviewing internal processes and dealing constructively with conflict.

In the case of the newsletter project, you may need to think about ways of setting up the project. Would it be possible to have a team awayday? If so, what would the themes of the day be? Perhaps you could work backwards from the finished product. How do team members envisage the newsletter in terms of aim, goals, content and look? Can they come up with an appropriate design and name for the newsletter? Then, what needs to be done in order for this to be produced? Some ground rules for working together may also need to be set at an early stage. Some throughput-related questions are set out in Box 8.3.

Box 8.3 Throughput-related questions

What can you do to build a sense of belonging among the team members?

How will the group communicate? (Face-to-face, email, group software?)

Do any ground rules need setting up? How can this be done?

What established procedures for decision-making are there?

Will there be a team leader? How will the person be chosen?

What tasks need to be performed to complete the project?

What maintenance behaviours does the group need to exhibit to get the job done and to benefit and develop from the experience?

Who will be responsible for ensuring that the different tasks and maintenance activities are performed?

Are there structures and systems in place to review processes?

Outputs

See also: Reviewing and evaluating team performance, in this chapter

Outcomes can be examined in terms of task performance, individual performance and other (incidental) outcomes.

Task performance. This may be judged on a number of criteria, such as quality of the formal outputs or objectives. In this case a product (the newsletter) and the time taken to perform the task are the criteria.

Individual outputs. These may include personal satisfaction and personal development and learning.

Other outcomes. These include transferable skills to apply in future to other teamwork. They include, for example, experience of effective teamwork and task-specific skills.

In general, it is always appropriate to evaluate outcomes. In this case you may need to think about:

Evaluating the newsletter itself. Was it well-received?

Evaluating individual outcomes. Have members developed transferable skills that they can take to new projects?

Evaluating other outcomes. Has the experience enhanced team members' ability to work in a team?

Some output-related questions are set out in Box 8.4.

Box 8.4 Output-related questions

Has the team completed the task it was given?

Has it kept to cost and to time?

What has the team learned from this experience?

Should the team now be broken up or could it go on to another activity?

What have individuals learned from the experience?

Have members experienced an effective team?

Have any learning and development needs been identified? How can they be addressed?

Have members developed transferable teamworking and other skills?

Where can these skills be used in the organisation?

The open systems model of teamwork shows us how effective teamwork can offer benefits to organisations and staff. However, it also shows us that these benefits do not occur without effort and planning. Managers need to ensure that the right team is put together to perform a given task and that it is given appropriate tasks. They also need to secure the freedom, resources and support for the team to undertake the task. The model alerts managers to both the micro and the macro issues they will need to be aware of in managing effective teams.

Other sections of this chapter cover in more detail particular aspects of inputs, throughputs and outputs. *Team roles* deals with putting a team together, an input issue; *Managing team processes* mainly deals with throughputs and *Reviewing and evaluating team performance* deals with output issues as well as ongoing review of a team as it carries out its task.

Team roles

Glenda's troublesome team

Glenda recalled looking around the meeting room with satisfaction on the first day that her team met, feeling pleased that team members, between them, had the appropriate skills for the task. Three months later, however, Matt who had been chosen for his expert knowledge, never seemed to be able to see the 'bigger picture' – the entire task in context. As a result he occupied himself with detail and technicalities, and missed seeing important implications. Rob and Sara were quite the reverse but were argumentative. Jenny seemed uncommitted and Steve seemed to have lost all his initial enthusiasm. Glenda's initial hopes of delivering high-quality results had turned to worries about whether the task could be done to an acceptable standard.

A team is more than a set of individuals with the appropriate skills. People bring to the team not only their knowledge and skills but also their personal attributes and the ways in which they behave, contribute and relate to others. A popular idea is that these individual characteristics should be taken account of in constructing teams. While we may not be in a position to select team members, according to Meredith Belbin we need to consider these behaviours when selecting a team. A person who is known to be confident and enthusiastic is likely to behave in the same way when he or she joins a team. If all team members behave in the same way, then not only is conflict likely but the quality of the task is likely to suffer.

By ensuring a balance of behaviours or 'roles' there is a greater likelihood that the team will perform well. Belbin's research (1981) (developed and slightly amended over the years) identifies nine clusters of behaviours, or roles. He suggests that individuals will be more effective if they are allowed to play the roles they are most skilled in or most inclined to play, although they can adopt roles other than their preferred ones, if necessary.

Each role has both positive and negative aspects. The nine roles are:

1 The implementer, who turns ideas into practical actions. Implementers may be inflexible, however, and may have difficulty in changing their well-thought-through plans.

2 The co-coordinator, who clarifies goals and promotes decision-making. Coordinators often chair a team. They can sometimes be manipulative and delegate too much work to others.

3 The shaper, who has the drive and courage to overcome obstacles, and 'shapes' others to meet the team's objectives. Shapers may challenge others and may be aggressive at times.

4 The plant, who solves difficult problems. Often creative and unorthodox, a plant will come up with ideas but may have difficulties communicating them.

5 The resource investigator, who explores opportunities and develops contacts. However, initial enthusiasm may not be maintained to the end of the project, and detail may be overlooked.

6 The monitor evaluator, who observes and assesses what is going on and seeks all options. Often working slowly and analytically, monitor evaluators come to the 'right' decisions but can be cynical and dampen the enthusiasm of others.

7 The teamworker, who listens, builds relationships and tries to avoid or reduce conflict between team members. Considered to be the 'oil' that keeps the team running smoothly, teamworkers are good listeners and diplomats. They can smooth conflicts but may not be able to take decisive action when necessary.

8 The completer finisher, who searches out errors and omissions and finishes on time. Often perfectionists, completer finishers are self-motivated and have high standards. They can worry about detail and can be reluctant or refuse to delegate work.

9 The specialist, who provides knowledge and skill. Specialists can be passionate about gaining knowledge in their field. However, their contribution to the team may be narrow and they may not be interested in matters outside their own field.

The weaknesses of Belbin's framework are that people's behaviour and interpersonal styles are influenced by context: that is, the other people in the team, the relationship with them and by the task to be performed. Moreover, research into the validity of Belbin's nine roles has shown that some are not easily distinguishable from one another and that the roles fit more easily into the more conventional framework of personality traits (Fisher *et al.*, 2001).

However, Belbin's framework has been very influential on organisational and managerial thinking about team building and development (although it is not the only one). Such frameworks are helpful in guiding the composition of a balanced team. When, as a manager, you have no control over the composition of a team it is important to discuss with team members their strengths and weaknesses and preferred working styles.

The life cycle of a team

Managing a team means managing it through the ups and downs of the team process from beginning to end. The idea of different 'stages' of team development is useful in understanding what the team needs and how best to provide support. The stages of team development were most famously described by Tuckman and Jensen in 1977. They are:

1 'Forming': the pre-team stage where people are still working as individuals.

2 'Storming': the stage of conflict that many teams need to go through to achieve their potential. During this stage the team becomes more aggressive and challenges previously agreed or taken-for-granted rules and restrictions.

3 'Norming': the consolidating phase in which the team works out how to use the resources they have to apply to the task.

4 'Performing': the optimal stage in which the team works well and strives to be even better by concentrating on the development of the team, individuals and the task in hand.

5 'Adjourning' (sometimes also referred to as 'mourning'): the stage when the team disbands and individuals move on to other responsibilities.

Your role as a manager in supporting and encouraging the team through each of these stages is set out in Box 8.5.

Box 8.5 Team stages: the manager's role

Forming

Your focus is to help the team members to get to know each other and put everyone at ease. Minimise fears, confusions and uncertainties by clarifying the goals, roles, responsibilities and relevant procedures. Discuss concerns and expectations: team members who have worked in teams before may bring specific expectations, worries or prejudices.

Storming

Listen to problems, provide feedback which acknowledges all points of view, and encourage the team to work towards shared goals. Attempts to suppress conflict are likely to disrupt team processes. The storming phase is really an opportunity to resolve conflicts and, if carefully managed, can help the team become more cohesive.

Norming

Ensure that rules and norms are arrived at by consensus and that they help the team's effectiveness. Time given to the creation of new rules by which the team wants to operate will make later stages more efficient. Facilitate team cohesion and ensure that each team member identifies with the team's purpose and values.

Performing

Evaluate team effectiveness by looking at individual and team efforts, satisfactions and successes. The team will be concerned with productivity, efficiency and potential. Praise the team for its successes. It is preferable to reward the team rather than individual team members in order to promote harmony and cohesion. Rewarding individuals can lead to competitiveness and hostility.

Adjourning (or mourning)

Provide feedback on how well the team has done, what team members have learned and how they are likely to cope with new challenges. If it is appropriate, encourage team members to maintain links with each other and develop their relations through new activities and projects.

Tuckman and Jensen's team stages are not always so clearly defined. For example, if new members join during the project, the team may need to return, at least in part, to the forming stage while performing at the same time. A variety of other changes may cause storming in well-established teams. However, the idea of team stages can be useful in anticipating what kind of support a team may need at a particular time.

Managing team processes

What steps do managers need to take to ensure that their teams are working effectively on a day-to-day basis? We set out the most important ones below.

Team goals and objectives

A team needs clear goals that members believe are important and worthwhile. A team is more likely to be effective if it can participate in developing team objectives and work out how they are to be achieved, even if the team's overall goal has been imposed from above. Discussions should lead to action planning, including specific milestones, timetables and monitoring activities to keep the team focused and to create an appropriate sense of urgency. Defining a measurable output gives the team a framework to work within.

Ground rules

The team needs to establish a mutually-agreed working approach. The means of participation and expectations of the team experience should be agreed on. Discussions will inevitably consider the norms and values held by the team and what rules are needed to preserve these.

Team members will also need to discuss process issues, such as how the group evaluates and self-regulates itself (that is, how any performance issues will be addressed) and how conflicts are managed.

Allocating tasks

The allocation of tasks, responsibilities and priorities of individual team members is usually done, at least partly, through joint discussion and negotiations in the team. If the team has a manager, it will be the manager's responsibility to see that this is done effectively. Usually the process will be supported and strengthened by regular supervision and appraisal. Key questions for the manager to ask are:

1   Has work been fairly distributed between team members?

2   Have roles and responsibilities of team members been decided?

3   Has each individual member taken personal responsibility for at least some aspect of the team task?

(Source: adapted from West, 2004)

Developing individual contributions

Based on their prior experience, team members will bring assumptions and ideas about how teams should operate, what is expected of them and what they can expect from the team-working experience. These assumptions, ideas and expectations may not be appropriate to the current situation. Conversations are essential to bring to the surface any possible tensions. Questions for the manager to address here include:

See also: Team roles, in? this chapter

1   How well do the tasks allocated fit with the person's preferred 'role(s)'?

2   Who has the skills and experience to handle a particular task competently and efficiently?

3   Who will find the task useful for their development?

4   What further training, development or support might an individual need?

Task and maintenance activities

One way of monitoring the successful functioning of teams is to look at two different types of behaviours. Task behaviours are those that aim to achieve the project or overall tasks set. Maintenance behaviours are those that keep the team running smoothly. It is important that both types of behaviours are present. Some examples are shown in Table 8.3.

Table 8.3 Task- and maintenance-oriented behaviours

Task	Maintenance
Proposing Proposing ideas or courses of action that help the achievement of the task	*Gatekeeping* Making a positive attempt to bring a person into the discussion or making an equally clear attempt to prevent a person from being excluded
Building Adding to other people's proposals	*Encouraging* Behaving or responding in a warm and friendly way
Disagreeing Contesting proposals that seem to be misconceived and might work against the achievement of the task	*Resolving conflict* Being ready to compromise and accept what others want to do
Giving and seeking information Providing data and opinions relevant to the task achievement	*Giving feedback* Giving positive feedback on feelings and opinions
Summarising Summarising a discussion or the group's progress	*Recognising feelings* In general, recognising that people have personal feelings about their work

Finding a balance between the two types of behaviours can be difficult. Managers may need to work hard to control the emergence of individuals' personal interests, motivations and agendas which can be detrimental to team working. Trust between team members can help individuals to suppress their personal interests for the good of team development and performance.

Developing trust

A reasonable degree of trust is an essential ingredient of any successful relationship. Without trust, communication will deteriorate because people will begin to hide their views or try to impose them.

Each member of a team must take some responsibility for the development of trust, although team leaders and managers have the greatest responsibility and the greatest influence. Trust is likely to develop when people listen to and respect each other's views, irrespective of whether or not they agree with them. Then they are able to share their ideas and views without fear of recrimination.

A team manager can help to ensure the development of trust by involving team members in setting team and individual goals and by giving the team members the necessary autonomy to carry out their tasks without undue interference. Managers should take care, however, that delegating

See also: Reviewing and
evaluating team
performance, in this
chapter

See also: Managing
conflict, in this chapter

responsibility to team members does not result in *abdicating* responsibility –
that is, ceasing to monitor the performance of team members. A team must
also have ways of monitoring and giving feedback on the performance of its
members. Any effective team will need to conduct regular reviews.

The higher the level of trust a group has, the easier it will be to deal with
conflict when it (almost inevitably) occurs.

Arriving at consensus in a team

Conflict is perhaps most likely to arise in team work during decision-
making. You can help to avoid unnecessary conflict by ensuring that
individuals see and understand the logic of what you are proposing, by
exploring and discussing the proposals and by making sure there is
agreement before proposals are finalised. Some guidelines are:

1 Present a position logically, pointing out strengths and weaknesses and
   illustrating with examples.

2 Try to avoid using your extra power as team leader or manager.

3 Demonstrate the benefits as well as any disadvantages of the proposal.

4 Avoid changing your mind or agreeing with something because this is
   easier than promoting or defining what you regard as a good proposal.

5 Remember that consideration of a variety of ideas and opinions is likely
   to be constructive.

See also: Making
decisions, Chapter 3

6 Make sure that everybody has access to all the information needed to
   reach considered opinions.

Sometimes during the life of a team, conflict can run so high that
communication is impaired and intervention may be necessary. At such
times, the team will need to examine its own progress. Here, the manager
or leader will need to:

- ensure that behaviour between members is appropriate

- reinforce and support desirable behaviour

- be prepared to raise the issue of inappropriate behaviour

- create a sense of fairness by empowering or sharing power across
  team members

- make sure the team goals are shared.

(Source: adapted from Hill and Farkas, 2001)

Some tips on leading and managing teams

Team leaders and managers need to make sure the task is done and that the
team develops in ways that benefit both the task and the experience of
individual team members. Figure 8.3 illustrates how the task, the team and
the individual are always linked. For example, team members' satisfaction
will be derived not only from the achievement of tasks but also from the
quality of team relationships, team morale, trust and team spirit, and the
more social aspects of teamwork.

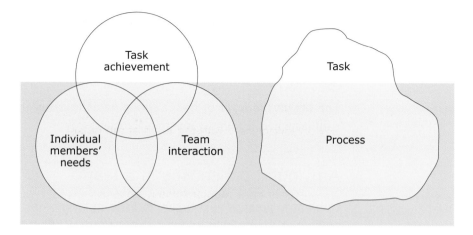

Figure 8.3 The internal elements of team effectiveness

(Source: Adair, 1983)

Different leaders will inevitably have different styles and approaches to leadership. Some leaders may tend towards a more directive style, wanting to tell team members what to do. The danger here is alienating the team and not allowing room for creativity and spontaneity. The challenge for a leader who adopts this style will be to try to involve team members more and to seek their opinions. Other leaders may adopt a democratic approach, asking questions and getting people involved. The danger here is that debate drifts too much and no clear direction emerges. The challenge is to develop structure. Leaders may also differ in their degree of involvement in the task. However, successful and effective team leaders have some common characteristics. These include:

- listening to team members
- questioning them to understand their point of view
- being responsive to feedback.

Similarly, there are reasons why team leaders fail (Hackman, 1990, 2002). These are set out as reason and remedies in Box 8.6 with additional contributions by West (2004). Because of the overlap between leadership and management, some remedies cover management issues.

Box 8.6 Why team leaders fail: reasons and remedies

Reason: Calling the performing unit a team, but really managing them as individuals.

Remedy

- Assign individual responsibilities but coordinate them so that the efforts of individuals combine to form the whole-team product
- Alternatively, assign a team task and give members responsibility for determining how that task should be completed.

Reason: Exercising too little or too much authority: a typical mistake is giving a team too much autonomy early in its life when direction is needed and then intervening too heavily later when the team is not performing well.

Remedy

- Work closely with the team at the outset
- Draw up ground rules, including the amount and timing of management intervention
- Agree on a regular review process.

Reason: Assembling a large group in which structures and responsibilities are not clear.

Remedy

- Make sure that a well-designed team task is in place, that the team is balanced and suitable for the task and that members have clear and unambiguous information about the extent and limits of their authority and accountability. Team members will then not do things that are not required or make decisions that are not appropriate for them to make.

Reason: Specifying challenging team objectives but providing too little organisational support.

Remedy

- Ensure that resources and support are available
- Hold regular team reviews
- Ensure provision of individual training and development.

Reason: Assuming incorrectly that members already have the skills to work well as a team.

Remedy

- Conduct a team skills audit early in the team process: this can be a simple identification and review of members' skills
- Address any training and development needs that emerge from this
- Encourage open discussion about individual strengths and weaknesses and team roles.

(Source: adapted from Hackman, 1990, 2002 and West, 2004)

A checklist

A useful checklist for team leaders and managers is set out in Table 8.4.

Table 8.4 A checklist for team leaders and managers

Action	Purpose
Create conditions for team effectiveness	The team has a clear mandate or purpose
	The team structures itself to do the work efficiently
Agree goals	Performance expectations and objectives/outputs are clear
Facilitate communication	Participation is monitored; those who are not participating are encouraged to do so
	Different conversational and participation styles are encouraged
	There is active listening (the focus is on what is meant rather than how it is said)
	Influence is based on task-relevant knowledge and skills rather than external status and personal dominance
Adopt a rigorous decision-making process	Sufficient time is spent identifying and framing the problem, task or project
	Information and alternative solutions or methods are thoroughly examined
	Team members are aware of and happy with the decision-making process used
Develop appropriate working methods	Constructive task conflict is encouraged and supported
	Collaboration is encouraged
	The team is a 'safe' place to share information and ideas
	Reflection on team process is encouraged
	Mistakes are a source of learning
Be sensitive to team diversity	Team members make an effort to understand and adapt to each other's working styles
	Team members understand how demographic differences such as culture and age might influence participation and influence
	The team has processes for utilising diversity
Manage context	There is action to remove external barriers to the team's effectiveness
	There is action to provide the resources the team needs and to promote the team's interests with key stakeholders.

(Source: adapted from Hill and Farkas, 2001)

Managing conflict

Conflict will occur almost inevitably in groups and teams – and between individuals who do not necessarily work together in a group or team. Conflict can arise through:

1 Misunderstandings between individuals; these often arise by accident.

2 Differences in beliefs and values; these may be personal beliefs or values, or may arise from structural divisions in the organisation, for example, production and marketing.

3 Differences of interest and ambition; such differences can result in competition for power, status and resources.

4 Interpersonal differences: people have different personalities and temperaments.

5 Feeling and emotions: people may have strong feelings and emotions but disguise them in work settings by talking about 'the principle of the matter'. Conflict itself can arouse emotion, leading to further conflict.

Not all conflict is destructive, however. Some conflicts are best discussed openly: managed constructively, such discussions can lead to deeper understanding and better decisions. The problem is that conflict tends to be seen in terms of win–lose – that is, one argument will win and the other will lose. But it is possible to reach an outcome in which elements of both arguments are accepted – a win–win situation. Negotiations over pay are a simple example: employers may agree to pay employees more in exchange for changes in working practices. For win–win outcomes, however, there need to be mechanisms for open discussion and fair decision-making. The likelihood of resolving conflict depends on the behaviour of those involved. To understand this better, it can be helpful to classify people's responses to interpersonal conflict in five categories (Figure 8.4). These categories reflect the balance between cooperation (attempts to satisfy the other person's concerns) and assertiveness (attempts to satisfy your own concerns).

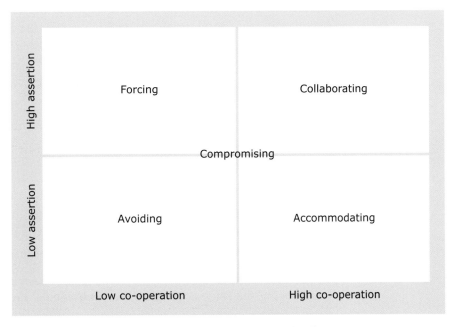

Figure 8.4 A two-dimensional model of conflict behaviour

(Source: based on Ruble and Thomas, 1976, and Whetten and Cameron, 1984)

Forcing represents the wish to satisfy one's own needs at the expense of others' needs. It may involve the use of formal authority, physical threats, majority rule, or disregarding the claims of the other person. This form of conflict management usually results in hostility and resentment and is an extreme example of a win–lose strategy. Nevertheless, sometimes it is necessary – in matters of health and safety, for example, or at times of crisis.

In contrast, accommodating satisfies the needs of the other person at the expense of one's own needs, often to maintain friendly relations. It may work when the quality of the relationship is more important than other considerations. However, it can lead to difficulties: discipline is seen to be negligible, decision-making becomes difficult and you lose respect and self-esteem – a win–lose situation.

Avoiding potential conflict is a common response to confrontation, particularly if a manager lacks self-confidence. It is the classic lose–lose situation, creating frustration and tension because issues are never resolved. Its use is normally justified only when an issue is unimportant or when time is limited.

Compromising seeks to obtain partial satisfaction for both parties. It is the preferred strategy of many managers since it avoids some of the adverse consequences of other behaviours. It is particularly useful in complex situations and where there is time for negotiation and discussion.

The only truly win–win strategy is collaborating, seeking to find solutions that are understood and appreciated by all parties. The focus is on the problem, not on personalities, blame or fault. It requires you to be both assertive and cooperative, and works when there is time to establish a collaborative environment.

Ways to deal with conflict

Once you have identified a disagreement and understood why it has arisen, you then have to decide what to do about it. You will need to consider a number of factors, including the seriousness of the conflict, the timescale (whether it needs to be resolved quickly or not), the ideal or preferred outcome, and your own power and preferences, strengths and weaknesses. If the conflict is relatively trivial or is a 'healthy' disagreement, you may decide that it is better to let it run its course. However, if there is a danger of the conflict escalating and becoming destructive, you will want to act. You have three choices: to ignore it, to prevent it occurring, or to resolve it.

Non-intervention. This is quite common and can be successful. However, there is always the risk that the conflict will become destructive; failure to intervene may make the situation worse.

Prevention. Your chances of preventing conflict will increase if you create a climate in which people seek win–win solutions. You can contribute to this by:

- establishing common goals: identify higher-level goals on which all people can agree
- changing the roles or groupings of individuals: this can remove sources of conflict
- improving communications by encouraging an atmosphere of debate and questioning.

Resolution. When conflict is not constructive you may have to intervene to find a solution by:

- facilitating: this will usually involve allowing individuals to explain their feelings and encouraging them to put their conflict in perspective

- imposition: people can sometimes be forced to behave differently through a threat of disciplinary action; however, this may not resolve the cause of the conflict and may cause further problems in the future

- negotiation: this involves bringing people together to seek and agree a solution; it is likely to require concessions from both sides, and may benefit from creative approaches to find a solution to the problem.

These different approaches to resolving conflict are illustrated in the example in Box 8.7.

Box 8.7 Managing conflict

Johanna groaned as she read the memo from the HR Director saying that all staff would be required to keep worksheets for activity costing. She had expected this, but she knew it would cause massive opposition from staff. After some thought, she asked Barbara, her secretary, to visit staff members to ask them approximately how much time they expected to spend on each project. Barbara would complete and send the worksheets. This way Johanna would avoid conflict with her staff, while still providing the information needed.

Just as Johanna finished reading the memo, the fire alarm went off. Two hours later, after the fire brigade had left, she was looking at the kettle with its burnt cord – no major damage had been caused, but it had seriously disrupted work. After lunch she wrote a memo to all staff in the building: no personal electrical appliances would be permitted. There were perfectly adequate kitchens on each floor, and the safety risk was too great. She was therefore content to impose a solution.

She then went to talk to Monica and Andrew, both members of the same project team who were complaining angrily about one another. Andrew, recruited for his technical knowledge, had told Johanna earlier in the day that he could not work with Monica because she had too little experience and she seemed unwilling to take his views seriously. Monica had complained about Andrew's disruptive behaviour and lack of technical knowledge. Johanna suggested to her that if she were to be successful in the organisation she needed to develop the ability to work with people like Andrew. He had experience that she lacked, and his skills would be needed to implement the project. Johanna suggested that Monica gave weight to Andrew's views in team meetings, and gave him clear accountability for parts of the project. Later, she told Andrew that his experience was vital to the success of the project, and that he should see part of his role as guiding and developing team members such as Monica. Johanna would talk to Monica and Andrew again in a week. It was important that these two learned how to work with each other, so she would take the time to facilitate this.

Reviewing and evaluating team performance

Evaluating team performance is an important element of team working. It can take a number of forms, such as: reporting on progress informally at weekly team meetings, group reviews at key stages along the way, and full and formal external evaluation once the project is completed. Encouraging the team to take responsibility for this evaluation process makes it much more a part of everyday work and less of a management control exercise. Managers and teams need to agree what needs to be reviewed and evaluated, how it is to be done and how it can help the team to be more successful.

Here we present a number of approaches for reviewing team progress and processes and for evaluating team effectiveness at the end of a team task or project. We suggest you use whatever seems most suitable for your purposes.

Adair's model of team work (1983) is useful as a framework for reviewing and evaluating because it highlights the interdependency between the task, the team and the individual in achieving team effectiveness. Questions to consider are:

The task

- Are there enough resources and internal and external support (external climate)?
- Is the task fully understood? Has it been broken down sufficiently into component parts?

The team

- Are there the right constituent parts to achieve the current task?
- Has the group formed well?
- Are team members communicating well and reviewing their progress regularly?

The individual

- Are individuals learning from the experience?
- How are they dealing with their expectations, hopes and fears of this team-work experience?
- Are there issues from previous group-work experiences that need addressing?
- Do they have enough support and development opportunities to perform and develop their roles?
- Are they aware of the consequences of their individual actions in working with or against team processes?

West (2004) proposes that there are two fundamental dimensions of team functioning: the *task* the team is required to carry out and the *social factors* that influence how members experience the team as a social unit. He suggests that for both of these to work effectively teams need to:

- review objectives and find ways of achieving them
- reflect on the ways in which the team provides support to members, how conflicts are resolved and what the social climate of the team is like.

West has developed a questionnaire, set out in Box 8.8, to measure how well these two factors are working. He suggests it is completed individually without consultation. It could then be used as a means of identifying and agreeing problematic areas to work on.

Box 8.8 Team function questionnaire

Rate on a scale of 1 (very inaccurate) to 7 (very accurate) how each statement describes the situation in your team. Add up the scores for the task dimension and the social dimension separately. If more than one person completes the questionnaire, divide the total *for each dimension* by the number of people who complete the questionnaire to calculate an average for each dimension. Compare the average score for each dimension with the values shown at the end of the questionnaire. The questionnaire can also be used to compare different teams.

Task dimension

We review our objectives

We regularly discuss whether the team is working effectively together

The methods we use to get the job done are often discussed

In the team we modify our objectives in light of changing circumstances

We often change our team strategies

How well we communicate information is often discussed

We often review our approach to getting the job done

We often review the way decisions are made in the team

Social dimension

We support each other when times are difficult

When things at work are stressful the team is very supportive

Conflict doesn't last long in this team

We often teach each other new skills

When the pressure is on, we 'pull together' as a team

Team members are always friendly

Conflicts are dealt with constructively

People in the team are quick to resolve arguments

High 42–56

Average 34–41

Low 0–33

(Source: adapted from West, 2004)

Observing group processes

Another method for reviewing and evaluating team processes is through observation. A method suggested by Boddy (2005) is that one team member observes the team for an hour and keeps a careful record of what members say or do. They also note how other members react and how that affects the performance of the team. Suggestions on what to observe are listed in Box 8.9.

Box 8.9 Reflecting on group interaction – some questions to consider

Who spoke?

How?

How were the roles allocated?

How were decisions reached?

What stated or unstated rules were being used?

What was the climate (or atmosphere) in the group like?

How did you personally feel during the activity?

(Source: adapted from Boddy, 2005)

An observer who may or may not be the team leader or manager could look out for unhelpful personal behaviours. Sometimes it is difficult to see whether a particular action is a maintenance-oriented or a self-oriented behaviour: that is, whether it is intended to maintain harmony in the group or to satisfy personal needs. Some examples of self-oriented behaviours, as described by Kakabadse et al. (1988), are given in Table 8.5.

Table 8.5 Self-oriented behaviours

Attacking/defending	Attacking or rejecting others' positions or defensively strengthening one's own position
Blocking/stating difficulties	Placing blocks or difficulties in the path of others' proposals or ideas without offering an alternative proposal or giving a reasoned argument
Diverting	Moving the discussion away from areas in which you feel your position is threatened or weak
Seeking sympathy/recognition	Attempting to make others sorry for you, and therefore willing to support you, or actively attempting to gain positive feedback on the value of your contribution to the group process
Withdrawing	Refusing to make a contribution
Point scoring	Winning petty triumphs over other members to enhance your status

Table 8.5 continued

Overcontributing	Monopolising discussion in the group; using the group process to satisfy individual power and control needs
Trivialising/diluting	Picking on minor faults in others' proposals or contributions in order to undermine their position.

(Source: Kakabadse *et al.*, 1988)

Identifying and discussing such behaviours (and providing evidence to support your claims) can be constructive. The questions set out in Box 8.10 relating to how comfortable individuals feel in the team could be incorporated into such a discussion.

Box 8.10 Satisfaction with team social processes

Does the team provide adequate levels of social support for its members?

Does the team have constructive and healthy approaches to conflict resolution?

Does the team have a generally warm and positive social climate?

Does the team provide adequate support for skill development, training and the personal development of all its members?

(Source: West, 2004)

End of project evaluation

Bateman *et al.* (2002) suggest six areas for the investigation of team effectiveness, which can be evaluated on an ongoing basis, retrospectively at the end of a project or at a specific stage in the group-working process. These are:

Team synergy. There is a shared sense of purpose and identity.

Performance objectives. There are clear performance objectives in terms of budgets, activity or throughput levels, which are monitored.

Skills. Team members are adequately trained and are competent to do their work. They are also flexible.

Use of resources. All resources including people, buildings and equipment are used effectively and to their full potential.

Innovation. The team constantly looks for ways to improve products and systems of work.

Quality. There is a high level of customer awareness; standards are identified and monitored.

Statements relating to these six areas of investigation are shown in Table 8.6. They can be used for group review discussions and as a means of identifying problematic areas for further investigation.

Table 8.6 Shared purpose and identity

Statement	Yes/no
There was a common sense of purpose	
Members were clear about their roles	
There was effective communication	
Individuals felt valued as members of the team	
Individuals felt proud to be a member of the team	
Morale within the team was high	
There was effective and appropriate leadership	
All the individuals performed to the best of their abilities	
There was a willingness to be flexible and perform other roles and jobs	
Members of the team felt that they were fully utilised	
The team had the resources it needed to do the job	
Team members were encouraged to be innovative	
Problems were quickly identified	
The team was quick to address the problem once identified	
Problem solving was seen as an opportunity for learning and growth	

(Source: adapted from Bateman *et al.*, 2002)

Team reward

Team evaluation, both internal and external, can be used as evidence that a good job is being done. Rewarding team effort is not always easy, however. Traditional appraisal systems focus on individual performances, so in some appraisal processes there is a danger that insufficient importance is given to contributions to teamwork. Nonetheless team leaders and managers can take time at the end of a task or project to celebrate the success of the team.

The benefits

Evaluation and review provide a means of identifying and dealing with task and team issues in a timely way. They allow team members to demonstrate progress as well as to voice any concerns. Post-task evaluation is a means of disseminating project achievements to colleagues and stakeholders. It is also a way of focusing on lessons learned which need to be carried forward to future projects and also to identify any training and development necessary. Team evaluation and review need to be approached with care, however. The more the team itself can have ownership of this process, the less threatening it will be and the more it will just seem part of everyday group processes.

Modern forms of groups and teams

Working at a physical distance from colleagues, managers, partners and clients is becoming a feature of the way we work. More and more members of teams are not physically located in the same workplace. Such teams are often referred to as 'virtual teams'. The reasons for this change in working practices include:

- organisation-wide initiatives that reach across national boundaries
- changes to organisational structures due to mergers, acquisitions and/or downsizing
- entering new markets
- offering possibilities for homeworking
- the need to reduce costs
- reducing the time taken for a product or service to reach its intended market.

In such situations, co-location of team members in the same workplace may not be possible, and it may not be possible for team members to travel regularly to meet face to face.

What is a virtual team?

A virtual team is one whose primary means of communicating is electronic, with only occasional phone and face-to-face communication, if at all. However, there is no single point at which a team 'becomes' a virtual team (Zigurs, 2003). Virtual working offers benefits to both organisations and individuals. Benefits to the organisation include:

- people can be hired with the skills and competences needed regardless of location
- in some cases working across different time zones can extend the working day
- it can enable products to be developed more quickly
- expenses associated with travel and relocation can be cut
- carbon emissions can be reduced.

Benefits to the individual include:

- people can work from anywhere at any time
- physical location is not a recruitment issue
- travelling expenses and commuting time are cut
- relocating is unnecessary.

Managing and facilitating virtual team processes – guidelines for managers

See also: Communication and new technology, Chapter 2

Challenges for virtual groups include communicating effectively across distance, which may involve learning how to make full use of all of the communication technologies available to the group in question.

A typical mistake when moving to virtual working is to believe that only small adjustments to established working practices will be required. This may result in managers failing to think through and plan for working virtually; this can result in reduced performance and heightened stress among team members. Successful virtual working means analysing and agreeing on communication practices, using the communication technologies available and building trust in the virtual team. Although dependent on technology, virtual teams are more likely to fail through lack of the development of 'soft skills' (that is, the social processes).

Guidelines for managers in helping teams through virtual team-working processes are set out below.

Trust

As with conventional teams, the building and maintenance of trust between members is vital.

Ways to facilitate the building up of trust include:

- initial face-to-face start ups (with team-building activities)
- periodic face-to-face meetings
- visits to each other's workplaces
- establishing clear codes of conduct and ground rules
- recognising and publicly rewarding performance
- taking care with the tone and language used in emails to reduce the risk of being misunderstood
- ensuring that team roles are made clear to everybody
- discussing and clarifying team goals
- making use of conference calls for in-depth discussions.

Accountability

Associated with trust is the accountability of individual team members. This needs to be based on agreed measurable outputs not on 'presentism' – that is, joining in communication without making any significant contribution.

Team building

Virtual teams need a clear and distinct team identity. When an organisation creates a face-to-face group, the organisation's day-to-day processes give it identity; for example, the room bookings system says 'Supplier Payments IT Team 14.00 – 16.00'. The meeting's agenda includes items such as 'Report from the Supplier Payments IT Team'. Members of the Supplier Payments IT Team also identify with the team; they see themselves as part of the team.

The external identity of virtual teams is often less visible than in the above example, and there may be less opportunity for virtual teams to build their own identity. Ideas for helping a team build an identity include:

- using visual material and photographs in communications
- having a message board and photos of team members with some biographical background
- designing a team logo
- celebrating successes with the whole team
- sending out news items on matters of interest for the whole team
- having a team blog.

Multicultural groups and teams

When groups or teams comprise people from just one culture, there are often agreed but unspoken social, organisational and national ways of behaving that do not need to be explained. It can usually be assumed that everyone has a common understanding of what a group is, how it will work, and how leaders and followers will behave. But such assumptions do not hold true when people are from different cultures.

In France, the common assumption is that the authority to make decisions comes as a right of office or rank, while managers in the Netherlands, Scandinavia and the UK often make their decisions in consultation with others and may be prepared to be challenged.

When creating multicultural groups or teams, managers need to consider the following points:

1 While professional skills are important, you may want evidence of a person's ability to work with others

2 Provide the team with initial support – for example, bring the whole team together for two days with the specific aim of:

- providing them with an awareness of cultural differences and their impact on organisational style and systems, management style, decision-making and interpersonal behaviour
- helping them become aware of their different roles, preferences and strengths and how these can complement each other
- building an international micro culture through exploring culture and cultural differences
- identifying methods of communicating swiftly and effectively
- developing a set of ground rules for maintaining group effectiveness when working together and when working apart.

Realistic ground rules for such a team might include:

- do not make assumptions; if you do, check them
- do not be impatient
- allow time to express yourself
- have the courage to challenge
- learn more of the others' cultures
- give and ask for feedback

- try to eliminate stereotyping
- take a positive attitude
- accept the differences.

(Source: based on Neale and Mindel, 1992)

Virtual and multicultural groups and teams present challenges not only because their creation and management are more demanding but often because organisations and managers have no prior experience to draw on. There will be no substitute for seeking information, clear thinking and good planning if such initiatives are to be successful.

Chapter 9 Recruiting and selecting staff

The importance of managing recruitment and selection well

People are a valuable resource for most organisations and good people can provide a competitive advantage. It is therefore important that this resource is managed well. In small organisations the managers manage people, possibly with the help of advisers from outside the organisation when an issue seems complicated. When an organisation has 100 staff or more, strategic managers have the option of adding people management specialists to the workforce. These specialists, whose job titles will include Personnel, or Human Resources (HR), are there to help managers take better decisions about the management of their staff. Some managers are very positive about the help that HR specialists can give, while others are less so. The creation of an HR unit in an organisation can result in people management decisions being taken away from managers. This can be so in recruitment and selection.

Bad recruitment and selection decisions are likely to be costly. If a person is unable to carry out the job they were chosen for there will be costs of various kinds for the organisation and the individual. For the person recruited the impact will be:

- negative feelings about their new job (and probably the organisation)
- the need to find a more suitable job
- possible loss of their new job
- loss of their previous job
- possible costs to the person's family – moving house, moving school, leaving friends.

For the organisation the costs will be:

- cost of additional training
- time and cost of managing the performance of the individual
- time and expense of recruiting again
- managing the ill-feeling of other employees who feel the wrong person was chosen.

See also: The problem with problem-solving and decision-making, Chapter 3

This suggests that all recruitment and selection decisions should be systematic and rational, and be the best possible ones we can make. As managers, we can see that this is likely to be so only sometimes: at other times we will take a satisficing approach if the situation calls for it. Our decisions will be contingent on the situation: where a job is simple, not client-facing and is likely to last only two weeks we might be willing to choose someone after five minutes' discussion. If we are recruiting a deputy manager whom we expect will take our job when we are promoted, whose work will be vital to achieving the work group's objectives, and who may work for the organisation for many years, we may well spend 50 hours on recruitment and selection activities.

A powerful HR department may demand that managers take a standard approach, however. At each stage in this chapter you will need to bear in mind your organisation's HR policies and how flexible they are. Standardisation can be useful but it can also present managers with a lack of flexibility. Some standards are likely to be based on employment legislation, of course, to guard against discrimination of applicants on the basis of age, race, and so on. The manager will have no flexibility over these. Our aim in this chapter is to present you with good practice in recruitment and selection: the extent to which you follow it will depend on such factors as organisation policy, employment legislation and the nature of the job to be filled.

Key features in recruitment and selection

Recruitment and selection are two parts of a process which starts long before a job is advertised. Recruitment begins with identifying work that needs to be done. Figure 9.1 shows the main stages of recruitment and selection. Job analysis involves examining the job that needs to be done. Job description refers to the statement of what a person who takes on the job will do and what they will be responsible for. The person specification sets out the skills, abilities and experiences that a candidate needs to be able to do the job. Only then is the position advertised. Then the process of sifting through the applications begins and removing some candidates (normally on the basis of a mismatch between the person specification and a candidate's skills, abilities and experience). Shortlisting follows and then the selection process which results in one person – the 'right' one – being offered and accepting the job.

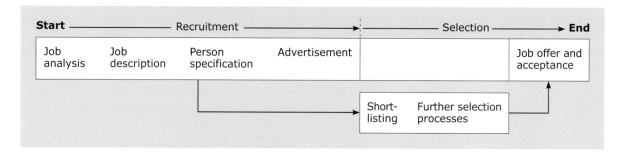

Figure 9.1 The recruitment and selection process

Common mistakes and assumptions

The key to effective recruitment and selection is preparation: knowing the job and what is required of someone to perform it well. Without careful preparation, it is easy to make mistakes and assumptions about who is needed. There are several dangers here. One is that you may fail to identify the best candidate. This can arise from not having clear and relevant criteria for suitability which are relevant to a job. Assumptions about class, gender, ethnic group or physical ability that result in rejection of otherwise suitable candidates can contravene employment laws. At other times, objectivity can be compromised by an organisation's traditions about the 'type of person' considered to be suitable, although it is important that the qualities of the successful applicant match what the organisation requires.

The recruiter's perception can also be influenced by the similarities between themselves and a candidate. When this happens, a candidate who attended the same college or university as the recruiter may have an advantage over other candidates. A common mistake is to be too influenced by one positive or negative attribute of an individual and ignore other factors. When a person is influenced by a positive attribute in another person it is called the 'halo' effect. When a negative attribute is influential, it is called the 'horns' effect – a bias first recognised by Edward Thorndyke in 1920. In the context of recruitment, an example of it might be a recruiter who believed that it was very important for applicants to be very formally dressed for the job interview. The horns effect would bias the recruiter to miss the positive attributes of a candidate who was rather informally dressed, and to focus on the less favourable attributes. The halo effect would bias the recruiter towards someone dressed smartly and might lead them to ignore or underplay some of the candidate's weaknesses.

Thus, if you are to choose someone who is suitable and likely to perform well in the job, poor preparation, incorrect assumptions and biases are likely to prevent you from achieving your goal. But is there more to consider than the job and task requirements and abilities, skills and experience needed?

Person–job fit or person–organisation fit

The traditional approach to recruitment and selection is to make the requirements of the role very clear and then find a candidate who satisfies those requirements. This is person–job fit. It is often easier to identify when the fit is poor as in the following example.

The demanding PA

Kerry, Marketing Director of Caresure, was delighted to appoint Angela as her Personal Assistant. Angela was highly-qualified for the job and scored very well on tests at the interview stage. Although she was very efficient in the job, problems soon arose. Other staff complained that she was condescending towards them. Kerry dismissed this at first but then more complaints were made, this time that Angela was rude and demanding. The general observation was that Angela treated more junior staff quite differently from more senior staff. Kerry suddenly remembered that she had not asked Angela at her interview about the type of organisation she worked in previously. Caresure took a team approach to its work and valued interpersonal skills.

A different approach is person–organisation fit. Here there is a recognition that the person needs to fit the broader organisation – they may move on to jobs in other parts of the organisation. Here we need to look at the match between particular characteristics of a person and of an organisation: for example, between the person's personality, attitudes and values and the organisation's values, goals, structures, processes and culture including pace and ways of working (see, for example, Carless, 2005). An example of such a 'fit' is illustrated by the example below.

Ed's mission

Ed, a conscientious and outgoing person with strong social values, was a project worker working with young disadvantaged people. Now that the project funding was coming to an end, he was looking for a career move. He studied advertisements and visited the websites of medium-sized organisations which he thought would have opportunities for promotions. But he was also looking for an organisation whose values he liked. Finally he successfully applied for a job as a student support officer at a local college. It offered training for the person who 'could help students with poor attendance records to re-engage in the learning process and realise their potential' – the mission of the college for all its students.

Note that person–organisation fit means that a person might be successful in one job in one organisation but not necessarily in a similar job in another. Recruiters need to think beyond whether someone simply has the technical skills to perform in the job and assess their fit with the culture of the organisation. The recruiter should explore the reasons why a person has performed well in their existing job and consider whether similar conditions apply in the new job. However, the danger of person–organisation fit is that it carries the danger of rejecting people who could do the specific job well.

Does a position need to be filled?

The question may need to be asked: does the vacant position need to be filled just now, or at all? Reallocation of work, internal promotion or temporary transfer could be used to cover the tasks associated with the vacancy. A vacancy also provides an opportunity to consider the way work is organised and the skills the organisation needs to secure its future success.

Ways of filling vacancies or getting work done other than by employing full-time staff are outlined below:

- Temporary staff. This may be appropriate if a person is needed only for a short period and the job does not require specialist skills. A temporary member of staff may be the most cost-effective option. Many organisations have links to one or more agencies that can provide temporary staff at short notice.
- Contract staff. This usually means offering a fixed-term contract from six months to a number of years. The main advantage is that the staff member leaves when the work is complete. The disadvantage is that, if there are too few long-term staff, the workforce may have little organisational knowledge and commitment.
- Consultancy staff. For some specialist roles, organisations may choose to bring in consultancy staff. The advantage of consultants is that they are usually highly-skilled individuals who are quickly able to work out what is required. The disadvantage is that they are normally very expensive.
- Outsourcing. Some organisations may consider outsourcing some or all of their functions to other organisations; for example, IT, HR, finance, or management of buildings.

There are disadvantages to each of these approaches:

- temporary workers are thought to be less reliable than permanent employees
- temporary or short-term workers need in-house training but may not get sufficient training so their skills level may remain low
- job insecurity and stress can lead to lower morale and lower productivity.

Advantages include employment flexibility which can enable organisations to be more efficient and competitive.

Job analysis and the creation of a job description

To find the 'right' person for a job, recruiters need accurate information about the job. In organisations with a structured approach to recruitment this information will be available from previous recruitment. Some updating may be all that is needed. If the present job holder is available, then they may have helpful information to add. Alternatively, people whose work relates to the job being considered may be useful sources of information. However, the organisation may not have this information. The job may be new, it may have changed or it may be that previous selections for it have not been successful, because the job was significantly different from what managers believed. Job analysis involves examining a job systematically to identify what is done. There is no single way of doing this but asking about the role is usually the preferred method. Figure 9.2 sets out a comprehensive process for job analysis and person specification, although here we focus on job analysis.

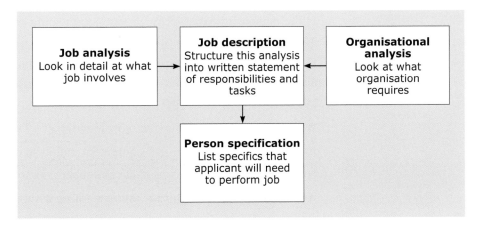

Figure 9.2 Stages of job analysis and person analysis

You will need to remember that, in information gathering, as the value of information increases so does the cost of producing it. The point will be reached where the increased cost of resources allocated to job analysis is less than the additional value of the information gained. Assess carefully what would be the extra cost of getting additional information, how this information would reduce the chances of a mistake in selection and what would be the cost of making such a mistake.

Asking about the job

Here are some suggested questions for finding out about the job. Although the list is already long, there may be other questions that are important in your setting.

What is done within the role?

When and where is it done?

How is it done?

Who does the role-holder report to?

Is the role holder responsible for managing anyone and if so who?

What and how does the person communicate and to whom?

Does the person have any responsibility for planning and organising and if so of what or whom?

Does he or she provide any general administrative support and if so what?

Does the role involve any monitoring and reporting and if so of what and whom?

Does the role involve any evaluating and decision-making and if so of what?

Does the role involve any financial budgeting and control and if so of what?

Is the person responsible for producing, creating or developing anything and if so how much and of what?

Does the person have responsibility for maintaining or repairing things and if so what?

Does the person have any responsibility for quality control?

What are the health and safety considerations?

Is the person required to use equipment and systems?

Is there a requirement for self-development – if so in what area?

Are there any responsibilities that do not fit within the general role?

The questions can be asked in an interview with the job holder, or in a written pro forma. If you feel that the information you receive is not accurate, then you might also speak to the person's supervisor, or arrange for the job to be observed, or for the workload to be measured. If you feel that you have not found the key work in a job, then asking about 'critical incidents' may be useful.

In the 'critical incidents technique' (Flanagan, 1954) you ask individuals to identify the critical incidents in their day-to-day job. This has the advantage of identifying the relative importance of aspects of the job, and the frequency with which they occur. For example, the interviewee might mention the difficulties experienced when the computer system failed for two days, or of regularly having to take urgent action to staff a hospital ward adequately.

More time-consuming methods of getting information are to devise a questionnaire that job holders fill in, or to create a checklist of activities that job holders mark to show how many times in a day they would carry out a particular activity. Such checklists may be available in your organisation but care should be taken so that activities are not missed simply because they do not appear on the checklist.

See also: Person specification, in this chapter

When carrying out a job analysis it is also necessary to consider the broader organisational requirements: these can be as important as the specific ones for the job itself. Consider what the organisation needs from the job holder such as creativity, flexibility, the ability to work in a small team, and so on. It is important to think beyond the technical aspects of the job to the cultural aspects of the organisation. The organisational analysis will feed primarily into the person specification, although there may be aspects that appear in the job description, which is discussed below.

Job description

A job description states what the job holder is responsible for and what they are required to do. If you decided that it was cost-effective to update an existing job description, then this part of the recruitment and selection process is easily completed. If not, then you will need to write a job description based on a job analysis. There are many pro formas for job descriptions. An example job description follows; the headings are given in Box 9.1 and details added in Box 9.2.

Box 9.1 Job description headings

Job title:

Department and location:

Responsible to:

Summary of role:

Specific responsibilities: (the main part of the document, possibly more than one page)

Box 9.2 Detailed job description

Job title: Retail buyer

Department and location: Housewares Department; York, UK

Responsible to: Marketing Director

Summary of role: Responsible for planning and selecting the range, type and quantity of houseware products according to customer demand (e.g. price, quality and availability), trends, store policy and budget.

By fully understanding customer needs, you will maximise profits and provide a commercially-viable range of merchandise at competitive prices. Keeping up to date with market trends and reacting to changes in demand are key elements of the role.

Specific responsibilities:

- Analyse consumer buying patterns and predict future trends; seek knowledge and information about competitor activity, products and pricing
- Liaise with Marketing Director and sales teams to forecast, plan to meet and supply demand
- Regularly review performance indicators with sales
- Compile reports and sales forecasts, and analyse sales figures, using purchasing and sales information and IT systems
- Manage plans for stock levels, reacting to change in demand and logistics
- Seek and meet suppliers, negotiate terms of contract and negotiate and manage service level agreements
- Maintain relationships with existing suppliers and source new suppliers
- Attend trade fairs, at home and abroad, to select and assemble new collections of products
- Liaise with other departments in the organisation to ensure resourcing and services in order to complete projects and to ensure efficient administration of contracts
- Comply with packaging and transport regulations, health and safety regulations and company policies on ethical and sustainable trading, and be aware of international trading issues
- Monitor and manage quality and quality assurance systems in relation to houseware products
- Participate in promotional activities
- Liaise with shop personnel to ensure product/collection supply meets demand
- Seek merchandise feedback from customers
- Train and mentor junior staff according to company policies, HR procedures and employment law.

(Source: adapted from Prospects, 2009)

There is no one right way of setting out job descriptions and you may find that the ones used in your organisation look different and may be more detailed in comparison. An accurate job description has various uses outside the recruitment process: for example, it can be used to review staff performance in appraisals or to assess training needs when someone new starts with the organisation. In the recruitment process, the job description leads on to the next stage: specifying the type of person you are looking for to fill your vacancy.

Person specification

See also: Job analysis and the creation of a job description, in this chapter

A person specification sets out the skills, abilities and experience a person must have to carry out a job. It is derived from a job description.

The person specification is important in your attempt to achieve efficiency, effectiveness and equity in the recruitment process. A well-written person specification helps recruiters in the following ways:

- it helps to maintain objectivity
- it assists with the design of an effective advertisement
- if it is supplied to applicants, then they are better able to decide whether they have the qualifications, experience and skills required to make an effective application
- it enables some unsuitable candidates to 'deselect' themselves, particularly if key selection criteria are set out in the advertisement
- it provides clear criteria for shortlisting and final selection
- it avoids the need to shortlist large numbers of applicants because the criteria are unclear
- it can be used to generate interview questions
- it can be used to inform feedback to non-shortlisted and unsuccessful candidates
- it can be used when investigating any subsequent complaints from unsuccessful applicants.

The person specification should be as specific as possible, be justifiable in relation to the job needs and not be unnecessarily restrictive. Criteria are usually split into 'essential' and 'desirable' with essential criteria being those that a candidate must possess in order to carry out the role and desirable criteria those that would help the candidate to perform the role better.

As you add essential criteria, you increase the difficulty of attracting suitable applicants (you may also be increasing the wage or salary the successful recruit can demand). It is useful to restrict essential criteria to those that are needed immediately. Alternatively (or in addition) you can increase the number of applicants by making it clear that training will be provided to help the recruit gain essential criteria. For example, if an airline pilot to fly Airbus 320s is required, the essential criteria could be specified in more, or less, restrictive ways:

Essential that the applicant holds the certificates to fly an Airbus 320 and has at least 200 flying hours on 320s in the last year. (This is the most restrictive essential criteria.)

or

> Essential that the applicant holds the certificates to fly a short-haul passenger jet and has at least 200 flying hours on such a plane and is willing to retrain at our expense.

or

> Essential that the applicant holds the certificates to fly a jet plane and has at least 200 flying hours and is willing to retrain at our expense. (This is the least restrictive criteria.)

Broad headings for person descriptions include the following:

> *Qualifications*. Those necessary to undertake the role; for example, a safety certificate, a driving licence.
>
> *Technical skills*. Any technical skills necessary to undertake the role; for example, word-processing skills.
>
> *Personal skills*. These can be wide-ranging but usually include such things as communications skills.
>
> *Experience required*. Prior experience necessary to be considered for the role.
>
> *Knowledge*. Particular knowledge required for the role.
>
> *Organisational requirements*. Specific requirements to meet the person–organisation fit.
>
> *Special circumstances relevant to the role*. Specific requirements related to the role itself; for example, must be prepared to work occasional Saturdays.

What is listed should be specific and, as far as is possible, measurable. If you are unable to make a judgement on whether someone fulfils a criterion then it should not be included in your person specification. It should also be applied consistently, throughout the recruitment process to all applicants.

Many organisations have a standard approach to person specifications, so you may have ready-made guidelines and format. If you need to develop your own person specification format, remember that the exact format is less important than making sure you capture what the suitable applicant requires in order to perform the job. However, care should be taken that the content is up to date. Legal requirements may have changed since the standard format was prepared. An example in the UK is the introduction of age as an unacceptable way of discriminating. This has affected many existing specifications which state that 'x years' experience are required'. An example of a person specification is set out in Table 9.1.

Table 9.1 A person specification from the UK Office of National Statistics

Criteria	Essential (E) or desirable (D)	Method of assessment. For example, application form, test, presentation or certificate.
3.1 Qualifications and education		
Member of CIPD or the willingness to obtain	D	Certificate/Application form
3.2 Experience		
Significant recruitment and selection experience to include competency-based interviewing, pre-sifting, telephone interviewing and quality-assuring recruitment documents.	E	Application form/Interview
Evidence of implementing innovative solutions to tackle volume recruitment and using targeting to attract applicants.	E	Presentation/Interview
Coaching and guidance of line managers on recruitment processes, policies and procedures.	D	Interview
Designing and implementing a detailed recruitment plan, for example, recruitment targets, advertising methods, analysis of pay issues, diversity targets and timelines.	D	Application form/Interview
Experience of utilising information technology to extract critical management information for informed decision-making, for example, Excel, Lotus Notes, Word, PowerPoint.	E	Application form
Evidence of utilising a wide variety of advertising techniques and selection methods, for example, brand advertising, internet, targeted advertising.	E	Application form/Interview
Previous experience of leading and managing a team.	E	Application form/Interview
3.3 Relevant knowledge		
Knowledge of recruitment issues affecting the wider government, for example, re-deployment of posts.	D	Application form/Interview

Table 9.1 continued

Strong knowledge of recruitment, policy and employment legislation, for example, age legislation, diversity, etc.	E	Application form/Interview
3.4 Relevant skills		
Negotiate and build relationships with key stakeholders.	E	Application form/Interview
Produce innovative and creative ideas for improving copy for advertising of external vacancies.	E	Interview
Results driven, for example, meeting recruitment targets.	E	Interview
Communication skills both written and verbal, for example, delivering presentations, representation at senior meetings, ability to write business cases and adverts. The ability to coach and advise users of the recruitment system.	E	Application form/Interview
Organisational skills, for example, be able to plan achievable timetables and work on a variety of recruitment campaigns at any one time.	E	Application form/Interview
Team working, for example, sharing best practice with other recruiters and supporting each other when recruitment volumes are high.	E	Test at the interview stage
3.5 Other requirements (hours of work, travel, etc.)		
Flexible to travel to the other Office for National Statistics sites when required.	E	Application form
Part-time – 18 hours per week.	E	Application form

Notes:

CIPD refers to the Chartered Institute of Personnel and Development.

'Wider government' refers to the wider UK government.

Competency-based person specifications

Many large UK organisations have moved from specifying knowledge, skills and attributes in person specifications to specifying competencies. The example provided demonstrates the use of a competency-based person specification. This approach focuses on the competencies required to do a job and places little or no emphasis on personal characteristics. Recruiters then seek objective evidence of the competencies to perform the job effectively.

A disadvantage of this approach is that while a candidate may satisfy all the categories of competency listed, the person may not have suitable personal qualities such as willingness and motivation, or may have a poor attitude towards others.

Diversity and regulation

The aim of good recruitment and selection should be to recruit a suitable candidate for the role; however, it is always important to ensure that you meet diversity regulation requirements when recruiting. In the UK, these include employment equality (age), equal pay, working time, race relations, sex discrimination, employment rights and disability discrimination. Information about these laws and regulations can be found via the internet on government websites or usually through your own organisation. If you work outside the UK, you will need to seek information on the laws and regulations relevant to your country.

Marketing the job vacancy

Recruiting suitable people to your organisation relies on effective marketing of positions to be filled. Marketing of jobs is often not under the control of the manager, however, and it is easy to see why this is so. An organisation may be concerned about 'employer branding' when communicating with potential applicants. Jenner and Taylor (2008) define this as what makes the organisation 'desirable and different as an employer'. This uses the idea of consumers having positive responses to product brands such as Nokia, IKEA or Oxfam International, and applies it to employees' and potential employees' feelings about working for an organisation. In such cases, the manager is likely to be required to follow particular organisational policies and procedures. There may even be standard formats for advertisements, or preferred marketing methods and communication channels. IT companies are likely to make use of ICT not only to reach an appropriate target market of candidates, but because the media used carry important brand messages.

The role of the manager – beyond providing a job description and a person specification – also depends on whether the organisation has a HR department and the extent of the services it provides, such as marketing and administration. Many organisations, whether or not they have HR departments, use recruitment agencies (see Box 9.4). These agencies may take the job description and person specification and then carry out all the stages that follow: marketing the post, processing applications, shortlisting and selecting from the shortlist and providing the organisation with a choice of one or two suitable applicants.

See also: Job analysis and the creation of a job description, in this chapter

Whatever, the involvement of the manager, however, your knowledge of good practice is essential. It will help you to review, assess and perhaps help to improve the effectiveness of processes and practices that, after all, are designed to ensure that you find the most suitable person for the position you want to fill.

Attracting applicants

Recruiting suitable people to your organisation relies on two things:

- finding the best ways of reaching your target audience
- communicating in a way that attracts appropriate candidates who have the skills, attributes and knowledge needed to do the job while dissuading those who do not.

Too many applicants can make your shortlisting process too time-consuming. Equally, too few can leave you with too little choice. Your aim should be to get a reasonable number of suitable candidates.

Advertising is the primary way of reaching potential candidates but this may be only a first step in the communication process. It is good practice to provide potential applicants with more details about the job, how to apply and what information they need to provide. The internet is likely to play a part in both advertising and provision of this further information: most forms of advertising have a web-based element and many organisations have their own websites. Thus potential applicants can get further information easily (and can research the organisation, too). Some may make contact by phone or email. All are communication opportunities and if these are used well they should influence the likelihood of suitable applications.

Table 9.2 lists the main ways in which job vacancies can be advertised, together with the advantages and disadvantages of each method. Note how the various methods provide access to a wider field of applicants as the 'reach' of advertisements increases.

Table 9.2 Ways of advertising job vacancies

Method	Advantages	Disadvantages
Recommendations of existing staff	Inexpensive Quick The recommended person may be very suitable	Biased May not satisfy anti-discrimination laws where these apply if this is the sole method used Very limited group of candidates considered
Internal advertisements through: Intranet sites Email Notice-boards Internal newsletters	Inexpensive Quick A lot is known about candidates Can reduce induction and training costs once someone is recruited	New people may not be reached and new ideas do not come into the organisation It can lead to difficulties if existing staff are rejected

Table 9.2 continued

Headhunters or executive search consultants. These seek out and approach prospective candidates on behalf of a client organisation. They can also research a prospective candidate	Good for filling top jobs Useful when ideal applicants are not looking for a job Discreet: an organisation can seek candidates without advertising this fact Exploration of interest can be done before further parts of the selection process are carried out Can be used to research prospective candidates	Very expensive: 35–50% of the first year's salary is not uncommon Can be seen as unethical
Employment agencies and state-funded job centres	Usually free or inexpensive Useful for routine jobs	Can have a poor reputation and therefore organisations may be less likely to use them for non-routine jobs Some are based locally so candidates in other locations may not see the vacancies
Local and national newspapers and specialist publications. These usually have an internet site as well as the publication itself	Attracts a wider pool of potential candidates Attracts new people and new ideas into your company Can gain publicity for your company Your job can be advertised alongside similar positions and may compare favourably By carefully selecting your publication you can gain access to a wide range of people in your target audience Still a major way of attracting applicants	Can be expensive (although this depends on the type of advertisement you place) If advertising in a specialist publication these may only be published monthly leading to a delay in the recruitment process
The internet There are a number of different ways of using the internet some of which have already been explored. Others include: Advertising on the jobs section of an organisation's website Advertising on a job site on the internet	Relatively inexpensive (or no cost if your own organisation's website is the only one used) Where an organisation's website is used for advertising, a link can be provided to other parts of the website giving additional information about the organisation	Internet sites can be accessed globally. The number of applicants may be overwhelming if the advertisement is not sufficiently specific Targeting is more difficult because the internet is a 'broadcast' medium with no particular target group. Choosing the appropriate external website can help

The advertisement

Most people expect advertisements to emphasise the good features of what is being marketed and say less about the problems. However, it is important not to oversell a job. Claiming that a job is more attractive than it is can result in individuals leaving after a short time and then criticising your organisation for many years.

To avoid overselling, the content of your advertisement should aim to do two things to maximise its effectiveness. It should encourage suitable people to apply for the position and it should discourage unsuitable people from applying. It is unfair to suggest that applicants will be considered suitable when they are not. They may have spent many hours preparing their applications; much time can be wasted, too, when you have to read unsuitable applications. The information in the advertisement should be taken largely from the job analysis, job description and person specification. Ideally, the content should cover that suggested in Box 9.3, if the budget allows for this. The ways in which the content is set out are likely to reflect the medium you are using, but normally the most important information is placed first.

Box 9.3 Contents of a job advertisement

The advertisement should be factual, truthful and relevant. Suggested items include:

- the job title, in terms likely to be familiar to the reader; avoid jargon
- the name of the organisation, the nature of its activity and the location of the job
- the salary and fringe benefits; where possible, state the salary range
- the aims and responsibilities of the job
- the qualifications required and the experience needed – this will be a summary of the person specification
- genuine promotion prospects
- how applications should be made; for example, asking the applicant to send a CV or to request an application form and further information
- the closing date, if there is one, for applications
- the organisation's website address if it has one.

(Source: adapted from Ludlow and Panton, 1991)

Anti-discrimination legislation in many countries applies to most stages of the recruitment process, including advertising. The legislation in place will differ from country to country but it is likely to be illegal to discriminate, either directly or indirectly, on many grounds including ethnicity, disability, colour, gender, sexuality or marital status. Care should be taken that your advertising does not discriminate either directly or indirectly; most HR departments will check this for you.

Advertisements often link into the wider marketing and public relations work of an organisation. If linked to a company website, an advertisement can give a richer picture of an organisation than an advertisement alone can provide and so it is important to maximise this opportunity. Cober *et al.*'s study of the 'best companies to work for' (2004) chosen by the US magazine *Fortune* found that such organisations included information about organisational culture, goals, values, work environment and the history of the organisation.

The applicant's contribution

There are four main ways to obtain the information needed from applicants to assess their suitability for a job. These are asking them to:

- complete an application form
- write a letter of application
- provide a curriculum vitae (CV)
- attend an initial interview.

A letter of application and CV are usually required together. The strengths and weaknesses of each method of getting information are set out in Table 9.3.

Table 9.3 Four main ways of getting information about the applicant

Method	Strengths	Weaknesses
Application form	Can be designed to focus on the person specification It can be cost-effective for the organisation It is what applicants expect	May take time to compile Time-consuming for the candidate – a good candidate may not have time to apply
Letter of application plus CV	Will attract an applicant with little time Cost-effective for the applicant, provided the applicant has a CV and has kept it up to date	May not be cost-effective for the organisation if all the information needed for shortlisting is not included
Initial interview	Cost-effective for both the organisation and the applicant for simple jobs Appropriate for jobs which do not demand a high level of literacy and which may attract candidates with poor literacy skills	If interviews last for more than a few minutes, initial interviews may be an expensive option, depending on the number of applicants

Candidates make decisions too

Selection is often regarded as the process by which organisations choose between individuals. However, candidates are also making choices: about whether to apply for the job, attend an interview and accept a job offer. The approach you take when attracting applicants will influence these decisions. It is important, therefore, to treat candidates in a sensitive and responsive manner. You will need to pay attention to the recruitment materials, the job description and how candidates are treated during all parts of the process.

Shortlisting job applicants

There will usually be a need to create a shortlist of candidates from those who have applied for the position. Shortlisting has two aims. The first is to reject all applicants who do not match the essential criteria in the person specification. The second is to consider in more detail the applicants who do match the essential criteria.

In the UK it is usual to shortlist up to six applicants per position. This can best be achieved by approaching the task systematically. The person specification will have set out the criteria on which to assess applicants. The application form, if used, should have been designed to record the relevant information. A pro forma for shortlisting like the one in Table 9.4 is useful for approaching this systematically. It is particularly helpful if the shortlisting is carried out by a team or a selection panel.

Consider the example of a person specification for a paid campaigner in a voluntary organisation. How might shortlisting be done if fifty people applied? Since only the applicants who meet the essential criteria can be successful, the first assessment can be limited to these criteria. In the second assessment, desirable criteria are considered. One approach would be to shortlist all the applicants remaining. Another would be to look at the information provided by all the remaining applicants until six with all the essential criteria and, say, at least half of the desirable criteria are identified.

There are two situations in which you might take a different approach. The first is when there are internal applicants – people who work for the organisation – or people who previously worked for the organisation. Many organisations will interview such candidates. There are several reasons for interviewing internal candidates: it shows respect; it is useful to know why a person wants to change jobs; and it lessens the risk that a person will leave the organisation if there is no response to their application. The second situation is one where applicants work for a competitor. Interviewing them might reveal useful information about the competitor. You may consider this suggestion unethical.

Shortlisting can either be done as yes/no, or with a scale such as strong, acceptable, poor. Table 9.4 gives the example of four candidates who have applied for the campaigner job and how their applications have been assessed against the criteria in the person specification.

Table 9.4 Example of a completed pro forma for shortlisting

Criteria (essential (E) or desirable (D))	Candidate A	Candidate B	Candidate C	Candidate D
Degree-level education (D)	Degree in Psychology	Doctorate in Sociology	Educated to A-level	Degree in Mathematics
Experience of working or volunteering in a campaigning organisation (E)	Has worked mostly in government organisations. Has some recent volunteering experience	Has no experience of working in a voluntary organisation	Has good experience of working in a voluntary organisation on a paid basis	Has long experience of working in voluntary organisations as a volunteer
Experience of working with volunteers (E)	Has managed a team of volunteers	Has no experience of working with volunteers	Has some limited experience of working with volunteers	Has worked alongside other volunteers. Has never managed a team of volunteers
Experience of carrying out research (E)	Has led two research projects	Has good research experience with publications	Has worked on research projects Has not led any research projects	Has some research experience
Experience of working with politicians and government units (D)	Extensive experience based on career in government organisations	Extensive experience based on former career	Limited experience	No experience
Experience of setting up events and meetings (E)	Some experience of setting up meetings Has never organised an event	Extensive experience based on former career	Has organised events on a regular basis in former organisations	Has experience of organising events
Word-processing skills or ability to be self-sufficient in terms of administration (E)	Able to use word-processing packages and has managed own administration in the past	Used to having secretarial support. Unable to use word-processing packages	Highly-proficient at a number of computer packages and fully able to provide own administrative support	Able to use word-processing packages and has managed own administration in the past

Having looked at the candidates in this way it should be much easier to assess their relative suitability for the role (on paper at least). An assessment of each candidate is given below.

Candidate A

Candidate A has a possible weakness in the area of event management and has less voluntary experience than the other candidates, but could be shortlisted on the basis of other strengths.

Candidate B

Candidate B is well-qualified academically but lacks experience of voluntary work – a key criterion – and so would probably not be shortlisted.

Candidate C

Candidate C is weak in two desirable areas – qualifications and experience of working with politicians and government units. Whether Candidate C is shortlisted will depend on the value placed by the recruiters on the candidate's experience of working in voluntary organisations.

Candidate D

Candidate D appears to meet all the essential criteria and is likely to be shortlisted.

While it is necessary to use information from application forms, it is important to recognise that the information may be only partly correct. George and Marrett (2004) found that in 40–70% of CVs they studied, applicants exaggerated their claims. Broussard and Brennan (1986) found that the areas most commonly misrepresented on CVs were job history, job responsibilities, job titles, pay and academic qualifications. Few academic studies have been carried out on CVs. One of the best-known studies was carried out by Goldstein in 1971. In this study the information given by candidates on application forms and CVs was compared with that subsequently collected from their previous employers. Goldstein found that of CVs sampled:

- 57% claimed higher salaries and/or different job responsibilities
- 57% overstated the duration of their employment
- 50% had understated the number of jobs they had held (Cascio, 1975)
- 37% gave reasons for leaving that were different from those given by previous employers
- 33% gave incorrect information about their marriage date
- 17% claimed to have had jobs in organisations where they had never worked.

Most people go for some 'impression management' on their CVs without necessarily lying. Carefully reading a CV can help to identify some of the issues that arise and in many cases these can be checked out at the selection stage. It should be a recruiter's aim to check out all information by at least one other method during the recruitment process. For example, qualifications can be checked by ensuring that certificates are provided. Where necessary, education providers can be contacted. For some jobs, it may be advisable to use pre-employment screening agencies which will carry out checks for you.

Some roles or organisations require that certain checks are carried out by law. For example, in the UK anyone working with children under the age of 16 has to be checked by the government's Criminal Records Bureau. In some other organisations that are part of the critical national infrastructure certain checks on applicants have to be carried out by law. Guidance on this type of organisation or employment can be found on the internet.

Selecting applicants

The aim of the selection process is to find out if the candidate is interested in the job and is competent to do it. A selection process also has the following functions:

- to explain the work of the organisation, the job and any features such as induction and initial trial periods
- to set expectations on both sides, including a realistic discussion of any potential difficulties (if appropriate)
- to give candidates the information they need to decide whether they want the job being offered.

Here we consider the main selection methods for roles at middle and lower levels of an organisation.

While in the UK the traditional model of recruitment outlined above has changed little for many years, the selection methods used by many organisations have been updated significantly as more research has been carried out into the effectiveness of these methods (Robertson and Smith, 2001). However, interviews are still the preferred method of recruitment for most organisations.

No selection method is perfect but some are better than others and some are useful in specific circumstances. We consider some of the most commonly-used methods, more than one of which is normally used. The cost of selection methods differs and we have grouped the methods by high and low cost.

Low-cost selection methods

Interviews

The oldest and most well-used selection method is the interview. However, it can also be one of the least effective. The 'traditional' interview, which largely involves a friendly discussion between the interviewer and candidate with little structure, is a poor predictor of later job performance. It can also be biased against certain groups (Schmidt and Hunter, 1998). Despite this, interviewing remains the most popular method of recruitment in nearly all countries in the world. It is also worth noting that candidates see interviews as a fair method for recruitment and it can be an effective way of clarifying a candidate's understanding of a role.

There are ways of making an interview a much better method for decision-making. One improvement that can be made is structuring the interview around the person specification or job competences and ensuring that the same questions are asked of all candidates. A further improvement is 'situational' interviewing in which candidates are asked how they would behave in certain situations. Research has shown these to be more valid than an interview that is just structured.

See also: Designing and conducting a selection interview, in this chapter

Work samples

Work samples are a widely-used method of selection. Applicants perform selected tasks that are similar to those performed on the job (Ployhart, 2006). Samples can predict performance well, because of their close link to the real work. Candidates may not enjoy work sample tests, but they see the close link between the work done in the role and the test and they usually regard the tests as fair. Another advantage of work sample is that they have been shown to have almost no ethnic bias in the sense that they focus on task performance (Potosky *et al.*, 2005). Three examples of work samples are set out below.

Examples of work samples

1. A person applying for a job as a chef is asked to cook a meal to a set of specifications and within a particular time. The finished meal is then assessed against criteria.

2. Candidates applying for a role as a manager are asked to prepare a presentation setting out their plans for the department they will be managing should they be successful. Their performance in terms of both the presentation and the planning are then assessed by the recruiters against a set of criteria.

3. Candidates for a clerical role are asked to prioritise a set of items in a timed 'in-tray' exercise and say how they would deal with the items of highest priority. Answers are then assessed against criteria.

Work samples need to be thought through carefully: it is important to have a clear idea of what you want to assess and to be sure that the work sample will test what it is supposed to test. Other critical factors when designing a work sample are that the instructions to candidates are clear and that a reasonable time is allowed for the test. For this reason, tests should always be tried out first with someone similar to the candidates. It is also important that the assessment criteria are clear and that people assessing candidates have a common understanding of the criteria. If not, then rating of candidates can be unsystematic. A disadvantage of work samples is that, because they are such a precise measure of someone's ability in a particular role, they are not a good predictor of how they will perform in other roles in the future. It is rare, therefore, that they are the only method used in selection.

References

These are statements about the candidate by previous employers or respected people. Previous employers will usually be willing to state some facts, such as the jobs done and the period of employment. Many organisations have found that the opinions of respected people are not safe sources of information. Your organisation is likely to have a policy on references.

Higher-cost selection methods

Psychometric tests

Psychometric tests are many and varied and can range from testing verbal, numerical or spatial abilities (aptitude tests) to assessing someone's personality (personality tests). These two main types are considered below. It is important to note that, in general, candidates tend not to like or trust psychometric tests. Such tests are therefore rarely the sole source of information collected, though not only for this reason.

Aptitude and ability tests

Aptitude tests have the big advantage that they are tried and tested methods of assessing someone's ability in a certain area and can provide a much more accurate and less biased assessment of qualities than other methods (Schmidt and Hunter, 1998). The key to using such tests, however, is ensuring that the ability you are measuring, for example, verbal reasoning, is a good predictor of job performance – and that the test you are using measures what it is supposed to. You will also need to make sure, of course, that the aptitude or ability you are testing for is required in the job. High verbal reasoning ability may not be needed by someone performing a largely-manual role. General mental ability, which reflects an individual's ability to plan, reason, process information and exercise self-control, is a good predictor of performance (Schmidt and Hunter, 2004). The disadvantages of these aptitude and ability tests are that candidates can practise taking tests (various websites offer this service) and when used in selection such tests require specialist knowledge and training to administer, adding to the expense of the recruitment process.

Personality tests

Personality tests are used for selection on the assumptions that certain jobs require a combination of particular personality traits and that tests can identify them. The most common personality tests take the form of questionnaires designed to rate respondents on various dimensions. The most respected tests cover the five broad personality dimensions – agreeableness, conscientiousness, emotional stability, extraversion/introversion and openness (to ideas, for example). Tests of conscientiousness are good predictors of productivity and performance (Hirsh, 2009). The other personality dimensions may be good predictors of performance in particular jobs: a degree of extroversion is likely to be important in marketing jobs and openness (to ideas, for example) in jobs where creativity and innovation are needed. Most reputable personality tests need to be administered and scored by trained and licensed users. Personality tests should not be the only method used for selection because many are in the form of self-report questionnaires. These require unbiased responses which are unlikely to be given in highly-competitive situations. Some tests developers now 'fake-proof' their questionnaires by getting respondents to choose between equally desirable responses (for example, Hirsh and Peterson, 2008).

Assessment centres

Assessment centre are based on two principles: that a number of different ways of assessing candidates will be more reliable than just one and, because several assessors are normally involved, several assessors will be more accurate than a single assessor. Typically, assessment centres are organised over one or two days and can contain a mixture of aptitude tests, interviews, practical tasks, presentations, group work, role play and work on case studies. They can be used to assess team-working, communication skills, leadership, initiative, decision-making, integrity and creativity, for example. The advantage of assessment centres is that candidates are more likely to feel they have been assessed in depth and fairly. The disadvantages are that they are not useful in situations where there are very few candidates and their effectiveness depends on how well the tasks and tests fit the job to be filled.

Choices and bias

When considering selection methods you will need to consider whether it is a good measure of a person's skill and abilities, and how well it will predict performance. You will also need to consider whether candidates think that a test measures what it is supposed to. This is known as face validity. A further consideration is whether candidates believe that a test is fair. Candidates prefer tests over which they feel they have some control, such as interviews, and can feel uncomfortable when they feel they have no control – for example, personality tests (Bertolino and Steiner, 2007). Some methods may discriminate against people: for example, those with disabilities, those in some ethnic minority groups or older candidates.

Whichever methods are chosen, no selection process is perfect, but some methods are more likely to indicate the strengths and weaknesses of individual candidates.

Designing and conducting a selection interview

If candidates for a job vacancy are to be selected by interview, a number of decisions about the arrangements need to be made early in the selection and recruitment process. To increase the objectivity of interviews, some organisations hold several interviews with each candidate with different interviewers. The most complicated method involves the use of a panel interview. Here, a group of people interview the candidate at the same time.

Because selection interviews are not easy to conduct, it is preferable that everyone involved has participated in some kind of training: some organisations insist on this. Most managers believe they can interview competently but probably few have been assessed on their interviewing practice. Thus training for interviewers may need to be arranged. This will be particularly important if candidates are from different ethnic cultures.

Preparation for the interviews is important, too. Box 9.4 sets out factors to consider in preparing for an interview.

Box 9.4 Requirements of a good interview

What the interviewer(s) needs for the interview

- Job description, person specification
- Individual application forms, CVs, etc.
- Details of the employment contract and working arrangements.
- Information on general prospects, training, induction within the organisation

What the candidate needs

- Details of venue
- To be met on arrival
- Access to facilities: toilets, any special needs for candidates with disabilities, comfortable waiting area and refreshments

Interview location requirements

- Suitable room and layout: consider whether this should be formal or informal and what type of setting to create
- Freedom from interruptions and other discomforts and distractions, such as extraneous noise, uncomfortable furniture, extremes of temperature
- Appropriate access for people with special needs

A structured interview plan will enable the interviewer(s) to assess what they are looking for in the candidate and whether the person:

could do the job (assessment against the person specification)

would do the job (judgements of motivation and commitment)

would fit (elements of person–organisation fit).

To assess this, interviewers need to have a clear idea of the areas of questioning for each candidate to check that they meet the criteria. If the interviews are to be conducted by a panel, there also needs to be agreement on:

- the roles of those involved: who will chair the panel and how questions will be divided among the panel members
- how note-taking will be handled during and after the interview
- a disciplined approach to timing: enough time for each candidate and not too many candidates per day – no more than five is considered best.

Interviews have distinct and recognisable stages, and individuals have certain expectations about what should happen when, but you must try not to become routine or mechanistic in your approach.

Conducting a traditional interview

In a panel interview one member will need to take the chair; this person will then be responsible for starting, controlling and closing the interview. It is also the role of the chair to link and manage the contributions of the panel members, limiting contributions if necessary. Whether or not a panel is conducting the interviews, the direction and flow of interviews will need to be controlled according to how an interview is progressing, both to keep the interviewee talking and to ensure that you are obtaining the information you need. Always introduce yourself (and panel members) to the candidate and explain how the interview will be conducted. At all times interviewers need to use active listening skills, attending to what is being said and, where appropriate, summarising and checking their understanding.

See also: Communication skills, Chapter 2

A relaxed and skilful interviewer or panel chair will establish and maintain rapport with candidates.

Gathering information

Your main objective is to gather information. A practical target is to expect the candidate to talk for 70% of the time. The example in Box 9.5 describes the kind of conduct to avoid when interviewing.

Box 9.5 An unsatisfactory interview

David was really pleased to have been asked to an interview for the job of Project Manager. He spent a lot of time preparing for the interview, not only collecting all the information required for the application but finding out more about the organisation from its website. The first question he was asked by the interview panel was 'Describe your major weaknesses and what you have done to overcome them.' David struggled to respond. It was not a good start. A second member of the panel questioned him closely about his fluency in other languages but was sharply reminded by another interview panel member that the job they were interviewing for was not the international project position. The third member of the panel asked some relevant questions but, all the time David was talking, the panel member was looking through a pile of papers on the desk in front of him. David received a letter a week later offering him the job; he decided not to accept.

Effective questioning

Similar areas of questioning should be used for all candidates so that you can compare each candidate's match with the job description and person specification and allow comparisons to be made between candidates. A well-thought-out set of questions for candidates will be comprehensive. The questions will be grouped in a way that makes sense to candidates and will be easily distinguishable from one another. This makes the interview easier to manage: candidates are less likely to repeat the same information in different ways.

See also: Communication skills, Chapter 2
The level of detail you require will influence how you ask questions.

Questions can be broad (open questions) and will encourage the candidate to talk. An open question such as: 'Tell me what you like and dislike about working in your current role' will usually encourage a more lengthy answer than a closed one such as: 'Are you happy in your current role?' While the person is speaking you can listen for specific things you want to check on. When you find something interesting, you can wait for the candidate to finish speaking and then ask a probing question so that you receive a precise answer (a closed question).

Another common approach is the use of questions about specific incidents from the candidate's past that indicate the person's suitability for the current job. This is sometimes known as behavioural interviewing. It overcomes the problem of 'textbook answers' by candidates. Such answers are often prompted by questions such as (in the case of interviewing a project manager): 'What do you know of project management?' or 'How would you ensure that a project runs to plan?'. The skilful interviewee will take this opportunity to present their wide range of knowledge about project management approaches and techniques. However, this is not evidence of good project management in a previous role. Behavioural interviewing focuses on actual instances when a person managed projects and what they did to ensure the success of the project. A question such as: 'Tell me about the most complex project you have had to manage in the past' will open up the discussion. You could then follow up with probing questions. The interviewee might say: 'There was one particular project that was really difficult because we were working to such tight deadlines, but we met them.' The interviewer might then ask: 'What did you do personally to ensure that the deadlines were met?'. This approach produces information on what someone has done in the past and their skill in a particular area. This can be much more effective than asking questions that test only a person's knowledge.

Looking beyond suitability for the job

See also: The importance of managing recruitment and selection well, in this chapter

We have provided examples of questions about the job itself, but how can you assess the degree of fit between the person and the organisation?

Box 9.6 provides some examples of questions related to a candidate's fit with the organisation to ensure that, for example, the person will be able to work in teams, if this is the way the organisation conducts much of its work.

Box 9.6 Questions to assess the person–organisation fit

- Could you compare the cultures of the organisations where you have worked before and say how the differences affected your behaviour at work?

- Where were you happiest at work? What was it about the organisation that made you feel like this?

- Why did you decide to join each of the organisations you have worked for?

- What factors will cause you to decide whether or not to leave your current employer? (Interviewers should look for more than a motivation to join the new organisation as many people will stay in a place of work if they are happy there.)

- How is your effectiveness measured in your present job?

- What do you like and dislike about working in teams?

- What are the things you have regretted leaving behind at places where you have worked in the past?

(Source: based on Billsberry, 2000)

However, some of these questions are easy to predict and there is a risk of candidates being able to prepare answers in advance, especially if they have researched your organisation and know what type of person you are likely to be seeking.

Evaluating the information

As the interview proceeds you will need to assess whether the answers to your questions are producing useful evidence of job suitability or unsuitability. If you are not getting the information you need, you will need to be flexible and change the type of question you are asking.

Ending the interview

When you are satisfied that you have all the information you require, it is good practice to invite a candidate to:

- tell you about anything that has not been covered, or to expand on anything that has not been adequately covered (for example, something that the candidate has done and wants you to know about)

- ask *you* questions in order to clarify any features of the job or the contract being offered.

This may reveal relevant information and it will make the interview more satisfying for the candidate. After this, the interviewee needs to be told what is likely to happen next and when.

Ethics in recruitment and selection

Good ethical practice in recruitment and selection will ensure that your approach is seen as fair. Here are some principles to follow.

Competence of the selectors

You should be satisfied that those involved in the recruitment process are competent in their respective roles. This may mean training some people or, in the case of psychometric tests, ensuring that a qualified tester is used. Many organisations insist that all people involved in recruitment are trained, particularly in the area of interviewing. If you are using a work sample test, it is important to ensure that everyone involved in assessing a candidate has a shared understanding of the assessment criteria.

Respect for candidates

Treat your candidates with dignity and respect. Recruitment can be very stressful for some applicants and you should avoid selection methods that would cause undue stress. Ask an experienced colleague to assess your selection methods. Inevitably some individuals will be disappointed by a recruitment decision but this should be partly overcome by good feedback. Offer all candidates the opportunity to receive feedback following a selection process regardless of whether or not they were successful.

Informed consent

Every candidate should know in advance the details of the selection procedure and of anything they need to prepare in advance. Send all shortlisted candidates a letter outlining the process before the selection date (two weeks is normally sufficient). If possible, provide the contact details of a person who candidates can contact if they have questions. It is good practice to ask someone independent of the process to read through the instructions to candidates.

Candidates' right to withdraw

All candidates should have the right to withdraw from the process at any time without undue pressure being placed on them to continue. Some may withdraw when they receive details of the selection process, some may not attend the selection (or withdraw part-way through), and some may decide not to take up a job offer.

Confidentiality

All aspects of a recruitment process are confidential to the candidates and the recruiters. This means that the performance of candidates should not be discussed with a wider audience following a recruitment process. This is particularly important where candidates are internal to an organisation. Data gathered at the recruitment stage are likely to be governed by the data protection legislation in your country and organisation.

Selectors' knowledge of candidates

Those involved in the selection process need to be particularly careful when selecting from a group of candidates when they know one or more either personally or through work. It is important that others on the selection panel are aware a selector has knowledge of an individual so a decision can be made as to whether another selector would be more suitable.

In general, selectors need to be familiar with the requirements of the job to be filled and that these (and the performance of the candidates on the day) are the primary basis for decision-making. In designing and implementing a recruitment and selection process to seek and recruit the 'best' candidate, it is easy to forget ethical considerations.

Induction and socialisation

How can a manager help a new recruit to become a high-performing employee as efficiently as possible? Two processes that help to ensure this are induction and socialisation. Both are different aspects of what is known as organisational entry. Induction relates to adjustment, the initial process of becoming familiar with a new organisation or new role, while socialisation refers to adaptation, the process of adapting to the culture of the organisation (Billsberry, 1996).

Induction

Induction is the tangible part of organisational entry and has three aspects to it (which do not normally include job training):

Administrative. The main purpose here is to provide information about the job, the procedures and the organisation.

Welfare and employee support. The emphasis here is on providing any support the new employee needs in the early days of employment.

Human resource management. This 'educates' new employees about the company ethos, their individual accountabilities and the standards of performance required.

(Source: adapted from: Marchington and Wilkinson, 1996)

Induction programmes may also be necessary when individuals change roles or departments in organisations. The previous job holder may be able to pass on their knowledge to their successor. In these cases, organisation-level induction may not be required but individuals who change roles or departments are as likely to experience anxiety as those who are new to the organisation. Moreover, pressures on them may be greater because the organisation may have greater expectations of them.

Socialisation

Socialisation is the more intangible part of organisational entry. It has been described as 'the ongoing process of instilling in all employees the prevailing attitudes, standards, values and patterns of behaviour which are expected by the organisation and its departments' (Dessler, 2004). These will include the often unwritten and unstated ways of working and communicating in an organisation.

Socialisation cannot be easily managed because the 'rules of the game' are often not explicit and are learned only by exposure to the organisation's customs and traditions. If the people a new employee will work with have aims, values and standards that are aligned with those of the organisation, then a manager may decide to delegate socialisation to the new recruit's colleagues. If they are not, then the manager will need to be involved in the new employee's socialisation.

Roles in induction and socialisation

While the manager has a vital role to play in induction and socialisation others may be involved depending on the size and nature of the organisation. These can include:

- *The human resources department.* A HR department may issue staff handbooks, contract details, health and safety information, and so on. The line manager will need to know what information the department sends to the new recruit in order to avoid duplicated efforts.

- *Senior managers and supervisors.* Senior managers also need to be seen to support the induction process and to demonstrate their commitment to new staff, by, for example, taking part in formal induction courses.

- *Colleagues and other staff.* These employees can act as informal guides or mentors to the newcomer. Staff from different parts of the organisation might take part in formal induction programmes. Where the organisation has staff representatives or recognises trade unions, then these often make an input to induction by discussing their membership and services.

Whoever is involved in this process, it is important to monitor, review and evaluate it. Feedback should be obtained from all parties and the process adjusted as necessary. Regular contact with the individual, whether informally or as part of the supervision process, is one way of achieving this.

Understanding and managing induction

As a manager you will need to offer, or assist in offering new employees a structured and comprehensive induction. It will include the formal process of welcoming and orientating new employees so that they feel comfortable with their job as quickly as possible. The cost of failing to provide the necessary support may well be poor performance and, in some cases, early departure from the organisation. When people join a new organisation or start a new job or role they will have different emotions, expectations and challenges as the example below illustrates.

First day fears

I was really stressed on my first day in this job. I had to move away from my family and friends and I moved into my rented flat the night before. I wasn't even sure where to buy milk in the morning! I was also feeling anxious and full of doubts: had I done the right thing? Could I cope with new responsibilities? Could I do the new job well? Would my employers soon find out the things they did not learn at interview and regret appointing me? Was it a good idea to move from a job I could do well and enjoyed, and where I was respected? Could I afford the extra travelling costs?

Stress, excitement, apprehension and some disorganisation are typical experiences on joining an organisation. Dessler (1988) has identified some of the problems encountered by new employees.

- *Change.* A new situation will involve change and the greater the change the greater the uncertainty for the employee.

- *Unrealistic expectations.* The job may have been explained too positively, or not positively enough. As we said before, impressions will be formed in the early stages of the recruitment process and these may not match reality.

- *Surprise.* Some expectations may not be met or additional requirements may be communicated. Working conditions may not be as the recruit had believed.

As a manager, you can help newcomers overcome their doubts and anxieties by offering reassurance and information. Putting yourself in their position will help you understand their induction needs. First impressions, both good and bad, are remembered for a long time. Carefully designing an induction programme to suit the individual's needs is an important part of this process.

Planning an induction programme

Properly structured, induction programmes should provide a series of planned activities that fit the needs of all involved. They should begin on an employee's first day. Programmes will vary with the nature of the organisation, and the job. Dessler (2004) suggests that a successful induction programme should aim to do four things:

- make new employees feel welcome
- help them to understand the organisation in its wider context (including its past, present and future vision), as well as key policies and procedures
- make it clear what the organisation expects of them
- start the socialisation process of understanding the organisation's preferred way of acting and doing things.

A common mistake is to overload newcomers with more information than they can process. Some of the activities in a well-managed induction are set out in Table 9.5.

Table 9.5 Induction activities

Type of induction	Benefits
Initial briefing with HR manager or line manager, covering the main organisational policies and procedures	Provides a personal approach
Provision of 'Induction Pack' including key information about the organisation and/or an organisation handbook	The pack provides good reinforcement and can be referred back to later
General introduction courses for new employees	Provides a good overview of the organisation and a chance to meet others starting at the same time
Induction through different media, for example, online, video	Provides new employees with an achievable task on their first day. They can refer to the induction information again later if necessary
Induction interview with the line manager focusing on the role, how it fits with wider organisational and departmental goals	Provides a personal approach and the opportunity for the new employee to get to know the line manager, discuss training and development needs and career goals
Buddy system – the new employee is assigned a person, a 'buddy', who can act as a guide	Useful for reducing anxiety and it provides a personal approach. New employees can ask the buddy many of the questions they consider insufficiently important to ask their line manager
Meetings with key members of staff	Provides an opportunity to meet colleagues (but too many meetings can be overwhelming)

(Source: based on Currie, 2006)

Indications that an induction programme is working well include:

- new employees taking a short time to become effective in their jobs
- the speed with which employees adapt to their surroundings

- good interpersonal relations between new and longer-serving employees
- a reduction in staff turnover
- a satisfactory staff retention rate.

Monitoring the process can be done formally, or informally, during regular discussions that extend beyond the first few weeks of employment.

Understanding and managing socialisation

Wanous (1992) suggests that successful socialisation is a four-stage process.

1 *Confronting and accepting reality.* This involves the recruit assessing whether their expectations about the job and/or the organisation are accurate. If they are not, the recruit may experience conflicts between their personal values and needs and those of the organisation. It can also involve the recruit discovering which of their values and needs are acceptable and unacceptable in the organisation. An example of this is the realisation that the organisation demands higher standards of interpersonal behaviour than the new employee normally exhibits.

2 *Achieving role clarity.* This will involve the new recruit clarifying the new role and the expectations that others have of them. The recruit will need to understand the changes required of them and how performance is evaluated by the organisation. It may also involve learning to work within the organisation's structure.

3 *Coming to terms with the context.* This stage involves the recruit learning the behaviours that fit with the organisational culture – the way in which the organisation and people do what they do.
It may also involve resolving conflicts at work and between work and home; for example, working hours and travel.

4 *Feeling that socialisation has been successful.* This is indicated by feelings of high satisfaction, a sense of being involved and motivated.

Successful socialisation will result in new employees recognising that they have begun to fit in, that the feeling of being new is beginning to be replaced with a sense of belonging. They become committed and dependable, and they may also experience a change in their self-image and values. Harris and DeSimone (1994) offer a useful framework for managers to use in assessing successful socialisation. It focuses on three areas: organisational roles, group norms and expectations.

Organisational roles

Organisational roles influence how people fit into the organisation and help them to make sense of their own position, and to define what they must do to perform effectively. To help the newcomer to come to terms with the various aspects of the role a manager can:

- give a clear description of the job or task
- assess whether established ways of working need to be followed or if there is scope for innovation

- be clear about the types of behaviour that are acceptable at different levels in the organisation
- be aware of the role confusion likely to be encountered by the new employee and be sympathetic and supportive
- provide support through counselling, discussion and by reassuring the newcomer that doubt and confusion are quite usual.

Group norms

Group norms are (usually) unwritten and informal rules of conduct that become established over time. They help the group to function as a coherent unit in relation to other groups, offer a common identity for group members and, by making expected behaviour clearer, help members to avoid inappropriate behaviour. Adherence to some norms in groups may be considered essential, such as not questioning the group's efficiency in public or contributing to the tea and coffee fund. Other norms may be considered less important; for example, washing up the cups after meetings.

See also: Managing conflict, Chapter 8

The manager can brief the newcomer on the explicit group norms, but normally it is only through working in the group that the newcomer will internalise the group norms and behave appropriately. The manager may need to intervene, however, if conflict arises because the newcomer refuses to meet group demands.

Expectations

The individual's and the organisation's expectations are a key aspect of induction and socialisation. The formal aspects of what is required of an individual can be clarified during induction; for example, contractual requirements and hours of work. Similarly, the individual's formal requirements of the organisation are relatively easy to make clear: needing to be paid as agreed, requiring advance notice of overtime working, and so on. However, an individual can have expectations of an organisation or job that are not discussed. If these differ from what the newcomer experiences, then anxiety or confusion may result. This is likely to affect the individual's satisfaction, performance and commitment to the organisation. The manager can identify wrong or unrealistic expectations and deal with them by discussing the expectations and helping the individual to identify mismatches, and, where there is a mismatch, helping them to adjust appropriately if this is possible.

An organisation may have unrealistic expectations too, of course. If so, the manager needs to identify these and bring them into the open.

Although socialisation will be experienced differently by different people, the purpose of socialisation is to clarify a person's role, understand and accept group norms and patterns of behaviour. When, as a manager, you are able to see that a person is carrying out their role with relative confidence and has a sense of belonging, then you will know that socialisation has been successful. There is no cause for complacency, however: changes in roles, group structure or expectations may require you to attend to aspects of the socialisation process again.

Chapter 10 Managing performance
The performance management cycle

How can you ensure that the people you manage are meeting their work objectives and performance goals? A systematic approach to managing performance is the 'performance management cycle'. It comprises three stages.

Stage 1

Setting goals and clear objectives

Communicating regularly with staff

Discussing standards and expectations

Communicating goals and standards

Stage 2

Reviewing processes and performance

Improving current processes

Asking for ideas for improvement

Giving ongoing feedback (positive and corrective)

Documenting discussions

Stage 3

Performing yearly assessment of performance

Sharing written records with an employee

Conducting an appraisal discussion

Recording the results of the discussion

Planning and undertaking any agreed professional development

Stages 1 and 2 comprise day-to-day performance management which can often be informal, while Stage 3 is generally more formal, often involving information gathering and an annual meeting. Many organisations now recognise the importance both for the organisation itself and for the employees of designing and implementing performance management systems which suit their own contexts. Performance management has been described as:

> a process which contributes to the effective management of individuals and teams in order to achieve high levels of organisational performance. As such, it establishes shared understanding about what is to be achieved and an approach to leading and developing people which will ensure that it is achieved.
>
> (Source: Armstrong and Baron, 2004)

> a systematic and strategic approach to ensuring that employees' performance, as individuals and team members, enables the organisation to achieve a competitive advantage by producing the level and quality of products that lead to customer satisfaction and thereby the achievement of objectives and the ultimate realisation of strategy.
>
> (Source: Currie, 2006)

the process through which companies ensure that employees are working toward organizational goals, and includes practices through which the manager defines the employee's goals and work, develops the employee's skills and capabilities, evaluates the person's goal-directed behavior, and rewards him or her in a fashion that hopefully makes sense both in terms of the company's needs and the person's career aspirations.

(Source: Dessler, 2004)

Organising and performing the tasks set out in Stages 1–3 (above) is only one part of the process, however. The management of different people can be influenced by factors such as expectations, motivation, individual circumstances, age differences and culture, as the following example illustrates.

The human side of performance management

Ruth had two people reporting to her: Alex and Ella, both several years older than her. Alex had been appointed as a translator and had then become a project manager. He was very aware of his inexperience as a project manager and was very willing to learn. He had a family to support and job security was important to him.

Ella had been recruited as a project manager from a prestigious position in a government department. She felt a loss of status and influence on leaving the government job and felt that the experience she gained there was not appreciated or made use of in her current role.

Alex was eager to learn and to please and was initially quite demanding. Ruth worked patiently with him, setting objectives and identifying and addressing training. Once he became confident in his role, Alex took the initiative more and, although occasionally he made mistakes, he accepted the feedback and improved his performance.

Ruth's relationship with Ella was more difficult. Ella resisted Ruth's attempts at supervising her performance, believing she knew best how to get things done. Ruth was uneasy but did not intervene. Ella then made two serious mistakes. Ruth used these as opportunities to have several frank conversations with Ella and to establish regular supervisory meetings. Ella and Ruth were able to establish respect for each other and went on to develop a mutually-supportive relationship.

Performance management needs to be both *task-orientated*, to allow the manager to exercise control, and *person-orientated*, to recognise the rights and needs of individuals; for example, to have the appropriate resources for their work and to have someone to take an interest in what they are doing. Managers need to ensure that objectives are set (being task-centred), while at the same time supporting and developing staff so that they can achieve these objectives (being people-centred).

Task-centred activities

- Shaping – structuring the task.
- Target-setting – setting or agreeing specific goals and deadlines.
- Explaining and 'selling' policies and plans.
- Delegating tasks and responsibilities.
- Guiding the person doing the task – giving advice, being a role model.
- Limiting – setting boundaries; that is, making clear what the job involves and what it does not.
- Negotiating – matching individual ideas and needs with organisational policy.
- Resourcing – arranging the necessary resources.
- Monitoring.
- Acting on deviations from the plan.

People-centred activities

- Coaching – helping people to learn the work.
- Encouraging – listening supportively to ideas, boosting morale.
- Facilitating – getting introductions and putting people in touch.
- Counselling – giving assistance in exploring approaches to situations/ dealing with anxieties.
- Rewarding – giving recognition, having a say in pay and promotion.
- Representing – speaking on behalf of individuals.
- Evaluating – making judgements about an individual's achievements and potential.

Performance management is easier when there is good rapport between a manager and the people they manage. Establishing a good professional relationship will depend in part on the manager's interpersonal and communication skills.

A good relationship will help a manager know what motivates a person to work and perform well. Such relationships are helped by regular communication and dialogue.

Understanding how different people respond to performance management and their expectations of you as a manager will help you to judge how best to manage each individual. Judgements will also need to be made about how much management an employee needs: too much can frustrate and demoralise the person being managed (as well as being costly for the organisation), while too little is likely to be ineffective and can demotivate staff. Blending task- and people-centred activities is the art of people management.

Day-to-day performance management: supervision and monitoring

Regular monitoring and supervision are important activities for the manager: through them you assess the performance of the people you manage day-to-day. They are the processes by which you ensure that your staff are carrying out tasks you have set to the agreed standard, and that they have the necessary support and resources to do so. They allow you to identify and address problems early on, before they become significant.

The terms 'monitoring' and 'supervision' are often used interchangeably but refer to different functions. Monitoring means getting evidence that a task or job is proceeding well. This evidence is often checked against previously-agreed performance criteria. Supervising refers to 'people processes': for example, supporting, enabling and coaching individuals to help them do their jobs and meet goals.

See also: Planning and control, Chapter 4

Supervision

The supervisory process is partly directive and partly supportive. It consists of:

- supporting individuals and making sure they are adequately resourced and fairly treated
- enabling them to have some influence over their work
- seeing that they fulfil the organisation's objectives as well as their own
- ensuring that what is agreed is done.

Ways of structuring supervision

There are various ways in which supervision can be organised. Practical considerations, along with staff motivation, experience, competence, and the communication climate will all affect the method, or methods, chosen.

Continuous supervision

In some circumstances, some or all of the staff can be observed continuously. This may take the form of sampling the performance of individual staff continuously for a short time, as when, for example, a call centre supervisor listens to the telephone discussions between the employee and customers. Continuous supervision may be used because the supervisor spends a significant part of the day with the work group, for example, because one of the supervisor's roles is to handle the more difficult calls from customers. Employees who are learning the job may be supervised continuously, too. When continuous supervision is used, it is important to tell prospective employees during recruitment and selection because people who are experienced at what they do may not be comfortable with such observation of their work. A challenge for the supervisor is to be able to move between relating to staff as a work colleague and as a supervisor, particularly when a staff member is underperforming.

Intermittent supervision

Intermittent supervision can occur in situations in which a supervisor is present for only some of the time. This can happen when the supervisor travels to work group A on Mondays, work group B on Tuesdays, and so on. Alternatively the manager may 'manage by walking about', walking round the store, factory, hospital or warehouse one or more times a day. Staff can stop the supervisor as he or she passes and ask for help. The supervisor monitors activity, and may see good work being done, allowing for recognition and praise to be given. One challenge for the supervisor is how to support an employee in the times between visits. Another is how to supervise staff who work part-time or when you do not normally work, such as the weekend, early mornings, evenings or at night. Such staff often receive much less supervision.

Supervision by request

In the case of supervision by request, the supervisor is located in or near the workplace. When the supervisor's office door is open (or signals his or her availability for discussion in other ways) members of the work group are encouraged to call on the manager and explain any difficulties they may be having with their work. This method is efficient for staff, but it can mean that the manager is continuously interrupted. Further, employees may be unwilling to ask for help, or do not realise that they need help, and some may work at different times from the supervisor.

Planned supervisory meetings

In this form of supervision the supervisor meets each staff member individually by arrangement, usually face to face. In the UK it is common for staff in the public social and health care sector to have a substantial meeting with their supervisor every four to six weeks for an hour or more. This is usually guided by an agenda and written notes are made of what was discussed and decided. Supervisory meetings are considered to be good practice, thus we focus on these. However, other methods of supervision may be needed in addition where supervision sessions cannot take place frequently enough for the needs of the person or job.

Supervision sessions

Supervisory meetings can be formal or informal, but generally the underlying aims are to:

- build up *trust*
- allow for *discussion* and *negotiation*
- allow feedback on the work to be given *regularly*
- make clear what are the *joint responsibilities*
- allow *control* to be exercised and *support* to be given.

How can these aims be achieved? First, a working relationship needs to be established and regular contact made. Second, the manager needs to be assertive and to be able to handle assertive responses from the people who report to them. Third, there needs to be a genuine desire for supervision to be effective. All these may be present in intermittent supervision or supervision on request, but they are more likely to be achieved when time is set aside specifically for a supervision meeting.

The main purpose of a supervision session is to review what has happened since the last session and to discuss what has gone well or not so well. This will mean the manager will need to develop a set of revised objectives with the staff member, explain tasks that need to be done, agree targets and/or deadlines, give encouragement and guidance when needed and evaluate the results.

When and how supervision sessions are run will depend on various factors including the nature of the job or tasks to be performed by the person being supervised. Some guidelines for running an effective supervisory session are set out in Box 10.1. You will probably want to make supervision sessions fairly informal, but informality does not mean they should be held irregularly.

Box 10.1 Running a supervisory session

If possible, find a private place where you and the other person can speak freely and without interruptions.

Set aside sufficient time: this will signify the importance you attach to supervision.

At the start of a supervision session, agree on an agenda and how long you expect each item to take. Alternatively, have a standard agenda of regular items. This will probably include reviewing the work that has been done since the last session and reporting on any developments.

Make notes of what has been agreed and who is responsible for any action agreed. Close the session by confirming the action points. Do not forget that you are answerable to each other: each of you is responsible for carrying out the actions you have agreed to.

If a matter has to be left unresolved, make sure it is followed up.

Other supervisory tasks and responsibilities of the manager can include:

- *Patrolling the boundaries.* This means managing the interfaces with other parts of the organisation and the external environment (that is, learning how policies have changed and the implications for the work group and individual members of it).
- Providing the individual with *information* about changes and developments (and they should do the same for you).
- *Protecting* individuals when they need it, for example, from work overload caused by other people.
- *Challenging/developing* individuals when appropriate.

Factors that may affect the supervisory relationship include:

- Personal style. A person may have a tendency to act in a certain way whatever the requirements of a situation.
- The nature of the task.
- The ability and experience of the individuals involved.
- The nature of The Psychological Contract, that is, the stated and unstated expectations of the employee and the organisation.
- The level of authority the supervisor has over the person being supervised.

See also: The Psychological Contract, Chapter 6

- Physical distance or proximity. How much the manager and the person being supervised see of each other – they may not be in the same geographical location – will influence the relationship.
- The culture of the present organisation and that of previous organisations the individual may have worked for.

Each factor makes the relationship a supervisor has with each member of the work group slightly different. At times it may be necessary to exercise more control over a person's work, while at other times you may need to provide more support. Your ultimate aim is to enable individuals to become relatively independent and self-supervising. This means encouraging:

- self-reflection and analysis of their progress towards targets
- an awareness of any problems or benefits of their work
- an appreciation of the next set of priorities which need to be agreed.

Monitoring performance

One way of monitoring performance is management by objectives (MBO), first developed by Peter Drucker, the well-known writer on management. The principle of MBO is that, instead of watching over employees and telling them how to do their work, managers provide staff with objectives or targets to be reached. These objectives provide a clear set of standards against which to measure an employee's progress. They are sometimes known as key performance indicators (KPIs).

See also: What do managers actually do?, Chapter 1

The performance of employees is then measured by what they achieve. Objectives will be discussed and agreed, and action plans formulated, so it is clear how the work is to be carried out, what the deadlines are and what is needed to carry out the task.

When setting objectives, questions to consider include:

Are they challenging? (They should be something to aim for.)

Are they attainable? (They should not be unrealistic.)

Can they be measured? (How will you know whether something has been achieved or not?)

Are they relevant to the jobholder and the task? (There must be a clear and direct relationship to the person's job.)

Are the objectives SMART – that is, specific, measurable, agreed, realistic and timed?

MBO offers a way of managing performance that helps staff to exercise self-regulation and to correct mistakes themselves. However, periodic reviews by the manager to check on progress are important. MBO can be used as a framework for monitoring and supervision; carried further, it can be the basis of an organisation's way of working.

MBO: some issues to consider

MBO implies that all objectives or targets can be quantified or measured, but not every aspect of a job can be quantified or measured in this way. This is often the case in sectors such as health and social care, and in creative work.

Quantified targets can be provided for some areas of a job, of course, although this can lead to overemphasis on measurable aspects of a job while other aspects are neglected. Additional methods of assessing performance may also be needed, for example 360-degree feedback (CIPD, 2008).

See also: Preparing for the appraisal process, in this chapter

Another potential problem with MBO is that objectives, even though they need to be set jointly, may be set too high or too low. This can affect the morale of the individuals: they may feel discouraged if they fail to reach targets even if there are valid reasons why these could not be met. For example, there may have been changes in the external environment which could not have been predicted and which are outside the control of the employee and the manager.

MBO tends to emphasise the task rather than the person and probably reflects the time when MBO was first described by Drucker in 1954. Early in the supervisory relationship, and in some other circumstances, more emphasis may be needed on the person performing the task.

MBO is nonetheless useful for monitoring and supervision. When it is used across an organisation, managers will need to identify and address any potentially conflicting objectives.

Giving feedback on performance

Feedback on performance is a way of letting people know how effective they are, and helping them to perform better. Can you recall a time when someone asked you for feedback on their performance but you were unprepared and did so clumsily, causing upset or offence? Can you recall a time when someone gave you well-intentioned but negative feedback on your own performance at a bad moment or when you were least expecting it? If you do, you will know that giving (and receiving) feedback can produce intense emotion. It needs careful and skilful handling to be effective.

The ability to give and receive feedback skilfully will often be needed by managers during supervision and appraisal of staff, and in project evaluation.

What is meant by feedback?

Feedback is not criticism. Rather, it is a way of letting people know how well they are doing. It is important that an individual's performance is measured against agreed targets and standards and that potential problems are identified and explored. Feedback can be used to regulate an individual's performance. However, it is also an important way of supporting staff, helping them to understand what is expected of them at work and to make them feel valued. Feedback can focus on what a person has done well and what needs improvement.

Feedback may include the use and interpretation of data in order to assess and improve performance. Simply passing on factual information is unhelpful. For example, statements such as: 'You were down on your targets this month' or 'You did a good job there' provide little information on which a person can improve on poor performance or build on good performance. A manager will need to collect the necessary information to provide good quality feedback. There are opportunities for this as you go about your day-to-day routine, talking to members of your work group.

Giving feedback

Giving effective feedback requires good planning, interpersonal skills and an understanding of individuals and their circumstances. Consider the example below.

Understanding the individual

Mali found the experience of giving feedback to Doug and Janet challenging in different ways.

Janet would stare intensely at Mali and frown and sometimes she would interrupt and state her own view forcefully. Over time, Mali realised that the staring and frowning were Janet's ways of showing concentration and that her interruptions and forceful views revealed her commitment to the job rather than disagreement. As understanding and trust grew between them, Mali's feedback became well-received.

Doug always smiled and agreed with any feedback Mali gave him. Mali found this frustrating and felt he was agreeing to anything for an easy life. As she came to know Doug a little better, she found he had a lot of good ideas but rarely offered them. Mali realised that Doug was shy and needed encouragement to express his ideas.

Feedback can be part of any method of supervision – for example, a formal part of regular, face-to-face meetings – or it can be part of a mentoring or coaching relationship. Whenever it is provided, however, it needs to be *continuous, constructive* and *consistent* to be effective. It should praise strengths and achievements and cover areas for improvement. It should also be:

Relevant. It relates to the work situation or the skills required.

Right. It has been carefully thought out, is logical and factual, and is supported by evidence.

Rapid. It is related to current work and given at a time when it is still possible to effect change.

Destructive feedback often focusses on complaining and attacking and offers few, if any, positive suggestions. Often it is badly delivered; that is, it is well-intentioned but vague, badly-timed or ill thought-out. Examples include focussing on the personal attributes of the individual rather than the task, performance and work behaviours; being unspecific and failing to provide evidence or examples that support what is being said; and failing to make suggestions on suitable improvements. Destructive feedback should always be avoided.

Managers need to take care when communicating the need for performance improvement to several people in a work group, if only one of the group has created the performance problem. A common approach is to give individual feedback and then, later, explain the improvement to the work group without identifying the individual. This avoids the person feeling that personal criticisms have been made in front of colleagues. Similarly, when feedback includes praise, individuals may not like being praised in front of colleagues. Others may welcome it, however. Here, the manager needs to consider the impact on the whole work group: praising one member of a work group may seem like criticism of the performance of the other members.

Receiving feedback

Learning to receive constructive feedback and to act on it is as important as giving feedback. To benefit from feedback:

- Listen to what is being said and do not interrupt (there will be opportunities for you to respond).

- Avoid being defensive or overreacting.

- Use open and encouraging body language.

- Take the feedback in the spirit it was intended and do not look for other reasons for the feedback.

- Listen actively, asking for clarification and more information when necessary; try to get the whole picture.

- Try to recognise the value of what is being said.

- Accept the feedback and if possible thank the person who gave it; it may have been very difficult for them.

- Take the opportunity to respond – you may be invited to do this during the feedback or at the end.

- Try to avoid 'gut' reactions; take time to gather your thoughts.

- If you do not feel able to reply immediately arrange to do this soon afterwards.

You will need strategies for responding skilfully to invalid or destructive feedback. If a senior manager has given you this kind of feedback, you could simply note the feedback. At other times, the best option may be to say that the feedback is not valid, or destructive, and why, and manage the potential conflict skilfully. Possibly, the best option might be to ask to continue the discussion at another time (when you have prepared information to challenge their feedback, or when you or they are no longer angry).

Feedback is best given and received in circumstances where there is mutual respect and understanding and where the genuine expression of views is encouraged. This may assume a genuine rapport between the giver and receiver which, initially at least, may be difficult to establish.

Managing poor or declining performance

Dan's negative impact

Dan had never been the best-performing member of the team, but his work had always been adequate – until last month. He was late finishing a project report which he handed to Maureen, the project leader, too late for her to include some charts in her presentation to senior management. Then, Maureen discovered important omissions in the report. She hoped the missed deadline and errors would not happen again. Today, however, two team members had complained to her that Dan was not carrying out his work properly and this was having a detrimental effect on their own contributions to the project.

Poor or declining performance, as in the example above, is not easy to deal with. But the quicker it is identified the quicker it can be addressed, to avoid more serious consequences later for the organisation and the individuals concerned. Disciplinary or grievance issues often arise if such issues are not dealt with effectively.

Judgements about when to act can be difficult. As a manager, you may have had experience of poor or declining performance in a staff member and wished you had done something earlier. You may have had experience of intervening when it was not entirely necessary. Action needs to be based on an informed decision about a person's performance, so it is important to gather as much information as possible.

Once you have all the information to hand you can make an assessment of the overall performance of the individual whose performance is poor or declining. You have three main options:

- take no action
- act to correct performance
- revise the work standards set.

Option 1 Take no action

There may be a number of reasons for doing nothing and letting someone continue what they are doing. Positive reasons include:

- there are more important or urgent work issues to deal with
- the performance problem is not serious at this point
- any corrective action would risk making things worse
- it is not possible to establish reasons for the failure to meet standards
- the employee is likely to take note and correct it.

There are negative reasons for taking no action, however. The manager may dislike raising difficult issues and fear provoking conflict. The advice of a more experienced colleague often helps in such situations.

Option 2 Act to correct performance

See also: Managing conflict, Chapter 8

This option might involve any of the following:

- committing additional resources (including finding other staff to help)
- insisting that the work be done again or improved
- getting directly involved yourself to resolve difficulties
- changing procedures or working methods

- arranging additional training for the person
- changing work allocations so that a more experienced person can take over.

If you are in doubt about whether the performance constitutes poor performance seek a second opinion from a trusted colleague.

A manager's attempt to address poor performance should be positive and focus on what can be done by individuals to overcome the problems. The basic steps for dealing with poor performance are:

Step 1: Identify and agree on the problem.

Step 2: Establish the reason(s) for the problem. Is it caused by lack of support, understanding, ability, skill or an inappropriate attitude?

Step 3: Decide and agree on the action required; for example, developing skills, providing more guidance.

Step 4: Support the action; for example, by arranging assistance, coaching or training.

Step 5: Monitor performance and provide feedback.

Option 3 Revise the work standards set

The third option for addressing poor or declining performance is to review the work standards an individual has been set and to revise them if they are unrealistic. They may be unrealistic if, for example, deadlines have changed, if promised resources were not provided or if other staff fell ill. However, revising the standards can have a negative impact. It can:

- encourage the person concerned to ignore any future standards set
- remove a good incentive even if the standard cannot quite be achieved
- make someone who has exerted themselves feel it was a waste of effort
- produce feelings of failure
- affect other aspects of the department's work or that of other people.

One problem with these three options for addressing poor or declining performance is that they may not address its underlying cause. This may mean that some systematic problem-solving is needed. Causes may be technical, such as IT problems, poor materials or challenging customers, or it may be the result of demotivation, lack of training and development or personal issues. Monitoring and appraisal meetings are opportunities to discuss performance issues and causes.

Performance management and the appraisal process

Most organisations have some kind of system in place for monitoring performance and giving feedback to employees on their performance. In many organisations this system is a performance management cycle in which an appraisal process occurs annually. While we can picture the performance management cycle without an annual appraisal process, this would be unusual. The appraisal process provides the opportunity for setting and reviewing work objectives and individual performance with each employee. People who work in the organisation but are not employed by it, such as volunteers and contractors, may also be included in this appraisal system.

Appraisal has been defined as:

> a process that provides an analysis of a person's overall capabilities and potential, allowing informed decisions to be made for particular purposes.

> (Source: Gold, 2003)

> [a means of] evaluating an employee's current and/or past performance relative to his or her performance standards.

> (Source: Dessler, 2004)

A formal appraisal process is normally a structured set of activities held once a year, sometimes with an interim event every six months. While performance feedback will have been provided throughout the year, the annual process is more formal. By having a formally-arranged process, the importance of appraisal is made clear, and it is more likely that all parts of it will happen. The appraisal process is important in improving job performance by reviewing what is going well and what needs improving. The formal identification and agreement of learning and development needs make it more likely that the learning and development will happen. The process also allows formal time for the manager and employee to discuss ideas and views. However, the appraisal process has a significant cost, particularly in time, so managers must be clear that benefits are greater than costs.

The importance of appraisal

Why is it important to have a formal system in place when effective management involves monitoring and supervision all through the year? Although day-to-day management is important, more formal assessment provides an opportunity for formally documenting informal feedback, for reviewing performance, for learning from difficulties, for celebrating successes and for looking towards the future. It can also be a way for organisations to set and agree objectives at the level of the individual and ensure that these are aligned with wider organisational objectives. For organisations that emphasise 'talent management' the appraisal system provides a mechanisms to recognise potential and to retain and reward staff.

See also: Induction and socialisation, Chapter 9

Appraisals and performance management are also part of the socialisation into an organisation that continues after an initial induction programme.

Delays in holding an appraisal should be avoided. A manager may postpone an appraisal to give priority to an operational crisis but those affected may conclude that the manager's commitment to appraisal is not strong.

See also: The
communication climate,
Chapter 2

The necessary communication climate

For appraisal – and performance management in general – to be effective, an open communication climate is usually necessary.

Here, people feel they can speak freely without fear of being criticised; suggestions are welcomed and acted on and mistakes are used as an opportunity to learn. Communication climate problems or interpersonal difficulties between appraiser and appraisee can sometimes make formal appraisal difficult in organisations where everyone is appraised. Here, alternative approaches include involving an HR specialist or an alternative manager who the appraisee will accept. In some cases, the employee may ask for an independent mediator, or for the support of a representative of their trade union.

Training for appraisers

It is generally recognised that specific skills are needed in appraisal meetings. Many managers become effective and efficient appraisers. However, even if good training is provided, managers with low commitment to successful performance management can readily forget their training. It is not easy for organisations to monitor appraisers' competence in appraisal meetings.

The appraisal meeting

Appraisal meetings can be very effective. Some are not, however. Common reasons include:

- lack of organisational commitment to performance management
- the aims and benefits of appraisal are not properly understood by the appraiser or the appraisee
- the process is hurried and little significance is attached to it by the appraiser, the appraisee or both
- the appraisee feels unable to discuss performance issues with the appraiser
- the appraiser is not sufficiently familiar with the appraisee's work
- actions agreed during the appraisal meeting are not followed through afterwards.

Disagreements

Factors such as a closed communication climate, unclear objectives, incomplete monitoring information and unskilled appraisers may well lead to disagreements in the meeting. It is usual for the process to include ways of handling disagreements. These normally include a way for the appraisee to record that the manager's evaluation is not accepted. Then, another manager, often more senior, or an HR specialist, will review the situation. However, if the communication climate is not open, an individual who privately disagrees with an evaluation may well decide that using the disagreements process is too risky or not worth the effort.

Action

A successful appraisal meeting may well identify the need for training, a change of job, changes in objectives, or just practical issues such as the need for a different desk or chair. The appraiser will have the authority and resources to implement some of these changes, but probably not all. It is important for the appraiser to be realistic about what courses of action can be taken. It is good practice to explain the relevant decision-making process and timescales with the person being appraised and to agree how progress will be monitored and communicated.

Monitoring

Many organisations recognise that accurate documents summarising the appraisal meeting have many uses. In an organisation which has implemented talent management, the document will add to the information enabling the talent managers to make best use of the organisation's human resources. If senior managers allocate time to studying these documents, there is an opportunity for:

- high-performing staff to receive direct praise and recognition, usually a very positive experience
- the managers of low-performing staff to be asked to provide periodic progress reports, ensuring that the low performance is actively considered.

Appraising people who are not employees

In most organisations, the work is done mainly by employees, but there are good reasons for using different sorts of people to do your organisation's work. We need to consider specifically the appraisal of volunteers. These people may or may not be familiar with appraisal in other organisations where they work or are volunteers. For each type of non-employee you will need to analyse, discuss and agree, before the arrangement starts, how the performance management and appraisal of them will be divided between you, and other managers inside and outside your organisation.

The appraisal process is a potentially helpful tool for both managers and employees as a way of structuring discussion on performance, identifying difficulties and training needs and agreeing actions. It is a process which helps to ensure that employees 'know and understand what is expected of them, have the skills and ability to deliver on these expectations, are supported by the organisation to develop the capacity to meet these expectations and are given feedback on their performance' (Armstrong and Baron, 2004). However, the process can go wrong if it includes hidden agendas and is not transparent and evidence-based. Managers may need the help of senior managers and specialists to create a climate in which the benefits of appraisal can be expected to exceed the costs. Above all, managers need to understand the purpose and nature of the appraisal process, and prepare for and manage it effectively for it to work well.

Preparing for the appraisal process

The appraisal process is normally part of a year-long process of performance management which needs careful planning and preparation. As a manager, you will have an important role in communicating to each employee the purpose and benefits of appraisal and what to expect.

Consider the following case in which problems in the process can be identified before and during the appraisal meeting.

An unsatisfactory process

> Peter, the organisation's representative in Vienna, and his line manager, Christopher, scheduled their annual appraisal meeting for the day on which they both returned on a night flight from an international conference in Washington. Twenty minutes before the scheduled meeting, Christopher, with much more formality than normal, solemnly handed Peter a sheet containing his thoughts on Peter's performance for discussion at the appraisal meeting. Peter, in an attempt to lighten the atmosphere, said, 'Oh, did you write this on the plane?'. Christopher coldly replied, 'It doesn't matter where I wrote it' and walked away. The document consisted of a report on Peter's performance showing that it was barely 'satisfactory'. It did not refer to what Peter considered to be his key achievements and successes. There was anonymous negative criticism with no supporting evidence. Fifteen minutes later, Peter was called into Christopher's office for the appraisal interview. Peter was tired and felt nervous because of Christopher's behaviour and his report. He felt that an unethical process of gathering feedback on his performance had been going on that he knew nothing about. He also felt unprepared because he had not been asked to produce his own report and now had little time to put forward a positive case. The meeting did not go well for Peter and he left the organisation a few months later.

Mistakes and misconceptions can upset the smooth running of the process and make appraisals unsuccessful. An important issue raised by this case is the type and nature of evidence and feedback used.

Collecting evidence

In most organisations, individual line managers carry out one-to-one appraisals with their staff. This has advantages for both parties and it is usually argued that the manager or team leader is the person best placed to comment on the individual's overall contribution and performance. In organisations where there is no one obvious appraiser, the appraisee may be consulted to recommend the person who best knows their work.

See also: Planning and control, Chapter 4

Information collected as part of day-to-day monitoring of performance (which should also have been addressed and discussed as it occurred) can be used, too.

Evidence may include:

- **Observation and involvement.** You notice a good climate in the meetings the appraisee runs. Their work colleagues never seem to have negative things to say about them. Their workplace is tidy and their communications with you are clear and effective. Or, you see that backlogs are building up, overtime has had to be worked, or that customer complaints are increasing. These symptoms may be traced to an individual, or may signify underperformance in the department as a whole. Equally, low or high performance may be due to factors such as resourcing.

- **Questioning and discussion.** You can identify levels of performance by discussion with individuals and teams. This will confirm everyone's knowledge and understanding of what is required and will help to keep people informed of what is happening and why. Discussion is essential when problems emerge, especially in a complex area of work, but if it involves asking standard questions, then routine reporting may be preferable.

- **Routine statistics and reporting.** Details such as output or weekly sales figures can be compared with previous performance or checked against the expected or budgeted figures. This checking of reports is a useful discipline for managers to develop, although much depends on their accuracy and timeliness.

- **Your own statistics.** These are your own figures, relating to your section or department. They may show the highs and lows of output that may reveal trends not shown elsewhere. However, you must be sure they are relevant to the performance of the person being appraised.

- **Other reports.** These could include regular reports from internal committees and meetings, and complaints or queries from customers and/or suppliers. Exception reporting is another option. These reports concentrate only on areas where performance is not as expected and draw attention to performance that is either below or above these expectations. As with routine statistics, you need to receive these reports promptly and regularly and be confident of their accuracy.

Performance is often measured against organisational objectives, or key performance indicators (KPIs). One way of appraising these is to concentrate on a measurable set of targets and objectives that an employee has achieved.

Some organisations carry out what is known as a 360-degree appraisal. It involves seeking feedback from a variety of different sources of higher and lower status and of the same status as the appraisee (hence the term '360-degree'). Thus, sources will include peers, people who report to the person being appraised, the line manager and others who are familiar with the person's work. These will sometimes be customers or clients. This concept is popular because it is seen as providing a fair and rounded view of performance. It has the advantage of providing a wider range of feedback, and sources are not normally identified. The wider information can reduce the possibility of the halo and horns effects: for example, when a manager focusses too much on evidence of a good or poor aspect of performance, ignoring contrary evidence about other aspects of it.

It can also help in identifying and prioritising learning needs. A disadvantage is the cost of gathering and collating evidence.

For the 360-degree process to be effective, it is important to decide at the outset on what behaviours and competences are to be assessed, who can provide this feedback and how the information can be collected (by, for example, a confidential questionnaire). A 360-degree feedback questionnaire may consist of a series of statements about the individual's performance, to be rated on a scale of 1 to 5 (CIPD, 2008). The questions should be short, clear and relevant to the person's job and the questionnaire may also include space for free comments. The questionnaire is sent to up to 10 colleagues and contacts, although three or four may be sufficient. The results are written up usually without identifying particular sources of information, and given to the individual.

Done well, 360-degree feedback can challenge the recipient's perception of their skills and performance and provides motivation to change. For example, others may rate aspects of a person's performance more highly than the person does. It can also indicate areas for improvement, which are hard to challenge because they are fully supported by evidence. A person may not have realised that an aspect of their behaviour has such an impact on their performance.

In order for such feedback to be taken seriously and lead to changes in behaviour, contributors need to be regarded as credible by appraisees. It is always good practice to ask those who are giving information to provide examples of the behaviours, skills or performance that they are commenting on. This makes the feedback more robust and also helps the individual to make changes.

Documentation

It is essential to give adequate advance notice of appraisal meetings and to help staff to prepare. They (and you) will need to be clear about the purpose of the appraisal and to agree a plan or agenda.

Performance systems sometimes break down if the paperwork is excessive. It is best to keep forms as simple as possible. Any written feedback should be given to appraisees several days beforehand to give them time to consider the feedback carefully. Some organisations use an appraisal preparation form that appraisees complete a week or more before the meeting. This might ask them to assess their own performance over the period in question and to provide constructive comment. The completed form can then be used as a basis for discussion at the meeting. An example is shown in Box 10.2.

Box 10.2 An example of an appraisal preparation form

What objectives did you agree at your last appraisal meeting?

How successful have you been in achieving these?

What have been your main achievements since your last appraisal?

What constraints and/or difficulties did you encounter in this period?

What might help you to deal with these or overcome them?

Which parts of your current work do you most enjoy and least enjoy?

What training and development activities have you undertaken since your last appraisal?

How have these helped you to do your job better?

In what areas of your job could you further develop your skills, knowledge or experience?

Are there any additional responsibilities you would like to take on in the next 12 months?

Would these involve any additional training?

In summary, performance management systems help both managers and individuals prepare for appraisal. Evidence needs to be collected from various sources, and individuals need to reflect on their performance, learning and development since their last appraisal. The use of standard procedures may help the smooth running of the preparation process. In addition, care needs to be taken by managers to avoid some of the faults that can lead to bad appraisal experiences.

Conducting the appraisal meeting

There is no one 'best way' of conducting appraisal meetings: managers need to think about how to conduct them in a way that leads to an open discussion about what a person has achieved and agreement on ways forward.

How formal or informal the event will be depends on organisational practice and culture. Because the appraisal meeting is outside everyday work discussion, it is likely to be relatively formal. If serious issues of poor performance are expected to be raised, a more formal atmosphere may be preferable. It is also important to structure the meeting well and leave sufficient and uninterrupted time to conduct it; this helps to demonstrate to the appraisee that the meeting is important: it is after all their job and their performance of it that is being discussed. It is important to have an agenda and to leave time for anything that you or the person being appraised may want to raise. A typical structure for an appraisal meeting is set out in Box 10.3.

> ## Box 10.3 A typical structure for an appraisal meeting
>
> Explain the form and purpose of the meeting
>
> Discuss the job's objectives and demands
>
> Discuss the extent to which the objectives were achieved
>
> Discuss ways to help the employee better achieve the objectives
>
> Agree and set new objectives to be achieved by the next appraisal meeting
>
> Discuss training and development needs
>
> Summarise the discussion and points agreed

For the meeting itself a neutral but private space – for example, a meeting room which can be booked – is recommended. Your aim is to create a rapport and encourage the appraisee to talk, so it is important for you to listen actively.

See also: Communication skills, Chapter 2

In each part of the meeting use open questions to help the appraisee talk about their work and performance. Suitable open questions – those that are almost impossible to answer with yes or no or with a one-word answer – normally include the words what, why and how:

What (What was your biggest achievement this year?)

Why (Why do you think it was so successful?)

How (How did you manage to produce X within budget?)

At the end of the session the discussion should be summarised verbally. This needs to include what has been agreed and what actions, if any, both parties need to take; for example, arranging specific training. Objectives for the period before the next appraisal should also be set. These need to be written down and a copy given to the appraisee.

Typically, a well-structured meeting lasts about an hour. However, meetings might need to be much longer than this, or everything that needs to be said may take only half an hour. An example of how a one-hour meeting can be structured is given in Table 10.1.

Table 10.1 An example of a meeting schedule

Time (minutes)	Activity
0 to 5	icebreaker
5 to 20	revisiting of objectives
20 to 30	achievements since the last appraisal
30 to 40	setting objectives for next 12 months
40 to 50	planning and training and development needs
50 to 60	questions or comments; summary; end session

Outcomes of appraisal

Normally objective setting is a key outcome of the appraisal meeting. Some organisations do this at different times in the performance management year; for example, when pay and bonuses are reviewed. In this case, the appraisal meeting will consider these objectives. Appraisees must be able to come away from the appraisal with a clear idea of what they need to do in the following year. The plan needs to be SMART – specific, measurable, agreed, realistic and timed. The manager should summarise the main points in writing and give them to the appraisee in the form of a report. Issues discussed may be sensitive and it is usual for there to be clear, well-enforced rules on who may see the report.

Additional meetings and conversations

In some cases it is not suitable or possible to discuss all the aspects of a person's performance in an appraisal meeting and further meetings may be necessary. Two examples are:

Training needs. Although training needs are often discussed and decided during the appraisal meeting, a further meeting may be needed to explore learning needs or for drawing up a personal development plan or for career planning.

See also: Identifying learning needs, Chapter 11

Reward reviews. In organisations that implement performance-related pay (PRP) or competence-related pay, a process is needed to review evidence and discuss performance with the employee. Some organisations save time by adding pay discussions to the appraisal meeting. If appraisees are seeking a pay increase, there are significant pressures on them to present their performance as positively as possible, however. An appraisee might decide not to remind the appraiser about mistakes and learning needs. Because of the conflict between the purposes of appraisal and pay-review meetings, many organisations keep them separate. However the pay-review meeting may draw on information and evidence used in the appraisal meeting.

Appraisal meetings have the potential to be a rewarding experience for both parties if well-planned and carefully-handled.

Chapter 11 Learning and development at work

The need to learn

Learning is the process by which people gain knowledge and skills throughout their lives, in and outside work. It is crucial both to organisations and people: to organisations because workplace learning is now often seen as a competitive strategy; to individuals because it improves their performance and their employability. Thus, the field of training and development has shifted its focus to more integrated and systematic approaches that aim to deliver better overall performance (Berge *et al.*, 2002).

Managers have a larger role to play in this new systems approach to performance improvement. The days of putting large numbers of staff through the same training programme are disappearing or gone.

Some training is not optional, of course. Teaching staff critical processes and procedures (for example, health and safety) must be done. But placing emphasis on learning in all areas of work – for example, if employees are involved in continuing professional development and sharing knowledge – means that organisations are best placed to react quickly to changing situations. They are likely to be able to produce a new product or service or to respond to changing demands more quickly than competitors. Creating a 'culture of learning' helps the organisation to gain or maintain competitive advantage or, in the case of a not-for-profit organisation, to meet changed needs faster and more fully. Further, organisations that offer training and development programmes, which include opportunities to train on the job and to improve skills and employability, can attract and retain high-quality staff.

To maximise the benefits of workplace learning and development, managers need to know how to facilitate learning, and support and encourage the people they are responsible for, even if training and development is organised and delivered by others who are sometimes in different organisations.

What drives learning?

Many learning needs arise as organisations develop and change, as technologies are invented or are improved, as climate change and sustainability provide an impetus for adaptation, and as individuals take on new responsibilities. In modern, flexible organisations employees may need a larger range of skills to perform a wider range of tasks. This means the ability to learn easily and quickly is increasingly required among new recruits. However, there is also less stability for employees: the idea of a job for life is disappearing and people often have several careers in their working lives. Learning needs to be life-long if people are to develop and maintain their employability by acquiring up-to-date transferable skills they can use in other jobs and roles.

Types of work-based learning

Learning at work can take different forms, from training in a specific technique to a long period of professional and personal development through, for example, coaching or mentoring.

It can also take place outside the workplace, with the new knowledge being applied back in the workplace.

The following examples illustrate some different forms of on-the-job and off-the-job learning.

Jay's learning

At the end of Jay's second week in his new role as a customer call-centre manager, he was asked to produce a report on how the new customer records system was working. Jay produced a set of notes but was unsure of how to write a report from them. Jay explained his problem to Sabia, a senior administrator, over lunch. Later Sabia gave Jay a written report: 'Here's quite a good example, Jay. Take a look at the structure and the headings and just organise your notes under those. On the front page, here, is an executive summary ... an overview of the key points, really. If you want me to have a quick look at your report before you submit it, that's fine.'

Health and safety provision

Laxmi is responsible for health and safety and training in a hospital. She has to ensure that all staff learn the necessary health and safety procedures and can act quickly and efficiently in an emergency. Laxmi's job involves ensuring that individuals have the right balance of technical and practical training. Different methods are needed for these. Staff must learn rules and procedures and be able to use a simple checklist when making inspections. They must also know how to react promptly in emergencies and be able to make quick decisions without consulting a manual. What would be needed in the case of a toxic chemical leak? What would be needed if staff and patients were at immediate risk of injury? All the training has to be highly-structured. Some of it is classroom-based and some it is in the form of repeated practice. Furthermore, the training must comply with state regulations on employee health and safety training.

Ash's course

Ash entered his organisation some years ago with a university degree in history. In recent years more people have entered the organisation with business and management qualifications. Ash is a skilful manager and has much experience of managing which he has learned on the job. However, he began to feel increasingly insecure about his lack of formal management knowledge. He has started a part-time Master of Business Administration (MBA) at a local university. He sees this as an opportunity to improve his day-to-day management practice by applying at work what he learns on the course.

In the first example, Jay has to learn a new skill, report writing. There are no written instructions to hand, so he draws on the experience of a colleague who already has this skill. With the help of his colleague he familiarises himself with something which he can use as a model. He also secures 'briefing time' with Sabia who will look at his work and help him develop report-writing skills by commenting on his work. Sabia will pass on the organisation's conventions of report writing.

In the second example, Laxmi's job involves making sure that members of staff have read the manuals on health and safety rules and regulations and have taken part in the relevant training programmes. However, she must also make sure that staff are able to apply instantly the information in the manuals in an emergency. Thus, she has to organise realistic practice in which the staff carry out simulations of emergencies many times.

In the third example, Ash takes part in formal learning outside the organisation but applies the learning to his day-to-day work. The form of study offers him the opportunity to try out new ideas and techniques in his work.

These examples illustrate different methods of learning, each relevant to the type of knowledge and skills needed. They range from informal learning supported by colleagues, to written instructions, formal training courses, drills and practice as well as external, structured, academic learning.

Almost all learning falls into these two broad categories: formal and informal learning. Formal learning is normally conscious and structured while informal learning is often less systematic: people learn through doing and through working with, talking to and observing others.

The learning organisation

As noted earlier, many organisations need to be able to anticipate and respond to the demands of the external environment. To do this, a number of organisations, such as Hewlett Packard and Ford, have attempted to become 'learning organisations'. These have been described as organisations in which 'people continually expand their capacity to create the results they truly desire, where new and expansive patterns of thinking are nurtured, where collective aspiration is set free and where people are continually learning how to learn together' (Senge, 1990). The learning organisation refers to a specific set of practices intended to achieve this. Key components of the learning organisation concept are that it advocates:

- a climate in which individual members are encouraged to learn and develop their full potential
- a learning culture which is extended to include customers, suppliers and other stakeholders
- a human resource development strategy which is central to business policy
- a continuous state of organisational transformation.

(Source: based on Pedler *et al.*, 1991)

Of what use and relevance are these ideas to practising managers? According to Caplan (2003), the concept of the learning organisation has helped people to see learning as something they take control of, rather than something that is done to them by being sent on training courses. What might it be like to work in a learning organisation? The case set out in Box 11.1 illustrates how some principles of the learning organisation operate at an individual and work-group level.

Box 11.1 The learning organisation in practice

When Anthony got his new job he immediately noticed many positive differences between his new employer and his former one. On the first day he was given a schedule for his personal induction programme as well as a schedule of all staff training events. Then, at his first meeting with his line manager, Funmi, he was encouraged to rate his existing skills against those needed to do the job. As gaps were identified, they drew up a training and development plan to address Anthony's needs. His manager also suggested that he had a mentor. They discussed who might be appropriate, but the choice of mentor was left to Anthony.

As the weeks went by, Anthony noticed that Funmi often reflected on her own actions, analysing her own behaviour and its effects. She encouraged staff to do the same. She regularly coached Anthony, guiding him towards more effective performance by support and questioning. This encouraged him to think about his own performance and, where appropriate, to find new ways of doing things.

At team meetings, there were regular debriefings and discussion on what improvements were needed. Members shared and developed ideas through discussion and new challenges were seized as a new team-learning experience rather than being given to one individual to deal with. New solutions were arrived at quickly and innovatively. As a result, Anthony felt more inclined to admit to his own shortcomings and share his ideas. He also felt positive towards this organisation, which was prepared to spend time and money on his professional development.

Making a difference

Individual employees, supported by their managers, need to recognise that they can have a substantial impact on the learning culture of the organisation by embracing 'learning organisation' concepts. This idea is reflected in the work of Peter Senge, the best-known proponent of the learning organisation whose book *The Fifth Discipline* (1990) achieved best-seller status.

Senge describes five disciplines that employees need in order for an organisation to be a learning organisation.

Box 11.2 The five disciplines

Systems thinking

Systems thinking is a way of understanding the interrelationship between all the processes and activities of an organisation. It helps provide a full and clear picture of the problems, issues and situations that managers face and is a useful problem-solving tool.

Mental models

Mental models are the frameworks or theories we develop to understand the world and which inform our actions. We are often not conscious of these models, so Senge suggests we develop the skills of reflection as a means of revealing (and changing) them.

Shared vision

Shared vision is an agreed and shared understanding that leads to a shared identity in an organisation and shared vision for it. It is important for staff and managers to know what the organisation's vision is, what they are doing to get there and what more could be done.

Team learning

Team learning involves skilful dialogue and discussion among team members to build an integrated and properly functioning team. Team learning is considered vital in organisations where teams, not individuals, are the 'learning unit'.

Personal mastery

Personal mastery is about individuals in the organisation taking responsibility for their own learning and development. They need to work out what they want to achieve and how to achieve it. This means identifying learning needs, seeking opportunities to meet them and making the most of these opportunities.

See also: Learning from everyday experiences, in this chapter

The relationship between individual and organisational learning is complex: individuals need to have some ownership of their learning while organisations need to emphasise learning for specific business-focussed reasons. Training and development may sometimes imply a strategic, top–down decision, conceived and implemented by senior management. However, the concept of the learning organisation, which advocates total employee involvement in a collaborative process towards shared values or principles, is an important counterposition. So, although the concept of the learning organisation is perhaps vague, idealistic and insufficiently business-focussed, it is useful in understanding the relationship between the individual and the organisation. It is a concept which real organisations can aspire to but may not be able to achieve because of lack of resources (Easterby-Smith and Araujo, 1999). However, there may be tangible benefits in developing elements of it to encourage creativity, innovation or flexibility.

Knowledge and adult learners

Work-based learning involves the acquisition of different forms of *knowledge* that improvements in work performance require. These types of knowledge need to be understood, along with differences in approach to learning by individuals, in order to match training and development, and methods, to the needs of the individual and the job.

Types of knowledge

Three types of knowledge, namely explicit knowledge, procedural knowledge and tacit knowledge, all play their part in work-based learning.

Explicit knowledge can be expressed in words and numbers and can be communicated. Formal and systematic explicit knowledge includes product specifications, scientific formulas, computer programs, documented best practices, the formalised standards by which an insurance claim is adjudicated and the official expectations for performance set out in written work objectives (Nickols, 2000).

The content of this textbook is made up entirely of explicit knowledge (although the authors have used other forms of knowledge, too, to compile it). Explicit knowledge can be acquired through formal education but the application of this knowledge to specific situations may also require specific training. Some explicit knowledge can be learned by rote, which may be necessary – for example, in the case of learning a set of safety rules.

Another form of knowledge is procedural knowledge. It cannot be articulated easily. Classic examples of this are riding a bicycle and throwing a clay pot on a wheel; in the workplace, operating machinery can often require procedural knowledge. Few tasks require solely procedural knowledge, however: in many cases, although one might be able to read a manual, effective performance is acquired only after practise. The learner may sit with a skilled operator first to observe the process and then carry it out under supervision.

A third type of knowledge, known as tacit knowledge, is acquired through practise and long experience and cannot be written down or fully articulated. Thus, it is difficult to pass on to others. Tacit knowledge has been described as 'personal, context-specific and hard to formalise and communicate' (Nonaka and Takeuchi, 1995).

The tacit knowledge of experienced employees is often the key to skilled performance although it is difficult to capture and control because, for those who possess the knowledge, it is taken for granted. There are, however, examples of how tacit knowledge can be captured and applied or made explicit. Nonaka and Takeuchi tell how Matsushita Electric could not build an electronic bread maker that kneaded the dough properly. Finally an engineer was assigned to work with one of Japan's premier bakers and under the guidance of this master baker the engineer was able to design a machine that effectively mimicked the baker's craft.

This example also illustrates that knowledge of one type can be transformed into another. Another example is learning to touch type: the novice follows a diagram of the keyboard (explicit) and keeps a check on output (explicit), correcting finger positions as necessary to type accurately (explicit). After becoming skilled, the person may be unable to draw a diagram of the keyboard (implicit), and can say where the keys are only by imagining typing a sentence that contains every letter of the alphabet (procedural).

Adults as learners

Learning in the workplace can be quite different from the formal learning that took place at school. There are also differences between school-age and adult learners. Knowles (1980) identified four characteristics of adult learners that distinguish them from children (and how they learn).

Adult learners are:

- self-directive: they prefer to be in control of what is learned and how it is learned
- experienced: they recognise that they can draw from experience when they learn, applying past learning to current problems
- ready to learn: they are more interested in learning things that seem urgent or relevant
- problem-centred: they are more interested in learning in situations in which they want to understand better or behave differently.

However, some adults may have had poor prior learning experiences and can be anxious about training and development. They may also have poor learning skills – that is, they have not learned effective ways of learning. Adult learners may need to develop such skills. Meggison (1996) uses metaphors to illustrate adults at different stages of learning–skill development.

Sleepers have not yet developed their capacity for learning. These learners will need specific encouragement and support.

Warriors persistently pursue predetermined learning goals but will follow *only* these goals and do not diverge from them as situations and needs change. They need to become more flexible.

Adventurers are open to learning and take a spontaneous but haphazard approach to learning. They need to become more systematic and organised learners.

Sages use the ways of both the warrior and the adventurer, combining both planned and spontaneous learning.

People can move from being one type of learner to another according to their engagement with learning, the development of flexibility and the ability to be systematic and organised. Managers can use these metaphors to try to understand people's current learning skills and to help improve them.

How people set about learning will be influenced by a number of factors, in addition to their learning skills. People have preferences about the way they like to acquire knowledge, although what needs to be learned may be best taught or acquired using particular methods. For some people and tasks demonstrations are preferable. For other people and tasks a more conceptual approach may be preferred, such as reading technical or other material to acquire an overview or a theoretical understanding. For yet other people and tasks, the use of diagrams or pictures instead of text is better, or handling the objects or walking through the relevant workplace and experimenting may be preferable. Personal preferences about methods of learning are not fixed and will change according to the type of knowledge to be acquired: a person is likely to approach learning to use a new mobile phone differently from learning how to conduct a performance appraisal. Priorities, time and prior experience will also have an influence on people's approach to learning.

Barriers to learning

Individuals' lack of learning skills are not the only way in which learning can be hindered. There are a number of barriers to adult learning which will need to be considered and removed or reduced. Some major barriers to learning are:

Perceptual: not seeing that learning is needed.

Cultural: accepting things the way they are.

Emotional: fear or insecurity – for example, about the learning activity, or having to use the new skill or knowledge afterwards.

Motivational: unwillingness to take risks during learning or afterwards.

Cognitive: previous learning experiences were not positive.

Intellectual: limited learning preferences or poor learning skills.

Expressive: poor communication skills which can have a negative impact on quality of interaction between the learner and the trainer.

Situational: lack of opportunity, for example, no time or no suitable coach or trainer.

Physical: place and/or time of learning opportunities are difficult for the learner – for example, the learning opportunity provided is a weekend workshop at a branch office and the learner has family commitments.

Specific environment: unsupportive line manager/colleagues.

(Source: adapted from Mumford, 1988)

Some of these barriers can be overcome by ensuring that the environment in which learning is done is safe – that is, unthreatening. Learners need to be permitted to make allowable mistakes: this also helps them to take considered risks. Barriers can also be reduced by accepting that people will learn at different speeds, and that some will need more help and encouragement than others. Flexibility of approach in training and development programmes is also important. Variety not only avoids overuse of a single approach to learning, but makes training and development more accessible and interesting to everybody involved. If you use a 'talk-it-through' style in training sessions, for example, consider providing written materials, using diagrams and organising role play, depending on the tasks or skills you are trying to get staff to learn.

People can adapt their approach to learning, of course, according to what needs to be learned, how much time they have and their interests and priorities. The challenge for managers is to understand all these factors and to appreciate that learners may require different forms of support.

Learning from everyday experiences

Everyday work experiences are the raw material of work-based learning. You and your staff can learn from them, identify the learning and skills needs and find ways of meeting them. Many of the skills acquired will be transferable and can be applied to other jobs. Here we address ways in which individual employees can develop as learners by thinking about work experiences and turning them into learning opportunities. We cover two key concepts that describe ways of doing this: 'the experiential learning cycle' and the 'reflective practitioner'.

Experiential learning cycles

Deliberate and structured learning have been conceptualised as 'experiential learning cycles'. One of the best known is that of Kolb and Fry (1975) which describes the transformation of experience into knowledge.

We have a concrete experience which we first need to make sense of. (A concrete experience is a real experience; perceptible by the senses.) We do this by creating a theory about it, from which we make predictions about what might happen next time. This model or theory is a conceptualisation – an abstract concept – created by reflection. Once we have developed this conceptual model or theory, we can test its soundness through action. This produces more concrete experiences on which to reflect. An example of the cycle in action is set out in Box 11.3.

Box 11.3 Experiential learning in action

Yesterday, Betsy submitted her proposal for a new training programme. She had made cases for new training schemes several times before to the previous director of training and development, and most had been accepted. This time, however, there was a new director, Joyce. Today, Joyce had returned the proposal with a polite note: 'Please could you make a case for this training programme: as it is, it will be hard to support.' Betsy was surprised, upset and a little confused. Later she asked an experienced colleague, Gianpiero, to look at the proposal with her. He pointed out how a 'case' needed to be built, using evidence and logic, and structured in a particular way. Betsy went away to consider her proposal, and the diagram Gianpiero had drawn indicating the structure, type of content required and how each part of a case related to the other. Gradually Betsy understood how a structured and persuasive case was constructed. Before then she had thought of making a proposal as more like making a good suggestion. She now saw the need for identifying a need, putting forward clear reasons for meeting the need, and setting out how it might be met. Then she rewrote her proposal and sent it to Joyce. 'Much better, Betsy,' Joyce said later, after she had studied the proposal. 'I'll let you know the outcome after the budget meeting next week.'

There is little evidence, however, that adults *naturally* work their way round the experiential learning cycle. It is very much an idealised model of learning. Frequently people learn by what is known as trial and error: they simply do something and if the result is negative they try something different without much thought about what happened and *why*. That is, they move backwards and forwards between the 'testing' and 'concrete experience' part of the experiential learning cycle. Asking *why* something has happened is the key to learning. In this way we reframe our understanding and act differently next time on the basis of new understanding. This is the most important feature of conscious learning, although often we ask *why* only when an outcome of an action does not match our expectation (or perhaps someone else's expectation).

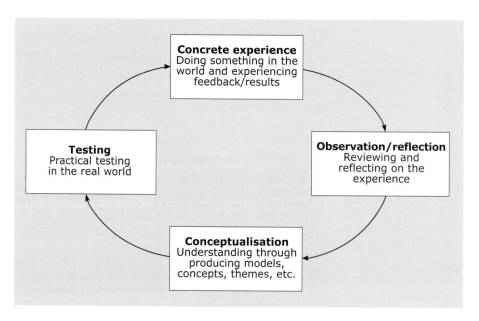

Figure 11.1 The experiential learning cycle

(Source: Kolb and Fry, 1975)

We can, however, ask *why* at any time: why am I doing this, in this way? This is the essential feature of problem-finding and improving what we do (and know). Kolb and Fry's model (Figure 11.1) is useful in showing us what we *should* or *could* do to maximise learning. Managers can use it to support staff learning, by encouraging observation, reflection and conceptualisation. Box 11.4 sets out a way of progressing round the learning cycle. Talking through a problem, as shown in the example, is an important means of learning. This social aspect of learning overcomes a weakness with experiential learning cycles (and some other methods of reflective learning) which represent learning as a solitary activity. It is important when colleagues help one another to 'work round' the learning cycle, however, that there is an open communication climate.

See also: The communication climate, Chapter 2

An advantage of taking a more social approach to experiential learning is that all those involved can learn from the experiences of others.

Box 11.4 Progressing round the learning cycle

1 Accept responsibility for your actions and be willing to challenge your usual responses to a situation.

2 Explore, expose and understand the differences, or contradictions, between your current responses and those you consider to be more desirable or those that might be more effective.

3 Channel any uncomfortable feelings about the conflict between actual and desired practice into a determination to take appropriate action to change your practice.

4 Explore your attitudes, beliefs and actions.

5 Work through any negative feelings.

6 Understand new ways of viewing and responding to the situation.

7 Work out how these insights can change your response to the situation and your practice.

8 Change your response and practice.

(Source: adapted from Johns, 2000)

Your new understanding should now incorporate your personal experience. Your understanding will continue to grow, of course, as your experience grows. If you are studying formal management theory, this can help you to reduce what is known as the 'theory–practice' gap – the gap between formal theory and its application in practice. Formal theory in management is often set out in terms of what is expected or ideal. While actions need to be informed by good theory, managers will often need to adapt theory in order to apply it to suit different situations and circumstances.

The idea of learning from experience has also been developed by Chris Argyris and Donald Schön through their concept of single- and double-loop learning (Argyris and Schön, 1978). In single-loop learning, if something goes wrong you identify *what* the immediate problem is and correct it. In double-loop learning, you identify what went wrong but then you go further, also asking *why* it went wrong.

In other words, single-loop learning is the first response in solving a problem, whereas double loop learning involves a second step: an investigation into the underlying cause. Double-loop learning is about asking why, and goes beyond the specific experience to ask why things are done in the ways that they are and how they can be improved.

Ideally, learning is a continuous and iterative process of evaluating what you have done in order to find ways to make improvements for next time. This is central to Schön's concept of the 'reflective practitioner'.

Schön (1983) distinguishes between two types of reflection: 'reflection-in-action' and 'reflection-on-action'. The first is the process of thinking about an issue or problem when it is happening and you must react. It is thinking on your feet. The second is the process of understanding the issue or situation after it has happened to inform future action.

The following example illustrates the use of both reflection-in-action and reflection-on-action.

Two types of reflection

Thomas was surprised to hear loud voices in the corridor outside his office. He saw two members of his team arguing about the new shift-work system.

Thomas's immediate reaction was that he could, and perhaps should, stop the argument. As he walked towards them he had a number of thoughts: Why was he doing this? Was it because senior managers would think he was a poor manager if they heard of the argument? Was it because he liked both team members and was unhappy to see them behaving in this way? Was it because he knew that they both had work to do? Was it because the noise was distracting him from his own work? Was it appropriate to take action?

His calming words seemed to stop the argument. As he walked away, Thomas came to the conclusion that he was right to act and that his reasons for acting had probably been a mixture of all of the above, with the main reason being the need to get the two team members working again.

That evening he noted that his reflection so far had not shown him the real cause of the disturbance or what he might do about it. Thinking about that led Thomas to decide to talk to both team members individually and to investigate the deeper causes of the tension between them.

The first part of this example describes the immediate thinking – 'in-action' – and the types of questions that might be asked immediately before making an intervention. The second part of the example describes Thomas's thinking back 'on-action'. After the event he took time to reflect, leading him to further investigation which would reveal the causes, including any larger or systemic problems.

Keeping a learning diary – or at least noting down in writing an event or a week of events – can help the process of reflecting on experience and actions. Useful questions to use as prompts are set out in Box 11.5.

Box 11.5 Reflection prompts

What were the most meaningful or stressful events of the week?

What might have caused them to happen and who was involved?

What is your interpretation of them?

What actions did you take?

What were the outcomes of your actions?

How successful were they?

What further or follow-up action might you need to take?

What would you do differently in the future?

What further skills, knowledge and understanding do you need to be a more effective manager?

How can you acquire these?

Write a brief action plan of how this can be done.

(Source: adapted from Collin, 2007)

Being a reflective learner means knowing how to draw out learning from a work-based experience or incident so that you can use it in your future activities, increasing your knowledge and skills. Workplace incidents are opportunities for learning. The challenge is not to miss them because you are too busy to attend to them or to help and encourage others to do so.

Identifying learning needs

See also: Managing poor or declining performance, Chapter 10

Managers will often need to guide and help employees in identifying their work-based learning needs, planning how to meet these needs, and reviewing and evaluating their learning. Suggested questions to use with staff in a training- and development-needs analysis are set out in Box 11.6. The questions refer to 'skills' and work best with well-defined jobs requiring specific skills or techniques, although it is possible to consider all job-related knowledge.

Box 11.6 Training- and development-needs analysis questions

1 What does your job involve?
   What is the purpose of the job?
   What are the areas of responsibility?
   What are the key activities and tasks?

2 What are the key skills needed to do this job?
   Identify those that are *essential* for the job.
   Identify those that are *desirable*.

3 What skills do you already have which help you to do the job well?
   List existing skills.
   Describe relevant past experience.
   List relevant qualifications.

4 What are the gaps between the key skills needed to do this job and those you have?
   List all of these.
   Highlight the most important gaps.

5 What training needs are emerging?
   What can you and others do about addressing these training needs?

This systematic approach can help you to identify and prioritise training and development needs based on organisational requirements. However, it cannot work unless individuals are prepared to learn new skills or techniques. Where training resources are not available in the organisation, external commercial providers or small business support agencies may be able to provide help. Job roles in small organisations tend to be less well-defined and cover a large range of skills which cannot be covered by formal training and development. However, it is still important to identify training and development needs and to try to meet them.

Another way of identifying learning needs is to develop a personal development plan. The method is associated with continuing professional development (CPD) for the development of professionals.

Continuing professional development (CPD)

The UK Chartered Institute of Personnel and Development (2008) describes CPD as a personal commitment to keeping one's professional knowledge up to date and improving skills throughout one's career. The principles of CPD are:

Development should be continuous, the professional always actively seeking improved performance.

Development should be owned and managed by the learner.

Development should begin from the learner's current learning state – learning needs are individual.

Learning objectives should be clear, and where possible serve organisational as well as individual goals.

Investment in time required for CPD should be regarded as being as important as investment in other activities.

(Source: Whittaker, 1992)

CPD results in a professional development plan (PDP) which is 'owned' by the individual employee but drawn up in discussion with the line manager. It should focus on setting clear learning objectives and on choosing from a range of learning methods and be prioritised according to practical realities. Mayo (2004) suggests that PDPs have four separate inputs of needs arising from performance, new requirements in the current role, career aspirations and desires for personal development.

CPD is a two-part process. The CPD *record* lists the activities carried out over the last 12 months, why they were undertaken, what was learned and how this learning was or is applied. The *personal development plan* then sets development aims and objectives and a proposed action plan for the next 12 months. It should include resources required, success criteria, and target dates for review and completion.

Examples of the CPD record and personal development plan for Sue Smith, a project manager, are set out in Tables 11.1 and 11.2. Note that keeping a record requires commitment because there may be a hundred or more activities to consider each year. Since many people start diaries and then no longer find time to continue them, the decision to start a CPD record will require careful thought, as will the amount of detail to include. One approach to encouraging record keeping is for samples to be read by the line manager from time to time. Another is for each record to be considered before and during the annual appraisal interview.

Table 11.1 Sue Smith's CPD record

Key dates	What you did	Why	What you learned from this	How you used or will use this. Any further action needed
March	Wrote a proposal for external funding to support the development of a new project	To develop proposal writing skills To raise the standing of my department by winning external funding	I learned that this is a specialist skill which I do not have!	I have asked for help with the next proposal from someone with experience and will attend a day's training
April	Became a mentor to a new member of staff	To increase my awareness of the processes of being a mentor and to develop my skills in this area	That it is difficult to listen objectively and not jump in with solutions	It has demonstrated the importance of making time to support and develop others and how much you can learn from it. I read about and am trying to practise active listening

Table 11.2 Sue Smith's development plan

What I want/need to learn	What I will do to achieve this	What resources or support I will need	What my success criteria will be	Target dates for review and completion
Learn more about different approaches to mentoring	Attend a mentoring conference	Can apply for a development grant to do this Would need to arrange someone else to do my urgent work on my day away	To take away a skill or technique to use in my next mentoring session	End of May
Write a successful funding proposal	Work with Ron who has more experience of bid writing	Support from other members of team in providing evidence, help from finance with costing, help from John with proof-reading	My next proposal to reach the shortlist process	End of June

When guiding others through this process and going through the process yourself you will need to develop SMART (specific, measurable, agreed, realistic and timely) objectives – for which there are resources (time and money). Unlike Sue's plan, PDPs should clearly state who is responsible for each action on the plan, and these actions should then be reviewed regularly, preferably two or three times a year. Columns could readily be added to Sue's plan to record these.

The benefits of the CPD process are that, by tracking learning, professional development becomes evident. It can be used in preparing and gathering evidence for performance appraisal meetings. The focus on training and development is a useful means of keeping track of career goals and progress towards them. It also helps the individual to highlight gaps in knowledge, skills and experience. However, the CPD process takes time and discipline to keep it going. It also assumes support from management and that money and time are available for relatively continuous professional development.

Learning and development activities

Identifying training and development needs of staff is one thing: meeting them in order to improve performance and performance outcomes to meet the needs of an organisation is another. What methods might a manager consider? There are three main categories: on-the-job techniques, off-the-job techniques and on-or-off-the-job techniques.

On-the-job methods are practised on a day-to-day basis or as part of a tailored programme of learning. They include job instruction and demonstration, observation, shadowing, delegation, job rotation, planned experience (such as assignments and projects, and secondment), and coaching and mentoring. Off-the-job methods take staff away from the workplace. These methods include talks, discussion, role play, simulation, group exercises, and workshops as well as formal courses. On-or-off-the-job methods can include instruction, question and answer sessions, action learning, assignments and projects, guided reading, and computer-based learning which can be interactive.

Here we offer a selection of approaches to two of these methods: on-the-job and on-or-off-the-job. Some are social and collaborative, others are more individual and many will work as well for managers themselves.

On-the-job and on-or-off-the-job methods

On-the-job and on-or-off-the-job methods, if they are to have the desired effect on skills and performance, must involve

- preparing the learner (and often the trainer)
- providing opportunities for the learner to practise the new skill or skills
- supporting the learner
- following up progress.

The training or development opportunity should also be offered at the right time. This can sometimes mean offering just-in-time training and development immediately before individuals need it so new knowledge and skills can be applied before they are forgotten. Some methods, for example, coaching and mentoring, can include both just-in-time learning and reflection on experience. Opportunities to practise new skills and apply new knowledge during or soon afterwards are crucial.

Job instruction and demonstration

Job instruction involves explaining and demonstrating, followed by the learner practising under guidance. Explanations should be as simple as possible. Use whatever media are appropriate, for example, films, charts diagrams and other visual aids. For the demonstration, particularly where a skill is to be learned, the operation is slowed down and each element in the process is indicated, together with the order in which it needs to be done. Demonstrations are best repeated two or three times (Armstrong, 2006). Practise consists of the learner imitating the instructor and then repeating the operation under guidance until the learner performs to an acceptable level in terms of quality, speed and attention to safety. Job instruction may look very basic, but is vital in the acquisition of a number of skills in organisations – and in many professions including medical surgery.

Learning by observation

Learning by observation is a related method of learning still in common use in organisations. Here the learner simply observes: it can be useful where a procedure cannot be explained easily. However, there are disadvantages: the person being observed may pass on bad habits or may be unwilling or unable to slow down sufficiently to explain what is being done. This method of learning therefore needs careful management and supervision.

Shadowing

Shadowing is another popular technique of watching another person while they work. In this way an employee can gain an understanding of a different job or role – for example, in a different department. This allows the employee to see the work being done and gain, or at least see, skills in practice. Shadowing can be used to inform job choices or to develop cross-departmental understanding. It can also be used when a person needs to learn to perform a role they will be taking on, as illustrated in Box 11.7. It can be used at many levels in an organisation. Shadowing is not easy to plan and the cost of covering a person's duties may be high.

Box 11.7 Shadowing the boss

Tamara was a project manager who worked closely with her line manager, Ian. She ran her own project at head office but helped Ian to coordinate the running of other projects in the regions for which Ian had overall responsibility. Ian was due to retire in six months. It was decided that Tamara would move into Ian's position when he left. In the meantime she would shadow Ian in order to train for the job. Ian started to delegate tasks to Tamara and to hold regular discussion sessions with her. She began to travel to the regions more often, taking on more of Ian's supervision responsibilities.

Delegation

Delegation involves giving another person the authority for a task that you are normally responsible for. It has the advantages of releasing time for other activities and of developing staff. For delegation to be effective, it needs to be carefully planned. First, it is important to identify the most appropriate person for the task to be delegated. People's availability and how the task fits with their other areas of work will need to be considered. There might be someone who would welcome a chance to demonstrate their ability, perhaps because they are preparing for promotion. Alternatively, delegation might be an opportunity to offer a challenge to a member of staff who has become bored with their routine work.

Once an appropriate person has been identified, you will need to agree on the goal, set clear objectives and establish a method of measuring how well the job is done so that you can provide feedback. You remain responsible for the delegated task, however: you are not giving up responsibility. For employees, delegation can enlarge and enrich their jobs. However, delegation can go wrong – for example, if insufficient communication takes place or if the task delegated is not achievable.

Job rotation

Job rotation involves encouraging members of a team to work proficiently in each other's jobs. This creates greater flexibility in a team – team members become multiskilled and are able to cover for each other – and it can result in greater understanding of the workings of the team or organisation. By building the skills in individuals, job rotation can address skills shortages and gaps. It is also a means of reducing boredom and of improving motivation and job satisfaction, particularly if everyday tasks are repetitive.

However, job rotation can lead to a short-term reduction in productivity while individuals learn new skills.

Assignments

Assignments are specific tasks that a person carries out at the manager's request as a means of extending the person's experience. A person whose job involves supplying information could be asked to find out what the recipients of this information (the internal customers) expect from their internal suppliers. The results of the assignment can then be used to improve the form or content of information supplied, or the channels used. Clear guidelines should be provided for assignments – what is to be done, the purpose and what kind of output is required. Assignments can be linked to coaching so that learning from the assignment can be reinforced and applied.

Projects

Projects are normally broader than assignments and only general guidelines are given: they are designed to encourage initiative in seeking and analysing information, in originating ideas and in preparing and presenting the results of the project. Projects might include an investigation into a company policy issue or an operating problem. Projects can be carried out by individuals or groups. They provide staff with an opportunity to extend their learning. Assignments and projects can be used following off-the-job learning as a means of applying new knowledge back in the workplace.

Secondment

Secondment is a similar process to job rotation but takes place over an extended time period. It usually involves the job holder leaving their workplace to work for another department or organisation for a fixed term. There is often a structured procedure for learning and feedback. Secondment allows for exchanges of ideas and exposure to different systems and practices. It must be planned for so that it is possible to release and replace the person being seconded.

Action learning

Action learning was developed by Revans (1998) to train managers. It involves a group of colleagues or individuals with common work-related interests who meet at regular intervals to work on a problem or issue that a member of the group has. Intense questioning is used to help the person who has the problem to reframe it and plan a series of actions. The success or progress of the actions is reported back at the next meeting. An example of how action learning operates is set out in Box 11.8.

Box 11.8 An example of action learning

Six managers took part in action learning as part of a leadership development course. After an initial trust-building day, they had six action learning sessions each lasting six hours. Each person arrived with a problem they wanted to discuss, such as exercising leadership in retaining staff, implementing appraisal systems or succession planning. No time limits were set for how long each problem would take, but generally the six managers would work on two or three problems during a session. First, the people whose problems had been discussed in the previous session would report back on the actions they had agreed at the last session and say what had worked, what had not and how they now perceived the issue. In some cases this led to another problem being put forward for the current session.

Second, another person with a problem would spend 10 minutes describing a current issue. The group would first ask clarification questions to seek information and then use open questions to encourage the person to explore the issue. Then the person would be encouraged to decide on some actions. The results of these actions were reported back at the next session.

Action learning involves a considerable time commitment and belief in the process. It also requires patience and discipline: the temptation to impose views and suggestions on the person with the problem must be avoided so that they can develop their own solutions. A high level of trust among participants is also needed.

Coaching

See also: Coaching and work-based learning and development, in this chapter

Coaching is a method of developing skills and is normally carried out by a person's line manager or senior person. It can be carried out one-to-one or with groups of about four to eight people, normally in a series of short, frequent sessions over a limited time. Typically, coaching is driven by the coach in terms of what the coach wants a person or group of people to learn. It can be used in conjunction with other on-the-job, off-the-job or on-or-off-the-job methods of training and development.

Mentoring

See also: Mentoring and personal and professional development, in this chapter

Mentoring focusses not on the development of skills but on personal and professional development – for example, developing capabilities to deal with difficult people. Mentoring is usually carried out by a more experienced person who is not an individual's line manager and it is broader than coaching. It can help mentees to explore their role in the wider organisation, for example. Mentoring is driven by what the learner needs at any given time. Mentors can act as collaborators, working alongside the mentee, as goal setters, as challengers by pushing the mentee to think more deeply, and as 'critical friends' by giving honest feedback. Mentoring is normally carried out over a longer period than is coaching and is time-consuming. Mentors require training and mentors and mentees need to be carefully matched.

E-learning

A wide range of training and development courses and programmes are available outside the workplace. They can be costly and time-consuming, however, not tailored to individuals, and much of the learning can be forgotten by the time a person has the opportunity to use their new skills or knowledge. Internal courses can have the same disadvantages if they are not tailored to individual or small group needs. Distance learning and e-learning, however, can overcome at least some of these disadvantages and can be used just-in-time, that is, just before a person needs particular skills or knowledge. At its best, e-learning provides learning which is more accessible, flexible and adaptable to individual circumstances (Collin, 2007), although personal discipline is needed, as well as time. Organisations using a 'blended learning' approach – that is, combining e-learning with other approaches such as face-to-face sessions – report the most success with e-learning (CIPD, 2004).

The likely impact of each method will depend on the match between the type of skill or knowledge needed and the method itself, how customised the method is, and, where appropriate, how frequently sessions take place. Learning is more effective when done in short regular sessions than in a single long one.

Coaching and work-based learning and development

Coaching is a commonly-used technique for training and development in the workplace. It is a way of transferring knowledge and skills from a more experienced person to one who is less experienced. It provides the person being coached with insights into new techniques or ways of working, develops their skills, helps them to learn from mistakes and workplace crises, and monitors their progress and recognises (and celebrates) their successes. It can be used to develop a wide range of skills, including those of management and leadership. The growing popularity of coaching and the development of coaching cultures in organisations mean that it is becoming more common for managers to coach their own staff. This can be a planned activity or an informal response to an opportunity.

Coaching is appropriate in the workplace when:

- a new project or assignment is given
- an error has been made
- a new member joins the team
- people feel a lack of confidence
- there is a change in technology or business process
- individuals or the team wish to improve their performance.

(Source: adapted from Clutterbuck and Megginson, 2005)

Coaching is designed to enhance and develop the performance of individuals, helping them to cope with situations such as those above, or at a higher level, with managing change, business transformation, restructuring, growth and technological development (Caplan, 2003).

Coaching is usually carried out by a person's line manager. An alternative is a senior person who is familiar with the individual's day-to-day work and who can give immediate feedback and guidance. External coaches can be used for specific purposes, for example, for executive or life-style coaching and for leadership.

Coaching is often referred to as mentoring but there are some important differences. These are set out in Table 11.3.

Table 11.3 Differences between coaching and mentoring

Coaching	Mentoring
Focus on specific knowledge, skills, task	Focus on professional development and progress
Usually short term	Usually longer term
Concrete feedback, e.g. on a specific piece of work	Intuitive feedback, e.g. a feeling on a given situation
Develops skills, e.g. managing a specific project	Develops capabilities, e.g. dealing with difficult people
Driven by coach, e.g. what the coach needs the person to develop in order to do the job	Driven by mentee/learner, e.g. what is currently bothering them
Shows where you went wrong	Helps you to work it out yourself

(Source: adapted from Clutterbuck and Sweeny, 1998)

The roles of a coach include:

Motivator: encouraging the person being coached to improve and achieve, perhaps by getting them to imagine what it would feel like to be more successful and effective

Goal-setter: helping the individual to break things down into manageable, achievable steps

Observer: giving accurate helpful feedback

Friend: developing a sufficient level of trust to allow discussion of serious problems.

(Source: Clutterbuck and Sweeny, 1998)

It is usual for the coach and the person being coached to spend time together that is protected and uninterrupted. The first task is to define the problem or what needs to be done. After the person being coached has explained the situation, questions of clarification are asked. Then gentle questioning is used to explore whether the individual has considered other courses of action. This is designed to develop broader thinking.

New ideas are offered but the individual is encouraged to seek his or her own solutions. The coach resists saying 'I would do ...' unless specifically asked for advice. This continues, if necessary, until the problem is redefined and a decision is made. Information may be provided to help the individual act on the decision. Any action to be taken is agreed and summarised.

A popular approach to structuring a coaching session is the GROW model developed by Whitmore (2002) and Downey (2003).

Table 11.4 The GROW model

Stage	Description	Questions
Goal	Decide area to concentrate on Establish objectives Identify longer term goals	What is your long-term goal? How much control do you have over this goal? When do you want to achieve it by? What is your short-term goal? When do you want to achieve it by?
Reality	Review the history Invite self-assessment Check assumptions Identify obstacles	What is happening now? Who is involved? What have you achieved? What are the constraints to moving forward?
Options	Explore full range of options Encourage different perspectives Offer suggestions Ensure choices are made	What options do you have? What are the advantages and disadvantages of these options? Which option appeals to you most?
Will	Plan the actions Agree time frame Measure commitment Decide what support is needed	What are you going to do? Will this address your goal? When are you going to do it? What prevents/constrains this from happening? How committed are you to doing this (on a scale from 1–10)?

While the GROW model is helpful in structuring the coaching conversation, Clutterbuck (2004) suggests that the coaching role can be much broader and can include the creation of opportunities to practise new skills, observation and feedback, and the provision of support when the person being coached experiences setbacks.

Advantages of coaching are that it is a highly flexible way of learning that is tailored to the needs of the individual. Not all people learn from coaching, however, and one-to-one relationships may be less comfortable than group-based developmental activities. Some coaches want to impose their own views or try to discourage a person from taking actions that did not work for the coach, even though the circumstances are different.

Mentoring and personal and professional development

Mentoring is a popular form of personal and professional development in organisations. It is increasingly used for leadership development and has been seen as offering significant benefits for leaders, including role socialisation, reduced feelings of isolation, improved leadership skills and leadership-capacity building (Stead, 2005). It is often carried out by a person more experienced than the mentee and who is not the individual's line manager. Unlike coaching, mentoring does not focus on the development of specific skills. It can cover a range of broader issues related to work, learning approaches, styles and skills, and management of the organisation, service or industry.

Models of mentoring

There are different approaches to mentoring which assume different relationships between mentor and mentee.

The European Collegiate model is 'off-line help by one person to another in making significant transitions in knowledge, work and thinking' (Clutterbuck and Sweeny, 1998). The mentor may be more experienced but may not have superior status. The mentor acts in a non-directive manner to help the mentee become self-reliant. The relationship encourages a two-way learning process.

The North American Traditional model focusses on career rather than personal development, the mentor is often more experienced and the relationship can be a rather directive and one-way learning process. It is a process in which the mentor is responsible for overseeing the career development of the mentee.

In both models, the attributes required of a mentor include:

- a strong motivation to assist the development of others
- considerable and acknowledged experience in the skills being mentored
- the ability to identify the strengths and weaknesses of the mentee and the ability to formulate developmental or remedial activities
- the personal skills necessary to build a relationship with the mentee and to carry out mentoring.

Types of mentoring arrangements may vary according to the needs of the mentee and the skill and experience of the mentor. However, the individual relationship needs careful planning and negotiating. Mentors and mentees should be matched according to the type of mentoring relationship required and should discuss how they both see and imagine the mentor/mentee relationship. Mentors play some all of the following roles:

Door opener/broker/advocate

Coach

Counsellor

Advisor

Sounding board/listening post

Guide

Role model

Tutor

Provider of information/knowledge/wisdom

Provider of managerial and/or emotional support

Confronter of problems, behaviours and relationships.

(Source: Mumford, 1993)

They can perform the following functions in the mentor/mentee relationship:

Collaborator working alongside the mentee

Goal-setter helping the mentee to set their own goals

Challenger, by encouraging the mentee to think more deeply about an issue

Critical friend, by giving honest feedback that others are too shy or embarrassed to give.

(Source: Clutterbuck and Sweeny, 1998)

The case in Box 11.9 illustrates how a mentee might choose a mentor and some of the benefits of having a mentor.

Box 11.9 Wanted: a challenger and critical friend

Molly is an experienced project manager who joined her current organisation a year ago. She has recently been chosen to lead a major new project that will involve major organisation change. It is likely that the project will not be welcomed by long-serving staff. Molly feels excited by the challenge and happy to have been chosen for the role but is aware of her lack of organisational knowledge and history. Molly has been offered a mentor of her choice to support her during the project. She has decided she needs a mentor who is familiar with the distinctive history and culture of the organisation, and with how staff might react to change and why. She needs to know whether her ideas will be acceptable and where she can be innovative. She realises she is looking for both a challenger and a critical friend.

Olga has been in the organisation for 20 years and has worked in all the departments and with all the main managers. She sits near Molly and they have met over coffee several times. They share quite similar views but Olga has sometimes gently challenged Molly, giving her honest feedback on how she thought Molly's ideas would work, given the organisational structures and people involved. Molly thinks that Olga would make a good mentor because she needs someone she can trust both to challenge and support her through this project.

To choose the type of mentor you need, Pedler *et al.* (2007) suggest you write down the names of people who have helped you in the past and then note your responses to the following questions:

What did you receive from these people?

What did you look for in these people?

What career stage are you at now?

What sort of help for learning do you need now?

What would you like to receive from a mentoring relationship?

This will help you to identify *what* you need from a mentor. To choose your mentor, Phillips-Jones (1982) suggests that you:

- evaluate yourself as a prospective protégé by identifying the sorts of needs and demands you might have
- identify some potential mentors
- prepare for the obstacles that they might raise
- approach possible mentors.

The benefits of mentoring need to be assessed against some potential disadvantages. Mentoring requires considerable time and commitment as well as careful management. Not all senior staff will be suitable or will want to act as mentors, and mentoring relationships may not be successful. Mentoring is usually viewed as optional and treated as a private, one-to-one activity, but if the relationships are informal (rather than a formalised part of professional development) this can lead to allegations of unfairness and favouritism by others. Whether formal or informal, being mentored can also be a negative experience for the mentee if, for example, the mentor expects his or her suggestions to be taken up and does not react well when the mentee makes different choices, or takes credit for the mentee's ideas. Eby *et al.* (2000) list five broad types of problems including:

- a mismatch between the values or personalities of the mentee and mentor
- lack of interest or self-absorption
- manipulative behaviour by the mentor
- lack of mentoring expertise
- poor attitude or personal problems.

One solution is to train mentors. Some public sector organisations in the UK, particularly in the education sector, offer mentor training packs which can be found on the internet. Mentoring can be used as part of a strategy for staff development, as in this case, but in some organisations there is a risk that there will be insufficient commitment and a lack of suitable mentors.

Evaluating learning

Evaluating the effectiveness of planned learning and of training and development initiatives is important to ensure that time, money and other resources have not been wasted. Training and development can be ineffective for a number of reasons, for example:

- the learner does not yet have sufficient commitment, prior knowledge or ability to benefit
- the training and development method chosen was not suitable
- the content was not relevant
- what needed to be learned was poorly presented or taught
- the new knowledge acquired was not applied
- the learner was not supported
- the application of the new knowledge made no difference to performance because the learning need was wrongly-identified in the first place.

The most popular model of evaluating the effectiveness of training and development is based on the classic framework developed by Donald Kirkpatrick (1959). The model has four levels, shown in Table 11.5.

Table 11.5 The Kirkpatrick four-level model of evaluation

Level	What is measured	How it can be measured	Issues and questions typically addressed
Level 1: Reaction	How the participants reacted to the training and development	Asking individuals or groups for feedback Feedback questionnaires*	Readiness Enjoyment Relevance Use of time Style/timing Participation Effort needed Practicality or potential for application of learning
Level 2: Learning	How much participants improved their knowledge and skills, or changed their attitudes	Reports from supervisors Workplace assessment (if training and development has taken place off the job) Pre- and post-training tests (suitable only for technical or easily-measurable skills and learning)	Did the learning opportunity offer what it was supposed to in terms of improvements? Are there improvements other than the planned ones, for example greater confidence, motivation, commitment, team spirit?

Table 11.5 continued

Level 3: Behaviour	How much participants changed their workplace behaviour	Observation by supervisors or the line manager Reports from others, e.g. peers, supervisors or line managers or customers/ clients Self-assessment questionnaires*	Has the learning been applied? Is the participant aware of changes? Is the difference noticeable to others (or can it be measured, e.g. speed, work volume, accuracy)? Has the change been sustained over time? Could the person now teach/train someone else (if appropriate)?
Level 4: Results	The organisational benefits	Interviews with senior managers Inspections (for example, quality inspections) Statistics	Impact on key performance indicators such as sales or timescales Impact on quantifiable performance such as costs, staff turnover, customer complaints, non-compliance Restructuring and new initiatives

* Free, generic questionnaires can be found on the internet.

Ideally, as Kirkpatrick now accepts, evaluation should begin at Level 4 and work through to Level 1 by asking the following overarching questions:

Level 4: What business results do we want?

Level 3: What workplace performance changes are needed?

Level 2: How can we ensure that learners perform as needed?

Level 1: How can we deliver instruction that appeals to and engages learners?

In major training and development programmes, responsibility for evaluation lies with senior management, the trainers, line managers, the person who is responsible for training and development in the organisation, and the learners. In these situations, the responsibility of the line manager is to identify work needs, be involved in developing the learning opportunity, support the learner and review performance progress.

It may be ideal to evaluate effectiveness at all four levels but it is too costly. Level 1 evaluations are commonly used by organisations while less effort is made for Levels 2 and 3 evaluations (Goldstein and Ford, 2002), and little at Level 4. However, when training and development involves only a few learners or a single individual in your own work group, it should be relatively easy to evaluate at Levels 1, 2 and 3, provided what is being learned is easy to measure, for example, some types of technical skill.

Kirkpatrick's model is a popular one because it adopts a systematic approach and simplifies the process of evaluation by focussing on gathering information *after* the planned training and development has taken place (except where pre-training tests of skill or knowledge are used). A particular benefit for commercial organisations is that the information gathered can be used to assess whether, in business terms, particular outcomes have been met (Bates, 2004).

Criticisms of the model

However, Kirkpatrick's model leaves many evaluation questions unanswered, especially where a key question is: are we doing the right thing and are we doing it well? For many organisations, including not-for-profit organisations, this is an important ethical consideration. Bates, drawing on the work of many other researchers, has summarised the criticisms of the Kirkpatrick model.

The information gathered is unlikely to be relevant to ethical questions. As a result, employees and other stakeholders may be put at risk; for example, if ineffective health and safety training activity is continued on the basis of misleading information. The model does not address the question of how training and development can be modified in ways that increase its potential.

The model assumes a causal relationship between training and development and its impact. It does not consider the influence of the individual or the situation or context before, during and after the training and development. Factors include the culture of an organisation, the organisation of the work unit and its goals and values, interpersonal support for learners during training and development, the climate for the application of skills and knowledge or the adequacy of the material resources, such as materials, tools and supplies. All have been found to influence the effectiveness of training and development processes and outcomes.

The model does not evaluate effectiveness. For example, at Level 1, learners' satisfaction cannot be regarded as effectiveness, particularly when learning can be difficult and uncomfortable. Rather, learner reaction measures may be used by trainers as an evaluation of their own performance (so trainers have a personal interest in making sure that learners' reactions are positive). At Level 2, tests used may be inappropriate (Tamkin *et al.*, 2002). What is easy to measure is often what is measured. At Level 3 many of the factors set out above will affect the application of learning. At Level 4, the impact of short episodes of learning – for example, of one to two days – are unlikely to be detectable. Desirable outcomes may take time to develop.

What is needed, Bates suggests, is information that not only assesses the effectiveness of training and development but also helps to improve its effectiveness in meeting its goals. How then should managers approach the evaluation of training and development in order to do this?

An alternative: the CIPP model

A well-developed alternative to Kirkpatrick's model is that of Daniel Stufflebeam (2002). Called the CIPP model, it covers context, input, process and impact, but has been extended to effectiveness, sustainability and transportability (whether the training and development under review can be used in other parts of the organisation). Evaluation begins at the planning stage of training and development and involves all stakeholders (those who have an interest in the training and its impact) in a comprehensive but complex process. Some of the key aspects of particular value for managers are set out below. The term 'instruction' refers to training and development whatever its form; the term 'assess' refers to measurement or judgement as appropriate.

Context

Identify and clarify needs of those likely to benefit from instruction.

Assess the goals of the planned instruction.

Ensure that needs and goals are well-matched.

Input

If possible, identify a similar instruction initiative and evaluation findings for comparison later.

Assess the strategy of the planned instruction in terms of feasibility of meeting needs and goals: can it deliver what's needed?

Make funding requests as necessary.

Process

During training and development, monitor, observe and make a record of learner progress.

Use the process of evaluation to control and strengthen staff activities that will improve the effectiveness of learning and performance change.

Use the process of evaluation to strengthen the design of the instruction.

Impact

Periodically interview key stakeholders to assess the wider impact of learning/performance change.

Use this information to judge whether the instruction is addressing the needs of stakeholders.

Effectiveness

Assess positive and negative outcomes of instruction (intended and unintended) by interviewing key stakeholders.

Assess the range, depth, quality and significance of impacts on key stakeholders.

Use this information to assess whether plans for further instruction and activities should be changed.

Use the same information to assess the effectiveness of instruction.

If possible, compare effectiveness with similar instruction initiatives.

Sustainability

Evaluate sustainability by interviewing instructors and staff to assess the extent to which the contribution made by instruction is embedded in work practice and continued over time.

Use this information to inform future plans and budgeting for continuation of instruction.

Transportability

Assess the transportability of instruction – whether it can or could be successfully adapted and applied elsewhere – by working with potential adopters, first to inform and establish whether the instruction is relevant to them and then assisting with adaptations.

The use of Stufflebeam's full set of checklists would be costly and justified only in the case of a major evaluation. However, the key aspects above can be used by managers in small-scale evaluations using observation and discussion. The method allows changes to be made to ongoing or regular training and development initiatives.

See also: Evaluation: how well are we doing? Chapter 4

The 10 checklists (and checklists for other forms of evaluations) are available from the website of The Evaluation Center at Western Michigan University. Stufflebeam's full set of checklists include ones for meta-evaluation – an assessment of how good the evaluation is – and synthesis, which draws together the findings of an evaluation to inform the full range of audiences about what was attempted, and accomplished, what lessons were learned and the bottom-line assessment of the programme.

Chapter 12 Organisational culture
What is organisational culture?

Ann's frustrations

> Ann, a 30-year-old Dutch nurse, is three months into a six-month mission in Africa with Médecins Sans Frontières-Holland (MSF). Volunteers like Ann are attracted by the unbureaucratic and democratic nature of the organisation and the focus on emergency work that shapes the image of MSF and the practices of fieldworkers. Working long hours is the norm. Ann starts her day early with a cup of coffee but has no time to drink it. Patients have already arrived and the new doctor has started work. She is frustrated because he wants to do things his way rather than listen to the experiences of others who have been there longer – a particularly important norm in MSF where people work for the organisation for only a short time. Lack of bureaucracy sometimes comes dangerously close to lack of professionalism and there is often a lack of clarity about tasks and responsibilities. Later Ann reflects on the fact that it seems hard for the volunteers, now that the emergency is over, to adapt to the routine work of the vaccination programme. Frustrated with problems in her team and feeling overworked, she feels a little distant from the stated values and policies of the organisation.
>
> (Source: adapted from Hilhorst and Schmiemann, 2002)

The above example captures something of the way that organisations work: 'The way we do things round here'; that is, how groups and individuals combine to get things done in a particular way. This is shaped by the unwritten, *shared* attitudes, behaviour patterns, practices, expectations and values which form the basis of *organisational culture*.

The example illustrates how corporate culture – the purpose, stated values and policies of the organisation decided by directors – is interpreted by workers: stated principles *shape* practice, are embedded in practice and are perpetuated *through* practice. This response to corporate culture becomes the unstated culture of the organisation's workers – the organisational culture. The example also illustrates that organisational culture does not instantly change when circumstances fluctuate, that newcomers need to learn how to 'fit in' and that our personal values may (or may not) match the stated values of the organisation.

We are most familiar with the idea of culture as something that exists at a national or ethnic level. This culture shapes the way we think, feel and behave and what we value, by focussing our attention on what it considers important to attend to. It teaches us – through others – how to interpret, feel about and describe our perceptions and experiences and how to behave in socially-accepted ways. It provides the language we use to describe our perceptions and experiences. In terms of evolution, this kind of *collectivism* makes sense for survival: it acts as social glue, helping to maintain relationships, to reduce uncertainty and to guide action.

See also: Induction and socialisation, Chapter 9

Organisational cultures are not as deep or enduring as national or ethnic cultures, although these may influence organisational culture. Nonetheless, organisational culture appears to shape the norms and practices of those who work in an organisation: there is shared learning from shared history and this shared learning is passed on to newcomers to the organisation in a process of socialisation. Like national cultures, organisational cultures are thought to develop from the need to reduce uncertainty, guide action and maintain relationships. The 'founding fathers' of an organisation will have strongly shaped a culture. Other significant influences include the prevailing national or ethnic culture, the need for an organisation to find its niche in the marketplace, what the organisation does and how it does it. A daily newspaper depends on speed and may sacrifice quality at times; a hospital depends on quality of health care and may at times sacrifice speed. There will be constant pressure to change the ways in which things are done – and therefore the organisational culture – to 'fit' the external environment better as it changes. A hospital may have to adapt to permanently reduce waiting lists for surgical procedures without compromising quality. The use of new technology will require a newspaper to adopt different ways of working.

Thus, a prevailing organisational culture, or an aspect of it, may not be the 'right' culture when an organisation needs to adapt quickly to work in a different way. This different way might be to respond to increased competition, to reach new markets, or to improve the quality of products or services or to introduce new ones, or in cases where two organisations merge. Thus, there will be times when managers find they need to change attitudes, norms and practices.

Dimensions and types of organisational culture

What does organisational culture 'look like'? We sense that one organisation is different from another organisation not only because in *this* organisation it is almost unthinkable to make decisions without consultation and in *that* organisation competition between individuals is rife. But what can we say precisely? A feature of the study of organisational culture is the lack of agreement about what it really is and how best to scrutinise and describe it.

Some writers such as Schein emphasise the dimensions of organisational culture. Schein (1992) argues that there are three 'levels' of organisational culture and seven dimensions.

Levels and dimensions

Schein's levels of culture are categorised by their visibility.

Behaviours and artefacts. These are the most visible signs of culture and include:

- symbols including status symbols, such as company cars and reserved parking places, artefacts such as the organisation's logo, the architecture and interior design, the technology used

- the stories and myths that circulate and the jargon and humour used
- rituals such as the office party
- non-verbal behaviours such as greetings, gestures, dress code.

Espoused beliefs and values. These are less visible than behaviours and artefacts. Beliefs are propositions for which we often have no evidence but which shape our perceptions. Values are ideals, principles or standards that people hold or live by. Organisational or collective beliefs and values often reflect the beliefs and values of leaders. They become shared over time by the workforce and may be 'taken for granted' and take the form of assumptions. For example, leaders and people in the organisation may believe that, in general, performance is improved by offering a pay increase. As a result, managers will have a view (a perception) about performance and pay. Beliefs and values shape what people think and do, how they interpret events and deal with them.

Underlying assumptions. These are taken-for-granted truths and are not visible, even to ourselves unless we think carefully about them. Leaders and managers who believe the answer to improving performance is to offer a pay increase are probably making an assumption that people are mainly motivated by money. There may be an assumption that all employees can improve their performance, given support and time, or conversely, that it is difficult for people to change. Staff will make this assumption, too.

The idea of levels attempts to define culture. However, the emphasis on artefacts as a visible part of organisational culture has been criticised (Haukelid, 2008) because changes to them may not mean that norms, values and basic assumptions have changed. Indeed, this writer defines culture in terms only of 'endowing experiences with meaning' – that is, making sense of experiences. The emphasis on values (and assumptions) has been criticised, too. Research by Hofstede (2001), for example, suggests that organisational cultures can be better defined by practices than by values. This is because values tend to be shaped early in life by family culture long before a person joins an organisation. Nonetheless, organisational values are likely to be expressed in organisational practice.

Schein's seven dimension of culture are set out as questions in Table 12.1.

Table 12.1 Schein's dimensions of organisational culture

Questions to be answered	
The organisation's relation to its environment	Does the organisation see itself as dominant, submissive, harmonising, or searching out a niche? *Example*: We are aggressive market leaders
The nature of human activity	Is the 'correct' way for humans to behave to be dominant/proactive, harmonising, or passive/fatalistic? *Example*: We're expected to take the initiative here

Table 12.1 continued

The nature of reality/truth	How do we define what is true and what is not true; and how is truth ultimately determined in both the physical and the social world? *Example*: Opinions and traditions count here
The nature of time	What is our basic orientation in terms of past, present and future, and what kinds of time units are most relevant for the conduct of daily life? *Example*: Tomorrow is always too late
The nature of human nature	Are humans basically good, neutral or evil, and is human nature perfectible or fixed? *Example*: People are greedy: it's human nature and they won't change
The nature of human relationships	What is the 'correct' way for people to relate to each other, to distribute power and affection? Is life competitive or cooperative? Is this the best way to organise society on the basis of individualism or collectivism? Is the best authority system autocratic/paternalistic or collegial/participative? *Example*: Here, you do what you are told
Homogeneity versus diversity	Is the group better off if it is highly diverse or if it is highly homogeneous (similar), and should individuals in a group be encouraged to innovate? *Example*: Diversity is good for our organisation

Asking such questions in relation to your own organisation is useful, allowing insight into its overall culture, even though the number and type of dimensions are disputed. Schein's view is that the culture of an organisation explains behaviour that is not easily understood and which may be irrational, and that once a culture exists it usually determines the types of leader who succeed previous ones. In this way, culture is perpetuated.

Taxonomies of culture

A different approach is to try to classify organisational cultures by type. Two well-known and enduring classifications are those of Deal and Kennedy (1982) and Handy (1985) building on earlier work by Harrison (1972) and expanded by others.

Deal and Kennedy consider two dimensions: the speed of feedback on performance and reward, and the degree of risk or uncertainty over outcomes. They identified four types of organisational culture placed on a matrix according to these two dimensions (see Figure 12.1).

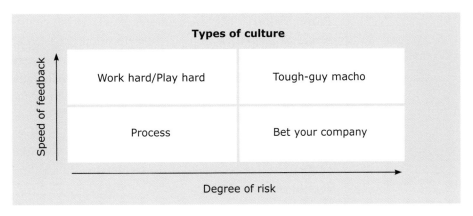

Figure 12.1 Deal and Kennedy's two dimensions of culture

The tough-guy macho culture. This culture is typified by fast feedback and reward and high risk. Organisational examples include brokerages operating in financial markets, venture capitalists, media and publishing, management consultancy. Employee stress may result from the degree of risk. Characteristics include a short-term orientation, little learning from setbacks, and distrust among colleagues.

The work-hard/play-hard culture. This culture is typified by fast feedback and reward and low risk. Organisational examples include property and car sales and computer/IT companies. Employee stress may result from the speed and quantity of work rather than uncertainty. Characteristics include an orientation towards action, reward for persistence, the sacrifice of quality for quantity, little long-term planning, a focus on clients or customers, and a lack of thought and attention.

Process culture. This culture is typified by slow feedback and reward and low risk. In an organisation with this culture, there is often a focus on the way things are done. Examples include insurance companies, banks, heavily-regulated industries and public sector bureaucracies such as local government. Employee stress may result from frustrations with systems and internal politics. Characteristics include use of jargon, orderly and punctual behaviour, attention to detail, and caution and protectiveness which are responses to absence of feedback.

Bet-your-company culture. This culture is typified by slow feedback and reward and high risk. In organisations with this culture timescales are long and there is emphasis on preparation and planning. Organisational examples include biotech and pharmaceuticals companies and others involved in science and technology. In these companies research and development can take years, not months, and research programmes may be abandoned at various stages. Employee stress results from the level of risk and the long delay in feedback. Characteristics include respect for authority and technical competence, slowness, consultative by top–down decision making, vulnerability to short-term fluctuations and cash-flow problems.

Other attempts to classify organisational culture have generally resulted in identifying the four types that Handy/Harrison described based on unwritten but shared rules of behaviour. These four types are set out below, together with the organisational structures with which they tend to be associated. Structure refers to how responsibilities for different functions and processes are divided up between different departments, work groups and individuals (see Box 12.1).

ннн

Figure 12.2 Power culture

Power culture. This concentrates power at the centre, like a spider in the centre of a spider's web. The organisation exists to enable the decisions of those at the centre to be carried out. It is often a very personal culture in the sense that communication is between individuals rather than between formal job holders or departments. Often dominated by a charismatic leader or founder, the culture relies on individual responses and interpersonal commitments. Care is taken to employ the 'right sort of people' who will 'fit in'. Organisations with a power culture often feel like extended families. The culture is associated with organisational structures that allow operational control over resources.

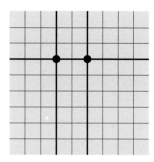

Figure 12.3 Task culture

Task culture. This culture has a job or task orientation and can be thought of as a matrix or net. Much power and influence lies at the intersections of the strings in the net. Employees typically belong to different teams for different purposes. Problem-solving is a feature of a task culture as employees deal with new situations to which tried and tested formulas cannot be applied. Coordinators and project team leaders are central figures. The culture is associated with a decentralised organisation structured for entrepreneurship and achievement.

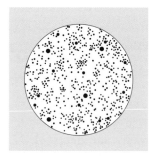

Figure 12.4 Person culture

Person culture. In power and task cultures the purpose of the organisation takes priority. In contrast, a person culture puts individuals and their interests first: the organisation is a resource to use to enhance their talents and abilities. This culture can be thought of as a constellation or cluster of stars. Cooperatives of artists, academic think-tanks or consulting partnerships may possess a person culture in which people are motivated by their own personal and professional values. Managing collective interests is often regarded as a chore rather than as a mark of distinction, status or leadership. The culture is associated with the need for collaboration, hence the lack of structure or of choice regarding structure.

Figure 12.5 Role culture

Role culture. This type of culture is quite the opposite of person culture. Individuals have roles to play and communication tends to be formalised into systems and procedures, both horizontally and vertically within the organisation. It can be thought of as a Palladian-style building as the diagram shows. An organisation possessing this culture is more likely to be managed than led. Certainty, predictability, continuity and stability are highly-regarded in such a culture and professionalism and reliability are valued above independence and initiative-taking. Training and development are important. The culture is associated with a highly-structured organisation with formalised working arrangements to increase efficiency via smooth administration.

Box 12.1 The structure of organisations

Structure refers to the arrangements for the way in which an organisation's activities are divided between staff and the way in which the efforts of staff are coordinated and controlled. Structure provides a framework for allocating responsibilities and authority. An organisation chart is a graphic description of an organisation's structure. An example of a chart is shown in Figure 12.6.

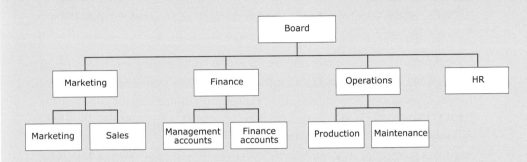

Figure 12.6 An example of an organisational chart showing a functional structure

The chart shows the span of control of the different parts of the organisation. It is an example of a functional structure, appropriate when people involved in different functions such as marketing or finance need to communicate regularly with each other. Other types of structure are based on products and or services – staff are grouped on product or service lines – or geography where staff are grouped according to their physical location. Thus, organisational charts can show products/services, branches, sites, locations, departments, work groups, and even individual people. A matrix structure, shown in Figure 12.7, combines functional and product/service structures. A project structure looks similar.

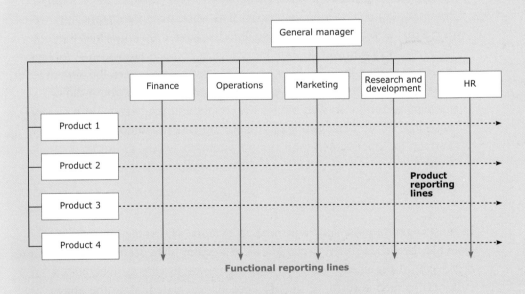

Figure 12.7 An example of how a matrix structure might work

Organisational structures can be 'tall' and hierarchical, with vertical lines of communication and interaction, or 'flat', with horizontal lines of communication and interaction. Most Western organisations became flatter in the last part of the twentieth century. Structure is equated with bureaucracy which the sociologist Max Weber (1947) regarded as 'legal-rational authority'. The structure of organisations can be stable when conditions do not change very much, but may change as they grow or decrease in size. In unstable conditions, an organisation's structure may be 'organic' with continual adjustments being made.

Just as in national cultures which are likely to vary from region to region, community to community, group to group and family to family, organisational culture has 'levels'. Smaller units within an organisation may have different cultures – for example, in functional areas such as marketing or operations – or in professional areas – for example, IT or engineering. The extent to which an organisation has a single common culture depends on the extent of common experience. There are likely to be sub-cultures that are independent of one another and which may conflict. Consider, for example, health care services in which doctors and managers may have very different cultures.

A weakness of these classifications, however, is that they are based on the impressions of management consultants rather than systematic study. The nature, dimensions and causes of organisation culture remain subjects for debate. However, there is broad agreement that there is *something* about organisations that leads some to achieve extraordinary improvements in, for example, quality, productivity or innovation. Fortunately for the manager, cultural change does not have to be tackled at the level of the whole organisation – at *that* level, all the manager can hope to do is to identify and minimise any negative impacts of it on the work group.

Ideal or 'above-the-norm' cultures

A safety culture

All the staff interviewed at the Swedish air traffic control centre thought the reporting culture was very good. The open dialogue meant they were not afraid of reporting safety problems because they knew that the organisation's aim was to look for solutions to such problems. A highly-developed three-level reporting system was in use, where the lowest level of reports were those written when operators wanted to share their learning experiences with others who might find themselves in a similar situation. At the other two levels, reporting was mandatory. Further, through the applied self-monitoring system, individual air traffic controllers were obliged to update their practical and theoretical knowledge.

(Source: adapted from Ek *et al.*, 2007)

In most organisations, staff will need to *comply* with something, for example, health and safety regulations or keeping data secure. In some organisations the need is so great that organisation-wide systems and a culture of safety, security or quality need to be created, as in the above example of the Swedish air traffic control centre. Nuclear power stations need to guard against malfunction and the risk of malicious attack; a computer manufacturer may make a strategic decision to improve and maintain quality to retain its share of a market in which customers demand product reliability. Whilst decisions about safety, security or quality will be taken by senior management and embedded in systems and procedures, the safety, security or quality culture will be the product of the behaviours, beliefs, values and practices of staff.

Quality, safety or security cultures can be thought of as 'above-the-norm'. The terms 'quality', 'safety' and 'security' can mean simply the degree to which something consistently meets requirements, set by the organisation or by law – or much more (see Box 12.2). In the last century the idea of quality moved from inspection to statistical quality control (sampling) to more comprehensive approaches. In organisations which have adopted what is known as total quality management (TQM), quality is so deeply embedded that it is regarded as everybody's job. In strategic quality management, quality is generally related to competition or pressure from customers rather than purely internal standards. These two quality systems originated in Japan and arrived in Europe via the USA.

Box 12.2 Definitions of quality

There are many different definitions of quality which, when summarised, can refer to 'perceived' quality (the experience of quality by the customer or client), the measurable characteristics of a product or service, the customer or client's perspective on 'fitness for use', fitness for purpose, conformance of the product or service to a specification, and value for money. Quality, then, can mean excellence (based on perceptions), or lack of defects (based on conformance) or value for money (Jackson, 1998). Quality is also considered to be relative to what something should be. Quality can refer to decisions, documents, information, outputs or processes in addition to products and services.

Whilst there are many potential benefits from the successful implementation of quality cultures and systems, there are significant costs and difficulties. First, we consider the benefits, then the difficulties. It is useful to remember that there is a 'quality industry' which needs to promote its 'quality products' in order to make profits.

Strategic quality management has led to recognised standards (CIPD, 2006). Organisations can seek to comply with the internationally-recognised standards; for example, ISO 9001, the generic name for a family of standards for implementing a quality management system. ISO 9001 is used by over 670,000 organisations in 154 countries. The second most popular global standard (ISO 14001 Environmental Management Systems) is used in over 90,000 organisations in 127 countries. Many international standards are based on the original British Standards. There are thousands of standards covering a wide range of areas and sectors. In the UK there are over 800 British Standards relating to the food industry alone, covering areas from food safety to occupational health.

Being inspected regularly and gaining certification is used by organisations for improvement and often to demonstrate publicly that they consistently achieve the standards they have set for themselves. The United Nations Secretariat earned ISO/IEC 27001:2005 Information Security Management certification in 2006 in order to improve its management of ICT security and to demonstrate this good management to the world (BSI Management Systems, 2008).

Taylor Bloxam, a UK print company which won the BSI British Standards ISO 14001 Environmental Management Systems award in 2008, wanted to reduce waste by using less, reusing and recycling, buying materials locally and regionally, improving energy efficiency and ensuring environmental awareness among employees (Taylor Bloxam, 2008).

Annual awards can demonstrate world-class standards. McNulty Offshore Construction, one of Europe's leading makers of equipment for offshore structures, has health and safety and the environment as core values. It meets ISO 14001 for safety and in 2007 won the British Safety Council Sword of Honour, one of only 40 organisations worldwide to do so – and for the tenth year in succession (McNulty Offshore Construction, 2008).

In general the introduction of quality standards requires training, team building, changes in work patterns and cultural change. The ISO 9000 quality management standard is based on eight management principles:

- customer focus
- leadership
- involvement of people
- process approach
- systems approach to management
- continuous improvement
- factual approach to decision-making
- mutually-beneficial supplier relationships.

The steps an organisation needs to take are to:

- define why it exists
- determine key processes
- establish how these processes work within the organisation
- determine who owns these processes
- agree these processes throughout the organisation.

The UK Chartered Institute of Personnel and Development describes the standards as essentially a management control procedure. It involves recording all the key processes in the organisation – for example, design, production and distribution – so that the quality of products and services meets the needs of customers, consumers or clients. The result is a quality manual setting out the organisation's quality policies, procedures and every system that affects the quality of the service or produce delivered. Staff training is critical to ensure that staff understand the role of the manual and the benefits of the system, and know how to upgrade and improve procedures. The final step in the ISO programme is an independent audit to see that the system is working as described in the manual and that it meets ISO 9000 requirements.

The European Foundation for Quality Management (EFQM) Excellence Model, launched in 1992 and regularly updated, is even more demanding than ISO 9000. An organisation also has to heed the results: what the organisation is achieving for its employees, customer satisfaction, and impact on society and business achievements. The model requires a full preparation and accreditation process (and also offers an annual award). It is a tool for:

- self-assessment
- a way for an organisation to compare itself with other organisations (benchmarking)
- a way of identifying areas for improvement
- providing a basis for creating a common vocabulary and way of thinking in the organisation
- providing a structure for the organisation's management system.

The benefits of certification are the confidence generated among suppliers and customers or clients and the cost-benefits that flow from improved quality, as well as marketing benefits. However, the certification approach to quality has shortcomings:

- it can be bureaucratic
- compliance may become an end in itself
- it is expensive
- it does not guarantee the product or service (which could still be faulty)
- it does not improve quality on its own.

Some argue that quality management systems are a necessary prerequisite to TQM. TQM adopts the view that quality will improve only if all employees and activities of the organisation are involved. This is what 'total' means. To see quality through the eyes of customers, consumers or clients, the organisation must also know what its customers want. Building a relationship with customers and getting closer to them is vital. In this, TQM highlights the role of staff who deal directly with customers. However, TQM also addresses the chain of staff who form the links that eventually lead to the external customer or consumer. If quality is maximised along this chain, then ultimately the customer or consumer will be satisfied. Changes in customer requirements can be communicated backwards along the chain which, ideally, stretches back to suppliers who are external to the organisation. In this, good communication is essential. This is the meaning of Q in TQM. Then there is management, the M in TQM. Senior managers need to develop a written quality strategy for their organisation which:

- makes clear the broad aim and long-term goals of its TQM
- defines how TQM fits into its corporate objectives and strategy
- describes the actions needed to implement TQM
- indicates the resources needed.

Senior managers also need to demonstrate their personal commitment to TQM by participating.

TQM requires the full and positive participation of employees. This may take the form of regular group or team activities (for example, quality circles) where staff work out ways of improving quality in their part of the organisation. There is no one best way to implement TQM but there are some common features, such as team work. Advocates of TQM say it is best underpinned by a quality management system such as ISO 9000.

The Deming Prize, which originated in Japan, and the Malcolm Baldrige Award, which originated in the USA, are offered annually to organisations practising TQM to the highest levels: these awards set 'standards' for organisations to aspire to.

It should be clear that successful implementation of TQM requires a supportive organisational culture, a culture of quality. In this kind of culture, blaming people who have caused quality problems will be discouraged: the important thing is to learn from mistakes which will need to be reported and discussed openly. Such an environment can be built only on mutual trust, with a management style that does not depend on blame or fear.

TQM is not without problems, however. These include:

Getting too close to existing customers. In trying to meet the needs of existing customers or clients, the needs of future customers may be neglected, leaving the organisation ill-equipped to meet a changing market. This may be particularly important where organisations are funded by governments which may change their requirements substantially, particularly after a change of government or leadership.

Increasing customers' control over staff. Because of the supremacy of customers or clients in TQM, it sees the main responsibility of staff as the satisfaction of customers. Staff may feel controlled via customers. This can put them at the mercy of customers, a tyranny that may be far worse than being at the mercy of managers.

Exploiting staff. Under TQM employees are expected to be a source of improvement as well as to perform their normal jobs. This can be stressful, and staff may feel excessively controlled by clients and customers.

Blocking more radical improvements. With no fear or personal criticism in the organisation, job security should be a feature of such organisations. Thus TQM should avoid the need for radical restructuring or cost cutting, but not doing so when necessary may not be in the interests of efficiency. In this respect, TQM is concerned with improving effectiveness rather than efficiency.

Quality as a fad. TQM probably amounts to what should be good practice. It can be argued, therefore, that TQM labels all problems as quality issues.

Cost. Inspection is usually done regularly by external assessors who charge a fee. The organisation has to spend time recording key processes.

When an organisation decides to improve quality in such systematic ways, whether through a set of prescribed standards or in other ways, the effect will be felt throughout the organisation. Although comprehensive manuals of procedure will have been introduced, the organisation is likely to become less bureaucratic and more flexible and creative, based on informal relationships and direct interaction between employees. Work is likely to be carried out by teams of expert staff – a task or project culture. The key features of a quality culture in addition to creativity and adaptivity are likely to be cohesiveness, participation and team work, which managers will need to foster.

Psychological climate

Are you trusted to take work-related decisions on your own? Do more senior managers involve you in the decisions they make? Would you say your organisation is quick to respond when changes need to be made?

When responding to questions such as these, you are describing your personal perceptions of the organisation you work for. These perceptions, together with all the others you have of the organisation and those of all the other staff, constitute what is known as the organisational or psychological *climate*.

How does the organisational or psychological climate differ from organisational culture – the unwritten, shared attitudes, behaviour patterns, practices, expectations and values that influence the way things get done? The organisational or psychological climate consists only of employees' perceptions of the organisational environment that result from their experience of working in the organisation. Some management writers prefer to use the term 'psychological climate' to emphasise this. Individual employees' perceptions will differ, of course, according to their status and which part of the organisation they work in.

Some researchers describe the psychological climate as a snapshot of an organisation in terms of the perceptions of employees while organisation culture constitutes the underlying reasons or causes for those perceptions. Psychological climate refers to the aggregate of individual perceptions. While it is hard to talk about the strength of organisational culture, the strength of psychological climate is said to depend on the degree to which individual perceptions are similar throughout the organisation – that is, shared. Because individual perceptions may fluctuate according to events and circumstances, some management researchers claim that the psychological climate is more volatile than the organisational culture. The perceptions of individuals can also be changed if they have good reason to change them. This means that managers are more able to change the climate than the culture (Davidson, 2003).

The concept of organisational climate is much older than that of organisational culture and there is more consensus about the nature of climate than there is on organisational culture. The main approach to studying psychological climate has been to try to identify its dimensions – those factors that contribute to it. Very many have been identified, but which ones appear to be most important? There appear to be eight broad factors that make the most important contributions:

1 **Autonomy.** This refers to the degree to which people are able to take individual responsibility, how closely they are supervised and the degree to which people can structure their own work.

2 **Cohesion.** This describes peer relations, cooperation, friendliness and warmth, sociability, spiritedness, lack of conflict and status differences.

3 **Trust.** This involves trust in leaders and the sensitivity of managers, openness and intimacy as opposed to aloofness.

4 **Pressure.** This describes the general pressure of the job, role overload and conflict, role ambiguity, how much emphasis is placed on production and achievement, the job standards required and the measurement of results.

5 **Support.** This refers to general support for an employee, the consideration of the leader and how the leader facilitates the work, the perceived distance of the leader from the employee, the influence of the hierarchy and management awareness.

6 **Recognition.** This describes recognition and feedback, opportunities for growth and advancement, rewards (and punishments).

7 **Fairness.** This relates to fairness and objectivity in the reward system, clarity over promotion, clarity of policies and the efficiency of the organisational structures, altruism (concern for the welfare of others) and egalitarianism (the belief that all people have equal rights and privileges).

8 **Innovation.** This refers to organisational flexibility as well as innovation, challenge, degrees of risk and security and orientation to the future.

(Source: adapted from Koys and De Cotiis, 1991)

These dimensions, drawn from a content study of organisational climate surveys, seem to be standing the test of time. A decade after Koys and De Cotiis, Davidson *et al.* (2001) identified the dimensions as:

- leadership
- facilitation and support
- professional and organisational esprit
- conflict and ambiguity
- regulations
- organisation and pressure
- job variety
- challenge
- autonomy
- work-group cooperation
- friendliness and warmth
- job standards.

Importantly, many studies of organisational climate show a relationship between climate and job satisfaction, work outcomes, stress, absenteeism, commitment, participation, sick leave and creativity.

Improving the psychological climate: what a manager can do

The idea of an organisational or psychological climate – the perceptions of employees about the organisation they work for – is of practical use to managers. Perceptions are possessed by individuals and can be shared by a team or work group. Some of these perceptions may concern aspects of organisational life over which a manager has little control. However, the

See also: What a
manager can do to
reduce pressure, in this
chapter

manager can influence other aspects of it. Here are some actions a manager
can take, based on the broad dimensions of the psychological climate –
autonomy, cohesion, trust, support, recognition, fairness and innovation. What
a manager can do to reduce pressure and stress is covered later in this chapter.

Autonomy

Trust people to make and take work-related decisions appropriate to their
role. Do not micro-manage them. Allow them to plan and prioritise their
work. Let them decide how best to do the job. This can be quite difficult for
managers because of their perceived reduction in control. However, when a
person responds well to increased autonomy, this self-control may be more
effective and efficient than the manager's control. How much autonomy you
allow a person to have will depend on the nature of tasks and whether there
are specific procedures to follow. Task requirements, performance targets and
expectations should be made clear (see 'Trust', below) and there should be
ongoing feedback on performance. Sometimes, you may have to redesign
tasks to allow a person greater autonomy without you losing too much
control. If the culture or rules of the organisation require you to take
decisions, then autonomy can be increased by asking people for their views
and discussing decisions with them.

See also: Learning and
development activities,
Chapter 11

It can be hard to trust people before you are confident that individuals are
competent at what they do. In such cases, it is best to assume that they can
be trusted (people normally respond well when they see that they are
trusted). However, initially it is wise to talk through with them how they
intend to plan and prioritise their work. Then the planning and prioritising
can be done with your support until you are confident that the person can do
this alone. Autonomy is not something people can be given; they will need
to develop the skill of dealing with it and understand the kinds of
responsibilities it carries.

Cohesion

Create strong relationships in the work group in order to develop:

- a willingness to work together
- loyalty between members
- a sense of unity
- commitment to goals and achieving them.

Goals need to be stated in terms of group or team goals not individual goals.
This helps members to understand that the goal is not achievable without
each other. Collaboration, including group problem-solving and decision-
making, also contributes to cohesion. If possible, make sure that group or
team members work near to one another to encourage closer relationships.

See also: Managing
conflicts, Chapter 8

Encourage agreement over ways of behaving, shared beliefs and values by
placing emphasis on similarities between group members. Be tolerant of
people and show them respect. Encourage them to be part of the team.
Be fair, cooperative and friendly. Managers who model these desirable
behaviours will create norms of behaviour that help to facilitate good
relations and positive interactions between employees. Another essential
element in creating cohesiveness is to handle conflict effectively.

Enhanced cohesiveness is usually the aim of awayday, team-building exercises when a work group spends time away from the workplace on team activities, such as outdoor pursuits, often unrelated to work tasks. Some management writers say that workplaces themselves need to be more fun, with more social events and community support activities, and by introducing regular activities such as casual dress days (Ford *et al.*, 2004). Managers can organise or promote work-group events such as celebrating the personal and professional milestones of individuals.

Not all attempts to enhance cohesions will meet with success. Cohesion is a psychological climate factor which organisational practices may significantly affect. For example, it may be difficult to achieve if an organisation links pay or other benefits to individuals rather than teams. It will also be difficult in some cultures, particularly those where deference to others is usual.

Trust

Trust is an expectancy that another person can be relied on. According to Lewicki and Tomlinson (2003) our ability to trust another person depends on:

- our own ability to assess whether the other person is capable of meeting our expectations
- our past experience of the other person – whether they have met our expectations before
- the degree to which we think the other person is sufficiently concerned about us to meet our expectations.

Thus it takes time to build a measure of real trust. The third factor – whether the other person has concern for us – can be helped by honest and open communication. This means being clear about our intentions and motives so that the other person can monitor them and allowing that person some autonomy by seeking their views (see 'Autonomy' above). Show concern for the other person's needs and interests. It is damaging to violate trust – for example, checking an employee's work while they are not there or without warning should be avoided – mainly because it is harder to rebuild trust. Note, however, that trust is two-way: the other person must be able to carry out his or her role competently, consistently and predictably. If you need to rebuild trust, then take action as soon as possible, apologise sincerely, do what you say you will do to mend the relationship and clarify future expectations. Above all, reaffirm your commitment to the relationship.

Support

Social support, the way in which you can support the employee's work and development, as well as facilitating work, are covered above: the absence of these types of support is potentially stressful. However, support is a thread that runs vertically through an organisation from top to bottom, and horizontally across peers and colleagues. The support you give to the staff you manage is considered the most important, particularly work-focussed support. Regular meetings are useful.

Non-work-focussed discussions with peers are also associated with perceptions of support. There is often mutual support among peers; however, the work group does not support the manager in the same way, so managers will need to seek their own sources of work and non-work support.

Recognition

Praise from a supervisor, team leader or line manager is highly valued by employees when it is perceived to be genuine. Indeed, some surveys place such expressions of gratitude above material rewards (which are nonetheless welcome!). Employees who receive praise, who feel that their line manager cares and that their job is important to the organisation are likely to feel more motivated and committed (Brun and Dugas, 2008). Recognition helps to produce more of the same desired behaviours and actions. Monthly, quarterly and annual recognitions are the norm for formal recognition in organisations but informal ones are much more frequent. Whether informal or formal, recognition works best when it is:

Specific. Let people know *exactly* what behaviours and actions they are being praised for.

Consistent. What is rewarded on one occasion should not be ignored on another; a person who models their behaviour on something that another person has been recognised for will justifiably feel overlooked.

Fair. Recognition must be available to all. In a sales team, recognition for the person who exceeds his or her target figures is appropriate (rather than the person achieving the highest sales). In a mixed team, however, all members need to be eligible for recognition of achievements above the norm. You will need to specify what constitutes above the norm so that all work-group members know they have the same opportunity.

Recognition often takes the form of a simple 'Thank you' but public recognition can be powerful (Heathfield, 2008). Ways of doing this include:

- saying 'Thank you' at a group meeting with a round of applause
- giving flowers or store vouchers
- setting out the recognition in a memo and emailing copies to the employee and the department head or CEO and placing a copy on record in the employee's file.

However, make sure that a person will not be embarrassed by public recognition. You can be strategic about recognition by deciding what kind of actions and behaviours you want to encourage and communicating your intention to work-group members. Other forms of recognition and acknowledgement include keeping employees informed, consulting and involving them in decisions and promoting their development.

Fairness

Fairness can be thought of as equity, or the absence of bias or discrimination. Many countries have laws governing discrimination on the basis of gender, age, race and religion. Beyond the unfairness of these kinds of bias, employees are said to make fairness assessments on the basis of social comparison. They look at what they bring to the job – their time, commitment, efforts, ability, and so on – and what they get in return, such as pay, esteem, responsibility, security and recognition. In doing so, they make comparisons with their peers.

Procedural fairness refers to the way employees are treated, how things are done and how decisions are made and indeed, it is claimed, all the processes and interactions that occur (Blader and Tyler, 2003).

Distributive fairness relates to rewards or outcomes, such as salary and promotion.

There appear to be no absolutes when it comes to fairness. People may assess equality and fairness relative to the situation. For example, short-term unfairness may be accepted because ultimately it will lead to greater overall fairness in a system. Employees might also regard themselves as being treated fairly while regarding the overall system as unfair. Individual perceptions of fairness will be different.

During all encounters, you will need to consider formal and informal aspects of fairness and their sources including:

- people's rights and dignity
- people's perceptions of how they are treated
- how decisions are made and their implications in terms of resources, workload, and so on
- fairness of formal rules and procedures
- how rules and procedures are implemented
- providing explanations; for example, giving people reasons for decisions in which they have not been able to participate
- polite and friendly treatment of others
- being sensitive to others
- conflict resolution.

Innovation

An organisation's orientation to innovation and creativity will help or limit what you can do at the local level. Innovation will be more likely in an organisation which:

- supports innovation and creativity from the top
- is willing to use resources to facilitate and implement ideas
- has good cross-functional cooperation and support
- is willing to take risks and deal with uncertainty and ambiguity
- ties creativity to rewards.

However, a 'climate for creativity' has a number of other facets on which you as a manager can have an impact. Hunter *et al.* (2007) summarise these as:

- a supportive and intellectually-stimulating work group in which relationships are characterised by trust, openness, humour and good communication, and a sense of cohesion
- a supervisor who is supportive of new ideas

- encouragement of debate and discussion of ideas
- challenging jobs or tasks but which are not overtaxing
- goals and expectations of creative or innovative performance
- autonomy and freedom for individuals in performing their jobs
- encouragement and support for participation

See also: Communication
skills, Chapter 2

- clear, open and effective communication between peers, supervisors and those supervised.

While you can have an influence over the local psychological climate of the work group, the extent of this influence will depend on how supportive the organisation is of the kinds of behaviours and actions that shape people's positive perceptions.

What a manager can do to reduce pressure

Pressure and stress

Paula's job in a school required her to spend long hours working with different age groups throughout the day and running a club for the children after school. Often, during the evenings she would prepare activities for her classes. Friends often told her that the job demanded too much of her and that she worked too hard. However, she loved her work and remained full of enthusiasm – though she tried to keep her weekends free and she enjoyed the long school holidays!

John worked in a local sports club which was open every day of the year from early morning till late at night. The staff worked in shifts. Although pay was not high, John was happy to have a job that allowed him to have access to a gym outside his working hours. He was a keen weightlifter and the job allowed him to train for competitions. The problem was that, when other staff were absent, John was often asked to work extra shifts. The additional time spent standing in for absent staff meant that he was not able to spend so much of his free time at the gym or to take part in competitions. He felt under pressure and was beginning to feel stressed.

Most jobs are associated with pressure of some kind. But as the examples above illustrate, the general pressures and demands of a job do not necessarily lead to stress. Stress relates to the way in which an individual responds to pressure. It is important to note, however, that pressures and demands can be excessive: that is, they would cause stress in most people. Excessive demands and pressure have been found to increase staff turnover and absenteeism, reduce work performance, increase poor timekeeping and produce more customer complaints. In countries such as the UK the law makes it the responsibility of organisations to ensure that employees are not made ill by their work. Studies of work-related causes of stress have identified 12 common ones. These are set out below, together with suggestions about what a manager can, or cannot, do about them.

Demands of the job. Job demands are the physical, psychological, social or organisational aspects of a job that require sustained physical, mental and emotional effort or skills (and without which, the job cannot be done). Examples include decision-making, working with customers, constantly monitoring machines or computer screens, or working on highly-unstructured tasks. Job demands are not necessarily stressful in themselves (though some may be). Some writers on management suggest that high demands will lead to stress if employees have little control over their work. The term work–life balance refers to people being able to find satisfaction both at work and in their life outside work. To achieve work–life balance, people need a measure of control over when, where and how they work. Work hours and patterns may need to be addressed here. Other writers suggest that a high degree of effort that brings low rewards in terms of pay, recognition or promotion will result in stress. Whether stress is the result of low control or rewards, organisational policies may limit what you as a manager can do.

Role conflict. Employees have work roles and personal roles and sometimes these can conflict. For example, a person may have one set of responsibilities that requires them to attend a number of committee meetings and another set that involves improving the productivity in the work group. Or it may be that a person's work role gives them some control over the activities of a colleague who is also a friend. Again, there is little a manager can do about these types of role conflict. However, you can ensure that there is role clarity. Further, a friendly and supportive work environment lessens the negative impact of role conflict and there is much you can do to create and maintain such an atmosphere.

Role ambiguity. This occurs when people are uncertain about some aspects of the jobs and their responsibilities, what is expected of them and how to organise their time. Sometimes the uncertainty extends to lack of clarity over the job role and goals. You can do much here to clarify a person's role and reduce ambiguity.

Having too much or too little to do. There are two types of work overload – simply having too much to do in the time available, or being unable to perform a task owing to a lack of skill or resources. Work underload also comes in two forms – having too little to do to fill the time available, or having tasks that are so boring and repetitive that an employee is understimulated. Here, you will need to investigate to see what can be done. Solutions are likely to range from time management to job redesign to ensure that people who you are responsible for have task objectives that are adequate and achievable within the agreed work hours. Where possible, employees need to have some control over their pace of work and to be consulted over work patterns, including when breaks can be taken.

See also: Job analysis and the creation of a job description Chapter 9; Managing your time, Chapter 1

Responsibility for others. This is a pressure which often applies to managers, who are responsible for those staff who report to them or work-group members: managers must motivate, organise, monitor performance, lead the work group, listen and communicate, to name but a few management tasks. Having decided to become a manager, there is little you can do about this unless the responsibilities are excessive. Perhaps more stressful are situations in which people (not only managers) are given responsibility without control.

Lack of social support. Negative events are perceived as less negative if a person has friends and supporters who care about and accept them, and provide support when needed. You will need to create a cohesive work group in which members can speak openly and in which asking for help is not considered a sign of weakness. The most effective support for employees comes from managers (Moyle, 2006). An interesting feature of support is that people's perception that support is there if needed is more important than the actual support given when difficulties arise.

See also: Managing team processes, Chapter 8

Lack of participation in decisions. When decisions that affect people's jobs are merely 'passed down' and they have no control over them, feelings of helplessness and alienation are likely to result. A manager can ensure that work-group members participate in the decision the manager must take, if the culture and rules of the organisation allow this. Where decisions are passed down from a higher level, managers can lessen the negative impact by providing as much information as possible, finding out and providing explanations for the decision, again if possible. Some sorts of decisions in organisations are often made without consultations: for example, mergers and takeovers. There may be some situations in which employees may prefer not to be consulted: for example, who in the work group will lose their job when an organisation must downsize.

See also: Performance management and the appraisal process, Chapter 10

Poorly-managed performance appraisals. Both not having one's performance appraised, and receiving negative feedback without being told how to improve one's performance can be sources of stress. Managers can ensure that their staff receive constructive feedback on their performance, even if an organisation does not have a system of formal appraisals.

Working conditions. Noise, heat and cold, lack of space, and so on are more stressful when they are unpredictable and uncontrollable. The perceptions of individual staff will differ, of course. In some cases there is little a manager can do about working conditions; in others, you will need to exercise leadership and discuss the situation with more senior managers. In the UK, the law sets out minimum standards of acceptability for working conditions, including safety.

Organisational change. Policy changes, reorganisations, mergers, downsizing of organisations and changes in structure often lead to uncertainty among employees. Further, work relationships and support networks are disrupted. Such changes are as likely to affect the manager as they are the work group. Timely information and communication of the reasons for change, the schedule and the impact on jobs are key components in reducing uncertainty. A manager can assist, and can provide some of the support required during the change.

Career development. Employees (and managers) can have realistic expectations about their career development but find their progress is disrupted by various factors. These can be organisational factors such as restructuring, or interpersonal factors such as a different relationship with a new line manager, or factors such as gender. These factors affect managers as well as staff they are responsible for. It is good practice to discuss career development during performance appraisals, ensure that career aspirations are realistic and agree on training and development needs and how they are to be met. This does not guarantee career development but ensures that an individual is ready to take career development opportunities as they arise.

Work–home conflicts. Most people regard themselves as having two main aspects to their lives: home and work. These may be in conflict when, for example, a family is unsupportive of a mother having a job, or an employee has to work over a religious holiday, or when work colleagues are intolerant of an employee wanting to arrange work hours around school times. A manager's efforts towards a cohesive and supportive work group will help in two ways: by promoting understanding and support from colleagues, and by encouraging individual commitment to the group which helps to prevent a person taking advantage of others because of a personal or domestic circumstance. What can be done to reduce work–home conflicts will depend on the rules of the organisation and culture, organisational, national and ethnic.

Pressure and stress: formal standards

In the UK the Health and Safety Executive, which has management standards covering work-related pressure and stress, summarises areas of stress under six main headings that can be acted on: demands, control, support, relationships at work, role and change (Mackay *et al.*, 2004). Its general advice to *organisations* is to ensure that *managers*:

- identify workplace stressors
- ensure good communication between management and staff
- ensure that all staff are sufficiently trained for the tasks they need to do
- provide staff with meaningful development opportunities
- monitor workloads, working hours and overtime to ensure that staff are not overworking
- ensure that staff take their full holiday leave entitlement
- deal with harassment and bullying (causing harm by coercion, intimidation or physical assault)
- be vigilant and provide support to staff experiencing stress outside work, for example, as a result of bereavement or marital breakdown.

(Source: based on HSE, 2008)

At the organisational level, interventions to reduce what managers and the law regard as unacceptable stress are generally of four types:

- policy, procedures and systems audits
- a problem-centred approach which means investigating particular issues such as sickness absence levels
- a wellbeing approach which identifies ways to create a healthy workforce
- an employee-centred approach in which individuals are provided with information and support to help them deal with workplace stress.

(Source: based on CIPD, 2008)

An example of the wellbeing approach is set out in Box 12.3. It illustrates a change that could happen only at an organisation level, not one that a manager could make in a single work group. Some of the HSE's intervention advice, however, could be taken up by managers, for example, organising stress forums where staff can identify problems and possible solutions: for example, adjusting work schedules to increase staff at times of peak demands, and team-building sessions (HSE, 2008).

Box 12.3 Flexible working at Toshiba

Toshiba UK pioneered flexible working in the UK allowing employees to adjust the time they start and finish work – a practice that helps working mothers in particular. Now, in addition, it encourages homeworking where possible and offers free broadband and wireless access to home workers. It promotes a healthy lifestyle in the workplace, offering counselling on health and welfare issues and allowing employees to 'pick and mix' benefits such as childcare provision, increased pensions contributions, additional holidays and gym membership. Toshiba believes this has helped it to reduce the number of absentee days per employee to 3.7 a year, fewer than half the national average for the UK services sector. Staff retention is also above the industry standard.

(Source: adapted from Pollit, 2006)

Chapter 13 The organisation and the external environment

The external environment

Fading flowers

> Greta opened her city flower shop eight years ago. Ten florists in that part of the city have closed recently, along with a number of shops in Greta's street. Each closure increases the concern of the business community in the area. Along with small businesses across the country, the flower shop is feeling the effects of a downturn in the global economy. For eight years Greta has relied on her bank to provide cash when she needed it. But now the bank and its competitors are no longer providing credit when Greta and the other small traders need it. As a result, they predict that small businesses will disappear from shopping centres and high streets, opening further opportunities for big businesses to increase their presence.

The case above illustrates the impact on one small business of the difficult economic situation that developed in the first decade of this century. Banks, which had bought risky investment packages, stopped lending to one another. Without money borrowed from each other, the banks stopped lending to their customers. The effects of what became known as 'the credit crunch' were felt in most parts of the world in one way or another. This is because the global economy is a highly inter-connected one in which even the closure of florists in London has an effect on growers and distributors of flowers in places such as South Africa.

Things that happen in the wider economy and in politics may often seem to have little direct relevance to the lives and work of most people. However, a range of external factors can affect an organisation's direction and performance. Economic and political factors are but two. Others include social and technological factors, as well as those relating to the natural environment. One major issue relating to the natural environment is climate change, which is becoming more important for organisations as they seek to attract customers by showing their concern and as they comply with new laws and standards. An understanding of the external environment of an organisation is critical to managers because it is the source of all important threats and opportunities faced by an organisation. It is not enough for a manager to understand the purpose, values, culture and structure of the organisation. Rather, it is necessary to understand why the organisation is like it is and behaves as it does, and this means understanding how factors in the environment have an influence.

Three environments

Organisations do not exist in isolation: they are part of a large and complex network of customers, suppliers, competitors and regulators. In addition, they are subject to changes in the economy, social trends, technical innovation, the political and legal settings in which they operate, and the natural environment from which they source their raw materials and to which they emit their wastes. We can represent this as three environments (Figure 13.1). The term 'stakeholder' refers to people or organisations who have an interest in the organisation and what it does.

Figure 13.1 The three environments

- The *internal environment* comprises the organisation itself, its staff, resources and facilities. The internal environment is said to be one that managers can control, but, of course, not all managers have control over all aspects of the internal environment, and many aspects of the internal environment are actually rather difficult to change.

- The *near external* environment includes customers, clients, contractors, suppliers and competitors, as well as intermediaries and other identifiable stakeholders. These cannot be controlled by managers but they may be influenced to some extent. They certainly often have the ability to influence the organisation and then its managers.

- The *far external* environment refers to factors that can be neither controlled nor easily influenced from within an organisation. These are often referred to by the acronym STEEP, which stands for social, technological, economic, environmental and political factors. (There are some other acronyms for these factors. It does not really matter which one you use as long as it helps you to remember what the factors are.)

Organisational boundaries

We all recognise that organisations differ in their structure and relationships with the outside world. These differences include where the boundaries between the internal and external environment lie. Some organisations have very large internal structures and do most things in-house, whereas others have only a small core organisation and outsource a lot of activities to other organisations in the near environment. Some examples are:

- IKEA, the Swedish household furnishings company, controls its global retail outlets and sells only its own-branded goods in them, whereas manufacturers of branded goods often do not own any retail outlets themselves but sell through retailers, including those operating via the internet. An example of the latter is Bosch, the German company which manufactures power tools and household appliances in addition to a range of other products including car parts and power tools.

- The French car manufacturer, Peugeot/Citroën, makes most of its engines in-house, whereas the USA's Ford motor company more often buys them in.

- Some local governments carry out services such as waste collection using their own staff, whereas others contract other organisations to do the work.

Organisational boundaries are not fixed. They can change in response to factors in the far external environment. Examples include:

- political and economic pressures that result in organisations in the public sector using outside contractors

- competitive pressure which may result in the need to reduce costs and a decision to outsource an activity because it is cost-effective to do so

- technological improvements that allow an organisation to do something more cheaply that was previously outsourced to another organisation.

Organisational boundaries may also change because something has changed in the *near* external environment (for example, a contractor has gone out of business) or because of a change in the *internal* environment (for example, a change of strategic direction within the organisation itself). An organisation's boundaries affect the tasks of all managers within it. For example, a manager at, say, a pharmaceutical company that outsources activities such as testing, sales and the manufacture of its drugs is likely to work with contractors and suppliers, and to be skilled in writing contract specifications and monitoring the contracts. A manager who works in an organisation that does all the above activities in-house is less likely to be skilled in these areas.

Often, in addition to not being fixed, organisational boundaries are not clearly defined. Sometimes it is not very easy to tell whether someone is a member of a particular organisation. For example, many business and management consultants work almost entirely with just one organisation and the organisation relies on their work as much as it does on that of the managers it employs. While the consultant is not technically an employee of the organisation, their function in that organisation may not be very different from that of a manager who is employed directly by the organisation. Similarly, workers can be supplied by outside organisations such as agencies. Some organisations, particularly not-for-profit ones, may share premises as well as staff and staff training initiatives. Small specialist commercial organisations may work together cooperatively to provide comprehensive car servicing and repairs.

Thus, drawing the boundary of an organisation can be difficult, because of the factors in the three environments that shape why an organisation does what it does and the arrangements it makes for doing its work.

Stakeholders and their interests

The environment in which organisations operate is a social one: it contains people and organisations with different needs, desires and interests. An important part of understanding an organisation and the factors that influence it is an awareness of stakeholders – those who have an interest in an organisation, what it does and how it does it.

These stakeholders can be internal or external to an organisation and their interests can conflict. For example, a company making large profits from producing electricity from fossil fuel can please shareholders who own the company. Employees of the company may be happy as a result of job security. Customers and politicians may be angry that energy prices are high. Groups campaigning for action on climate change may welcome high prices of energy created from fossil fuels but still be critical of 'profiteering' by a company which fails to invest sufficiently in alternative energy technology.

Our understanding of who are the key stakeholders of an organisation has greatly increased from the early twentieth century when only the owners and managers of organisations were considered to have a 'stake' or interest in the organisation. Then, political meetings throughout Europe would be interrupted by shouts of 'What about the workers?'. Towards the end of the century, reflecting the shift to a more consumerist society, the outcry from television and press was 'What about the customers?'. Throughout this period, there was a growing interest in the natural environment. The slogan was 'What about the environment?'. And during the entire twentieth century, the rationale for company mergers or acquisitions was 'to enhance shareholder value'. In a seminal book, Freeman (1984) argued that, during the course of the century, the understanding of who the key stakeholders of an organisation was widened to include *all* those who had a stake in the organisation.

Understanding and engaging with stakeholders and their needs and interests is not just a task for the senior management of an organisation. On the contrary, much regular engagement with stakeholders is done by middle and first line managers. For example, the manager of a small sewerage works might have to deal not just with internal stakeholders, such as employees and their line managers, but with external stakeholders such as the local community which is concerned about smells from the works. If the sewerage works wanted to expand, these external stakeholders might argue against any plan. Other groups of external stakeholders such as environmental activists who want changes in waste water collection and treatment might protest by writing to the sewerage works and the local planning authority, by distributing leaflets or by protesting outside the works.

Stakeholders have been defined as follows: 'A stakeholder in an organisation is … any group or individual who can affect, or is affected by, the achievement of the organisation's objectives' (Freeman, 1984). From this it seems immediately obvious that it is important for organisations and their managers to take into account their stakeholders' interests and expectations for two reasons. First, if stakeholders have the power to affect the organisation's objectives, then managers should pay attention to stakeholders' expectations. Second, if stakeholders are significantly affected by what the organisation does, then normal ethical and proper business conduct demands that the organisation monitors these effects to make sure that few are negative and many are positive. Figure 13.2 shows a typical stakeholder map.

Figure 13.2 Typical stakeholder map of an organisation

While this is a generic figure, it is possible to draw a similar, specific stakeholder map for a particular organisation or a part of an organisation.

When thinking about stakeholders it is useful to bear in mind the following important points.

> *All organisations have internal and external stakeholders.* Internal stakeholders include shareholders, employees, managers, directors, trustees. Other departments or divisions of an organisation can also be internal stakeholders. External stakeholders are those who are strongly linked to the organisation or are affected by it. These include customers/clients, suppliers, funders and possibly even competitors. External stakeholders also include those who are indirectly affected by the organisation: members of the community or the general public, or pressure groups. Note that it is possible to place all these types of stakeholders in the far, near and internal environment of an organisation.

See also: The external environment, in this chapter

> *Different stakeholders have different interests and these may conflict with one another.* We can easily recognise the conflict between the interests of employees, who want security of employment and increased earnings, and those of shareholders, who may be seeking cost reductions to increase their annual dividends. A similar conflict could exist between the interests of taxpayers and of those who receive publicly-funded services such as education or healthcare.

> *An organisation's culture, structure and control systems will determine how these conflicts are resolved.* In practice, the interests of one stakeholder group are often dominant. Commercial organisations are conventionally considered to be shareholder-led, although in reality directors' and senior managers' interests may dominate. Some service industries may be regarded as customer-led. Cooperatives – businesses which are owned and run by their employees and customers – tend to

be member-led. Power structures reflect the dominant stakeholder interests. These organisations have to work hard to ensure that the interests of other stakeholder groups are not ignored or forgotten.

Some stakeholder interests are protected by law, but not all. Owners and shareholders are protected by property and company law whereas the interests of other stakeholders are protected, if at all, only by regulation, contract or management discretion. In many countries, measures have been taken in recent years to adjust this imbalance: employment legislation provides increasing protection for employees; and environmental legislation and regulation protect the natural environment and often local communities.

All organisations have difficulty balancing the interests of their different stakeholders, particularly when groups differ in their power and influence. Mitchell *et al.* (1997) argue that managers pay more attention to those stakeholders they believe have greater power, legitimacy and urgency. 'Power' refers to the probability that one 'actor' in a social relationship is in a position to carry out his own will despite resistance from others. It can be based on the ability to exert physical force, the ability to use material or financial resources, or the ability to influence through symbolism, such as the influence vested in traditional roles. An example is the use of religious authority. 'Legitimacy' refers to a general perception or assumption that the actions of a person, group or organisation are desirable, proper, or appropriate. 'Urgency' refers to how pressing the expectations of a stakeholder are perceived to be.

Figure 13.3 shows seven different categories of stakeholder priority based on the extent to which stakeholders are thought to have the three attributes.

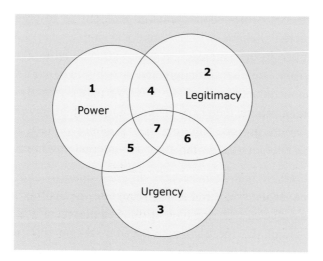

Figure 13.3 Categories of stakeholders

Areas 1, 2, and 3 in Figure 13.3 show those stakeholders with the lowest importance for managers. They have power *or* legitimacy *or* urgent expectations. They are called 'latent' stakeholders. Moderately important stakeholders (areas 4, 5, and 6) have two of the three attributes. They 'expect something' from the organisation, so are called 'expectant' stakeholders. The most important stakeholders are those who have all three attributes (area 7). These are called 'definitive' stakeholders. According to Mitchell *et al.* these stakeholders are likely to be given the highest priority by managers.

Not all stakeholder concerns can be given equal consideration because of limited money or management time. A consideration of power, legitimacy and urgency can help managers to decide which stakeholders to prioritise when making decisions or allocating money or time. However, those stakeholders with the greatest power or urgency are not always the ones who have the most legitimate claim. Mitchell *et al.* do not argue that prioritising stakeholders with the greatest power, legitimacy and urgency is what managers *should* do. Rather, they state that *in practice* these are normally the stakeholders who are given priority. But what happens in practice is not necessarily what should happen from an ethical perspective.

Mitchell *et al.*'s ideas about stakeholders are but one of three different forms of stakeholder theory. Donaldson and Preston (1995) distinguish between the three different forms:

> *Descriptive stakeholder theory* concerns itself with the question of whether and how managers take into account stakeholder interests (Mitchell *et al.*'s ideas are an example of this).

> *Instrumental stakeholder theory* concerns itself with the question of whether it is beneficial for organisations to take into account stakeholder interests (for example, because this will increase their reputation, or reduce the threat of stakeholders protesting against the organisation, and so on).

> *Normative stakeholder theory* concerns itself with the question of why it is morally right that organisations should take into account stakeholder interests.

Donaldson and Preston argue that only a normative or moral concern with stakeholder interests is ultimately sufficient as a basis for acting. Unfortunately they don't provide guidance on which stakeholder interests should be prioritised. Much will depend on the organisation, its stakeholders and the industry and the general external environment in which it operates. In general, it might be argued from the perspective of care ethics – that is, attending to and meeting the needs of those we are responsible for – that managers owe a particular duty of care to those stakeholders who are directly dependent on or affected by what the organisation does. These stakeholders would include employees, customers, the local community and those who are particularly vulnerable.

The concept of stakeholders is important for two reasons. First, it emphasises that stakeholder groups have different interests and that managers therefore have to balance these interests when making decisions. Second, it illustrates the relationship between organisations and the external environments in which they operate, in particular the near environment.

Understanding the external environment

What organisation has not experienced changes in bank interest rates or currency exchange rates, government policies, new regulations, changes in buyers' behaviour or the introduction of new technology? These external factors, however, are mostly felt inside the organisation in changes such as mergers or takeovers, or organisational restructuring. This is a paradox of organisational life: the greatest impact on organisations arises from changes in the external environment, yet the largest part of management time and effort is directed at the internal environment.

To be successful, organisations must anticipate possible changes and position themselves to deal with opportunities, challenges and threats in a proactive rather than a reactive way. It follows that managers who can understand and monitor their external environment are likely to be more effective. What are the main kinds of external factors that influence organisations? We consider five categories: sociological, technological, economic, environmental and political factors, known as the STEEP factors.

Sociological factors

Many of us live in a way quite different from that of our parents; the world in which our children will live and work as adults will be different again. These differences are due to demographic changes, patterns of work, household structure, patterns of consumption and gender roles. These sociological factors affect organisations too.

Demographic changes

In the West, birth rates and death rates are both declining (a characteristic of wealthy, mature societies). As a consequence a quarter of the population of Western Europe is over 65 years old. In contrast, less than a quarter of the population is under 20. More than three-quarters of disposable income in Western Europe belongs to people over 50 years old. This ageing of the population affects the demand for goods and services, the size of the workforce and the availability of labour. Thus, clothing industries and leisure activities targeted at young adults have a smaller proportion of customers, whereas the market for goods and services for the elderly increases (not just for retirement homes but also for leisure activities). Although birth rates are falling, overall populations in most countries are increasing (populations do not decrease until birth rates fall to 'replacement' rates).

Patterns of work

Our grandparents may have spent all their working lives employed by one organisation. Few people entering the job market now can expect lifelong employment with the same employer. Careers will consist of several jobs, often with periods of unemployment. There has been substantial growth in part-time jobs, most of them done by women. In most European countries the proportion of women in paid employment is now similar to the proportion of men.

Household structure

The traditional household of two parents and one or more children is no longer typical. Indeed, in the UK, it represents less than a quarter of households.

Patterns of consumption

The decline in traditional social structures (class, religion, family) has resulted in the emergence of 'lifestyle consumption' in which people express themselves through their purchasing and consumption behaviour. The importance of brands in influencing purchasing behaviour is evidence of this: customers choose brands to reflect and build their own identities.

Gender roles

The role of women has changed substantially. In the UK, the net growth in employment since 1960 has been accounted for almost entirely by women – but they have been less successful in reducing their unpaid work in the home and caring for their children and families. They are often employed in jobs with lower pay and fewer benefits.

Generalisations are useful for giving a broad view and, as here, they can be valuable in challenging some established beliefs. But very few of us are truly typical, and few organisations operate across the entire population of a country or region. There are still large numbers of families of parents and children. Not all women in work are in part-time jobs. Even though birth rates are declining there will be a market for toys and for branded jeans and trainers.

Technological factors

Few people's lives have not been affected by information technology (IT) which has changed forever the structure and nature of work. Rather than try to predict where IT will take us, it is more useful to focus on the process of technological change and its implications.

IT is removing the barriers of time and place. Whether you work for an airline in Italy, a bank in Romania, in telecommunications in India or insurance in Russia, you can expect to face competition from organisations which once would have been unable to enter your market.

IT creates new industries that are made possible only because of IT. These include the world of e-commerce where goods and services can be bought and banking can be done online.

Many traditional roles, such as secretary, bookkeeper, production planner and credit controller, are now solely or largely reliant on IT systems, and some jobs no longer exist. Importantly, IT has led to a massive change in the skills needed for desk-based jobs. Computer literacy and familiarity with an expanding range of software are essential for most of them. Organisations that fail to adopt IT are at a severe disadvantage as IT becomes standard.

Experience tells us that predictions of the impact of technological change are generally correct about the nature and direction of change, but are often overoptimistic about the speed of change. Examples of this are the predictions in the early 1990s of the paperless office and of the wholesale switch to homeworking: these are now more widespread, but have proceeded much slower than initially predicted.

Economic factors

The economic environment affects organisations in a number of ways. The main economic factors are:

- the rate of economic growth
- interest rates (the cost of borrowing money)
- inflation (increase in prices for the same goods and services)
- energy prices
- currency exchange rates
- unemployment.

The state of a country's economy affects all aspects of organisational life. It affects the level of demand for goods and services, and the availability and cost of raw materials, buildings and land and, most importantly, labour. The economy tends to move in cycles, and although we all know that these cycles exist, they are difficult to predict. Economic cycles – the swings from boom to bust – are undesirable because they create uncertainty and inefficiency in resource use and allocation. They are said to be the result of market inefficiencies, whereby production cannot increase sufficiently to meet increased demand. This leads to increases in the costs and prices of goods and labour (inflation) which reduce demand. The rate of economic growth then slows, and goods, services and labour move into surplus. Inflation falls, and a new cycle begins. The global financial crisis of 2008 is an example.

Organisations and individuals behave according to their expectations of economic trends. If the expectation of growth is high, organisations are likely to invest and expand and individuals are likely to spend more: these actions stimulate economic growth and so ensure that the expectations are met. Of course, the same happens in reverse: if the economy is expected to go into decline, organisations invest less and individuals spend less – and again the expectation is fulfilled.

Governments and central banks try to manage these expectations to reduce the instability of economic cycles, but the tools at their disposal are limited. They seek to establish stability by setting medium-term policies and economic goals. Governments use changes in the interest rate to try to achieve short-term adjustment in the levels of demand and investment. For example, in 2008/2009 the Bank of England reduced the key interest rates to the lowest levels ever to stimulate the economy.

Currency exchange rates can have a major impact on organisations. The exchange rate is the price of a particular currency, based on the supply and demand for that currency. If the domestic currency strengthens (that is, becomes worth more relative to other currencies), exporting becomes more difficult and foreign products are more competitive (cheaper) in the home market. If the currency weakens, exports are easier and opportunities may open up for new markets. However, imported raw materials will increase in price and costs can be expected to rise, increasing the rate of inflation.

Currency trading is often speculative leading to volatility in exchange rates. Many organisations try to minimise the risk created by changes in the exchange rate through forms of insurance. An important objective of the

European Union (EU) has been to reduce the damage caused by the instability of currencies through integration, first through the Exchange Rate Mechanism (ERM) and since 1999 through monetary union and the single European currency (the euro).

Environmental factors

Greater ecological (or environmental) sustainability is one of the most important and challenging tasks for modern societies. As businesses and other organisations are responsible for much of humanity's environmental impact, they are being asked to contribute significantly towards greater sustainability. All organisations depend, directly or indirectly, on the natural environment for resources, such as raw materials and energy. Ultimately, all human activity depends on a functioning natural environment. Whilst most managers have been trained to focus only on production and consumption, these exist only because there is an ecosystem to support them. If the ecosystem fails, then so do production and consumption. The environmental issues facing the world were summarised by Stead and Stead (1996) but we now must add the challenges of climate change, as shown in Figure 13.4. The implications of climate change for organisations will be significant.

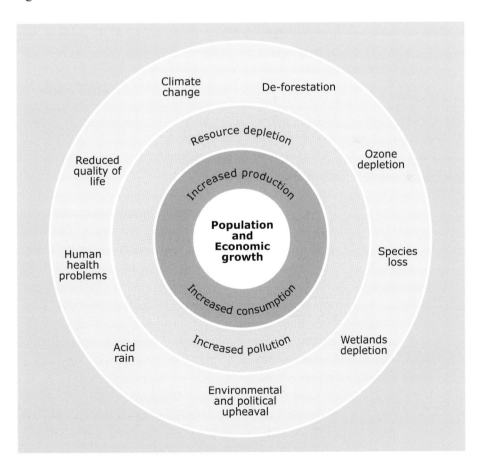

Figure 13.4 The environmental issues wheel

(Source: adapted from Stead and Stead, 1996)

As a manager you will need to be aware of at least some of these issues in order to make or implement appropriate decisions. In addition, there are a number of pressures and trends you will need to be aware of. These include:

Legislation. The main emphasis is on pollution control and waste disposal, but regulation also affects packaging, transport and distribution, and sources of materials.

Information. In recognition of the interests of local communities and the general public many organisations report regularly on their environmental performance. Larger companies carry out regular environmental audits and publish them in their annual reports.

Employees. Employees are interested in and concerned about the environmental impact of the organisations they work for and may create internal pressure to reduce environmental damage. Organisations can communicate with their workforces regularly by reporting back on actions.

Shareholders. Most shareholders of larger organisations are financial institutions, whose interests are driven by financial performance. In several countries, however, a category of ethical or 'green' investors is emerging. Organisations may wish to consider whether they should make themselves eligible for such investments.

Pressure groups. Pressure groups were a phenomenon of the late twentieth century. Many have broadened their focus from single issues and have become a permanent part of political life.

Customers. In some sectors customers are willing to favour 'green' organisations which are able to increase their market share or charge higher prices. A number of UK retailers market themselves on their environmental or ethical credentials, for example, by stocking more extensive ranges of organic or Fairtrade goods.

Political factors

If you think your organisation is not influenced by political factors, think again! If you work in the public services or the voluntary sector you will be aware of the political influences on your work. Commercial organisations, too, are powerfully influenced by political factors. This is because legislation affects most aspects of organisational life. Health and safety at work, equal opportunities and employee protection are three major examples of European law. Since the Treaty on European Union of 1992 (the Maastricht Treaty), regulations are applied across Europe in areas such as working hours and minimum wages.

Trading relationships are strongly influenced by political factors. The EU is an obvious example, but the World Trade Agreement is also of major importance. Embargoes on trade for political reasons can also have a commercial impact. Set out below are a number of political factors of which organisations and managers need to take account.

- In all countries, government is the largest employer and the largest purchaser of goods and services. In some sectors the government is often the only, or largest customer – for example, for defence, medicines and some social services.

- The level and nature of public services – for example, health services, education and police – are determined on political grounds.

- Governments continue to be significant players in the commercial sector – for example, in telecommunications, utilities, banking and transport. In economic or financial crises governments are often called on to provide financial support to vital industries such as banking. Sometimes they take control of private sector organisations if it is considered they are too important to fail.

- Governments continue to regulate many commercial industries – for example, through the appointment of regulators in the UK utilities sector, through the retention of a 'golden share' in telecommunications in Germany or, in France, through a network of government employees appointed to executive positions in industry.

- In many countries, local governments control planning permission for new buildings and developments and are in charge of local road networks and the provision of housing.

- Finally, governments set the levels of taxation – on the individual, on businesses, on property and on goods and services.

The STEEP model provides a useful framework for scanning the external environment to see what it is like now or what it will be like. As you identify the broad features of that environment, you need to ask yourself: 'What is the significance to the organisation of what I can see?'. If your STEEP analysis has focussed on the future, there are likely to be a number of features in the environment that you cannot be certain of. Then, you might want to ask 'what if...?'. STEEP analyses naturally lead to what is known as scenario planning.

As you will have noted, however, the distinction between STEEP factors is rather artificial. Many political decisions have an economic impact and almost all economic factors have a political dimension. Social behaviour is influenced by new technology and, in turn, influences political decisions. Environmental issues have strong social, political and economic elements; the implementation of acceptable solutions often depends on technology. However, how STEEP factors can affect your organisation and your role as a manager is far more important than being able to classify them.

Assessing the impact of STEEP factors

Managers need to identify factors in the external environment and assess the level of threat or opportunity that these factors present to an organisation, or part of it. To do this it is also necessary to identify the organisation's strengths and weaknesses: strengths can be used to take advantage of opportunities while weaknesses may need to be remedied.

A simple tool called SWOT allows you to identify these strengths and weaknesses and the opportunities and threats arising from the external environment – the STEEP factors (sociological, technological, economic, environmental and political). The tool is shown in Figure 13.5. Note that you will need to identify and gather information on STEEP factors in order to carry out a SWOT analysis.

The basic method used to carry out an analysis is this. First identify the organisation's strengths and weaknesses in relation to the STEEP factors. This will help you to answer the question 'Where are we now?'. Second, identify the opportunities and threats that the external environment presents to the organisation. This will help to answer the two questions: 'What opportunities exist because of our strengths?' and 'To what threats do our weaknesses expose us?'. Actions will involve assessing and taking advantage of opportunities and reducing threats by remedying weaknesses.

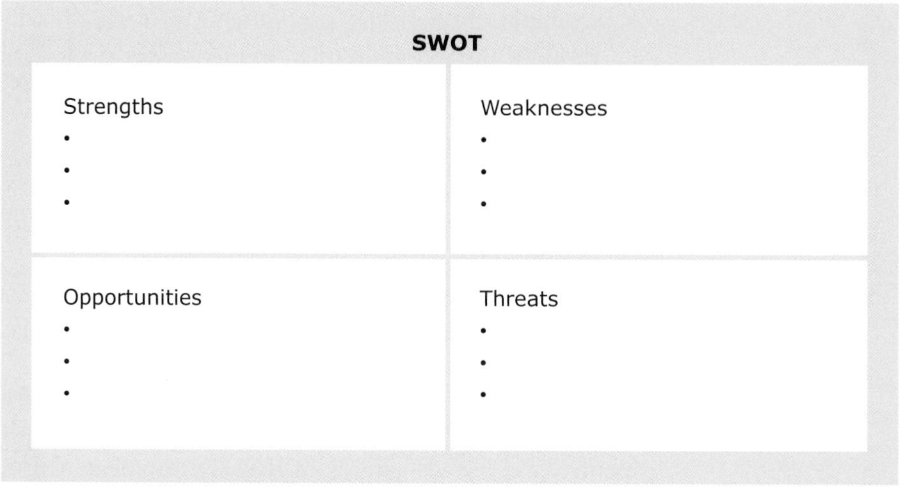

SWOT

Strengths	Weaknesses
•	•
•	•
•	•
Opportunities	Threats
•	•
•	•
•	•

Figure 13.5 The SWOT framework

Note that the two cells in the top row of the framework are labelled **S**trengths and **W**eaknesses; the two in the bottom row are labelled **O**pportunities and **T**hreats, hence the name, SWOT.

A useful tool for working out an organisation's strengths and weaknesses is Michael Porter's value chain (1980). The framework, used by managers for many years, allows them to look 'outside in' to identify the impact of STEEP factors on an organisation, and therefore, identify strengths and weaknesses.

A value chain shows the activities or functions in an organisation that contribute to the creation of the product or service that is delivered to external customers, consumers or clients. Its function is to expose the components of an organisation's activities so that managers can analyse and improve processes. The more that an organisation knows about these components, the better equipped it will be to find opportunities to reduce the cost of an activity or to improve the way in which an activity is carried out. In this way strengths and weaknesses are identified, often as costs and risks and vulnerabilities to STEEP factors. The framework can be used for part of an organisation or for a particular product or service. It can also be used to assess internal activities where inputs are from other parts of the organisation and outputs are for other parts of the organisation.

The five primary activities that are strategically important for the organisation are shown in Figure 13.6.

Inbound logistics	Operations	Outbound logistics	Marketing and sales	Aftersales service

See also: Input, transformations output, Chapter 4

Figure 13.6 The five primary activities in the value chain

(Source: Porter, 1980)

The first three 'primary' activities by themselves comprise an input / transformations/output model. 'Inbound logistics' refer to the flow of inputs to the organisation; 'operations' refer to the transformation of inputs into goods and services (the outputs). 'Outbound logistics' are those activities that deal with the initial storage and then the distribution of the outputs to the customers. The final two primary activities are concerned with the disposal of the outputs. 'Marketing and sales' comprise those activities that are intended to achieve the sale of the outputs while 'after-sales service' is directed towards people who have bought the output. The primary activities are supported by others which result in the fuller model shown in Figure 13.7. This includes four support activities, all of which will reflect the current state of technological development in the organisation. 'Procurement' deals with purchasing the inputs. 'Human resource management' deals with the management of the organisation's staff, and the 'organisational infrastructure' covers the other supporting activities. The 'value' in the value chain refers to what the market is prepared to pay for what an organisation produces. This determines the organisation's total revenues. The margin is the difference between the total revenues and the costs incurred in creating them. These financial aspects of the value chain need not concern us here, however: they can be hard to calculate when considering a small part of an organisation or a single activity.

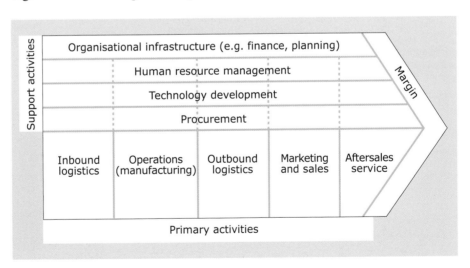

Figure 13.7 The value chain

(Source: adapted from Porter, 1980)

More recently the value chain framework has been developed by Porter and colleagues (Porter and Kramer, 2002, 2006; Porter and Reinhardt, 2007) to allow managers to look 'inside out' to assess the consequences of the organisation's activities on the wider natural and social environment. This is particularly important when organisations seek competitive advantage by adopting policies and practices that are less damaging to the natural environment or by accounting for the social (including environmental and ethical) consequences of their activities, known as corporate social responsibility. In the case of some not-for-profit organisations, competitive advantage may mean competition for funding or resources. Competitiveness can also be equated to efficiency and effectiveness which are important to all organisations, including those in the public and voluntary sectors.

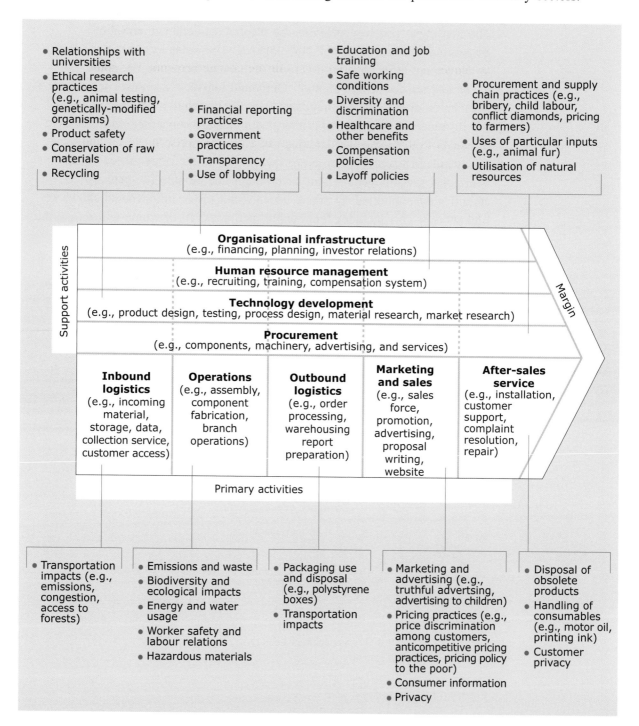

Figure 13.8 Looking inside out: mapping the social impact of the value chain

(Source: Porter, 1985)

Porter and his colleagues have considered in particular both social impact and climate change as political, social and competitive factors that organisations need to address as business issues. Changing weather patterns and political intervention to reduce carbon emissions increasingly affect the availability of raw materials, the size, growth and nature of demand, access to organisations that support one's own, what the organisation's competitors are doing, 'best practices' and rules and standards governing industry sectors. Organisations need to assess and reduce their vulnerability to climate-related environmental and economic shocks and to take initiatives to reduce the costs and risks that climate change presents. For some organisations, there will be opportunities to innovate; for others the response may be an operational one, such as using more efficient delivery vehicles; yet others might change an activity entirely, for example, by using technical solutions to diagnosis and treatment in after-sales service (Porter and Reinhardt, 2007). For many public and not-for-profit organisations, solutions will not be very different: such organisations might change their sources of inputs, redesign their activities or find different ways of delivering products and services.

Figure 13.8 shows the use of Porter's value chain as an 'inside out' framework for identifying the positive and negative social impact of an organisation's activities. It can be adapted for use in part of an organisation and in not-for-profit organisations.

It should be fairly straightforward to complete a SWOT analysis after using the value chain, either 'inside out' or 'outside in' to assess the primary activities in the organisation, or a part of it, or a single activity.

Chapter 14 Managing change
Types of change

Whether we like it or not, we and the organisations we work for seem to be in a constant process of change. Indeed, change has become a permanent feature in many organisations (Caldwell *et al.*, 2004). Some changes will affect the entire organisation while others will be small and confined to a single work group or process. For managers, change may be something imposed on them by senior management. Sometimes managers may be involved in implementing such changes, while at other times, managers will initiate changes over which they have far more control. When change is a common feature of organisational life, it is important for managers to understand it and know how to plan and implement it.

Although there is no single definition of the management of change, the idea of planning and implementation, normally through the use of strategy, structures, procedures, technology and tools and techniques, is a feature of many definitions, for example:

> the coordination of a structured period of transition from situation A to situation B in order to achieve lasting change within an organisation.

> (Source: BNET UK, 2009)

This distinguishes change management and the types of change involved from those that are routine alterations designed to restore or maintain the status quo. The 'change' in change management is one that creates a new status quo, regardless of the size of the change.

How can we categorise and characterise such change? Organisation-wide changes can involve changes to structure; for example, from a hierarchical one to a 'flat' one involving team work, or the way in which an organisation does its work. These large-scale changes can come about from external pressures including changes to the external environment. These might be sources of finance, economic conditions, increasing customer expectations or changes in laws or technology. They can also come about as a result of a desire to make operations more efficient, perhaps by using more technology and automation, in order to reduce costs. Whatever the driving forces, these sorts of change are often deliberate, planned and top–down – that is, led by senior management. Large-scale organisational changes are not usually continuous – with good reason! Normally they occur infrequently and so can be described as 'episodic'.

Other changes happen with more spontaneity, often when managers make small changes at the level of subsystems in the organisation. Such changes are often described as 'emergent' or 'incremental'. They can happen during an organisation-wide change, or as a result of the initiatives of individual managers in the normal course of their work. When managers across an organisation make a number of such changes over time, the changes are often cumulative, bringing about wider change in the organisation in the longer term. When this happens, the changes are incremental. Incremental changes can be continuous, as when an organisation decides to adopt quality management processes.

See also: Ideal or 'above-the-norm' cultures, Chapter 12

However, small changes can also be episodic and infrequent: a manager can make a change to the staff-selection or performance-appraisal process and then make no further changes. Some organisations adopt 'emergent change' as an approach to change in much the same way that other organisations prefer to use a planned approach. When an emergent approach is used, the many small changes made at a local level will be consistent with organisation-wide objectives for change.

Whether or not changes are large or small, planned from the top or more spontaneous bottom–up initiatives of individual managers, the reasons for them can be categorised in terms of two primary intentions: to remedy a poor situation or to improve on successes. An organisation may need to downsize to survive in a difficult economic situation, or a manager may want to redesign systems or work-group activities as a result of poor performance. Conversely, an organisation may want to expand a successful service, or a manager may want to make changes that build on successful ways of improving performance and productivity. In practice, the intention or result of a change may be to achieve both. We might want to remedy a poor situation and build on success, or build on success while remedying minor problems.

So change can be large- or small-scale, planned or emergent, a response to problems or to successes. A change may happen just once or a number of small changes can be incremental. Types and reasons for change can be combined in different ways. Ackerman (1997) distinguishes between the main types of change and their characteristics (Table 14.1).

Table 14.1 Types of change and characteristics

Type of change	Characteristics
Developmental: to remedy a problem or improve something	Can be planned or emergent/ incremental. Often focusses on skills or processes
Transitional: to move from an existing state to a desired state	Is planned. Is episodic
Transformational: to change structure, processes, culture and or strategy (and change the assumptions of the organisation/staff)	Is planned. Likely to be continuous because it may result in an organisation that continuously learns, adapts and improves

How successfully is change managed in organisations? The answer, according to Probst and Raisch (2005), is not well. They claim that the majority of major change programmes fail to meet expectations. Poorly-defined objectives, poor management or unrealistic expectations of what will be achieved are to blame. Stacey (1996) says that the problem with planned change is that organisations are complex environments in which managing change does not proceed by following a set of techniques and procedures. Rather, managing change involves dealing with unpredictability, conflict and inconsistency. Olson and Eoyang (2001) argue that many factors affect the outcome of a planned change; the behaviour of people cannot be predicted and it is uncontrollable; causes and effects cannot be mapped in a linear fashion; and decisions are based on tensions and organisational patterns. This differs from traditional models of change management where almost everything is regarded as predictable and controllable, where all causes and effects are linear and where effects can be traced to specific causes. Stacey suggests that two factors – agreement and certainty – influence whether a change will be simple to achieve, complicated, complex (where there may be many alternatives but little predictability) or simply chaotic (where actions are based on guesswork). This is shown in Figure 14.1.

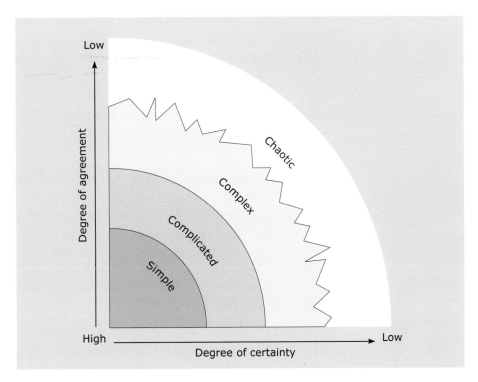

Figure 14.1 Agreement–uncertainty matrix

(Source: adapted from Stacey, 1996)

Most managers who initiate and manage local-level changes, which are likely to be emergent and incremental, are probably operating in the regions of Stacey's diagram where there are likely to be higher levels of agreement and certainty. But are there other ways of trying to determine the level of risk and disturbance a change might involve? Pennington (2003) suggests that risks and disturbance can be predicted by considering the degree of change (radical or incremental) and whether or not the change involves the organisation's core business activities. This is shown in Figure 14.2.

A radical change is one which an organisation or part of it changes in fundamental ways. It is sometimes referred to as a revolutionary change to contrast it with the more evolutionary nature of incremental change. In incremental change, underlying assumptions about an activity, processes, products or services, or about structure and culture, can remain unchanged while radical change depends on questioning these assumptions (Alvesson and Willmott, 2001). Another way of thinking about this is that in radical change there is discontinuity – a break with the past – but when change is incremental, there is continuity.

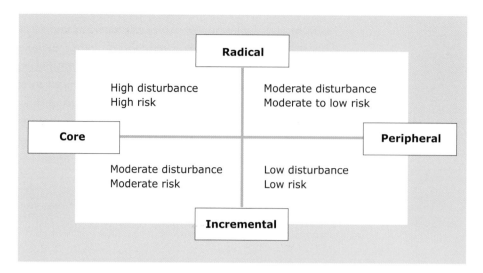

Figure 14.2 Type of change: disturbance and risk

(Source: based on Pennington, 2005)

A change to core activities is likely to create high levels of disturbance, whereas incremental changes to non-core, or peripheral activities, will usually be unexceptional. Most junior managers are likely to initiate and manage changes of this latter kind, graduating to those involving higher risk and disturbance as they rise to more senior management positions.

Anticipation and preparation

Stacey and Pennington provide useful tools for assessing whether a proposed change is likely to be simple to achieve, how much risk it carries and how much disturbance it will create. The most common changes that managers make are likely to be emergent and incremental, but, because these changes are said to occur spontaneously, does this also mean that careful consideration and planning need not be involved?

Consider the following example of a very small change.

The good idea that did not work

Younis thought about the tedious job he had to carry out over the next three days: negotiating holiday dates with the staff in the telemarketing section for which he was responsible. Younis suddenly saw the obvious solution. He would simply pin up a chart and let staff mark in their own holidays using a set of rules (no more than two people absent at any one time, no-one away during the peak season in May, and no-one to separate their annual leave entitlement into more than two periods of absence). He put up the chart that day and got on with important problems awaiting his attention.

The logic of Younis's reasoning was not obvious to his staff, unfortunately. Comments included: 'He's evading his responsibilities'; 'It's his job to decide who's needed when'; 'He's stirring up conflict between us'; 'What happens if I'm away when the list goes up?'; 'It's the only time I ever get to talk to him about my own affairs – he's keeping me away from him.' The next morning Jane, the Head of Marketing, asked to see him.

'I've had a deputation from your staff,' she said. 'They're furious with you for being what they describe as uncaring and arrogant. What happened?' Younis told her. Jane smiled. 'It's the old story,' she said. 'What seems logical to one person doesn't seem that way to another. If you're going to try to change a system, you'll have to ensure that people understand there's a problem before you give them your solution. You need to plan changes by anticipating problems and to prepare the way for the particular sort of change you're making.'

This example illustrates some of the main problems associated with any change a manager might make:

- people may not see the need for it or may think the reason is mistaken
- it may threaten practices that people value
- it may have unintended consequences
- it may threaten the interests of some staff
- whilst some people greet change with enthusiasm others dislike it.

Organisations need people who are 'change enthusiasts' because they are vital in stimulating and supporting change and making it happen. Organisations also need sceptics, however, who will resist misconceived proposals for change and who will scrutinise and improve them. Sceptics will ensure continuity in the organisation, too, when continuity is needed – as it often is. Many people will be neither enthusiastic nor sceptical: their reactions will depend on the circumstances and detail of the change and its consequences. Will it affect a person's job? Is it likely to mean more work? Often both positive and negatives can be seen at the same time.

Attitudes towards change

As managers, our attitudes towards change will be influenced by the role we play. Kanter *et al.* (1992) identify three different ones:

- *change strategists or initiators* who initiate and set the direction of change
- *change implementers* who are responsible for the coordination and implementation of the change
- *change recipients* who are strongly affected by the change and its implementation.

A manager's role will depend on the nature and size of a change, but non-managerial staff are most frequently the recipients of change. For managers, the roles are not necessarily mutually exclusive. Strategists may also be involved in implementation and vice versa, or the recipients of change may have some input into the change strategy or its implementation. However, change recipients usually have much less control over the change process, which is a common source of conflict and resistance. Passive recipients of change are less likely to share the sense of excitement about the change. Those in charge of the change may see its success as helping towards their professional advancement and may be less sympathetic to those who are sceptical or less enthusiastic. Indeed, if you have been the recipient of change that originates higher up the organisation you may have experienced such scepticism or lack of enthusiasm. You may also have experienced the discomfort of being expected to sell the change to your colleagues while having doubts about it yourself. If you have had experiences like these, you already have valuable knowledge you can apply when initiating and managing changes in the organisation you work for.

Planned and emergent approaches to change

Two dominant approaches to change in organisations have emerged over the years. The planned approach advocates careful planning and implementation while the emergent approach regards change as a more continuous and adaptive process. The planned approach is explored first.

The planned approach

The first and best-known approach to planned change was proposed by Lewin in 1951. He suggested that change had to be an iterative, collaborative process in order for it to be effective. In this way, change could be seen as a process of learning for those involved; that is, developmental.

Lewin suggested that change could be understood in terms of three phases: unfreezing, change or movement, and refreezing. The first phase involves getting people to accept that there is a need for change and preparing individuals and groups for the change. The second phase covers implementation, while the third phase involves embedding and consolidating the change. The approach assumes that organisations are stable and that the process of change moves an organisation between different stable states; that is, changes are transitional. While we may still find organisations that are stable, it is clear that most are unstable for most or all of the time. Bullock and Batten (1985) developed the four-phase planned model set out below.

1 *Exploration phase.* Exploration determines whether a change is needed. If it is, the necessary resources need to be put in place.

2 *Planning phase.* This stage involves the collection and interpretation of information to understand what the problem is, developing objectives for the change and deciding on the approach to be taken to achieve them. Key stakeholders are identified and involved.

3 *Action phase.* This is the implementation phase. Monitoring should take place and any necessary adjustments should be made to the approach to change, the activities or the objectives.

4 *Integration phase.* At this point the change becomes fully-integrated and embedded. Evaluation should take place to assess the effectiveness of the change.

The example in Box 14.1 shows the planned approach working in practice.

Box 14.1 The office move

Hans was a branch manager with a team of 20 staff. For some time the company had been concerned about costs and decided to move the branch to cheaper premises outside the city centre. Hans was asked to plan and oversee the change. First he visited the new premises. Then he approached his key stakeholders (his team) and gathered information about their concerns and expectations. He identified three main issues which would affect future working practices:

- the new offices were open-plan
- there would be fewer meeting rooms
- the new premises had no nearby shop where staff could buy lunch.

Hans devised a number of solutions. He developed a system for booking rooms, operated by his secretary. He also worked with his team to devise some rules for working in the open-plan environment. These included ensuring that mobile phones were set to silent when in the office and that meetings took place in the rooms available for booking. He also arranged for a catering company to deliver food at lunchtime.

When the move had taken place Hans monitored these new systems. It soon became clear that the system for booking rooms was cumbersome. It depended on the availability of Hans's secretary. Further, staff needed somewhere for short impromptu discussions. Each team member agreed to give up a little space to create an enclosed seating area. He also changed the booking system to an electronic one that could be accessed by all staff. For a few weeks, his secretary monitored the booking system until the change was embedded and working smoothly. Two months later, Hans began a short evaluation to assess the success of the move.

Lewin saw planned change as democratic, person-centred and collaborative. Recent criticisms of the planned approach have centred on the tendency for organisations to use a directive approach to change. While Lewin's ideas may be desirable it is easy to see that they might be time-consuming and impractical in fast-moving or urgent situations. Further criticism centres on the inability of the planned approach to deal with radical or transformational change, and that it underemphasises political conflict in organisations. Despite these criticisms, however, the planned approach continues to be a dominant one in change management.

The emergent approach

The emergent approach to change takes account of the complex and dynamic nature of organisations and the way in which they operate. It takes a less prescriptive approach than planned change (although planning is still regarded as important). Weick (2000) describes emergent change as consisting of continual adaptations and alterations that eventually produce fundamental change without the intention to do so. Emergent change occurs when people change routines, deal with contingencies and breakdowns, and act on opportunities in everyday work. Much of this change goes unnoticed, he says, because 'small alterations are lumped together as noise' in the otherwise uneventful day-to-day life of an organisation.

The emergent approach stresses the importance of bottom–up changes. However, it suffers from a lack of clear focus on the best way to achieve a change and there is no consensus among advocates on how organisations should put the emergent approach into action (Burnes, 2004). When emergent change is desired as an organisation-wide development strategy, senior managers will not develop detailed plans; rather they will work out options for change and for managing the change in a complex environment (Bamford, 2006). Detailed planning then takes place at the lower levels. The role of leaders and managers is therefore not so much to plan and implement change, but to empower the workforce to make changes. Local-level changes that are not part of an emergent-change programme also require leadership that allows managers to take initiatives, of course.

Those who support the emergent approach reject the idea of rules for change. However, they focus on five areas that help or hinder the change process. These are:

- *Organisational structure* – flatter structures encourage delegation and increase the likelihood of change taking place at all levels.
- *Organisational culture* – a 'culture of change' means that change becomes an accepted way of doing things (Clarke, 1994).
- *Organisational learning* – employees' learning creates pressure on managers to make changes.
- *Managerial behaviour* – managers need to move away from directing change to leading, facilitating and coaching.
- *Power and politics* – the emergent approach stresses the need for power and politics to be managed if change is to be successful.

One assumption of the emergent approach is that organisations are constantly changing and adapting. This is not always the case: organisations may need to adapt their processes to implement changes in legislation, for example, as they did across Europe during the late 1990s to meet the requirements of changes in data protection laws. In such cases, a planned approach may be preferable.

There can also be significant difficulties persuading managers to be less directive. Critics also argue that, while the planned approach largely ignores political and cultural factors in organisations, the emergent approach is too concerned about them.

Merging the planned and emergent approaches: a case study

In most organisations there will be a mixture of the planned and emergent approaches to change – by design or accident. An example of a mixed approach is provided by Orlikowski and Hofman (1997) in a case study of the introduction of technology to improve communication.

Planned and emergent changes at Zeta

In the mid-1990s Zeta was one of the top 50 software companies in the USA, with $100 million in revenues and about 1,000 employees. It produced and sold a range of software products to clients globally.

Specialists in the Customer Service Department (CSD) at Zeta provided technical support via telephone to clients, staff in the field, and others. This technical support could be quite complex often taking several hours of research to solve and involving a number of different departments. The CSD employed approximately 50 specialists and was headed by a director and two managers.

In 1992, the CSD purchased software to develop a new incident-tracking support system (ITSS) to help it log customer calls and keep a history of progress as the department solved customers' problems. Following a successful pilot of the new system, the CSD deployed ITSS throughout its department.

The new ITSS system was accompanied by planned changes in the specialists' and managers' work. Previously, only a brief description of the problem and its ultimate solution was recorded. Now ITSS allowed specialists to record every step they took in dealing with a particular problem. As specialists began to use ITSS, the focus of their work expanded from research and solving problems to research, solving problems, and recording calls and work in progress.

Whilst recording calls took time, it provided a rich database of information which could be searched for potential solutions. This new database also served as an unexpected and informal resource for learning by exposing the specialists to a wide range of problems and solutions. As one specialist noted: 'If it is quiet, I will check on my fellow colleagues to see what... kind of calls they get, so I might learn something from them... just in case something might ring a bell when someone else calls.' However, using the ITSS database as a sole source of information did pose some risk, because the accuracy of the information was not known. To minimise this risk, the specialists developed a set of informal quality indicators to help them distinguish between reliable and unreliable data. For example, solutions that were comprehensively recorded, recorded by certain individuals, or verified by the customer were considered more reliable sources of information than others.

Additionally, the new system helped departmental managers to control the department's resources. Specialists' use of ITSS to record calls provided managers with detailed workload information, which was used to justify staff increases and to adjust work schedules and shift assignments as necessary. ITSS also supplied managers with more-accurate information on specialists' work processes; for example, the particular steps followed to research and solve a problem, the areas in which specialists sought advice, and the quality of their solutions. As managers began to rely on the ITSS data to evaluate specialists' performance, they expanded the performance criteria. For example, the quality of work-in-progress documentation was included as an explicit evaluation criterion and recording skills became a factor in the recruitment process.

As the CSD understood the capabilities of the technology better, the managers took the opportunity to redistribute call loads, a structural change that had not been planned originally. Front-line specialists now took all incoming calls and solved as many of these as they could. They were partnered with more senior, second-line specialists. When the front-line specialists were overloaded or had calls which were difficult they transferred calls to their second-line specialist. These senior specialists were expected to monitor their front-line specialists' progress on calls and to provide help.

While this partnership idea seemed a good one, it was not successful. Front-line specialists were often reluctant to transfer calls, fearing that this would reflect poorly on their competence or that they would be overloading their more senior partners. Senior specialists, in turn, were usually too busy solving complex incidents to spend much time monitoring their front-line partners' call status or progress. In response, the CSD managers introduced a second structural change. They created a new role, that of an intermediary. These new specialists regularly monitored front-line specialists' call loads and work in progress, and reassigned calls as appropriate.

Another change resulted from all specialists now having access to the database of calls being worked on: they began to browse through each other's calls to see which ones they could help with.

Later, some of the senior specialists realised that the information in the system could be used to help to train new staff. These senior specialists created a training database of sample problems which newly-recruited specialists could work on. Using the communication capabilities of the software, these senior specialists could monitor their trainees' progress through the sample database and intervene when necessary. As one senior specialist noted: 'We can keep up to the minute on their progress ... If they're on the wrong track, we can intercept them and say: "Go check this, go look at that." But it's not like we have to actually sit with them and review things.' As a result of this new training system, new specialists could begin taking customer calls after five weeks instead of eight weeks.

An emergent change noted at this time related to the control of the ITSS database. An ongoing issue for the CSD was who (if anybody) outside the CSD should have access. This issue had not been anticipated before the introduction of the technology. It was some time before managers realised that their various responses to different access requests had created a set of rules and procedures for access.

Learning from experience

This case demonstrates a series of planned and emergent changes. The planned change was to develop the software and increase record-keeping. The emergent changes included enabling everyone to make useful suggestions immediately; improving the allocation of work and the use of senior specialists; and a training database which reduced initial training from eight to about five weeks.

By allowing some of the changes to emerge Zeta was able to learn from practical experience, respond to unexpected outcomes and capabilities, and adapt both the technology and the organisation as appropriate. In effect, Zeta's change model cycled through planned and emergent changes over time (Orlikowski and Hofman, 1997).

The feasibility of change

Change may look desirable. But is it always beneficial? 'New' and 'different' are not always better – and even if they are, the financial and other costs may sometimes be too high. So the first decision a manager needs to make is whether change is needed, whether it is feasible and, if so, the scope of the change.

We often make sense of change after the event, once the change has taken place. Many of the stories we hear about change, and much of the management literature on change are constructed with the benefit of hindsight. In the process, a great deal of simplification takes place. The reasons for the change seem clear because much of the uncertainty, confusion and disagreement that once surrounded it are forgotten or disregarded. We often hear about successful change but little about those changes that failed. Most studies of change are written from the perspective of those who made a change happen and rarely from the perspective of those who experienced the effects (Dent and Goldberg, 1999). The danger in this simplified view is that it can give a misleading impression of what managing change involves.

When initiating change yourself, you do not have the benefit of hindsight. You have to recognise the need for change and decide what sort of change is necessary. While much of the management literature sees change as a necessary response to poor performance, an economic threat or some kind of crisis, the reality is often not so clear. It may not be obvious that an organisation or a part of it is doing badly. Different people may interpret a situation in different ways. You may start with a sense that things are not right. This can present a dilemma: it can be difficult to decide whether and what kind of change is needed without discussion, but discussing the issues may itself cause concern among staff and customers. The desire not to raise difficult issues until you are sure it is necessary is one reason why changes are often delayed until there is a crisis.

The scope of change

Another problem for managers is defining the scope of any change project. What do you include and what do you exclude? Consider the example in Box 14.2.

Box 14.2 Unanticipated impact

Tom managed a team of administrators at a college. One of the team's tasks was to administer the registration process for new students. Tom was sure the team could be more efficient if the outdated computer program was replaced. He found a new system that would suit the needs of the task and trained his team, but soon there were complaints. Staff in the finance department were unhappy because the old system had linked directly into theirs and now they had to manually transfer information from one system to another. Members of the administrative team were also unhappy because the new system had changed the structure of the team and the roles people played. Tom realised he had not considered the scope of his change.

All aspects of an organisation are interconnected in some way. If you change the way that someone does an apparently self-contained task, you may soon discover that it has an impact on the work of another person or has implications for the way a job is graded in terms of the skills required and pay. Where do you stop? Leavitt's diamond (Figure 14.3), named after its originator Harold J. Leavitt, provides one useful tool for answering this question. Developed in 1964 it remains popular as a way of assessing scope. It shows the interconnection between an organisation's structures, systems, tasks and people: if you make a change in one area you need to consider the likely implications in other areas. A balance is needed. In the example of Tom, he could have assessed what impact the new system would have by discussing the proposed change with his team and initial stakeholders. Then he could have avoided problems instead of creating news ones.

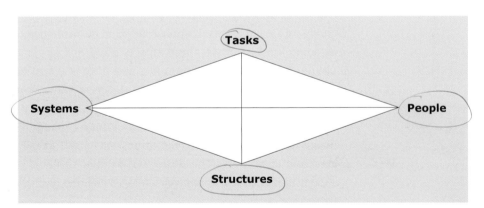

Figure 14.3 Leavitt's diamond: the interconnectedness of organisations

(Source: based on Handy, 1988)

Assessing the prospects: force-field analysis

As well as deciding whether a change project is worthwhile and what its scope and aims might be, you will probably have to consider whether it is feasible – will it be possible to make the change in your organisation at this time?

Force-field analysis is a useful tool for analysing change situations and assessing the prospects for change. Kurt Lewin who developed it suggested that we can consider any organisation or group as being held in balance, or equilibrium, between driving forces that are seeking to change it and restraining forces that are preventing movement and change (see Figure 14.4).

See also: Force-field diagrams, Tools and techniques

Driving forces   **Restraining forces**

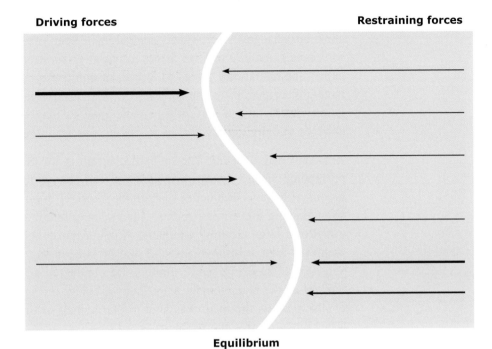

Equilibrium

Figure 14.4 Force-field analysis

(Source: based on Lewin, 1951)

This simple approach can be applied to many situations at an individual, group and organisational level, or even to wider assessments of social change. Where you are at present is at the point of equilibrium – the white line in the middle of Figure 14.4. If the situation is not currently changing, it is because the forces inhibiting change – represented by the arrows on the right – are equal to the forces that are driving the change – the arrows on the left.

When you are describing the various driving and restraining forces it often helps to assess their relative strengths (represented by the thickness of the arrows in Figure 14.4) and to cluster them under different headings. Some useful ones, with examples, are:

- personal – for example, ambition, fear of redundancy, loss of competence
- interpersonal – for example, A is an ally of B, but neither talks to C
- intergroup – for example, the production staff are suspicious of the marketing staff, or the research workers want to enhance their status
- technological – for example, the new computer system makes things economic that were not possible before
- financial – for example, resources are inadequate or, on occasion, new resources are available for a particular project
- organisational – for example, the structure of the organisation or physical location makes joint projects between two departments difficult

- environmental – for example, a forthcoming European Union directive will require changes in employment practices, or increased competition requires some response
- the climate for change – for example, there is a skilled champion of change in the work group, or the last change in the work group did not go well and the work group has too much work at the moment.

In your analysis, do not overlook long-term pressures that enable or constrain change. A force-field analysis will help you assess the prospects for change. Are the driving forces going to grow stronger? Is it realistic to expect the restraining forces to lessen, or could they increase? Once you have a clear picture of the forces, you may decide that your change project is not feasible at the present time. The analysis may lead you to revise the changes you are aiming for, or to direct your resources elsewhere.

A second way of using a force-field diagram is for identifying ways of promoting change – ways in which you can change the balance of forces in favour of change. Reducing restraining forces is often more effective than strengthening the driving forces. The example below concerns the retail outlet of a large clothing company. A new department store manager identified a large turnover of staff and he is keen to reduce this from 40% a year to less than 25% in 12 months. He conducted a force-field analysis with the rest of the management team (shown below in Figure 14.5). As a result of this analysis the team was able to plan which of the restraining forces to focus on to resolve the problem.

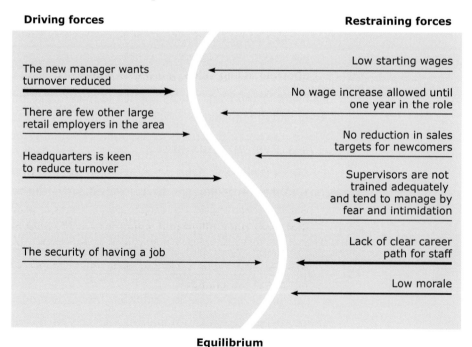

Figure 14.5 Example of a force-field analysis

(Source: adapted from French and Bell, 1999)

A strength of force-field analysis is its simplicity, but it needs to be used with some care. Writers on organisational change have challenged the idea of equilibrium. Given the complexity of organisations, there may be no such thing as equilibrium or a state of balance. Nevertheless, force-field analysis is useful as a snapshot of forces to help you to decide whether to act. The situation you find, however, may be different next time you look. The forces for change may also be different for different aspects of a change or in other parts of the organisation. It may be useful to carry out more than one force-field analysis.

Care also needs to be taken if you use force-field analysis with other people. When identifying someone or something as a positive or negative, helpful or unhelpful force, you will need to be sensitive to the dangers of people thinking in terms of opposing sides and of winning or losing. The aim of force-field analysis is not to create well-defined battle lines but to make a realistic assessment of the prospects for change. Introducing force-field analysis into a situation that is already tense could produce the confrontations and fixed positions that you were trying to avoid.

Five operational strategies for change

A new system: scenario 1

Bertingsall's had been planning to introduce a new stock and inventory system next year to improve efficiency. It would mean the loss of a number of jobs and the retraining of the small number of staff needed to work with the new system. Now, caught up in a difficult economic climate and with falling sales, there was a pressing need to reduce costs. The plan had been brought forward and implementation would begin next month with some urgency.

A new system: scenario 2

Bertingsall's had been planning to introduce a new stock and inventory system to improve efficiency. It would mean the loss of jobs, but with sales increasing and good prospects for expansion the company hoped that most back-office and warehouse staff could be given other roles and retrained. Remaining stock and inventory staff would need to be trained to use the new system. Bertingsall's wanted to ensure that staff affected did not resist the change.

In these two scenarios involving a required change, the change is the same but the circumstances are quite different. Will the same way of achieving the change work successfully in each case? In the first scenario, if the company does not act fast and decisively it could face bankruptcy. In the second scenario, the company has time to ensure that staff do not resist the change, which they may do if they regard the new stock and inventory system as impactful and negative. When a change is necessary in an organisation, or part of it, there is no one 'best way' of going about it. There are a number of different strategies a manager can use and your choice will reflect the particular change you want to make and the circumstances.

There are five classic operational strategies, distinguished by the degree to which a change is imposed on the recipients (Thurley and Wirdenius, 1973). These are set out below. Note that those that have a higher level of imposition on recipients are more likely to be used in planned or top-down change at organisational level, while those that involve people are likely to be used in an organisation that adopts an emergent strategy. However, any one of the five classic strategies might be used by a manager to make a change at a local level – a change that might be an emergent or incremental change, or a single, isolated change.

Directive strategies: management's right to manage change. Here, managers use their authority to impose a change and involve other people very little. The advantage of a directive strategy is that a change can be carried out quickly. The main disadvantage is that it does not take any account of the views of those affected by the change. As a result, valuable information may be missed and the likelihood of resistance to change is increased. This resistance may reduce the speed of the change or even undermine it. A further difficulty is that in some cases the authority of managers may be unclear. In these circumstances, managers will need to ask: 'What will happen if people say, "No, we won't do that."' If changes affect volunteers, they may simply leave the organisation.

Expert strategies: management of change as technical problem-solving. This strategy is often adopted when a change results from a technical problem that requires solution by experts, such as the introduction of a new information system. A special project team – often with a strong lead from management – is likely to implement the change, typically without much involvement of those likely to be affected by it. The advantages of expert strategies are specialist knowledge and speed: in theory, experts working in a relatively small group can implement a change quickly. A potential disadvantage is that the people affected by the change may not see the problem only as a technical one. They may not accept the legitimacy of the experts' knowledge or solutions. As a result, there may be resistance to the change.

Negotiating strategies: bargaining about change. This strategy involves a willingness to negotiate with other groups and to accept that adjustments and concessions may be needed. The adoption of this strategy does not remove a manager's responsibility for initiating and directing the change. However, it acknowledges that those who will be affected by the change should have some say in the change. It accepts that they have the power to resist the change. The potential advantage is that those affected by the change are less likely to resist it because they are involved. The disadvantages are that implementation may take longer and outcomes are less-easily predicted. The adoption of new work practices in return for increased pay and benefits is a typical example of a negotiating strategy.

Educative strategies: managing change by winning hearts and minds. This strategy involves changing people's attitudes (beliefs, feelings and values and dispositions to act in certain ways) so that they support the change and are committed to it. The emphasis is on winning over staff through persuasion, education and training. Sometimes organisational development consultants – specialists in the behaviour of individuals and groups – are brought in to assist in this process. The advantage of such a strategy, if successful, is that people will be committed to the change. A possible disadvantage is that it is likely to take much longer and require more resources than the three previous strategies.

Participative strategies: we are all involved in making the change. This strategy involves those affected by the change process. Although change may be initiated by managers, the individuals and groups implementing it or affected by it will have a say in the form and direction of the change. Again, organisational development consultants may be used to help with this process. There are several potential advantages of participative strategies. First, the change is more likely to be widely accepted because more people are involved. Second, through their involvement people are likely to become committed to and enthusiastic about the change. Third, the organisation has the opportunity to learn from the experience of a wide range of people. Fourth, there are more opportunities for people to learn from the change process. The main disadvantages of participative strategies are that the change is likely to take longer, to be more complex to manage and to require more resources. Further, the outcomes are likely to be less predictable.

The different strategies are not mutually exclusive and typically they are used in combination. For example, you may consult a group of experts and then use a directive strategy to implement the change. When changing working practices you might use educative strategies to try to convince staff of the need for change; negotiate some details of the change with trade union or employee representatives, and use participative methods to consider the details of implementation. Table 14.2 summarises the five different strategies and their main advantages and disadvantages.

Table 14.2 Five strategies for change management

Strategy	Advantages	Disadvantages
Directive	Relatively fast	Ignores the expertise, views and feelings of change recipients
Expert	Uses relevant expertise Relatively small group required Relatively fast to implement	Expertise may be insufficient Expertise may be challenged; if so, resistance is likely Speed of change likely to produce resistance
Negotiated	Change recipients have some say Resistance likely to be reduced	May be relatively slow Changes may have to be modified
Educative	People become committed to change May lead to improvements in the change	Relatively slow Likely to require more resources
Participative	Change more likely to be accepted People become committed to change More opportunities for individual and organisational learning	Relatively slow Change is more complex to manage Likely to require more resources

When deciding which change strategy to adopt, you will want to consider not only the particular circumstances you face but your own management preferences, too.

Factors affecting the choice of strategy

Why – and when – should you choose one change strategy rather than another? Each of the five strategies will be appropriate in different circumstances. Consider a continuum between fast and slow, shown in Figure 14.6. Directive strategies, which are at the fast end of the continuum, involve a clear plan of action, rapid implementation and minimal involvement of other people. Any opposition and resistance are simply overcome. Expert strategies are also towards the fast end of the continuum. Participative and educative strategies, which are at the slow end of the continuum, involve less clear-cut plans and sense of direction; they involve people in the change process and minimise opposition and resistance. Negotiation strategies are located in the middle of the continuum.

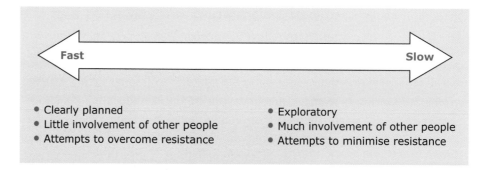

Figure 14.6 The change strategy continuum

There are several factors that will influence your choice of strategy. These include:

- the urgency of the situation – the more urgent and important the threat, the stronger the case for a fast strategy

- the degree of opposition that can be expected – the greater the opposition, the more appropriate a slower strategy, to prevent or overcome the resistance to change

- the power base of the change initiator – if the change initiator is powerful enough, it may be possible to maintain a fast strategy even in the face of opposition; otherwise a slower strategy may be needed to reduce opposition

- the need for information and commitment when designing and carrying out the change – a fast strategy presupposes that the change initiator knows, or can readily work out, what is required; if they do not, they will need to involve others and proceed more slowly.

(Source: based on Kotter and Schlesinger, 1979)

Strategies that are inconsistent with the demands of the situation will run into predictable problems. Changes that need the extensive involvement of others for their success but which are implemented quickly are likely to meet with resistance and will possibly fail. If the situation calls for urgent action, a strategy of extensive participation will slow down the process and reduce the chances of success.

Of course, the different factors may pull you in different directions. The situation may be urgent, requiring speedy action. At the same time, you may not have adequate information indicating that a slower strategy might be more appropriate. As ever, it is a question of judgement and balance, of weighing up probabilities and possibilities rather than applying a formula.

The eight-step process of change

Whatever type of change needs to be made it will require planning. This is so whether the change is dictated and controlled by senior management or is a more spontaneous incremental or emergent change which may be part of a change programme or the result of an individual managers initiative. John Kotters eight-step process of change (1995) is introduced here. It has been developed for transformational change, that is, a change in organisational culture resulting from changes to strategy and processes over a relatively long time. However, it is equally useful for smaller changes, though you will need to simplify the steps. The process may seem time-consuming but remember that the measure of success of an essential small change such as an office move for a team, or the introduction of a new system, is not simply whether the change takes place but whether staff happily embrace the change, help to make the change, find additional, unanticipated benefits and see further ways to make cost-effective improvements. The eight-step process will help you to achieve this success, even if you have used it in a considerably less complex way than Kotter suggests.

See also: What is organisational culture, Chapter 14

It can be used with any strategy for change. Figure 14.7 summarises the process. Although one step is shown as logically following another, the process is rarely linear.

Step 1: Establishing a sense of urgency

Crucially, this step is about encouraging people to recognise there is a need for change and to start considering possibilities. If necessary, free up old attitudes and beliefs. This may happen gradually, as when a need for change slowly emerges, or it may be brought about suddenly by a crisis or a major change in the organisation's environment – for example, legislation that makes previous practice impossible or a sudden upsurge in demand for services or a change in resources. Alternatively, the need may be caused by internal changes, for example, the sudden departure of a key member of staff and the realisation that the person was the only one who knew the job. What is common in these situations is the recognition that existing ways of doing things are no longer adequate to meet the circumstances the organisation faces.

In some cases you may need to create this sense of urgency yourself. If information is being kept from a group of people to keep them happy, you may need to bring some key facts to people's attention to make the 'status

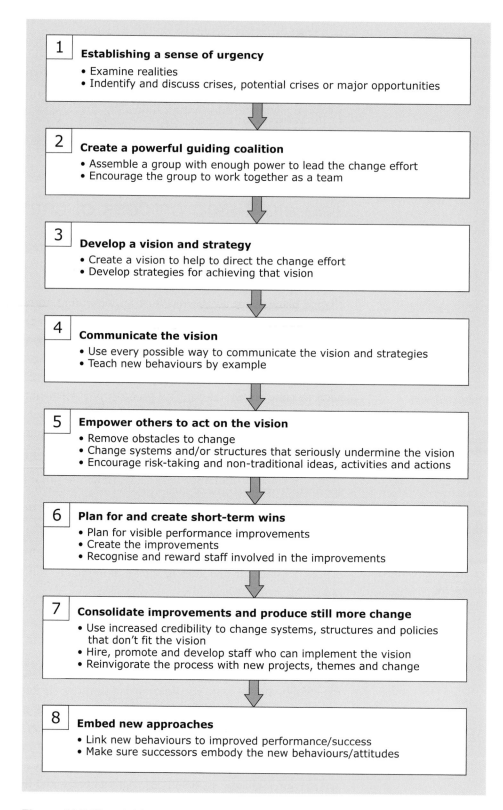

Figure 14.7 The eight-step process of change, adapted from Kotter, 1995

quo' seem more risky and unacceptable than taking a journey into the unknown.

If major change is needed, an important part of your role in this phase will often be to contain (neither rejecting nor reinforcing) the initial feelings and reactions to the need for change. Anger, resentment, outright opposition, denial, anxiety, sadness and excessive optimism are all common. As they are expressed and acknowledged, and the realities of the situation are gradually absorbed, more considered responses and proposals will usually be offered. At this point you will be in a better position to discuss and prepare more detailed plans for the change.

Acknowledging opposition and successfully working through initial reactions to the prospect of change cannot be avoided. This effort is essential because change cannot progress smoothly unless these reactions have been dealt with effectively. Some practical approaches that you can use to 'open up' and address resistance to change are examined later. Box 14.3 describes a tool you may find useful when considering whether conditions are right for a change to be acceptable.

Box 14.3 The change equation

The change equation was developed as a tool to highlight what is needed to initiate a change process. Although it is expressed as an equation, it is not a mathematical tool and cannot be used with numerical values. However, it provides a useful way to look at the conditions necessary if a change is to be acceptable. The way to use this tool is to think about the balance between each side of the equation. The basis of the equation is the simple assumption that people are rarely interested in change unless the benefits outweigh the costs.

In the change equation, A, B and C must be greater than D.

A = the individual's or group's level of dissatisfaction with the way things are

B = the individual's or group's shared vision of a better future

C = the existence of an acceptable, safe, first step

and

D = the costs to the individual or group.

Change is unlikely unless: **A x B x C > D** (the mathematical symbol > means 'is greater than').

You may decide, after applying the change equation to your project, that the balance between **A, B** and **C** on the one hand and **D** on the other is so unfavourable that change is impossible. However, you may see ways to alter the balance in your favour. It is then your job either to reduce **D** or to increase the sum of **A, B** and **C**. Let us examine each of the elements of the change equation briefly.

A Dissatisfaction with the way things are

If we want to initiate a change, we are normally dissatisfied with the current state. We may wrongly assume that other people share our dissatisfaction. If people are comfortable with the way things are, they are unlikely to support change. However, you may be able to persuade them that improvements would be beneficial.

B A shared vision of a better future

If change is to be sustained, the individual or group must have a vision of a better way of doing things. If the vision does not exist, or is unclear, then people will not strive to achieve it. If there are several different visions, energy will be continually dissipated in argument. Try to create a single, clear and shared vision.

C An acceptable, safe, first step

First steps are acceptable if they are small and likely to be successful. It must be clear that if these steps fail, the situation is easily and quietly retrievable. Even when there is a high level of dissatisfaction and a common vision which all would strive to achieve, the size of change needed and the risks involved can encourage inertia. Break the change task into small achievable steps and encourage people to focus on those.

D The costs to the individual or group

The costs may include: money, resources, time, energy, adverse personal and psychological effects. Remember, it is the perceived costs that are important, and what is trivial for some may be significant or even traumatic for others. But there will always be costs of one kind or another: for example, a change may be painful and unfair to some. You will need to consider how best to 'sell' the benefits of the overall change and to see if some costs to individuals can be reduced or compensated for in some way.

The change equation is regarded as the work of David Gleicher while at Arthur D. Little, the international management consultancy, during the 1960s. It was popularised by Beckhard and Harris (1977) and Dannemiller and Jacobs (1992).

Step 2: Create a powerful guiding coalition

Step 2 in the eight-step process is about working out who will be your key critics, opponents, detractors and supporters in the change process and how to address their various needs. Many change projects fail because they do not have the support of a key senior person or because the interests of various groups have not been met.

Stakeholder-analysis ideas and tools are the best way of analysing these key groups and identifying who you will need to influence the most to make your change project successful. It is particularly important to identify at this stage who needs to be involved and who does not. When you have done this, Kotter suggests that for large-scale changes it is important to create a change management team – a group with enough power to lead the change effort. This team may operate outside the normal hierarchy and involve people who are not part of senior management – the reason why Kotter refers to a *guiding coalition* rather than a team – so effective leadership is needed. You will need to help members of this team to develop a shared assessment of the problems and opportunities, to develop trust and to be able to communicate. For smaller changes, such a team may not be necessary but you will need to lead the change effectively using the results of your analysis to guide your actions.

Step 3: Develop a vision and strategy

The key to success here is to develop a clear and compelling vision or picture of the future that is relatively specific and easy to communicate. It will also need to be meaningful and inspiring to those who will be most involved in the change. The vision or picture should help to clarify the direction in which the organisation, or part of it, needs to move. Kotter's 'rule' is: if you can't communicate the vision to someone in fewer than five minutes and get a reaction that signifies understanding and interest, you haven't achieved this part of Step 3! From the initial picture, the guiding coalition develops a strategy to achieve it. Here is an example of a vision and a strategy.

A carbon-neutral vision

> In 2007, the UK-based clothing and food retailer M&S created a vision of an organisation that would be carbon-neutral in five years. The aim of the overarching strategy to achieve this was to provide a framework for many lower-level initiatives across the organisation and for employees to be aware of what they could do. Thus, the vision led to a 100-point plan for reducing carbon emissions. This led to a number of projects across the organisation, for example, encouraging employees to be aware of their carbon footprint when travelling to work.

Visions (and strategies) do not have to be organisation-wide or complex. A vision can be as simple as: 'Our customers can place orders by telephone from 07.00 to 22.00 seven days a week.' In working though the vision, other elements may be added to it, for example, abandoning activities that add little value. These new elements may come to light only after the first or subsequent 'draft' of the vision, as a result of discussion among members of the guiding coalition.

Step 4: Communicate the vision

Communicating the vision with a single meeting, by making speeches or through newsletters is unlikely to be effective by itself. Often during the change people are expected to make sacrifices as well as to help make the change. Hearts and minds need to be won over. Talking about the change in daily conversion and communications, and encouraging talk about it, is necessary. All communication channels need to be considered and every good opportunity should be used to have constructive and forward-looking discussion about the change and any new desirable behaviour. When the change is major and transformational, members of the guiding coalition need to 'walk the talk', that is, become living symbols of the new 'culture' that the vision embraces.

If the change will not be positive for everyone concerned, then the vision needs to be attended to. For example, if the change is likely to lead to job losses, it will help if your vision includes new growth possibilities and the commitment to treat fairly anyone who will be made unemployed. It will help, too, to communicate how people are contributing to the change.

Step 5: Empower others to act on the vision

Successful change to systems, structures and policies involves an increasing number of people as it progresses. This is because, for the change to succeed, staff themselves will often need to develop new ideas and approaches that fit with the change vision. However, they need to feel confident enough to do this: they will need to be sufficiently empowered to take the required risks. At the same time, obstacles that prevent staff from helping to make the change happen will need to be removed. Sometimes the obstacle is organisational structure, for example, job categories may be too narrow preventing people from making changes. Or the obstacle can be systems such as those for performance appraisal which may reward people for self-interest rather than for adopting the new vision. Sometimes obstacles to change involve individual people who may feel threatened by the change or who simply do not see the need for change. They may persuade others to resist the change, too. Obstacles and resistance are not necessarily easy to distinguish from one another. For example, a manager or team leader may place demands on a staff member, or members, which are inconsistent with the change effort (an obstacle). However, the manager or team leader may be making inconsistent demands because he or she is quietly resisting the change (resistance).

Addressing resistance

When you encounter resistance to a change, in many instances you will want to do two things: remove or overcome this resistance and encourage positive involvement with, and commitment to, the change process. However, just as opposition to change is not wholly negative you should not assume that involvement and commitment are self-evidently good. This may seem paradoxical, but consider the following points:

- What are the risks of over-commitment? Have you, for instance, encountered a person who is so enthusiastic about a particular change that he or she prevents others from becoming involved?

- Is it really necessary for everyone to be in full agreement with a particular change? There can be a tendency in some organisations, particularly if they have a participative culture, to spend a great deal of time ensuring that all individuals and sections 'own' the change. But, for changes that require modifications to individual attitudes and practices you may never achieve this. You may decide that implementing the change is a higher priority.

- Conversely, is it necessary for *all* opposition to be overcome or, at least, turned into some form of active commitment? Organisations normally live with different and competing priorities and concerns.

- Is there any reason why the processes of change should not also be conducted in ways which, in most cases, acknowledge and use constructively such diversity and differences of opinion? In other words, you may need to be selective in the efforts you make to overcome resistance and to develop a positive involvement and commitment to change.

A commitment plan is a chart used to show the level of commitment to a change required of various people and groups. Key individuals or groups affected by the change are listed down one side and across the top are four headings which indicate levels of commitment:

- Opposed or not committed – likely to oppose the change.
- Let – will not oppose the initiative but will not actively support it.
- Help – will support the change with time and other resources, provided someone else will take the lead.
- Make – will lead the change process and make it happen.

Each individual or group is rated with an 'O' to indicate their current position and an 'X' to indicate the commitment needed if the change is to be achieved. The difference between the two positions is a simplified measure of the work to be done to build the necessary support to advance the change. Sometimes it may be appropriate to reduce the level of commitment: leadership should move to other people; sometimes it does not really matter that people remain opposed or inactive.

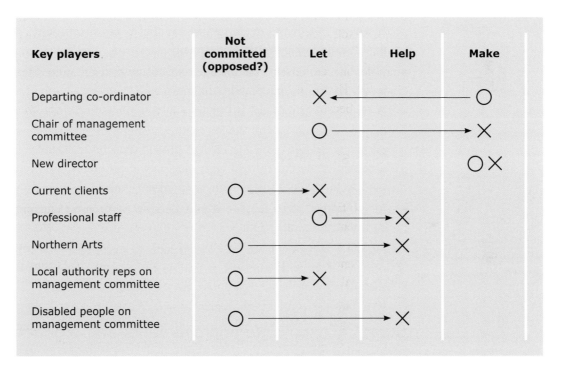

Figure 14.8 A commitment plan

See also: The feasibility of change, in this chapter

When combined with force-field analysis, a commitment plan can help you to be more precise about the extent to which commitment is necessary and with whom you need to build alliances.

Step 6: Plan for and create short-term wins

If the change is significantly large and transformational, it may take time to achieve. In this case there is a risk of loss of momentum and people may give up making the efforts needed or may even begin to resist the change. It is wise, then, to plan for short-term 'wins' so that staff can see evidence that their efforts toward change are successful. These short-term gains need to be planned for and they should be as unambiguous as possible, for example, particular quality or performance improvements. Establish the goals and then recognise and reward the achievement of them by those involved. Commitments to produce short-term wins help to keep up the level of urgency and they require the kind of thinking that can clarify or revise the change vision.

Incorporate these short-term wins into the overall plan and the way in which you manage the transition. Managing the transition will require all your skills as a project manager to implement the required change. The following checklist covers the key areas that need to be considered by you and your guiding coalition:

- Seek to maintain a climate for change in your organisation, department or section.

- Decide on the goals for the change – it is usually wise to avoid altering more than you need to, particularly as the need for further change may emerge.

- If the change is one that needs to be imposed, plan it in terms of what needs to be done, in what order and by whom, and draw up a timetable. If it does not, then develop a process that is consistent with, in particular, an educative or participative strategy.

- Calculate the cost of the change and ensure that there are the necessary resources to introduce and maintain it.

- Decide how to monitor the change process – try to anticipate where there may be difficulties and devise early-warning systems. Be alert to problems or signs that the change project may be in trouble. Reserve time and resources to deal with unexpected problems. Be prepared to modify the plans to deal with new circumstances.

- Identify what other factors, if any, need to be modified to reinforce and consolidate the change.

- Decide how to evaluate the change later to make sure that it has been successful. Include markers or criteria for overall success and for short-term wins.

Step 7: Consolidate improvements and produce still more change

It is important to monitor progress closely and report to everyone involved the successes that have taken place. Keeping people informed in this way is one of the best ways of maintaining momentum. If there is a loss of momentum, consider discussing this with those involved in the change to see if there are any major reasons for this. There may be a problem that was not identified earlier and which you or they can now correct. For example, it may become evident that some systems and structures are not consistent with the required change and you will need to work to change these too. Indeed, some changes may be larger than the initial one envisaged. This is where short-term wins will help: they will provide the credibility you will need to continue the change efforts.

Step 8: Embed new approaches

A major transformational change made will need to become 'the way we do things here' otherwise it will be short-lived and people will return to their previous behaviour. The change you make needs to become part of the culture of the organisation, or the part of it in which the change occurs.

You can help in two ways. The first is to try to show staff how the new approaches, behaviours or attitudes have helped improve performance. This helps people to make the 'right' links. To do this you will need to communicate to and discuss with staff why performance or quality is improving. The second is to take time to ensure that the changed approach, behaviours or attitudes can be embedded in the culture of the organisation, or department or team. To do this, you may need to ensure that the requirements for promoting staff reflect the new behaviours and attitudes. This is particularly important if the change leaders or champions need to be replaced when, for example, they themselves are promoted or leave the organisation.

Kotter's eight steps have been developed for changes that involve the entire organisation. They are relevant to smaller changes too, however. In such cases, the steps can be simplified and they should be less complex because fewer people are likely to be involved – but each step remains important.

Dealing with opposition

When managers are considering making a change in their organisation or their part of it, an important concern will often be how to quickly identify and deal with resistance and opposition by staff and how to gain their involvement and commitment. The management of change too easily becomes a matter of drawing up battle lines, of trying to win people over and to reduce opposition. Change does not always generate irreconcilable positions and conflict: debate and opposition can be constructive and may lead to improvements to the proposed changes.

People may resist change for many different reasons and opposition can occur at different levels in the organisation. As the example in Box 14.4 shows, managers themselves are often a common source of resistance.

See also: Ideal or 'above-the-norm' cultures, Chapter 12

Box 14.4 Resistance to change at Alpha Motors

Alpha Motors is a vehicle retail business with fifteen dealership companies. The dealerships in the group had autonomy in the way they were run. For all staff in the dealerships, a substantial proportion of their pay was based on sales performance.

However, the directors of Alpha Motors decided to implement quality-management systems to meet a European standard. This affected the dealerships. A quality coordinator was appointed in each dealership and a quality committee was set up in each department with one manager and one non-manager. The quality coordinators reported to both the manager of their dealership and to Alpha Motors' quality manager.

The process of establishing quality procedures met considerable resistance from the dealerships and the departmental managers. They resented the time taken by the process of writing quality procedures and frequently insisted (despite evidence to the contrary) that existing procedures met the new standards. Very little cooperation was given to the quality controllers. Many managers regarded the new responsibility given to their employees as a reduction in their managerial status. There was also poor cooperation between the departmental managers in the dealerships.

Two other factors contributed significantly to the resistance. These were the management reward systems and the autonomy of the dealership managers. First, managers' pay was contingent on monthly sales performance: quality measures played no part in the calculation. Second, the dealership managers were not used to intervention by head office in how they ran their businesses.

After three years, compliance with the European quality standard had not been achieved. The quality programme began to make progress only when the dealership managers were brought together to help to design the quality programme and (at their suggestion) bonus payments were incorporated into quality targets.

(Source: adapted from Fenton-O'Creevy, 2000)

Those in favour of a particular change – in this case the senior management of Alpha Motors – are often self-interested. They are likely to underestimate the impact of a change and to be intolerant of those who have a different opinion. Similar factors operate in resistance to change. Kotter and Schlesinger (1979) identified: parochial self-interest (that is, a narrow focus on personal concerns rather than the needs of the organisation); misunderstanding; low tolerance to change; and different assessments of the situation. It is easy for managers to regard opposition as misconceived or based on unreal fears and concerns. However, resistance can sometimes be justified and constructive. Managers will need, at least, to note the particular circumstances that give rise to the opposition. This does not mean they must agree with the opposition or must reach a consensus before continuing, but the meaning and significance of the opposition needs to be acknowledged. Table 14.3 summarises some other important reasons why people resist change.

Table 14.3 Reasons why people resist change

Reason	Explanation
Loss of control	People can feel that the change is being 'done to them' rather than 'done by them'
Loss of face	Change can result in people losing face or status
Loss of identity	People build identities around aspects of their job and the organisation. Removing important symbols and traditions can make people unhappy
Loss of competence	People can feel that their old competences are challenged and they lack the new competences to deal with the changed situation
Personal uncertainty	People experience uncertainty when they do not know what the change will mean for them and their job
Surprise	A sudden change is likely to make people sceptical and defensive
More work	Usually change means more work for those involved. If people are already overworked, this will be an important factor
Past resentments	People resist change if its source is someone with whom they have past grievances. Forcing through change can build up problems for the future
Unintended consequences	A change in one area can lead to unintended consequences in another
Real threats	Change can threaten an individual's or group's interests, for example, the closure of a project, or a part of an organisation or the whole of an organisation

(Source: based on Kanter, cited in Lorenz, 1985)

There are many methods or tactics that managers can draw on to address opposition. These include:

Avoid unnecessary change. Do not change things that do not need to be changed. In particular, be careful not to change things that have a symbolic value and are important to people's sense of identity unless you have to.

Communication and education. Try to communicate ideas about change early to reduce surprise and ensure that those likely to be affected understand what is happening. An education and communication programme can be invaluable as a forum for exploring conflicting perceptions and ideas about the proposed changes.

Involvement. Actively involving and engaging those who may oppose a change can be an important means of winning their commitment and support, particularly if they fear a loss of control or are worried about the likely consequences of the change. Managing participation is not always easy – people may be reluctant to switch from opposing a change to helping to make it happen. The scope of individual or group participation is important too: if people feel it is limited to those aspects of the change that matter least, then do not be surprised if they see it as tokenism or manipulation which become a source of further resentment.

Support and development. Another way to acknowledge opposition and respond positively is to be supportive when fears and anxieties are expressed. Also make allowances for periods of recuperation and readjustment at the end of a period of difficult change. It may be necessary to provide people with opportunities for retraining and development if they are to have the confidence and competences to adjust to the changes.

Bargaining. If, in your estimation, making a particular change is important enough to make a deal with those who are opposed to it, then bargaining and negotiation may be appropriate. In some instances you may be able to do this informally with individuals or small groups. At other times you may need to involve workers' representatives and engage in more formal bargaining. Try to make sure that concessions to one group do not lead to new demands from other groups.

Building coalitions and alliances. Be prepared to use your networks and build support for the change. Anticipate where opposition is likely to come from and which individuals or groups are likely to be influential, and try to win their support.

Manipulation and co-option. These tactics are the opposite of participation and involvement, because they are usually conducted behind the scenes. They may involve, for example, selective use of information, private deals and co-opting or buying off people who are likely to be the most outspoken in their opposition to change. Such tactics may have costs if it is later discovered by others that you made private deals or even if you are suspected of using them – costs to your own reputation and possibly to the standing of your group or even of the organisation. People may stop trusting you. Nevertheless, on occasions you may find that to achieve a particularly important change such an approach may be called for – while recognising that you may have to handle negative consequences at a later stage.

Explicit and implicit coercion. Finally, another way of implementing change is simply to act coercively and to use your position to force it through. Again, there will probably be costs: coercion may clash with some of the values of your organisation; it may lead to unwilling compliance and poor motivation; it may lead to later resistance; in voluntary organisations, volunteers may simply leave. Nevertheless, occasionally it may be necessary. There may be an element of coercion – albeit unacknowledged – in your use of other methods for dealing with opposition.

(Source: based on Kotter and Schlesinger, 1979)

Do managers choose from the full range of tactics according to the circumstances or do they adopt particular methods whatever the circumstances? Do they choose tactics that are usual in the organisation's culture? Many people believe that managers commonly choose manipulation and co-option. The reasons for this are not hard to find. They are probably rooted in the fundamental dilemma of change management: trust versus control. Managers know from experience (and management courses) that it is best to involve people, to offer them choices, to lead by consent. But they also know that staff and colleagues have their own interests and preferences and managers are frightened of losing control. So, at the same time as informing and involving people, managers also act unilaterally. They select, interpret and emphasise particular information in order to influence people, to pre-empt choices, to divide or exclude potential opponents, and so on.

While it is understandable that managers sometimes act in this way, this tactic causes problems. When people are manipulated they usually sense at least some of what is happening, with predictable negative consequences for their motivation and trust.

Is there an alternative? Manipulation and co-option may seem the easiest and quickest way to achieve your objectives. If the culture of the organisation emphasises this approach, you may find it hard to do otherwise. However, the longer-term effects on motivation and trust may mean that you will struggle with your next change initiative. When the organisational culture allows, it is generally best to be as clear and honest as possible with those involved about what has already been decided, and about what choices remain or can be influenced. This will bring benefits even if people are involved only in some aspects of implementation rather than the change decision itself. Be clear about the scope of their participation. This involvement will help to reduce the possibility of problems arising after implementation. Such problems are often much harder to resolve.

Tools and techniques

Introduction

This section of the book deals with tools and techniques to help you to:

- generate, organise and communicate ideas
- analyse situations, solve problems and make decisions
- organise and communicate information and data.

Graphs, charts, matrices, tables and diagrams are like pictures; they can 'speak a thousand words'. They are useful for expressing ideas and communicating them quickly to others. Some can be used as *visual thinking tools*. They are useful when you are trying to figure out, for example, how a system works, where your part of the organisation fits into that system, or the root causes of a difficulty in order for you to try to resolve it rather than simply deal with the symptoms. Other tools and techniques are processes that are useful to follow; some are checklists, and others are simply helpful tips.

They are set out in four groups. The first deals with graphs, charts and matrices. The second covers the kinds of diagrams that are useful for identifying, investigating and solving problems, and for mapping the 'boundaries' of a problem. The third covers methods for generating ideas and the fourth, checklists.

Graphs, charts and matrices

Line graphs

A line graph is a method of showing a relationship between two variables such as the output of an activity and the associated costs. There are some special terms that you need to understand in order to create and interpret line graphs. These terms include the axes, the origin, the intercept and the slope (or gradient).

Table 15.1 contains data about the output of an activity and the associated total costs. The relationship between the output and the total costs of producing the output is as expected: that is, the costs rise as the output rises.

Table 15.1 Output and total costs

Output	Total costs (£)
0	10
10	30
20	50
30	70
40	90

These data can also be displayed in a line graph, as shown in Figure 1.

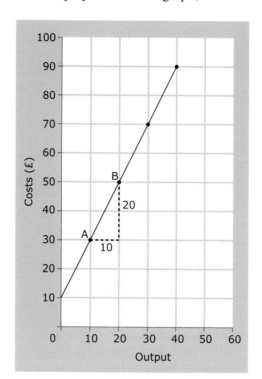

Figure 15.1 Output and total costs – a line graph

The horizontal and vertical axes

The total costs depend on the output, so the output is the 'independent variable' and the total costs are the 'dependent variable'. When there is a dependence of this kind, the independent variable is plotted on the horizontal axis, which is also called the x axis. In the graph, output has been plotted on the horizontal axis. The dependent variable is plotted on the vertical axis, also called the y axis. The total costs have been plotted on the vertical axis.

The origin

The origin is the point on the graph where the x axis value (the output) and the y axis value (the total costs) are both zero.

The intercept

When a line cuts an axis, the line is said 'to intercept the axis at' (the particular point). In this example, the line cuts the vertical y axis at £10, so 'the line intercepts the y axis at £10'. It can also be said that 'the intercept with the y axis is £10'.

The slope

The slope (or gradient) of the line describes its steepness. The steepness is measured by considering two points on the graph, A and B. The vertical distance between the two points is 20; the horizontal distance between them is 10. The steepness of the line is the ratio of these two distances:

vertical distance ÷ horizontal distance = 20 ÷ 10 = 2

In the example the slope is 2. This tells us that for every change of one unit in the value of x, there will be a change of two units in the value of y.

When you know the intercept and the slope, then you have a complete picture of the line. The particular graph in the example can be described mathematically as follows:

$y = 2x + 10$

In this equation the slope of the line is 2, and the intercept on the y axis is 10. The equation shows that the total cost (y) of an output can be found by multiplying the output (x) by 2, and then adding 10.

Time series line graphs

In time series line graphs, data are plotted or organised along a time dimension. Time series graphs are used for displaying data that show cyclical fluctuations or changes, such as growth over time. Suppose that you wanted to present the data shown in Table 15.2 as a graph.

Table 15.2 Number of staff in an organisation

Year	1	2	3	4	5	6
Total	10	25	40	55	60	65

You would plot the data in a line graph like the one shown in Figure 15.2.

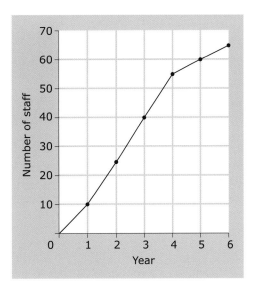

Figure 15.2 Number of staff – a time series line graph (large scale)

As a rule, the variable plotted on the horizontal (x) axis is the interval of time: for example, years, months or minutes. This rule leads to the use of 'time series' to describe this kind of chart. The other variable, in this instance 'Number of staff', is plotted on the vertical (y) axis. The points are then joined up to form a continuous line, which shows how staff numbers have changed in the organisation over the years.

Selecting the scales

The scales that are used determine the look of the graph. For example, if the horizontal distance between 'Year 1' and 'Year 6' shown in Figure 15.2 were doubled, the line would be stretched to double its present length. If the horizontal distance were halved, then the length of the line would be halved. Each of the graphs would be mathematically correct.

Now suppose that you had to draw a line graph of the staff in a second organisation using the data shown in Table 15.3. Figures 15.3a and 15.3b show two ways of presenting the data.

Table 15.3 Number of staff in an organisation

Year	1	2	3	4	5	6
Total	200	220	240	255	270	260

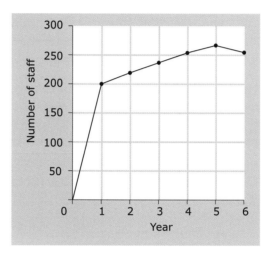

Figure 15.3a Number of staff – a time series line graph (small scale, compressed)

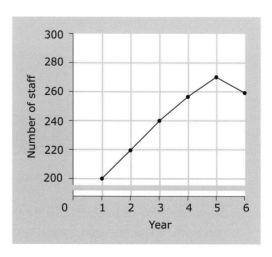

Figure 15.3b Number of staff – a time series line graph (small scale)

Although both of the line graphs are mathematically correct, they look different. The effect, in Figure 15.3a, of beginning from zero has been to compress the data shown on the y axis (from 200 to 260) and so make it harder to understand the graph. In Figure 15.3b the vertical scale begins at 200 and the scale has been extended so that the information presented in the graph is much clearer.

The presentation of data – the 'picture' of the data that is presented in a graph – varies according to the scales selected. Choose scales that are appropriate. As you examine a graph, pay particular attention to the scales.

Pie charts

A pie chart is a way of presenting *proportional* data in the form of a circle – the 'pie'. Each 'slice' shows its proportion to the whole. The whole itself must be finite and known: for example, the total number of staff in an organisation or the total IT maintenance budget.

Suppose that the staff of an organisation is comprised as shown in Table 15.4.

Table 15.4 The composition of staff in an organisation

	Number	**%**
Senior managers	20	10
Other managers	30	15
Administrative	70	35
Clerical	80	40
Total	200	100

You could show this composition in a pie chart like the one in Figure 15.4.

The area of a segment (or 'slice') of the pie chart corresponds to the proportion that the category occupies in the whole. For instance, the segment marked 'Other managers' occupies 15% of the whole pie.

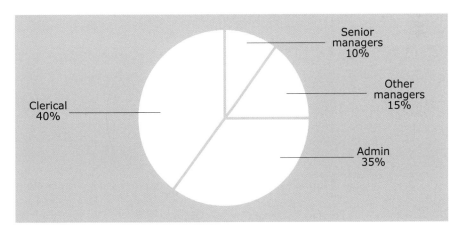

Figure 15.4 The composition of staff – a pie chart

You can use a pie chart when you want to show the components of a whole. It is possible to use a pie chart to illustrate the composition of the staff in an organisation because the data describe the whole organisation. Notice that the percentages add up to 100.

You could also use pie charts to show the composition of staff in an organisation in two (or more) years. Data are shown in Table 15.5, and data for each year are shown in two pie charts, Figures 15.5a and 15.5b.

Table 15.5 The composition of staff in an organisation

	(a) Year 1		(b) Year 2	
	Number	**%**	**Number**	**%**
Senior managers	20	10	35	14
Other managers	30	15	25	10
Administrative	70	35	60	24
Clerical	80	40	130	52
Total	200	100	250	100

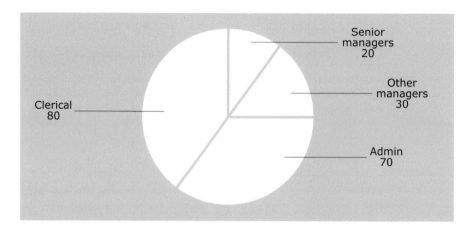

Figure 15.5a Composition of staff in Year 1 – a pie chart

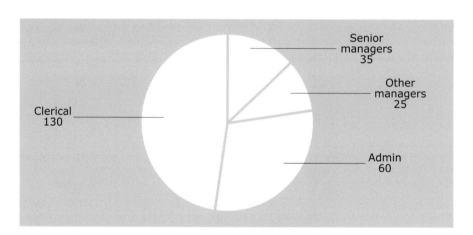

Figure 15.5b Composition of staff in Year 2 – a pie chart

The Year 1 pie chart (Figure 15.5a) is the same as Figure 15.4 because the data are the same. The proportion of senior managers is 10%. Their number increases in Year 2, so in Figure 15.5b, which represents that year, they account for 14% of the staff compared with 10% in Year 1. The 'Senior managers' segment is proportionately larger. The 'Other managers' and 'Admin' segments are smaller compared with Year 1, and the 'Clerical' segment is larger.

Bar charts

A bar chart is another way of presenting data. It is designed to show *frequency distribution*: for example, the number of staff in each of four categories in an organisation. You could present the data given in Table 15.6 in a bar chart as shown in Figure 15.6.

Table 15.6 The composition of staff in an organisation

Senior managers	20
Other managers	30
Administrative	70
Clerical	80
Total	200

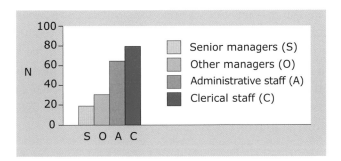

Figure 15.6 Composition of staff – a bar chart

You can see how the bar chart has been created. The four categories are marked on the horizontal axis, so the chart is built on that axis. An appropriate number scale is marked on the vertical axis. A vertical bar is drawn for each of the categories. The height of each bar represents the number of staff in that category. The width of each bar is the same. In the resulting chart we can see that the bar representing 'Senior managers' measures 20 on the vertical scale; that representing 'Other managers' measures 30; that representing 'Administrative' measures 70; and that representing 'Clerical' measures 80.

Of course, you can show more than one set of data on a bar chart. Suppose that you wanted to present the data shown in Table 15.7.

Table 15.7 The composition of staff in an organisation

	Year 1	**Year 2**
Senior managers	20	35
Other managers	30	25
Administrative	70	60
Clerical	80	130
Total	200	250

Then the bar chart could be shown as Figure 7a or as Figure 7b.

Figures 15.7a and **15.7b** Composition of staff in Years 1 and 2 – two bar charts

Notice the difference between the two bar charts. In Figure 15.7a the dominant relationship, the one that will catch the reader's eye, is the one between the four categories in each of the two years. The emphasis remains on the composition of the whole staff in each of the years. In Figure 15.7b the dominant relationships are those within each of the four categories. If you wanted to emphasise how the numbers in each category of staff had changed during the two years, you would choose the type of representation shown in Figure 15.7b.

Matrices

A matrix is an arrangement of 'cells' in rows and columns. A spreadsheet is a simple example of a matrix. Each cell is described by its position in a row and in a column; the row is given first and then the column, so 'cell 6B' on your spreadsheet is the one that occupies row 6 and column B. The size of a matrix is described by the number of rows and the number of columns. A 'two-by-two' matrix has two rows and two columns. A 'three-by-two' matrix has three rows and two columns.

Using matrices

A matrix can be a useful way of organising your thinking. Suppose that you were asked: 'How will you know when you have written a good report?' After careful consideration you decide that usefulness and quality of presentation are key measures by which you would assess a report. Then you could use a two-by-two matrix like the one shown in Figure 15.8.

The labels on the two axes of the matrix (the rows and the columns) are your two criteria, 'Usefulness' and 'Quality of presentation'. Each of the criteria can be divided into 'low' and 'high' so that you now have four cells, each of which describes a particular combination of 'Usefulness' and 'Quality of presentation'. The four combinations represented by the matrix are: low usefulness/low quality of presentation, low usefulness/high quality of presentation, high usefulness/low quality of presentation and high usefulness/high quality of presentation. You would know that you had written a good report if it could be placed in the high usefulness/high quality of presentation cell of the matrix.

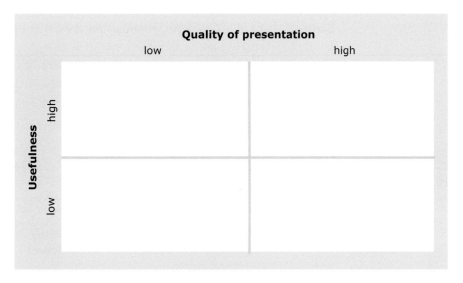

Figure 15.8 A matrix for judging a report

This two-by-two matrix describes the possibilities in a simple way ('high/low') and so enables you to think about them. The criteria ('usefulness' and 'quality of presentation') are the boundaries. Whenever you can confine the criteria (the boundaries) to just two, you can construct a two-dimensional matrix. You could also expand 'high/low' into three or more categories, or you could number your axes, for example, from 1 to 9, if you wanted to create a larger matrix than the two-by-two matrix in the example.

Evaluation matrices

When there are several courses of action, then one way of thinking clearly about the advantages and drawbacks of the different courses is to compile an evaluation matrix. There are six basic steps as set out in Box 15.1.

Box 15.1 Six steps to creating an evaluation matrix

1   List the various options.

2   Identify the criteria by which you will judge the options.

3   Give an importance weighting to each of the criteria. (The preferred option will be the one that has the highest weighted score.)

4   Give each option a raw score from 1 to 5 under each criterion. Write the raw scores in each 'raw score' column.

5   Multiply each raw score by the weight of each criterion in turn. This gives a weighted score for the option under each criterion. In the example below, the walking holiday is given a raw score of 1 for 'Happy children'. That raw score is then multiplied by the weight of the criterion 'Happy children' (5), to give a weighted score of 5 in that column.

6   Add the weighted scores across the row for each option. The option with the highest weighted score is the best option. If two options tie, then the choice must be made either (i) randomly between the tied options, or (ii) in some other way (perhaps by a review of the matrix).

Suppose that a non-for-profit organisation that offers holidays for deprived families is thinking about the next type of holiday it will offer next year. The organisation lists four options, including families staying at home and benefitting from locally-provided activities. It also lists four criteria and gives each an importance weighting on a scale of 1 to 5, where 5 is the most important and 1 is the least important. The evaluation matrix would look like Table 15.8.

Table 15.8 An evaluation matrix

	Criteria and their relative weighting									
	Happy children		Low cost		Happy adults		Easy travel		Totals	
	Weighting = 5		Weighting = 3		Weighting = 2		Weighting = 1			
Options	Raw score	Weighted (x5)	Raw score	Weighted (x3)	Raw score	Weighted (x2)	Raw score	Weighted (x1)	Raw score	Weighted
Walking holiday	1	5	3	9	4	8	4	4	12	26
Beach holiday	4	20	1	3	3	6	2	2	10	31
Stay at home	1	5	5	15	2	4	5	5	13	29
Holiday camp	5	25	1	3	1	2	2	2	9	32

Using the matrix

The results of the evaluation reflect the scores that are awarded to each option and the weightings that are attached to the different criteria. A change in one or the other (or in both) will lead to a change in the results. Accordingly, when you construct a matrix of this kind be sure to think hard about the scores and weightings. A matrix like this can be used in many ways: for example, when interviewing applicants as part of a selection process.

Diagrammatic representations

Force-field diagrams

A force-field diagram shows the opposing pressures (or forces) that are bearing on a situation. Within the context of planning and managing change, the diagram shows the forces which are supportive of change (the driving forces) and the forces which are likely to be unhelpful or resistant (the restraining forces).

The diagram

Suppose that a manager is planning or exploring the possibility of a change (in working practices, for example). The manager can represent the current situation as a vertical line. The driving forces, those forces or reasons that are supportive of a change, can be represented as arrows pushing the line to the right. The restraining forces, those forces or reasons that are likely to resist the change, can then be represented by arrows that are pushing the line (the current situation) to the left and are seeking to keep it where it is.

A general force-field diagram is shown in Figure 15.9.

Driving forces   **Restraining forces**

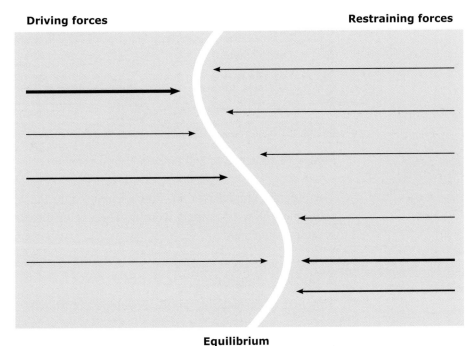

Equilibrium

Figure 15.9 A general force-field diagram

The thickness of an arrow can be used to show the strength of a force. The length of an arrow can be used to show how difficult it would be to modify the force. However, these conventions are not hard and fast. You can adopt them or you can use your own system. It is usual to explain your system in a note below your diagram.

How a force-field diagram can help:

- The diagram is a useful expositional or presentational device. When you are presenting an analysis or proposal, the diagram will enable you to describe (and distinguish between) the reasons for a change. It will enable you to do the same for the reasons why a change may be resisted.

- The diagram will be an explicit prompt for exploring the restraining forces. The more a manager finds out about these, and the earlier, the better placed the manager will be to find a way to deal with them. The idea of the restraining forces reminds a manager to look for and identify them.

Input–output diagrams

An input–output diagram shows the inputs to a system or to an operation and the outputs from it.

A first diagram

For example, think about the inputs to the running of a commuter rail operation and the outputs from it. The diagram might look like the one in Figure 15.10.

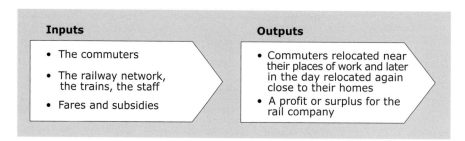

Figure 15.10 Inputs to and outputs from a commuter rail operation

The diagram emphasises the flow of inputs into the operation and the subsequent flow of outputs from it. The use of the arrows will establish this sense of movement.

A second diagram

This first representation can be developed in the way shown in Figure 15.11.

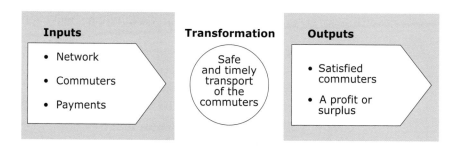

Figure 15.11 Inputs, transformation, outputs

Figure 15.11 includes a general representation of the process that transforms the inputs into outputs. In the example, the transformation is the movement of the passengers – the customers – from their home railway stations to the stations close to their work. The diagram can help your thinking in two ways:

- It emphasises the need for a transforming process – something must be done with the inputs in order to achieve the outputs.
- The transformation process is the reason for the existence of the organisation – it is the value that the organisation adds to the inputs.

You can apply an input–output diagram to an organisation or to a part of an organisation. You can apply it to your own work or to your activities outside work.

When you identify the inputs and the outputs, identify those that are sufficient for your purposes. Sometimes it will be appropriate to identify a relatively long list of both; at other times it will be sufficient to identify just the major inputs and outputs.

Systems thinking

'The whole is more than the sum of its parts' is a good place to start thinking about systems. A car is more than its individual components, a football team is more than a collection of individual players, and a family is more than a group of people who share the same name.

Each of these examples – the car, the football team and the family – can be seen as systems. Individual parts of a system are connected together in some way for a purpose.

An example of such a system is a local hospital catering system, which has the purpose of providing food for patients and staff as part of the hospital system for helping the sick and injured. But the idea of systems goes beyond collections of tangible components such as people, equipment and buildings that form part of various systems. Systems also include intangible items, such as ideas, values, beliefs and norms. These intangible things are factors in a system.

We can see that families have beliefs and behaviours that guide how they interact with each other and with those outside the family. Football teams and their football clubs have strong bonds of beliefs, loyalties and aspirations, and they show these in how they behave when they appear in their club colours. Their systems have tangible elements, such as the playing field, the seating areas, the players, officials and supporters, but also intangible elements, such as their hopes and fears, their history and songs, and their reputation.

We also think about a boundary around each system. This defines those things that are part of the system and those that are outside it. *Each element* of the system is connected to every other, affects how the system behaves, and is affected by it. *All members* in a family system are connected with the other members of the system (both the people and the intangible values and beliefs); they are affected by them, and have an affect on them too. In the larger family system there are a number of smaller systems: subsystems such as grandparents, parents and children.

Five key ideas about systems

Systems thinking will enable you to analyse complex issues in an illuminating way. It takes a whole (or holistic) view of a situation.

When you think of a system, bear in mind the following five ideas:

1 *Everything in a system is connected.* The elements of a system are interconnected. The members of a department or a voluntary group constitute a system. There are connections between the members. A system can comprise people, material objects, and intangible elements such as ideas or common sets of beliefs. The idea of a system emphasises the interconnections between the elements.

2 *A system does something*. A system is defined by what it produces. Every system has an output of some kind. Once again, the outputs may be tangible or intangible. When you think of a hospital as a system, then the outputs will include measurable improvements in health as well as immeasurable outputs in the improvements in people's feelings about themselves. The only valid components of a particular system are those that contribute to the specified output.

3 *Systems have a boundary and an environment*. The system boundary encloses those elements that make up the system. Think of the hospital example again. The boundary of the system will separate the elements that make up the system and interact with each other from the elements that are outside the boundary. The elements that are outside the boundary constitute the environment in which the system operates. In a closed system, elements in the environment affect the system but are not affected by it. However, systems are often open: elements in the environment affect the system, and the system can have an effect, albeit usually a lesser one, on the immediate environment.

4 *The system is defined by your interest*. What goes into and what remains outside a system is decided by your interest. For example, in the local hospital, the system that provides care for accident victims may include counselling support if you feel it is important. Your system may differ from someone else's if they feel counselling is not essential. The way that you express the local hospital as a system will reflect your understanding and point of view.

5 *A system can have one or more subsystems within it*. Your local hospital, for example, could include a catering subsystem (a tangible subsystem), as well as a subsystem which encompasses the values and standards that inform the medical practice in the hospital (an intangible subsystem).

A systems map

Mapping a system is like mapping a town. First we define the boundary and draw it on paper. The boundary separates those places inside the town from those outside. We do the same with the system. We show the system boundary with rounded corners to emphasise the imprecise nature of the boundary that separates those things that are interacting inside the system from those outside in the environment that have an effect on it.

We become selective when we draw a map. We consider the purpose of the map and choose a suitable scale. We include on the map only those things that are useful to our purpose.

Figure 15.12 shows the system boundary and the smaller subsystems inside the boundary. We include all those things that help our use of the map. A system is defined by what it does and shows only those components (those subsystems) that contribute to this output. The environment of the system lies outside the system boundary. In the environment of our system, we include all those things that are outside the system but have an effect on it.

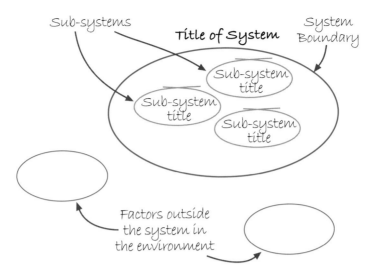

Figure 15.12 A typical systems map

In reality, the systems you consider at work may reside in your team. The near environment of the system will be the organisation you work for. Your system may be influenced by the structures and organisational cultures that surround you. Further away there may be important environmental factors such as national economic conditions or the legal and political framework.

Systems diagrams can become impossibly complicated if you try to include too many elements. Show only the most influential ones. Key points to consider when drawing a systems map are set out in Box 15.2.

Box 15.2 Important points about systems maps

1. A systems map shows the boundary of the system and the different subsystems inside the boundary. It may also show important influences outside the boundary, that is, in the external environment.

2. A map is a map. It does not have arrows showing relationships or influences between the subsystems.

3. The scale and the detail depend on the purpose of the systems map. Keep the map as simple as possible to aid clarity.

4. Ensure the map is clearly labelled. All boundaries and subsystems need to be clearly identified.

5. When changing a system, two drawings are needed: the existing system and the new system. To transform the existing system into the new one requires systems interventions.

Influence diagrams

Influence diagrams show the influences, from within the organisation or from outside it, that bear on a person or unit.

The model

Figure 15.12 shows some of the influences that bear on an organisation. Of course, these influences are felt not by 'an organisation', but by people in the organisation. It is sensible, therefore, to talk about the influences on the management or on the manager within the organisation. Thus, Figure 15.13 shows the organisation as a system, while the manager and the other staff are shown as two subsystems within the main one.

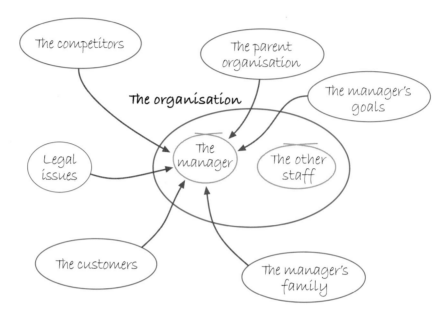

Figure 15.13 Influences on the manager of a firm – influence diagram

The diagram provides the opportunity to identify the external systems or bodies which influence the manager's thinking. Some of the external systems are to do with the organisation's business. They include the competitors, customers and legal rules within which the organisation must operate. If the organisation is a subsidiary, then the parent organisation will be a powerful influence. But other influential systems lie outside what is probably understood as the business. For example, it is sensible to include the manager's family (as an influence to represent the whole of the manager's private life). It will be equally sensible to include the manager's goals.

These two latter influences, the manager's family and the manager's goals, express the strength of this way of portraying the influences on a person's (in this instance, a manager's) behaviour. The range of the analysis is entirely up to the analyst – the person who draws the diagram – to decide. In the example, any system or body can be represented on the diagram if it exerts an influence on the person whose behaviour is being examined. Perhaps one member of the manager's family is particularly influential; in that case, that person alone can be represented, without the rest of the family. In the same way, the manager's goals could be amended to show a particular goal to which the manager is strongly committed. An influence diagram can also be used to explore and identify the extent to which the powerful people within the organisation (the senior managers) are sensitive to the forces outside the organisation which are bearing on the organisation.

Fishbone diagram

There are times when management problems seem too complicated and 'messy' to analyse. A fishbone diagram can be used by both individuals and groups to help to clarify the causes of a difficult problem and capture its complexity. The diagram will help to provide a comprehensive and balanced picture and show the relative importance and interrelationships between different parts of the problem. Box 15.3 sets out how to draw a fishbone diagram.

Box 15.3 Developing a fishbone diagram

1   On a wide sheet of paper, draw a long arrow horizontally across the middle of the page pointing to the right, and label the arrowhead with the title of the issue to be explained. This is the backbone of the fish.

2   Draw spurs coming off the backbone at about 45 degrees, one for every likely cause of the problem; label each at its outer end. Add sub-spurs to represent subsidiary causes. Highlight any causes that appear more than once – they may be significant.

3   Consider each spur and sub-spur, taking the simplest first, partly for clarity but also because a good, simple explanation may make more complex explanations unnecessary.

4   Circle anything that seems to be a key cause so that you can concentrate on it later. Finally, redraw the fishbone diagram so that the relative importance of the different parts of the problem is reflected by its position along the backbone. Draw the most important at the head end.

Figure 15.14 shows the possible causes of failure to meet project deadlines.

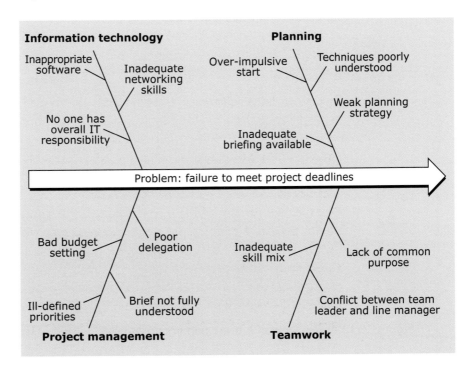

Figure 15.14 Failure to meet project deadlines – a fishbone diagram

We can see there are four main causes. These are the lack of teamwork, project management, information technology and planning. Each of these has been developed to show greater detail.

It is often helpful to develop the fishbone diagram with a group: the analysis and consensus may provide a basis for group action and learning.

Mind mapping

The term mind mapping was devised by Tony Buzan for the representation of such things as ideas, notes and information, in radial tree diagrams. These are sometimes also called spider diagrams. They are widely used – try searching the internet for 'Buzan', 'mind map' or 'concept map'.

Figure 15.15 shows an example adapted from a real problem-solving session (Buzan, 1982).

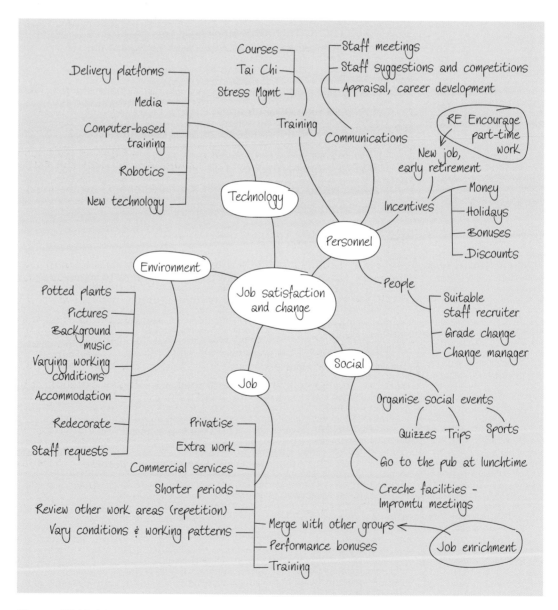

Figure 15.15 An example of a mind map from a problem-solving session

How to draw a mind map is described in Box 15.4.

Box 15.4 How to draw a mind map

1 Put your paper (ideally a large sheet) in landscape format and write a brief title for the overall topic in the middle of the page.

2 For each major sub-topic or cluster of material, start a new major branch from the central topic, and label it.

3 For each sub-subtopic or sub-cluster, form a subsidiary branch to the appropriate main branch. Do this too for ever finer sub-branches.

Tips

- You may want to put an item in more than one place. You can either copy it into each place or draw in a cross-link.

- Show relationships between items on different branches by, for example, coding them using a particular colour or type of writing.

- You can identify particular branches or items with drawings or other pictorial devices to bring the map to life.

There are several mind mapping software packages available. They make it easy to edit and rearrange the map; they can sometimes hold notes and documents associated with labels (so that they can act as filing systems); and some can switch between map and text outline formats. However, computer-based maps are less adaptable than hand-drawn versions (for example, you can't usually make cross-links).

Multiple-cause diagrams

As a general rule, an event or outcome will have more than one cause. A multiple-cause diagram will enable you to show the causes and the ways in which they are connected. Suppose, for example, that you were asked to explain why a work group was under-performing. You could use a multiple-cause diagram both to help you to construct the explanation and to present it.

Figure 15.16 presents a picture of the problem. It shows the connections between the elements, rather like a road map. If you can look at the diagram

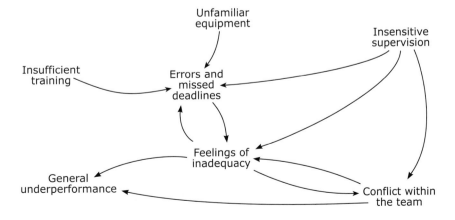

Figure 15.16 Why a work group is under-performing – a multiple-cause diagram

and say 'I can read that diagram, I can see how it explains the under-performance of the work group', then the diagram will have been effective as a means of exposition.

Using a multiple-cause diagram will help you to think about a problem, to explain the problem to other people, and to decide what to do about it. It will expose the connections between the events (including the loops – the occasions when one event leads to another which, in turn, reinforces the first). It will show you the possible routes into the problem. It will remind you of the complexity of the problem and it will help you to guard against taking an inappropriately narrow view of it.

As you construct and revise a multiple-cause diagram you will be reaching your own view of the problem. If someone else studied the problem they would probably draw a diagram that differed from your own. Different views of the nature of a problem mean that there will be different ways of addressing the problem.

Drawing a multiple-cause diagram

We can draw a multiple-cause diagram to explore and to communicate the complexity of a system, and to recognise that the effect of a particular system is normally the result of a number of different causes.

Figure 15.17 shows the multiple causes of poor sales performance from a team.

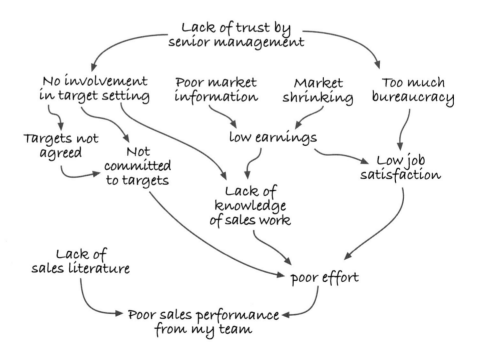

Figure 15.17 Causes of poor sales performance – a multiple-cause diagram

The first task in drawing such a diagram is to identify the output in which you are interested. Generally we take a single output or effect and examine the several causes leading to it. We could try to draw a multiple-cause diagram for two or more effects but the diagram would quickly become impossibly complex.

Having identified the effect we are exploring, we then add the first, or primary, causes of that effect. In this case, we have established two primary causes. These are lack of sales literature and poor performance. We then consider each of these and add their causes. We then move backwards through the different levels of causes of poor effort until we are satisfied that we have a comprehensive diagram to explain the multiple causes of the poor sales performance.

Box 15.5 sets out key points about multiple-cause diagrams.

Box 15.5 Important points about multiple-cause diagrams

1   We are examining the multiple causes of a single output, so all arrows lead along a path to the output.

2   There needs to be a logical cause-and-effect relationship between each link. For example, the link between low earnings and lack of knowledge of sales work may not be clear, and another element such as high staff turnover could be included in the path.

3   A single cause can have a number of effects. An example in the diagram is low earnings that lead to lack of knowledge of sales work and to low job satisfaction. Often these points are the key ones to address: an improvement (on low earnings) will lead to multiple benefits.

4   Consider how the diagram can be developed to make it more effective. Important paths can be highlighted – perhaps the lines can be coloured or made thicker. Key elements can be underlined or bordered.

Drawing multiple-cause diagrams helps in exploring and in communicating complex issues. Practice improves drawing skills and deepens understanding – draw one today!

Activity sequence flow diagram

One of the weaknesses of simple charts for planning and control, or for analysing activities or problem situations, is that they do not show how tasks are related to each other. Issues, functions, resources and so on may be recorded in 'balloons' or boxes that have some relationship to what is being investigated or considered, but the nature and direction of each relationship is not defined. Activity sequence diagrams define these relationships. They are useful in the early stages of analysis, particularly for collecting together preliminary thoughts and ideas prior to more detailed analysis. An example is shown in Box 15.6.

Box 15.6 Streamlining a process

Anja has just been appointed Managing Clerk at a legal practice. Her role also includes that of office manager. The legal practice has eight qualified solicitors, two part-qualified staff, Anja, and eight support staff – a receptionist, secretarial staff and two accounts clerks. The procedure for accepting new business is as follows. Potential new business is identified by telephone call or letter to the senior solicitor, Patrick. He decides which solicitor will handle the business and, after brief consultation, informs Anja. In turn, she informs the accounts department and it is recorded in the business record book. The accounts department then liaises with the solicitor chosen to undertake the work and produces an estimate. Anja then sends the estimate to the potential client. If the client confirms the business, this is noted on the business record.

Anja believes that the process could be streamlined, particularly for relatively-routine business. As a first task in her investigation, she draws up an activity sequence diagram to consider the current situation. Anja's diagram is shown in Figure 15.18.

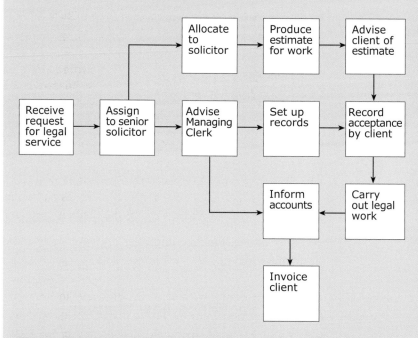

Figure 15.18 Activity sequence diagram – new business

The diagram shows how the component parts are connected and how they influence one another.

Task breakdown chart

A task breakdown chart is a useful planning technique that breaks down the task or project to be planned into its component parts. An example is given in Figure 15.19. You start with the whole job that has to be done and then ask the question: 'What are the two or three (or four or five) main elements that make up this piece of work?' Each one of those is then considered in turn and broken down in the same way to whatever level of detail is helpful to you.

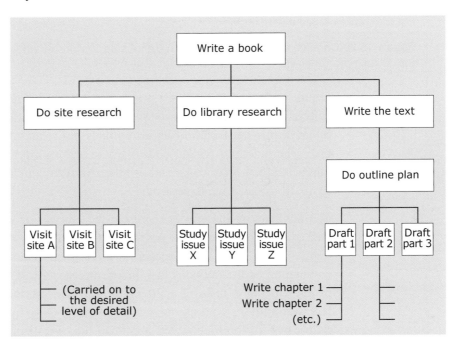

Figure 15.19 The first stages of a task breakdown chart for writing a book

The advantage of a task breakdown chart is that it follows a hierarchical approach. However, it may miss some ideas and concerns that occur to you, since they cannot be captured on the chart unless you annotate it.

Network or critical path analysis

See also: Gantt charts, in this section

For large or complex tasks it is necessary to know which tasks are critical to achieving the deadline; some tasks will depend on the completion of others, for example. Network analysis (or critical path analysis) is used to identify those tasks which *must* be started before others, those that must be completed on time, and those which are not critical on the completion of other tasks and can be delayed if resources are needed to keep the critical tasks on schedule. The 'critical path' is found as a result of the analysis of the network of tasks. This critical path also identifies the minimum time required to complete the project. It is a useful tool for both planning and managing projects. It is often used in conjunction with Gantt charts.

There are many computer software packages that can help a manager to carry out a network analysis but the principles are straightforward.

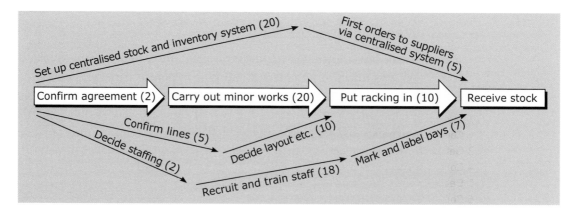

Figure 15.20 Converting surplus space for warehousing – a preparatory diagram for network (or critical path) analysis

Figure 15.20 shows part of a preparatory diagram for a critical path for converting surplus retail space into a warehouse. Each task is represented by an arrow; the length of an arrow does *not* relate to the duration of the task. The junctions (called nodes) where arrows meet would normally be numbered. You may come across other formats which use slightly different terms from those we have used.

The numbers on the arrows represent the number of working days it will take to complete each task. As you can see, there is one critical path highlighted. This is because each of the critical tasks depends on the completion of the previous task before it can start. If you add up the number of days for these tasks (2 + 20 + 10), you will see that stock cannot be received until 32 working days have elapsed. Only by changing the timescales for the highlighted tasks can the overall timescale be reduced. Gaining time on other tasks will not affect the calculation. Some key points to consider when drawing a network analysis are:

1 Some tasks depend on the completion of other tasks to enable them to start.

2 A string of such tasks makes a path through your plan, and that path has a very significant effect on the timescale for your project.

3 The path will tend to define the shortest feasible timescale for the accomplishment of the project, irrespective of the tasks elsewhere.

Gantt charts

Planning involves identifying the tasks that need to be done in the appropriate sequence. The most commonly-used tool for setting out the tasks in this way is the Gantt chart, a form of bar chart (see the earlier section on Bar charts). A Gantt chart is simply a grid with the tasks listed down the left-hand side of the page, a timescale across the top of the page, and bars to indicate the timing of each task (i.e. the length of the bar shows its duration). A bar chart for a warehouse project is shown in Figure 15.21.

For demonstration purposes, the chart is simplified. For example, far less work is involved in task 11, which is an automated one in an IT-based stock and inventory system, than in task 13, recruiting and training staff.

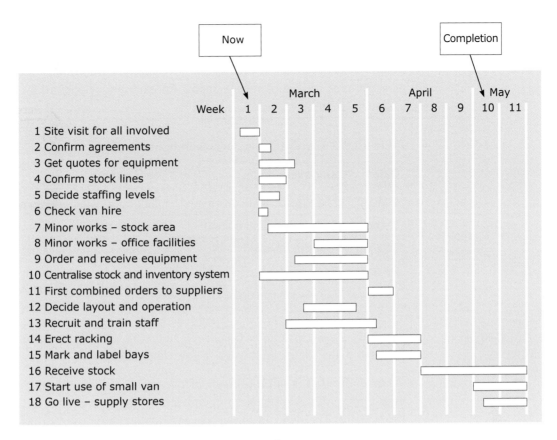

Figure 15.21 Gantt chart for a warehouse project

Gantt charts are adaptable. Some people show a dotted line continuation of a bar to indicate how far a task could overrun its set timescale without causing difficulty. Another variation is to leave sufficient space under each bar to draw in a second line in a different colour to indicate progress to date.

One of the main strengths of the Gantt chart is that it gives an overall picture of the work to be done on a single page. It can be broken down into sub-projects in the case of large, complex projects.

One of the weaknesses of the Gantt chart, however, is that it does not display how tasks are dependent on each other. In the example, task 7, minor works in the stock area (which would typically involve electricians and heating/air conditioning engineers in overhead work), probably needs to be completed before task 14, erecting the racking (special metal shelving for stock), is started; and that in turn needs to be complete before the stock comes in (task 16 on the chart). More information on the interdependence of tasks can be provided through a technique called network analysis.

See also: Network or critical analysis, in this section

Computer software is available for producing Gantt charts, often as a component part of project software which will carry out critical path analysis. Such software can automatically identify resourcing problems, such as when tasks involving one or more of the same people overlap. This is an important human resource aspect which needs to be considered when drawing Gantt charts manually, especially when projects involve small teams.

Key events table

Simple tables can be a useful means of *communicating* the overview of a plan, perhaps for senior management. An example of one, a key events list, is shown in Table 15.9.

Table 15.9 A key events list for a warehouse project

Date	Key event	Other events
9 March	Site agreed and confirmed	Other initial work in progress
8 April	Staff on site and trained	Goods handling equipment ordered
17 April	Racking installed	Bays marked and labelled
20 April	Receive stock	
15 May	Supply small stores	

See also: Gantt charts, in this section

The dates shown would be broadly in line with a Gantt chart for the project, although actual dates might vary a few days either way.

A key events list is not a primary planning tool. It should always be derived from a more detailed planning document, not least to ensure that the dates are realistic. The dates in the key events table can be used to indicate where you should be at a particular time or stage.

Generating ideas

Ways 'into' problems

There are two ends of the spectrum of difficulties we may face when trying to solve problems or make decisions. At one end is a blank sheet of paper and an accompanying blank mind; at the other is a tangled web of information, ideas, hunches, possible solutions and difficulties to avoid, which is seemingly impossible to tease apart.

Problems can often be difficult to analyse and resolve, especially when you are close to them. Here are some different methods you might try in order to *enter* a problem. Don't worry if using a method takes you only so far down the problem-solving route: if it has set you off on a productive line of thinking then it has been effective.

- *Start in the middle.* For example, you might begin by assuming that the work involved in developing a new system has been done. Then work forwards and backwards, working out how the system will operate, and how it might be developed.
- *Start with rival solutions.* Potentially, these could resolve the problem. Consider each and ask:

  Why would this solution work?

  Why would this solution *not* work?

By giving detailed consideration to each solution, you will work through some basic elements of the problem, which you can then focus on with more insight. The eventual solution you develop may be different from both the original ones, or combine the best elements of them.

- *Use metaphors*. What is the problem most like – a machine, an underground transport network, an eco system? You can use these metaphors to visualise aspects of the problem and how they are related, and to consider some possible solutions.
- *Share it*. Tell one or more people and invite them to tell you their thoughts. You will not really be asking them to solve the problem for you; rather you will be seeking different perspectives on it.
- *Work backwards*. Start with the desired solution and work backwards. This may be a good method to apply to the issue of quality improvement as well as problem-solving.

If you are having difficulties recognising the problem, then basic *problem-finding* techniques may help. Setting out to find a problem may seem odd – recall the old adage '*If it ain't broke don't fix it*' – but if you want to improve something and can't quite see how, then you will need to identify ways in which things can be done better.

Creative problem-solving, devised by Sidney J. Parnes in the 1950s and developed by many people since then, suggests the following stepped problem-finding method described by VanGundy in 1988. It is set out in Box 15.7

Box 15.7 Creative problem-solving

See also: Brainstorming, in this section

Step 1 Mess finding. Sensitise yourself (scan, search) for issues (concerns, challenges, opportunities, etc.) that need to be tackled.

Pose suggestions to yourself such as: 'Wouldn't it be nice if ...' and 'Wouldn't it be awful if ...'. Then brainstorm ideas to identify desirable outcomes and obstacles to be overcome. This is an 'opening up' or divergent technique. Conversely, narrow down or *converge* your thinking to highlight areas for improvement. For example, ask yourself a series of questions beginning with: 'In what ways might ...?'

Step 2 Gather information. Ask the five 'wh' questions (who, why, what, when, where), and how. Then compose a list of 'wants' and who expressed them (sources). List all the 'wants' as a series of questions and compile a list of possible sources of answers. Follow up these for each source, and list what you find.

See also: Mind mapping, in this section

Alternatively use mind mapping to sort and classify the information gathered. Then restate the problem in the light of your richer understanding of it.

Step 3 Problem-finding. Convert a fuzzy statement of the problem into a broad statement.

Step 4 Generate as many ideas as possible. Brainstorm ideas and identify promising ones.

Step 5 Select ideas. Shortlist the best ideas generated in Step 4.

Step 6 Gain acceptance for the ideas. Ask yourself how the idea or ideas you have just chosen can be presented persuasively and implemented. Action plans are better developed in small groups of two or three rather than in a large group (unless you particularly want the commitment of the whole group). For 'people' problems it is often worth developing several alternative action plans.

(Source: based on VanGundy, 1988)

Lateral thinking

Lateral thinking is a technique for trying to gain new perspectives. This is useful when you find that your thinking is in a rut such as when you 'go over the same ground' again and again and seem to make little progress.

Lateral thinking, a term coined by Edward de Bono, relies on a willingness to free your mind from its usual disciplined thought patterns and allow it to be stimulated into unpredictable and unaccustomed flights of imagination, which can sometimes be rich and innovative.

It advocates the suspension of all judgement until many ideas have been generated, on the grounds that one idea, although possibly 'wrong', can stimulate further ideas which might prove to be 'right'. De Bono argues that it is better to have enough ideas, even if some of them are wrong, than to be right by having no ideas at all (de Bono, 1982). Similarly, he suggests the deliberate use of 'discontinuity' as a way of triggering new lines of thought. Totally random words can be thrown into the melting pot in the hope that they will spark off new ideas.

The restructuring of problems is also a valuable device for compelling you to look at them in a new light in the hope of coming up with a new solution. 'What if the problem were not to achieve this but to avoid that?' 'What if this factor did not constrain us, what would we do then?' 'What if we did not have to make this assumption?' 'What if that rule did not apply?'

In these ways, it may be possible to redefine a problem or situation. For example, the problem of how to reduce graffiti in the lifts in high-rise residential housing can be redefined as potential problems of:

- how to reduce the time available for scribbling
- how to encourage creative graffiti
- how to make people think someone is watching
- how to use the lift for information collection
- how to occupy people's minds.

Such redefinitions can be achieved using brainstorming (see below). Redefinitions of a situation open up the possibilities for dealing with it in ways that would not have been apparent, and may catch the imagination of those whom the solution is designed to target.

For some people, lateral thinking is a way of life and they are entirely happy to allow their ideas to roam around in apparently unconnected ways. Others, however, may find it very different from their normal ways of thinking and therefore hard to adopt.

Classical brainstorming

Brainstorming is a method of generating ideas and can be used for a wide variety of situations, from problem-solving to making the most of a new opportunity that has arisen. Brainstorming can be carried out by one or many people. The key to successful brainstorming is to separate creative thinking from judgemental thinking. Ideas generated by creative thinking are only later assessed by judgemental thinking to identify the best or most appropriate.

These two principles – suspension of judgement and the generation of as many ideas as possible – lead to four practical rules:

1 *No criticism*. This is to ensure that judgement is deferred, and it is the most important of the four rules. It precludes not only explicit criticism, but also any spoken or unspoken gestures or actions that express criticism, or that any participant feels are critical.

2 *Freewheel*. Expression of ideas must be uninhibited. Whatever comes to mind is welcomed, including random thoughts, images that are funny or apparently irrelevant.

3 *Go for quantity*. The more ideas that are generated and recorded, the more chances there are of finding one that is likely to succeed.

4 *Hitch-hike*. As well as contributing your own ideas, it is important to build on those of others. This encourages the improvement and elaboration of ideas and enhances group interaction.

Only when you have an exhaustive list, that is, no one can think of any more, should you begin to sift through and gradually discard some. However, it is useful to take one or two offbeat or seemingly senseless ideas and try to turn them into useful ones. This 'wildest idea' technique, developed by Rawlinson (1981), can sometimes lead to valuable suggestions. Rawlinson reports that, in a brainstorming session on how to attract customers into a shop, a wild idea was that the staff threw nails on the road outside the shop to stop buses. This led to a number of additional ideas such as asking the bus companies to place a bus stop outside the shop, arranging an upper-floor window display that could be seen by passengers on double-decker buses, and placing advertisements on buses.

Brainstorming sessions can be structured. The procedure for the classical form is set out in Box 15.8.

Box 15.8 Basic procedure for brainstorming

1 Well before the meeting, a suitable problem statement is developed, and a suitable group (of five to ten participants) is selected and invited. A person to record the ideas at the session is identified.

2 Two or three days before the meeting, participants receive a note giving the background to the problem, a problem statement, how the session will run and the four brainstorming rules.

3 The room is set up appropriately. The recorder prepares a good supply of pre-numbered blank sheets of flip-chart paper (or equivalent).

4 The session starts with a review of the brainstorming format, the four rules, and a warm-up session (unrelated to the problem).

5 The problem statement is displayed prominently with a brief question time for clarification. The four rules are repeated.

6 Participants call out ideas as they occur to them, and the recorder writes them down. The facilitator checks that the four rules are followed. It is important the recorder is seen to record every idea (including quiet asides, jokes, and so on) in the contributor's words, or an agreed re-phrase. It helps if the contributors signal each idea clearly and adjust their pace so that there is time to record each idea. It is usually best that the recorder does not contribute, though in a very small group s/he might do so. End the process when the flow of ideas begins to run dry – it should certainly not exceed 30 to 40 minutes.

7 As a separate activity, collate, sort and evaluate the ideas generated in any suitable way, providing the original participants with copies of the results.

Brainstorming is a simple technique, but it is not necessarily easy to apply. It can seem stylised and artificial, and careful handling may be necessary to overcome people's reluctance to engage in games of this kind. The leader needs to be committed to making it succeed, and be able to guide the group through the various stages. The group members should preferably bring a variety of experience and expertise, but the technique is unlikely to succeed if the members of the group are from a wide range of levels of management – the presence of senior staff may constrain the juniors and vice versa. In these circumstances a structured approach such as the nominal group technique may be preferable. Similarly, the presence of non-participating observers is likely to act as a constraining factor. People need to feel free to sound silly and frivolous if they are to brainstorm without restraint.

See also: Nominal group technique, in this section

It is a technique that must be introduced with care and sensitivity. Participants and facilitator need to be skilled and compatible, since adverse group processes can severely reduce its effectiveness.

Nominal group technique

See also: Brainstorming, in this section

The nominal group technique has the advantage that it allows everyone to participate actively in generating ideas and expressing their preferences, and may be appropriate where forceful individuals or status differences inhibit involvement. The steps are set out in Box 15.9. Unlike brainstorming, participants both generate ideas and evaluate them. The procedure may seem rather elaborate but it has been designed to separate idea generation from evaluation, to deal with disagreements safely (with the focus on ideas not individuals) and to provide a sense of *closure* to the process. It is particularly useful in temporary work groups which have to make complex decisions, such as inter-departmental or inter-agency groups, and it has been widely-used in many settings, including community development.

Box 15.9 Nominal group technique (NGT)

NGT has the following stages:

1 **Preparation.** Select groups of six to ten members. Larger groups can be divided up. Give each group a flip-chart.

2 **Brief group members.** Outline the technique and explain the task or question under consideration. For example: 'Our task is to devise new ways of campaigning for a safer environment' or 'Our task is to identify the key problems which lead people discharged from prison to re-offend'.

3 **Silent generation of ideas.** The group members are asked to write down their ideas silently and independently (allow 5–10 minutes).

4 **Round robin to record ideas.** Ask each group member in turn for one idea. The group leader records all the ideas on a flip-chart, using brief statements in the original words of the person concerned whenever possible. Continue until everyone has offered all their ideas and a complete list has been made. At this stage the ideas are NOT discussed (allow 15–20 minutes).

5 **Brief discussion.** Taking one item at a time, members have the opportunity to eliminate obvious duplications, clarify the meaning of ideas, and defend or argue against ideas. Lengthy debates are discouraged as the purpose is to clarify ideas, *not* to resolve differences of opinion (allow 20–40 minutes).

6 **Preliminary vote on importance.** Each person is asked to rank, for example, the top five items in order of importance (the more items on the list the more 'priority items' participants can identify). This is usually done by giving each participant five slips of paper, on which they write their priority items, giving each an appropriate number of votes (five for first priority, four for second top and so on). The slips of paper are collected and the votes for each item are recorded on the flip-chart. This should be done without discussion. The totals for each idea are calculated and clearly displayed.

7 **Discussion of preliminary vote**. The vote is then discussed to examine inconsistent voting patterns and to provide an opportunity to discuss items which are perceived as having too many or too few votes. This allows members to clarify their positions and assures that split votes reflect genuine differences of opinion rather than differences in information or misunderstandings (allow 20–30 minutes).

8 **Final vote**. A final vote is taken as in stage 6.

9 **Selection of items**. Based on the votes, the most important items are selected. The group will need to use its own judgement and set ground rules for which items are included and which are excluded (allow 10 minutes).

10 **Aggregation of several groups**. If several groups are functioning, then their separate votes will need to be aggregated on one main list for final selection by the group as a whole.

Note: It is not always necessary to repeat the voting procedure, especially if a clear understanding of an agreement on the issues has emerged. The *times* given above are indicative only and will vary according to the size of the group and the nature of the issue being discussed.

The idea of different kinds of thinking being used is illustrated in Figure 15.22. You can see that you are using creative or 'divergent' thinking as you open up the possibilities, but you change to analytical or 'convergent' thinking when you start to narrow down the possibilities towards the final choice.

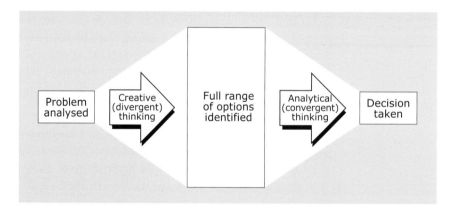

Figure 15.22 Creative and analytical thinking in the decision-making process

Decision trees

Decision trees are usually used to depict options: that is, the various courses of action available for solving a problem or making a choice between options in order to make a decision.

Figure 15.23 is an example drawn from the scenario set out below.

Decisions, decisions...

A university normally sends out leaflets to potential mature students for its wider access campaign. There has been a lot of criticism of the leaflets: they are in A3 format, so that they catch the eye, but they are difficult to fit into small envelopes. Some people argue that leaflets are not needed any more and that other methods are more effective. Advertising in magazines and on the internet have been suggested by some members of the marketing team, while others believe it would be better to run a poster campaign in public places such as libraries and on public transport. If the university continues with the leaflets, however, it could use an A4 design to better fit the envelopes. It would be cheaper to keep the old leaflet and make minor updates; a straight reprint would be the cheapest option of all. However, major changes ought to be considered because the leaflet is becoming out of date; in updating it the university may as well consider a new design.

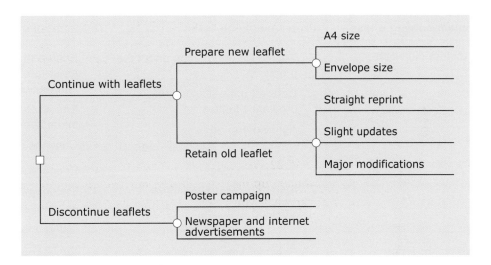

Figure 15.23 A decision tree

Figure 15.23 shows five separate decision points at which there were two or more options to choose from. Clearly, before a decision can be made each of the options has to be evaluated and likely outcomes have to be predicted. The figure allows this to be done with a fair amount of clarity. If something goes wrong, you can re-examine the decision made and ask whether the right one was taken. This is a simple technique that can be applied to many low-level problems where several, linked options are available. For complex problems, use other techniques.

PIPS: Phases of Integrated Problem Solving

PIPS, or Phases of Integrated Problem Solving, devised by Morris and Sashkin (1978), not only defines the various analytic steps required in problem-solving: it also defines the interpersonal activities needed for each step, as shown in Table 15.10, showing the distinction between problem-solving and interpersonal tasks.

PIPS is designed to be used with a problem-solving group and a facilitator, plus one observer to monitor the problem-solving tasks and another to monitor the interpersonal tasks. Ideally the observer roles should be rotated; for example, at the end of each phase the previous observers swap with others in the problem-solving group.

The authors of the PIPS technique also provide a questionnaire (considerably more detailed than Table 15.10) which all participants have for reference, but which the observers fill in. At the end of each step there is a general review of process issues, and members continue to the next step only when all tasks of the previous step have been adequately completed.

The full PIPS process may be good for training, but is probably too cumbersome for routine problem-solving. However, the general principle of placing explicit interpersonal goals alongside the task goals of any problem-solving method is extremely useful.

Table 15.10 Outline of PIPS activities, showing the distinction between problem-solving and interpersonal tasks

Problem-solving phase	Problem-solving tasks	Interpersonal tasks
1 Problem definition	• Search for information about the problem • Detailed understanding of problem situation • Agree group goals	• Ensure that all members of the group are involved in the information search • Encourage open sharing of information about the problem • Consensus building
2 Solution generation	• Brainstorm ideas • Elaborate and refine ideas • Develop tentative list of solutions	• Encourage all to brainstorm • Encourage 'no criticism' • Encourage cooperation when listing solutions
3 Ideas into action	• Evaluate strengths/weaknesses of each idea • Try combining good ideas • Select a tentative solution	• Avoid non-productive criticism • Resolve conflicts over combining/modifying ideas • Consensus building
4 Action planning	• List steps needed for implementation • Identify resources needed • Assign responsibilities for each step	• All participate in listing steps • Group adequately evaluates potential of available resources • Develop real commitments
5 Plan evaluation	• Develop success measures for each step • Timetable to measure progress against • Contingency planning in case steps need modifying	• All contribute to developing success measures • All comfortable with timetable • Real commitments for contingency plans
6 Evaluate product and process	• How well do effects of solution match original goals? • Identify any new problems created • Are any future actions needed?	• How much group participation is there overall? • Can members express themselves freely and offer support? • What has the group learned about itself?

Checklists

Checklists are useful to ensure that nothing has been overlooked. Checklists can be created for every activity and are useful both in recurring situations – in which it is worth making your own personalised checklist – and for unfamiliar situations in which it would be easy to omit something. For the latter situations, the best checklists have been compiled and tested by those who are very experienced. You can then annotate or add to them any special element of your task that you need to remember. Checklists are often in the form of questions – these help you to think. But remember, no checklist is infallible.

Problems: preliminary questions

When you are faced with what seems to be a problem or a situation that needs exploring it can be helpful to know the basic questions to ask. This list of questions is conveniently grouped under the 'wh' questions – who, when, why, what and where. The questions will help you to explore the situation and to gather and categorise basic information about it.

Who

- Who is affected by the problem?
- Who else has it?
- Who says it is a problem?
- Who would like a solution?
- Who would not like a solution?
- Who could prevent a solution?
- Who needs it to be solved more than you do?

When

- When does it occur?
- When doesn't it occur?
- When did it appear?
- When will it disappear?
- When do other people see your problem as a problem?
- When don't other people see your problem as a problem?
- When might it occur again?
- When will it get worse?
- When will it get better?
- When is the solution needed?

Why

- Why is this situation a problem?
- Why do you want to solve it?
- Why don't you want to solve it?
- Why doesn't it go away?
- Why would someone else want to solve it?

- Why wouldn't someone else want to solve it?
- Is it easy to solve?
- Is it hard to solve?

What

- What might change about it?
- What are its main weaknesses?
- What do you like about it?
- What do you dislike about it?
- What can be changed about it?
- What can't be changed?
- What do you know about it?
- What don't you know about it?
- What will it be like if it is solved?
- What will it be like if it isn't solved?
- What have you done in the past with similar problems?
- What principles underlie it?
- What values underlie it?
- What problem elements are related to one another?
- What assumptions are you making about it?
- What seems to be most important about it?
- What seems to be least important about it?
- What are the sub-problems?
- What are your major objectives in solving it?
- What else do you need to know?

Where

- Where is it most noticeable?
- Where is it least noticeable?
- Where else does it exist?
- Where is the best place to begin looking for solutions?
- Where does it fit in the larger scheme of things?

(Source: adapted from VanGundy, 1983)

Implementation checklist

Where you are implementing a plan, it is useful to carry out a series of checks to ensure that you have not missed any essential features. VanGundy (1988) and Isaksen *et al.* (1994) have provided checklists, but they approach implementation from slightly different perspectives, so both lists are included here.

Implementation checklist 1

Resources: Are resources (time, personnel, equipment, money, information) adequate for implementing this idea?

Motivation: Do others possess the motivation and commitment needed for successful implementation?

Resistance: Is the idea likely to encounter 'closed thinking' and/or resistance to change in general?

Procedures: Are there procedural obstacles to overcome?

Structures: What structural obstacles need to be overcome (for example, communication channels that might block implementation)?

Policies: What official/unofficial policies need to be complied with or changed?

Risk: How much risk-taking is likely to be tolerated by those responsible for implementation?

Power: Are there any power struggles going on in the organisation – even if unrelated to the idea – which might block implementation?

Clashes: Are there any interpersonal conflicts that might prevent or hinder the idea from being put into action?

Climate: Is the organisational climate one of cooperation or distrust?

(Source: adapted from VanGundy, 1988)

Implementation checklist 2

Relative advantage

Does my plan demonstrably improve on what's currently done?

What advantages/benefits might there be to accepting it?

Who may gain from it?

How will adopting it reward others or me?

How can I emphasise its benefits to all?

Compatibility

Does it show consistency with current practice/thinking?

Can it be shown to meet a particular group's needs?

Is it a better path to an already shared goal?

What group(s) would endorse it, its goals and actions?

Can it be named/packaged more favourably?

Complexity

Is it easy to understand?

Can it be explained clearly to different people?

Does it take long to communicate to others?

How might it be clarified, made simpler/easier to understand?

Can I demonstrate the new idea/object's ease of use?

Trialability

How can I reduce uncertainty concerning its new elements?

How can I try out sections, before deciding to use it all?

How can I encourage adopters to try part of it?

If it needs full adoption, but senior management insist on partial trials, what then?

How can I change it to make it more-easily tried?

Observability

How easy is it to find/obtain it? Is it visible?

Can it be made more visible? How?

How can I make it easier to understand?

How can I best communicate it?

Are there reasons for not making it visible now?

Other questions to help gain acceptance for the plan

What other resources could help? How can I best use them?

What important obstacles are there? How can I overcome them?

How can I deal with challenges/opportunities it creates?

What might initiate action? And the next steps?

How can I build feedback into it to allow future improvements?

(Source: adapted from Isaksen *et al.*, 1994)

References

Chapter 1

Adams, J., Hayes, J. and Hopson, B. (1976) *Transition: Understanding and Managing Personal Change*, London, Martin Robertson.

CIPD (Chartered Institute of Personnel Development) (2008) Absence Management Annual *Survey Report* [online], http://www.cipd.co.uk/subjects/hrpract/absence/absmagmt.htm (Accessed 25 November 2008).

Drucker, Peter F. (2004) 'What makes a good executive?', *Havard Business Review*, pp. 58–63.

Fayol, H. (1949 [1916]) *General and Industrial Management* (trans. Constance Storrs from the original *Administration Industrielle et Générale*), London, Pitman.

Jennings, E.E. (1952) 'A study of the relationship of some aspects of personality to supervisory success', Ph.D. dissertation, The University of Iowa. Retrieved 3 December 2008 from Dissertations & Theses @ CIC Institutions database (Publication No. AAT 0181809).

Katz, R. (1986) 'Skills of an effective administrator', *Harvard Business Review*, March/April, vol. 64, issue 2, p. 198.

Kotter, J.P. (1999) 'What effective general managers really do', *Harvard Business Review*, March/April, vol. 77, issue 2, pp. 145–59.

Management Standards Centre (2002–2004) *Management Standards* [online], Management Standards Centre, http://www.management-standards.org/ (Accessed 3 December 2008).

Mintzberg, H. (1971) 'Managerial work: analysis from observation', *Management Science*, October.

Stewart, R. (1982) 'A model for understanding managerial jobs and behaviour', *The Academy of Management Review*, vol. 7, issue 1, pp. 7–13.

Chapter 2

Akkirman, A.D. and Harris, D.L. (2005) 'Organisational communication satisfaction in the virtual workplace', *Journal of Management Development*, vol. 25, issue 5, pp. 397–409.

Austin, J.L. (1962) *How To Do Things With Words* (ed. J.O. Urmson and Marina Sbisá), Cambridge, MA, Harvard University Press.

Bartels, J., Pruyn, A., de Jong, M. and Joustra, I. (2007) 'Multiple organisational identification levels and the impact of perceived external prestige and communication climate', *Journal of Organizational Behaviour*, vol. 28, pp. 173–90.

Bennett, M. (1987) 'Towards ethnorelativism: A developmental model of intercultural sensitivity' in Paige, M. (ed.) *Cross Cultural Orientation: New Conceptions and Applications*, University Press of America, pp. 27–69.

Berry, G.R. (2006) 'Can computer-mediated asynchronous communication improve team processes and decision making: Learning from the management literature', *Journal of Business Communication*, vol. 43, issue 4, pp. 344–66.

Boone, R.T. and Buck, R. (2003) 'Emotional expressivity and trustworthiness: The role of nonverbal behaviour in the evolution of cooperation', *Journal of Nonverbal Behaviour*, vol. 27, issue 3, pp. 163–82.

Bouwman, H., van den Hooff, B., van de Wijngaert, L. and van Dijk, J. (2005) *Information and Communication Technologies in Organisations*, London, Sage Publications.

Bremner, S. (2006) 'Politeness, power, and activity systems: Written requests and multiple audiences in an institutional setting', *Written Communication*, vol. 23, pp. 397–423.

Brown, P. and Levinson, S.C. (1987) *Politeness: Some Universals in Language Usage* (Studies in Interactional Sociolinguistics), Cambridge University Press.

Bull, P. (1983) *Bodily Movement and Interpersonal Communication*, New Delhi, John Wiley & Sons.

Chartered Institute of Personnel and Development (2006) *How engaged are British employees? Survey Report*, CIPD, London [online], http://www.cipd.co.uk/subjects/empreltns/general/_hwngdbremp.htm?IsSrchRes=1 (Accessed 16 January 2009).

Daft, R.L. and Lengel, R.H. (1986) 'Organizational information requirements, media richness and structural design', *Management Science*, vol. 32, issue 5, pp. 554–71.

Daft, R.L., Lengel, R.H. and Trevino, L.K. (1987) 'Message equivocality, media selection, and manager performance: Implications for information systems', *MIS Quarterly*, September, pp. 355–66.

Deaux, K., Dane, F.C. and Wrightsman, L.S. (1993) *Social Psychology in the 90s*, Pacific Grove, CA, Brooks/Cole Publishing.

Decety, J. and Jackson, P.L. (2006) 'A social-neuroscience perspective on empathy', *Current Directions in Psychological Science*, vol. 25, issue 2, pp. 54–8.

Dimmick, J., Kline, S. and Stafford, L. (2000) 'The gratification niches of personal e-mail and the telephone', *Communication Research*, vol. 27, issue 2, pp. 227–48.

Fahlman, Scott, personal website [online], http://www.cs.cmu.edu/~sef/sefSmiley.htm (Accessed 22 October 2008).

Fulk, J., Schmitz, J. and Steinfeld, C.W. (1990) 'A social influence model of technology use' in Fulk, J. and Steinfield, C.W. (eds) *Organizations and Communication Technology*, Newbury Park, CA, Sage, pp. 117–40.

Gibb, J. (1961) 'Defensive communication', *The Journal of Communication*, vol. 11, issue 3, pp. 141–8.

Gibson, D.R. (2008) 'How the outside gets in: Modeling conversational permeation', *Annual Review of Sociology*, vol. 34, pp. 359–84.

Goffman, E. (1967) 'On face-work: An analysis of ritual elements in social interaction', Interaction Ritual, Pantheon Books. Reprinted in *Reflections*, vol. 4, issue 3, 2003, pp. 7–13.

Guild, W.L. (2002) 'Relative importance of stakeholders: Analysing speech acts in a layoff', *Journal of Organizational Behavior*, vol. 23, pp. 837–52.

Hall, E.T. (1959) *The Silent Language*, New York, Anchor.

Hollingshead, A.B., McGrath, J.E. and O'Connor, K.M. (1993) 'Group task performance and communication technology: A longitudinal study of computer-mediated versus face-to-face work groups', *Small Group Research*, vol. 24, issue 3, pp. 307–33.

Ley, R. (2006) 'Speak up and call the shots', *The Times*, 2 September.

Murray, S.R. and Peyrefitte, J. (2007) 'Knowledge type and communication media choice in the knowledge transfer process', *Journal of Managerial Issues*, vol. 19, issue 1, pp. 111–33.

Ohala, J.J. (1984) 'An ethological perspective on common cross-language utilization of F0 of voice', *Phonetica*, vol. 41, pp. 1–16.

Patterson, M.L. (2003) 'Commentary. Evolution and nonverbal behaviour: Functions and mediating processes', *Journal of Nonverbal Behaviour*, vol. 27, issue 3, pp. 201–7.

Robertson, E. (2005) 'Placing leaders at the heart of organizational communication: A model to improve internal communication climate', *Strategic Communication Management*, vol. 9, issue 5, pp. 4–37. First published in *Strategic Communication Management*, vol. 1, issue 1, 1997.

Sacks, H., Schegloff, E.A. and Jefferson, G. (1974) 'A simplest systematics for the organization of turn-taking in conversation', *Language*, vol. 50, issue 4, pp. 696–735.

Schegloff, E.A., Jefferson, G. and Sacks, H. (1977) 'The preference for self-correction in the organization of repair for conversation', *Language*, vol. 53, pp. 361–82.

Shannon, C. and Weaver, W. (1949) *The Mathematical Theory of Communication*, University of Illinois Press.

van den Hoof, B., Groot, J. and de Jonge, S. (2008) 'Situational influence on the use of communication technologies: A meta-analysis and exploratory study', *Journal of Business Communication*, vol. 42, issue 4, pp. 4–27.

Wilkins, R. (2005) 'The optimal form: Inadequacies within the Asiallinin (matter of fact) non-verbal style in public and civic settings in Finland', *Journal of Communication*, vol. 55, issue 2, pp. 383–401.

Chapter 3

de Bono, E. (1982) *Lateral Thinking for Management*, Harmondsworth, Penguin.

Drucker, P.F. (1955) *The Practice of Management*, London, Heinemann.

Fradd, E.H. (1988) 'Achieving change in the clinical area: Supporting innovation', *Senior Nurse*, vol. 8, no. 12, pp. 19–21.

Harris, R. (2008) *Case study – 'assumption articulation'* [online], http://gloriahuston.org/ps/quotes.html (Accessed 28 May 2008).

March, J.G. (1978) 'Bounded rationality, ambiguity, and the engineering choice', *Journal of Economics*, vol. 9, pp. 587–608.

March, J.G. (1981) 'Decision-making perspective: Decisions in organizations and theories of choice' in van de Ven, A.H. and Joyce, W.F. (eds) *Perspectives on Organization Design and Behaviour*, New York, John Wiley, pp. 205–44.

Peckham, M. (1996) 'Teams: Wrong box, wrong time', *Management Development Review*, vol. 9, issue 4 [online], http://www.emeraldinsight.com/Insight/ViewContentServlet? Filename=Published/EmeraldFullTextArticle/Articles/0110090405.html (Accessed 28 May 2008).

Simon, H.A. (1960) *The New Science of Management Decision*, New York, Harper Row.

Stewart, R. (1982) *Choices for the Manager*, Englewood Cliffs, NJ, Prentice-Hall.

Chapter 4

Bloor, K. and Maynard, A. (1999) *Clinical Governance: Clinician Heal Thyself*, London, The Institute of Health Services Management.

Brager, G.A. and Sprecht, H. (1973) *Community Organizing*, New York, Columbia University Press.

Bronte-Tinkey, J., Joyner, K. and Allen, T. (2007) 'Five steps for selecting an evaluator: A guide for out-of-school time practitioners', *Child Trends*, October [online], http://www.childtrends.org/Files//Child_Trends-2007_10_01_RB_SelectingEvaluator.pdf (Accessed 28 November 2008).

Centre for Social Research Methods [online], http://www.socialresearchmethods.net/ (Accessed 7 December 2008).

Charities Evaluation Service [online], http://www.ces-vol.org.uk/ (Accessed 28 November 2008).

de Bono, E. (1982) Lateral Thinking for Management, Harmondsworth, Penguin.

Drucker, P.F. (1955) The Practice of Management, London, Heinemann.

Fradd, E.H. (1988) 'Achieving change in the clinical area: supporting innovation', Senior Nurse, Vol. 8, No. 12, pp. 19–21.

Huf Haus [online] http://www.huf-haus.com/ (Accessed 28 November 2008).

Kepner, C.H. and Tregoe, B.B. (1981) *The New Rational Manager*, Princeton, NJ, Kepner–Tregoe, Inc.

Lindblom, C.E. (1959) 'The science of muddling through', *Public Administration Review*, no. 19, pp. 79–88.

McCollam, A. and White, J. (1993) *Building on Experience*, Edinburgh, Scottish Association for Mental Health.

National Bee Unit. https://secure.csl.gov.uk/beebase/ (Accessed 28 November 2008).

Quality Standards Task Group (QSTG) (1998) A 'White Paper' on Quality Standards in the Voluntary Sector, London, NCVO.

UK Evaluation Society [online], http://www.evaluation.org.uk/ (Accessed 28 November 2008).

Rawlinson, J.G. (1981) *Introduction to Creative Thinking and Brainstorming*, London, British Institute of Management Foundation.

Sargent, A. (1976) *Decision Taking*, London, Industrial Society.

Slack, N. and Chambers, S. (2007) *Operations Management*. Essex, FT/Prentice-Hall.

Van Gundy, A.B. Jr (1988) *Techniques of Structural Problem Solving*, 2nd edn, New York, Van Nostrand Reinhold.

Chapter 5

Lucey, T. (1991) *Management Information Systems*, DP Publications, London.

Martin, C. and Powell, P. (1992) *Information Systems: A Management Perspective*, New York, McGraw-Hill.

Miller, K.A. (2004) *Surviving Information Overload*, Grand Rapids, MI, Zondervan.

Strassman, P.A. (1985) *Information Payoff: The Transformation of Work in the Electronic Age*, reprinted with the permission of The Free Press, a division of Simon and Schuster. Copyright © Paul A. Strassman 1985.

Wurman, R.S. [online], http://www.wurman.com/ (Accessed 7 November 2008).

Chapter 6

Currie, D. (2006) *Introduction to Human Resource Management: A Guide to Personnel in practice,* London: CIPD

Herriot, P., Manning, W.E.G. and Kidd, J.M.(1997) 'The content of the psychological contract', *British Journal of Management,* Vol. 8 pp. 151–62.

Herzberg, F.W., Mausner, B and Snyderman, B. (1957) *The Motivation to Work,* New York, Wiley.

Maslow, A.H. (1943) 'A theory of human motivation', *Psychological review,* 50(4), 370–96.

Schein, E.H. (1978) *Career Dynamics: Matching Individual and Organizational Needs*, Reading, MA, Addison-Wesley.

Vroom, V.H. (1964) *Work and Motivation,* New York, Wiley.

Vroom, V.H. (1970) *Management and Motivation,* Harmondsworth, Penguin.

Watson, T.J., (2002) *Organising and Managing Work: Organisational, Managerial and Strategic Behaviour in Theory and Practice*, Harlow: Pearson Education Limited.

Chapter 7

Blake, R.R., Mouton, J.S. and Bidwell, A.C. (1962) 'The managerial grid', *Advanced Management Office Executive*, vol. 1, issue 9, pp. 12–15, 36.

Bolden, R. (2008) *Distributed Leadership in Leadership: the Key Concepts*, (ed. A. Marturano and J. Gosling), London, Routledge.

Department of Children, Schools and Families (2007) *Subject Leader Mentor Training* [online], http://www.standards.dfes.gov.uk/sie/si/SfCC/goodpractice/slmt/ (Accessed 14 January 2009).

Fiedler, F.E. (1967) *A Theory of Leadership Effectiveness*, New York, McGraw-Hill.

Fulop, L., Linstead, S. and Dunford, R. (2004) 'Leading and managing' in Linstead, S., Fulop, L. and Lilley, S. *Management and Organization: A Critical Text*, Basingstoke, Palgrave Macmillan.

Gabriel, Y. (2005) 'MBA and the education of leaders: the new playing fields of Eton?', *Leadership*, vol. 1, issue 2, p. 147.

Grint, K. (ed.) (1997) *Leadership: Classical, Contemporary, and Critical Approaches*, Oxford, Oxford University Press.

Grint, K. (2000) *The Arts of Leadership*, Oxford, Oxford University Press.

Grint, K. (2004) 'Twenty-first century leadership' in Cooper, C.L. (ed.) *The Twenty-first Century Manager: Changing Management in Tomorrow's Company*, Oxford, Oxford University Press.

Grint, K. (2005) 'Twenty-first century leadership – the God of small things; or putting the 'ship' back into leadership' in Cooper, C.L. (ed.) *Leadership and*

Management in the Twenty-first Century: Business Challenges of the Future, Oxford, Oxford University Press.

Hersey, P. and Blanchard, K.H. (1988) *Management of Organizational Behavior* (5th edn), Englewood Cliffs, NJ, Prentice-Hall.

Hosking, D.M. (1997) 'Organizing, leadership and skilful process' in Grint, K. (ed.) *Leadership: Classical, Contemporary, and Critical Approaches*, Oxford, Oxford University Press.

Mumford, A. (1997) *How Managers Can Develop Managers*, Aldershot, Gower Publishing.

Pedler, M., Burgoyne, J. and Boydell, T. (2007) (5thedn) *A Manager's Guide to Self Development*, Maidenhead, McGraw-Hill Professional.

Yukl, G. (2004) 'Tridimensional leadership theory: a roadmap for flexible, adaptive leaders' in Burke, J.K. and Cooper, C.L. (eds) *Leading in Turbulent Times: Managing in the New World of Work,* Oxford, Blackwell Publishing.

Chapter 8

Adair, J. (1983) *Effective Leadership*, Aldershot, Gower.

Bateman, B., Wilson, F.C. and Bingham, D. (2002) 'Team effectiveness – development of an audit questionnaire', *Journal of Management Development,* vol. 21, issue 3, pp. 215–26.

Belbin, R.M. (1981) *Management Teams: Why They Succeed or Fail*, London, Butterworth-Heinemann.

Bennett, R. (1994) *Organisational Behaviour* (2nd edn), London, Pitman.

Boddy, D. (2005) *Management: an Introduction* (3rd edn), London, Financial Times/Prentice Hall.

CIPD (2008) *Fact Sheet on Teamworking* [online], http://www.cipd.co.uk/subjects/maneco/general/teamwork (Accessed November 2008).

Fisher, S.G., Hunter, T.A. and Macrosson, W.D.K. (2001) 'A validation study of Belbin's team roles', *European Journal of Work and Organizational Psychology*, vol. 10, issue 2, pp. 121–44.

Hackman, J.R. (1990) *Groups that Work (and Those that Don't),* San Francisco, CA, Jossey-Bass.

Hackman, J.R. (2002) *Leading Teams: Setting the Stage for Great Performances*, Boston, MA, Harvard Business School Press.

Hill, L.A. and Farkas, M.T. (2001) 'A Note on Team Process', Harvard Business Online (for educators).

Ingram, H., Teare, R., Scheuing, E. and Armistead, C. (1997) 'A systems model of effective teamwork', *The TQM Magazine*, vol. 9, issue 2, pp. 118–27.

Kakabadse, A., Ludlow, R. and Vinnicombe, S. (1988) *Working in Organizations*, Harmondsworth, Penguin.

Katzenbach, J. and Smith, D. (1993) *The Wisdom of Teams*, Boston, MA, Harvard Business School Press.

Mabey, C., Salaman, G. and Story, J. (1998) *Human Resource Management: a Strategic Introduction* (2nd edn), Oxford, Blackwell Publishers.

Makin, P., Cooper, C. and Cox, C. (1989) *Managing People at Work*, London, British Psychological Society.

Neale, R. and Mindel, R. (1992) 'Rigging up multicultural teamworking', *Personnel Management*, January, pp. 36–9.

Peckham, M. (1996) 'Teams: wrong box, wrong time', *Management Development Review*, vol. 4, pp. 26–8.

Ruble, T. and Thomas, K. (1976) 'Support for a two-dimensional model of conflict behaviour', *Organizational Behaviour and Human Performance*, vol. 16, p. 145.

Schermerhorn, J.R., Hunt, J.G. and Osborn, R.N. (1995) *Basic Organizational Behavior*, New York, Wiley.

Tuckman, B. and Jensen, M. (1977) 'Stages of small group development revisited', *Groups and Organization Studies*, vol. 2, pp. 419–27.

Weiss, J. (1996) *Managing Diversity, Cross-Cultural Dynamics, and Ethics*, Minneapolis/St. Paul, MN, West Pub. Co.

West, M.A. (2004) *Effective Teamwork: Practical Lessons from Organizational Research* (2nd edn), Oxford, BPS/Blackwell.

Whetten, D.A. and Cameron, K.S. (1984) *Developing Management Skills: Managing Conflict*, New York, HarperCollins.

Zigurs, I. (2003) 'Leadership in virtual teams: oxymoron or opportunity', *Organizational Dynamics*, vol. 31, issue 4, pp. 339–51.

Chapter 9

Bertolino, M. and Steiner, D.D. (2007) 'Fairness reactions to selection methods: an Italian study', *International Journal of Selection and Assessment*, vol. 15, issue 2 (June).

Billsberry, J. (ed.) (1996) *The Effective Manager: Perspectives and Illustrations*, London, Sage/The Open University.

Billsberry, J. (2000) *Finding and Keeping the Right People* (2nd edn), London/ Milton Keynes, Prentice-Hall.

Broussard, R.D. and Brannen, D.E. (1986)

Carless, S. (2005) 'Person–job fit versus person–organization fit as predictors of organizational attraction and job acceptance intentions: a longitudinal study', *Journal of Occupational and Organizational Psychology*, vol. 79, pp. 411–29.

Cascio, W.F. (1975) 'Accuracy of verifiable biographical information blank responses', *Journal of Applied Psychology*, vol. 60, pp. 767–9.

Cober, R.T., Brown, D.J. and Levy, P.E. (2004) 'Form, content and function: an evaluative methodology for corporate employment websites', *Human Resource Management*, vol. 43, Summer/Fall issue, pp. 201–18.

Currie, D. (2006) *Introduction to Human Resource Management: a Guide to Personnel in Practice*, London, CIPD.

Dessler, G. (1988) *Personnel Management* (4th edn), London, Prentice-Hall.

Dessler, G. (2004) *A Framework for Human Resource Management* (3rd edn), New Jersey, Pearson Education.

Flanagan, J.C. (1954) 'The critical incident technique', *Psychological Bulletin*, vol. 52, pp. 327–58.

Goldstein, I.L. (1971) 'The application blank: how honest are applicant responses?', *Journal of Applied Psychology*, vol. 55, pp. 491–2.

Harris, D.M. and DeSimone, R.L. (1994) *Human Resource Development*, Fort Worth, TX, Dryden Press.

Hirsch, J.B. (2009) 'Choosing the right tools to find the right people', *Psychologist*, vol. 22, issue 9, pp. 752–755.

Hirsh, J.R. and Peterson, J.B. (2008) 'Predicting creativity and academic success with a "fake-proof" measure of the Big Five', *Journal of Research in Personality*, vol. 42, pp. 1323–1333.

Jenner, S. and Taylor, S. (2008) 'Employer branding, fad or the future of HR?', *CIPD Employer Branding Research Insight*, London, CIPD, pp. 7–9.

Ludlow, R. and Panton, F. (1991) *The Essence of Successful Staff Selection*, London, Prentice-Hall.

Marchington, M. and Wilkinson, A. (1996) *Core Personnel and Development*, London, Institute of Personnel and Development.

Ployhart, R.E. (2006) 'Staffing in the twenty-first century: new challenges and strategic opportunities', *Journal of Management*, vol. 36, issue 6, pp. 868–97.

Potosky, D., Bobko, P. and Roth, P. (2005) 'Forming composites of cognitive ability and alternative measures to predict job performance and reduce adverse impact: corrected estimates and realistic expectations', *International Journal of Selection and Assessment*, vol. 15, issue 4 (December).

Schmidt, F.L. and Hunter, J.E. (1998) 'The validity and utility of selection methods in personnel psychology: practical and theoretical implications of 85 years of research findings', *Psychological Bulletin*, vol. 124, pp. 262–74.

Schmidt, F.L. and Hunter, J. (2004) 'General mental ability in the world of work: occupational attainment and job performance', *Journal of Personality and Social Psychology*, vol. 86, issue 1, pp. 162–173.

Wanous, J.P. (1992) *Organizational Entry: Recruitment, Selection and Socialization of Newcomers* (2nd edn), Reading, MA, Addison-Wesley.

Chapter 10

Armstrong, M. and Baron, A. (2004) *Managing Performance: Performance Management in Action*, London, CIPD.

Beardwell, J. and Clayton, T. (2007) *Human Resource Management: a Contemporary Approach* (5th edn), Harlow, Pearson Education.

Burke, J. and Cooper, C. (2005) *Reinventing HRM, Challenges and New Directions*, London, Routledge.

Chartered Institute of Personnel and Development (2008) 360 Feedback [online], (Accessed 19 March 2009).

Currie, D. (2006) *Introduction to Human Resource Management: a Guide to Personnel in Practice*, London, CIPD.

Dessler, G. (2004) *A Framework for Human Resource Management* (3rd edn), New Jersey, Pearson Education.

Drucker, P.F. (1954) *The Practice of Management*, New York, Harper & Row.

Gold, J. (2003) 'Appraisal and performance management' in Bratton, J. and Gold, J., *Human Resource Management: Theory and Practice*, Basingstoke, Palgrave Macmillan.

Pinnington, A. and Edwards, T. (2000) *Introduction to Human Resource Management*, Oxford, Oxford University Press.

Chapter 11

Argyris, C. and Schön, D.A. (1978) *Organisational Learning: A Theory of Action Perspective*, London, Addison-Wesley.

Armstrong, M. (2006) *A Handbook of Human Resource Management Practice* (10th edn), London, Kogan Page.

Bates, R. (2004) 'A critical analysis of evaluation practice: the Kirkpatrick model and the principle of beneficence', *Evaluation and Program Planning*, vol. 27, pp. 341–7.

Berge, Z., de Verneil, M., Berge, N., Davis, L. and Smith, D. (2002) 'The increasing scope of training and development competency', *Benchmarking: An International Journal*, vol. 9, issue 1, pp. 43–61.

Caplan, J. (2003) *Coaching for the Future: How Smart Companies Use Coaching and Mentoring*, London, CIPD.

Chartered Institute of Personnel and Development (2004) *Elearning Survey Results Report*, London, CIPD.

Collin, A. (2007) 'Learning and development' in Beardwell, J. and Claydon, T. (eds) *Human Resource Management: A Contemporary Approach* (5th edn), Harlow, Prentice Hall/Financial Times.

Clutterbuck, D. (2004) *Everyone Needs a Mentor: Fostering Talent at Work*, (4th Edn), London, CIPD.

Clutterbuck, D. and Sweeney, J. (1998) 'Coaching and mentoring' in Lock, D. (ed.) (1998) *The Gower Handbook of Management*, Aldershot, Gower.

Clutterbuck, D. and Megginson, D. (2005) *Making Coaching Work: Creating a Coaching Culture*, London, CIPD.

Downey, M. (2003) *Effective Coaching*, New York, Thompson Texere.

Easterby-Smith, M. and Araujo, L. (1999) 'Current debates and opportunities' in Easterby-Smith, M., Araujo, L. and Burgoyne, J. (eds) *Organisational Learning and the Learning Organisation,* London, Sage.

Eby, L.T., McManus, S.E., Simon, S.A. and Russell, J.E.A. (2000) 'The protégé's perspective regarding negative mentoring experiences: The development of taxonomy', *Journal of Vocational Behaviour*, vol. 57, pp. 1–21.

Goldstein, L.L. and Ford, J.K. (2002) *Training in Organizations*, Belmont, CA, Wadsworth.

Johns, C. (2000) *Becoming a Reflective Practitioner: a Reflective and Holistic Approach to Clinical Nursing, Practice Development and Clinical Supervision*, Oxford, Blackwell Publishing.

Kirkpatrick, D.L. (1959) 'Techniques for evaluating training programs', *Journal of the American Society of Training and Development*, vol. 13, pp. 3–9.

Knowles, M. (1980) *The Modern Practice of Adult Education*, Englewood Cliffs, NJ, Prentice Hall Regents.

Kolb, D.A. and Fry, R. (1975) 'Towards an applied theory of experiential learning' in Cooper, C.L. (ed.) *Theories of Group Processes*, New York, John Wiley.

Mayo, A. (2004) *Creating a Learning and Development Strategy: the HR Business Partner's Guide to Developing People* (2nd edn), London, CIPD.

Meggison, D. (1996) 'Planned and emergent learning: consequences for development', *Management Learning*, vol. 27, issue 4, pp. 411–28.

Mumford, A. (1993) *Management Development: Strategies for Action* (2nd edn), London, CIPD.

Mumford, A. (1998) *How Managers Can Develop Managers*, Aldershot, Gower publishing.

Mumford, A (1988) 'Learning to learn and management self-development' in Pedler, M., Burgoyne, J. and Boydell, T. (eds) *Applying Self-Development in Organizations*. New York, Prentice Hall.

Nickols, F.W. (2000) 'The knowledge in knowledge management' in Cortada, J.W. and Woods, J.A. (eds) *The Knowledge Management Yearbook 2000–2001*Boston, MA, Butterworth-Heinemann (pp. 12–21).

Nonaka, I. and Takeuchi, H. (1995) *The Knowledge Creating Company*, Oxford, Oxford University Press.

Pedler, M., Burgoyne, J. and Boydell, T. (1991) *The Learning Company: a Strategy for Sustainable Development*, London, McGraw-Hill.

Pedler, M. Burgoyne, J. and Boydell, T. (2007) *A Manager's Guide to Self Development* (5th edn), Maidenhead, McGrew Hill Professional.

Phillips-Jones, L. (1982) *Mentors and Protégés: How to establish, strengthen and get the most from a mentor/protégé relationship*, New York, Arbor House.

Revans, R. (1998) *The ABC of Action Learning*, London, Lemos and Crane.

Schön, D.A. (1983) *The Reflective Practitioner: How Professionals Think in Action*, London, Maurice Temple Smith Ltd.

Senge, P. (1990) *The Fifth Discipline: the Art of Practice of the Learning Organization*, New York, Doubleday.

Stead, V. (2005) 'Mentoring: a model for leadership development?', *International Journal of Training and Development*, vol. 9, no. 3.

Stufflebeam, D.L. (2002) *CIPP Evaluation Model Checklist: a Tool for Applying the Fifth Installment of the CIPP Model to Assess Long-term Enterprises* [online]Western Michigan University, The Evaluation Center.

Tamkin, P., Yarnall, J. and Kerrin, M. (2002) 'Kirkpatrick and beyond: a review of models of training evaluation', Report 392, *Institute for Employment Studies* [online] October (Accessed 29 January 2009).

Whitmore, J. (2002) *Coaching for Performance,* London, Nicholas Brearley Publishing.

Whittaker, J. (1992) 'Making a policy of keeping up to date', *Personnel Management*, March, pp. 28–31.

Chapter 12

Blader, S.L. and Tyler, T.R. (2003) 'What constitutes fairness in work settings? A four-component model of procedural justice', *Human Resource Management Review*, vol. 13, pp. 107–26.

Brun, J-P. and Dugas, N. (2008) 'An analysis of employee recognition: perspectives on human resource practices', *The International Journal of Human Resource Management*, vol. 19, issue 4, pp. 716–30.

BSI Management Systems (2008) [online] (Accessed 14 November 2008).

Chartered Institute of Personnel Management (2006) http://www.cipd.co.uk/subjects/hrpract/general/hrqualstan?cssversion[online], Accessed 14 November 2008.

Chartered Institute for Personnel Development (2008) *Stress at Work* [online] (Accessed 18 November 2008).

Davidson, M.C.G. (2003) 'Does organizational climate add service quality in hotels?' The *International Journal of Contemporary Hospitality Management*, vol. 15, issue 4, pp. 206–13.

Davidson, M.C.G., Manning, M., Timo, N., Ryder, P. (2001) 'The dimensions of organizational climate in four and five Australian hotels', *Journal of Hospitality and Tourism Research*, vol. 25, issue 4, pp. 444–61.

Deal, T.E. and Kennedy, A.A. (1982) *Corporate Cultures: The Rites and Rituals of Corporate Life*, Harmondsworth, Penguin Books.

Ek, A., Akselsson, R., Arvidsson, M. and Johansson, C.R. (2007) 'Safety culture in Swedish air traffic control', *Safety Science*, vol. 45, pp. 791–811.

Ford, R.C., Newstrom, J.W. and McLaughlin, F.S. (2004) 'Making workplace fun more functional', *Industrial and Commercial Training*, vol. 36, issue 3, pp. 117–20.

Handy, C.B. (1985) *Understanding Organizations* (3rd edn), Harmondsworth, Penguin Books.

Harrison, R. (1972) 'Understanding your organization's character', *Harvard Business Review*, May, pp. 119–28.

Haukelid, K. (2008) 'Theories of culture revisited – an anthropological approach', *Safety Science*, vol. 46, pp. 413–26.

Health and Safety Executive (HSE) (2008) *An Example of a Stress Policy* [online] (Accessed 17 November 2008).

Heathfield, S.M. (2008) 'Employee recognition rocks: kick employee recognition up a notch' [online] (Accessed 17 November 2008).

Hilhorst, D. and Schmiemann, N. (2002) 'Humanitarian principles and organisational culture: everyday practice in Médecins Sans Frontières–Holland', *Development in Practice*, vol. 12, issue 3/4, August, pp. 490–500.

Hofstede, G. (2001) *Culture's Consequences* (2nd edn) Thousand Oaks, CA, Sage.

Hunter, S.T., Bedell, K.E. and Mumford, M.D. (2007) 'Climate for creativity: a quantitative review', *Creativity Research Journal*, vol. 19, issue 1, pp. 69–90.

Jackson, T. (1998) 'New-style quality is just a fiddle', *Financial Times*, 29 December, pp. 12–13.

Kleber, H. (1947) *The Theory of Social and Economic Organisation*, NY, Oxford University Press.

Koys, D.J. and De Cotiis, T.A. (1991) 'Inductive measures of psychologist climate', *Human Relations*, vol. 44, issue 3, pp. 265–85.

Lewicki, R.J. and Tomlinson, E.C. (2003) 'Trust and trust building', The Beyond Intractability Project, Boulder, University of Colorado [online] (Accessed 14 November 2008).

Mackay, C.J., Cousins, R., Kelly, P.J., Lee, S. and McCaig, R.H. (2004) 'Management standards and work-related stress in the UK: policy background and science', *Work and Stress*, vol. 18, issue 2, pp. 91–112.

McNulty Offshore Construction (2008) [online] (Accessed 14 November 2008).

Moyle, P. (2006) 'How to reduce stress in the workplace', *People Management*, August.

Pollit, D. (2006) 'Pressure management keeps down the stress at Toshiba UK', *Human Resource Management International Digest*, vol. 14, issue 5, pp. 29–30.

Schein, E.H. (1992) *Organizational Culture and Leadership*, San Francisco, CA, Jossey-Bass.

Taylor Bloxam (2008) [online] (Accessed 14 November 2008).

Chapter 13

Choueke, M. (2008) 'The credit crunch is really hitting home', *Sunday Telegraph*, 9 September, p. 2.

Crane, A. and Matten, D. (2007) *Business Ethics: Managing Corporate Citizenship and Sustainability in the Age of Globalization* (2nd edn), Oxford, Oxford University Press.

Donaldson, T. and Preston, L.E. (1995) 'The stakeholder theory of the corporation: concepts, evidence and implications', *Academy of Management Review*, vol. 22, issue 1, pp. 65–91.

Freeman, R.E. (1984) *Strategic Management: A Stakeholder Approach*, Boston, MA, Pitman.

Mitchell, R.K., Agle, B.R. and Wood, D.J. (1997) 'Toward a theory of stakeholder identification and salience: defining the principle of who and what really counts', *Academy of Management Review*, vol. 22, issue 4, pp. 853–86.

Porter, M.E. (1980) *Competitive Advantage*, New York, Free Press.

Porter, M.E. and Kramer, M.R. (2002) 'The competitive advantage of corporate philanthropy', *Harvard Business Review*, December.

Porter, M.E. and Kramer, M.R. (2006) 'Strategy and society: the link between competitive advantage and corporate social responsibility', *Harvard Business Review*, December.

Porter, M.E. and Reinhardt, F.L. (2007) 'A strategic approach to climate', *Harvard Business Review*, October.

Stead, W.E and Stead, J.G. (1996) *Management for a Small Planet: Strategic Decision Making and the Environment* (2nd edn), Thousand Oaks, CA, Sage.

Chapter 14

Ackerman. L. (1997) 'Development, transition or transformation: the question of change in organizations' in van Eynde, D.F., Hoy, J.C. and van Eynde, D.C. (eds) *Organization Development Classics*, San Francisco, CA, Jossey-Bass.

Alvesson, M. and Willmott, H. (2001) *Making Sense of Management*, London, Sage.

Bamford, D. (2006) 'A case study into change influences within a large British multinational', *Journal of Change Management*, vol. 6, issue 2, pp. 181–91.

Beckhard, R. and Harris, R. (1977) Organisational transitions: Managing complex change. Reading, Mass: Addison-Wesley.

BNET Business Dictionary Business Definition for: Change Management [online] http://dictionary.bnet.com/definition/change+management.html (Accessed 22 October 2009).

Bullock, R.J. and Batten, D. (1985) '"It's just a phase we're going through": a review and synthesis of OD phase analysis', *Group and Organization Studies*, vol. 10, pp. 383–412.

Burnes, B. (2004) 'Emergent change and planned change – competitors or allies? The case of XZY construction', *International Journal of Operations and Production Management*, vol. 24, issue 9, pp. 886–902.

Caldwell, S.D., Herold, D.M. and Fedor, D.B. (2004) 'Toward an understanding of the relationships among organizational change, individual differences, and changes in person-environment fit: a cross level study', *Journal of Applied Psychology*, vol. 89, issue 5, pp. 868–82.

Clarke, L. (1994) *The Essence of Change*, London, Prentice Hall.

Dannemiller, K.D. and Jacobs, R.W. (1992) Changing the way organizations change: A revolution of common sense. Journal of Applied Behavioral Sciences, 28 (4), 480–498.

Dent, E.B. and Goldberg, S.G. (1999) 'Challenging resistance to change', *Journal of Applied Behavioral Science*, vol. 35, issue 1, pp. 25–41.

Fenton-O'Creevy, M. (2000) 'Middle management resistance to strategic change initiatives: saboteurs or scapegoats?' in Flood, P.C. *et al.* (eds) *Managing Strategy Implementation*, Oxford, Blackwell.

French, W.L. and Bell, C.H. (1999) *Organization Development: Behavioural Science Interventions for Organization Improvement* (6th edn) Upper Saddle River, NJ, Prentice Hall, p. 176.

Handy, C. (1988) *Understanding Voluntary Organisations*, Harmondsworth, Penguin.

Kanter, R.M., Stein, B.A. and Jick, T.D. (1992) *The Challenge of Organizational Change: How Companies Experience It and Leaders Guide It*, New York, Free Press.

Kanter, R.M. cited in Lorenz (1985) 'Why people resist change', *Financial Times*, 29 May 2008.

Kotter, J.P. (1995) 'Leading change: why transformational efforts fail', *Harvard Business Review*, March-April, pp. 59–67.

Kotter, J.P. and Schlesinger, L.A. (1979) Choosing strategies for change. Harvard Business Review, March-April, 106–114.

Leavitt, H.J. (1964) 'Applied organization change in industry: structural technical and human approaches' in Cooper, W.W., Leavitt, H.J. and Shelley, M.W. (eds) *New Perspectives in Organizational Research*, New York, Wiley.

Lewin, K. (1951) *Field Theory in Social Science*, London, Harper & Row.

Olson, E.E. and Eoyang, G.H. (2001) *Facilitating Organizational Change: Lessons from Complexity Science*, San Francisco, CA, Jossey-Bass/Pfeiffer.

Orlikowski, W.J. and Hofman, J.D. (1997) 'An improvisational model of change management: the case of groupware technologies', *Sloan Management Review*, January.

Pennington, G. (2003) *Guidelines for Promoting and Facilitating Change* [online], LTSN Generic Centre, www.heacademy.ac.uk/assets/York/documents/resources/resourcedatabase/id296_Promoting_and_facilitating_change.pdf. (Accessed 25 January 2010).

Probst, G. and Raisch, S. (2005) 'Organizational crisis: The logic of failure' *Academy of Management Review*, vol. 19, pp. 90–105.

Stacey, R. (1996) *Strategic Management and Organizational Dynamics* (2nd edn), London, Pitman.

Thurley, K. and Wirdenius, H. (1973) *Supervision: a Reappraisal*, London, Heinemann.

Weick, K.E. (2000) 'Emergent change as a universal in organisations' in Beer, M. and Nohria, N. (eds) *Breaking the Code of Change*, Boston, MA, Harvard Business School Press.

Wheatley, M.J. (1992) *Leadership and the New Science*, San Francisco, CA, Berrett-Koehler.

Tools and techniques

Buzan, T. (1982) *Use Your Head*, London, Ariel Books.

de Bono, E. (1982) *Lateral Thinking for Management*, Harmondsworth, Penguin.

Isaksen, S.G., Dorval, K.B. and Treffinger, D.J. (1994) *Creative Approaches to Problem Solving*, Dubuque, IA, Kendall/Hunt.

Morris W.C. and Sashkin, M. (1978) 'Phases of integrated problem solving (PIPS)' in Pfeffer, J.W. and Jones, E. (eds) *The 1978 Handbook for Group Facilitation*, La Jolla, CA, University Associates Inc., pp. 105–16.

Rawlinson, J.G. (1981) *Introduction to Creative Thinking and Brainstorming*, London, British Institute of Management Foundation.

Rawlinson, J.G. (1986) *Creative Thinking and Brainstorming*, Aldershot, Wildwood House.

VanGundy, A.B. (1983) *108 Ways To Get a Bright Idea*, Englewood Cliffs, NJ, Prentice-Hall.

VanGundy, A.B. (1988) *Techniques of Structured Problem Solving* (2nd edn), New York, Van Nostrand Reinhold.

Acknowledgements

Grateful acknowledgement is made to the following sources:

Boxes
Box 9.2: Adapted from Prospects (2009) 'Retail buyer – Job description and activities', www.prospects.ac.uk;

Images
Chapter 4 Image 1: Courtesy of Huf Haus;

Chapter 4 Image 2: Courtesy of Central Science Laboratory, Crown Copyright;

Figures
Figure 1.1: Management Standard Centre (2008) 'Structure of the standards', Taking Management and Leadership to the Next Level, Management Standard Centre;

Figures 4.7 and 4.8: McCollam, A. and White, J. (1993) Building on Experience, Scottish Association for Mental Health;

Figure 5.3: Strassman, P. A. (1985) Information Payoff: The Transformation of Work in the Electronic Age. Copyright © Paul A. Strassman 1985;

Figure 5.4: Strassman, P. A. (1985) Information Payoff: The Transformation of Work in the Electronic Age. Copyright © Paul A. Strassman 1985;

Figure 11.1: Kolb, D. A. and Fry, R. (1975) 'Towards an applied theory of experiential learning', in Cooper, C. L. (ed.) Theories of Group Processes, John Wiley;

Figure 13.2: Crane, A. and Matten, D. (2007) Business Ethics, Oxford University Press Inc.;

Figure 13.3: Mitchell, R. K., Agle, B. R. and Wood, D. J. (1997) Toward a theory of stakeholder identification and salience: Defining the principle of who and what really counts, Academy of Management, vol. 22, No. 4. © Academy of Management Review;

Figure 13.4: Stead, W.E. and Stead, J.G. (1996) Management for a small planet, Sage Publications Ltd;

Figure 13.7: Porter, M. E. (1980) Copetitive advantage, New York: The Free Press;

Tables
Table 4.10: Brager, G. A. and Sprecht, H. (1973) Community Organizing, Columbia University Press;

Table 8.5: Adapted from Hill, L. A. and Farkas, M. T. (2001) 'A note on team processes', Harvard Business Online;